Byron and Or

Byron and Orientalism

Edited by

Peter Cochran

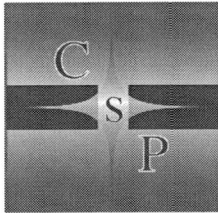

Cambridge Scholars Publishing

Byron and Orientalism, Edited by Peter Cochran

This book first published 2006. This second paperback edition first published 2008.

Cambridge Scholars Publishing

12 Back Chapman Street, Newcastle upon Tyne, NE6 2XX, UK

British Library Cataloguing in Publication Data
A catalogue record for this book is available from the British Library

ISBN (10): 1-84718-749-8, ISBN (13): 9781847187499

TABLE OF CONTENTS

PREFACE

Many of the papers in this book were given at a conference on Byron and Orientalism organised by the Newstead Byron Society and the Midland Romantic Seminar at Nottingham Trent University on April 15 2005.

I should like to thank Maureen Crisp, Keri Davies, John Goodridge, Ken Purslow, and everyone else who assisted in making the day a success. Also to Abu Ali, Anne Barton, Shobhana Bhattacharji, Vitana Kostadinova, Andrew Nicholson, Catherine O'Neill, Andrew Rudd, and Firas O. Shaer for their help with the book.

—P.C.

NOTES ON CONTRIBUTORS

Richard Cardwell is Emeritus Professor of Modern Spanish Literature at the University of Nottingham. Along with editing both a special bi-centennial issue of Renaissance and Modern Studies (1988) on "Byron and Europe" and Lord Byron the European: Essays from the International Byron Society, July 1994 (1997), he has published essays on Byron, Keats, and European Romanticism, including Byron's impact on Spanish writers. He is also the author of over one hundred articles and over twenty books and editions on nineteenth-century Spanish writers and literary history in the period 1800-1930 in Spain. He has lectured in Argentina, Denmark, France, Georgia, Holland, Portugal, Spain, and the United States, where he also taught as Visiting Professor. He is editor of *The Reception of Byron in Europe*, 2 vols, London-New York, Thoemmes-Continuum, 2005.

Peter Cochran is the editor of the *Newstead Abbey Byron Society Review*. He has lectured on Byron in London, Oxford, Cambridge, Newstead, Glasgow, Liverpool, Versailles, Monckton, Gdansk, Salzburg, Paris, St Andrews, Venice, Missolonghi, Delphi, Yerevan and New York, and published numerous articles on the poet. He is author of the Byron entry in the *New Cambridge Bibliography of English Literature*, and of the entries on J.C.Hobhouse and E.J.Trelawny for the new *DNB*. He edits Byron's works on the website of the International Byron Society

Jeremy Davies is a doctoral student at Queen Mary, University of London.

Allan Gregory is a practicing consultant engineer living and working in Dublin. He has studied Irish and English literature at University College, Dublin, where he received his BA, and subsequent Masters Degree in Anglo-Irish Literature and Drama. His poem, *Some Other Place*, originally written in Gaelic, on a family's trauma with Alzheimer's disease, was Ireland's contribution to Roma Tre University's Symposium on Peace for the Millenium. His literary "work in progress" is a biography of contemporary Irish poet Michael Hartnett. He is a regular contributor to International Byron Conferences, with specific emphases on the literary relationship between Byron and Moore.

Svetlana Klimova is an assistant teacher and a postgraduate at the University of Nizhnii Novgorod. She is writing a thesis on the history of translations of Byron's metaphysical dramas into Russian, with special attention those of Ivan Bunin. She has given papers on Byron's *Manfred* and *Cain* as translated by Bunin and other Russian interpreters, on Byron and chaos, on Byron and the metaphor of journey, and on the image of paradise in Byron's works. Other areas of interest include Milton, Coleridge, Pushkin, and Blok.

Seyed Mohammad Marandi is Assistant Professor in the Department of English at Tehran University. He has recently been appointed as head of the American Studies Department at the University of Tehran's Institute for European and North American Studies. He has written on Orientalism in nineteenth-century English literature, representations of Iran in the American media, and is currently working on a critique of Azar Nafisi's *Reading Lolita in Tehran*.

Robert McColl is a postgraduate at the University of Liverpool, writing a thesis on the historical romance in Byron and Walter Scott. He has written papers on Byron, place and space, Byron and abstinence, and knowing and telling in Scott. Other areas of interest include the Bible, Shakespeare and Dylan.

After a career as a consultant psychiatrist (Cambridge and the Middlesex Hospital), **Gerald Silverman** read history of art at University College London where he began to focus on the Jewish-Christian interface to be found in much art, literature and music; this being now the subject of most of his writing and lecturing. A teenage fascination with Byron was re-ignited in much later years on encountering Peter Cochran.

ABBREVIATIONS

To economize on space in the notes, the following abbreviations are used for the books referred to. See the Bibliography for further information.

Ashton: Thomas L. Ashton, *Byron's* Hebrew Melodies (London: Routledge and Kegan Paul, 1972).

Bagabas: Omar Abdullah Bagabas, *Byron's Representation of the Orient in Childe Harold's Pilgrimage, Don Juan, and the Oriental Tales* (PhD Diss.), (Essex University 1993).

BLJ: *Byron's Letters and Journals,* ed. Leslie A. Marchand, 13 vols, John Murray, 1973-94.

BoA: Byron, *The Bride of Abydos.*

Burwick and Douglass: Frederick Burwick and Paul Douglass, Introduction to George Gordon, 6th Baron Byron, and Isaac Nathan, *A Selection of Hebrew Melodies, Ancient and Modern*, ed. Burwick and Douglass (Tuscaloosa: University of Alabama Press, 1988).

Coleridge: *The Works of Lord Byron: A New, Revised and Enlarged Edition with illustrations. Poetry*, ed. E.H.Coleridge, seven vols, John Murray, 1898-1904.

CHP: Byron, *Childe Harold's Pilgrimage.*

CMP: *Lord Byron: The Complete Miscellaneous Prose*, ed. Andrew Nicholson, Oxford, Clarendon Press, 1991.

CPW: *Lord Byron: The Complete Poetical Works*, ed. Jerome J. McGann and Barry Weller, 7 vols Oxford, Clarendon Press, 1980-93.

CSL: *The Life and Correspondence of the Late Robert Southey*, ed. C.C.Southey, Longman, Brown, Green and Longmans, 6 vols 1849-1850.

DJ: Byron, *Don Juan.*

LR: Moore, Thomas. *Lalla Rookh, An Oriental Romance*, first edition, Longman, 1817.

Kidwai: Abdur Raheem Kidwai, *Orientalism in Lord Byron's 'Turkish Tales'*, Lampeter, Mellen Press, 1995.

Makdisi: Makdisi, Saree. *Romantic Imperialism: Universal Empire and the Culture of Modernity*, Cambridge, 1999.

Marchand:	Marchand, Leslie A., *Byron: A Biography*, 3 vols Alfred A. Knopf, New York, 1957.
Moore Letters:	*The Letters of Thomas Moore*, ed. Wilfred Dowden, 2 vols Oxford, 1964.
Moore Works:	*The Poetical Works of Thomas Moore Complete in one Volume*, Longman, 1855.
Oueijan:	Oueijan, Naji B. *A Compendium of Eastern Elements in Byron's Oriental Tales*, New York, Peter Lang, 1999.
Pratt:	*Robert Southey, Poetical Works, 1793-1810*, ed. Lynda Pratt, Pickering and Chatto, 5 vols. 2004.
RR:	*The Romantics Reviewed*, ed. Donald H. Reiman, Garland, 1972.
Sale:	*The Koran, Commonly called the Alcoran of Mohammed, translated by George Sale*, 1734, *Preliminary Discourse.*
Sharafuddin:	Sharafuddin, Mohammed. *Islam and Romantic Orientalism;Literary Encounters with the Orient*, New York, I.B.Tauris, 1994.
SoC:	Byron, *The Siege of Corinth.*
Vathek:	William Beckford, *Vathek*, ed. Roger Lonsdale, Oxford 1986.
Vail:	Vail, Jeffery. *The Literary Relationship of Lord Byron and Thomas Moore,* Johns Hopkins, Baltimore and London, 2001.

INTRODUCTION

BYRON'S ORIENTALISM

PETER COCHRAN

In the "romantic" period, "Orientalism" was a large concept, by no means to be defined with strict regard to the dictionary; and it is no more precise today. If Thomas Moore's Zoroastrian Fire-Worshippers in *Lalla Rookh* may be interpreted as a metaphor for Catholics, and if his Moslems may stand for oppressive Protestants, then Ireland – to England's West – is honorary Oriental territory (see the essay below by Alan Gregory). If we grant that, why should the barbarous and strange highland reaches depicted by Scott in his poems and in the Waverley Novels not be considered Oriental too? Byron, we know, associated both Greece and Albania with Scotland.[1] Aztec Mexico, as portrayed by Southey in *Madoc,* is still more barbarous and strange. Having thus granted the West and the North Oriental status, what of the South Pacific, as portrayed by Byron in *The Island?* The Scots Torquil and the Polynesian Neuha are both "children of the isles".[2] Toobonai is not so much to the East as to the South-East, not so much to the South-East as on the other side of the globe: but it offers what all self-respecting Oriental scenery does, namely, a depiction of territory which, whatever it *is*, is emphatically *not* Anglo-Saxon, Tory, Anglican, imperialist, or full of cant.

However, in this introductory essay, I mostly interpret "Oriental" in the narrow sense of "Eastern"; and naïvely, "Islamic Eastern". I am aware that there were other areas of Orientalism – Armenian, for example – in which Byron was interested, but the Islamic East informs the largest portion of

---

1: "He loved the mountains of Greece, because they recalled those of Scotland" (Teresa Guiccioli, *My Recollections of Lord Byron, and those of Eye-Witnesses of his Life,* tr Jerningham, New York 1869 p.359.) "The Arnaouts, or Albanese, struck me forcibly by their resemblance to the Highlanders of Scotland" (CHP II, st. 38, Byron's note).
2: Byron, *The Island*, II, 274.

the poetry he wrote deriving from the subject – as well, of course, as being the one most relevant to our concerns today.

***

There have been, in modern orientalist writings, a number of cant approaches hurled up, which try define what the "Orient" *is*. The Orient, says one of the most influential, is an object, an Other, which you, the subject, wish to "possess" and "penetrate". This crude sexual formula may be applied to any narrative in which an occidental male possesses and penetrates an oriental female, and enables the narrative to be used as a metaphor for western imperialist expansion into and forcible domination of eastern countries. The fact that many oriental females might (if approached tactfully), enjoy being penetrated and possessed by occidental males, is left out of the scenario as an embarrassment to the political metaphor.

Opponents of such an approach, aware of the advantages of cultural variety, write of the Orient as a place in which one can redefine one's self in new ways, not so much by penetrating and possessing it, as by "encountering" it, and in doing so, newly discovering oneself:

> ... if Orientalism is, for us, an "antiworld," a lush and necessary Other "against which we pit ourselves for definition," Byronic Orientalism involves a pitting of self against self.[3]

This may lead to a recognition that cultural variety is only skin-deep, so that the boundaries between "occidental self and oriental other" often blur, and the line between hitherto Eurocentric Self and Oriental Other becomes hard to see. The myth of Eurosupremacy loses its power in this version. The Orient is, or becomes, you. The "Eurocentric binary of self and other" becomes indistinct and disappears. East is West, and vice versa. There may be comic potential in this discovery that Orient and Occident are identical.

The Orient can also be a place of violence, of oppression, or contrariwise of romance, of lost innocence recovered, or of paradisal strangeness. But it can also be a place of romantic disillusion, of innocence lost all over again, or of paradisal strangeness evaporated: a subject not for romance but for satire, where the disparity between ideal and real is, again, a source of laughter. In the Orient, everything is

---

3: Frederick Garber, *Self, Text, and Romantic Irony: The Example of Byron* (Princeton 1988), p.82.

revealed as having the capacity to transmute into its complementary opposite – as happens in the Forest of Arden, or Bohemia, or Cyprus.

Now in order to discover the disparity between the Ideal and the Real, or for things to dissolve into their complementary opposites, or for the Binarism of Self and Other to evaporate, one often has in real life only to cross the road, or open an envelope, or go into the next room. It's true that Ireland and even Scotland were a lot further away from the metropolis then than they are now; but the specifically Oriental version of such a voyage of spiritual discovery should really involve adventures in eastern countries. The psychological adventures which Orientalism offers in theory are much more adventurous if we believe in the detailed presentation of the Oriental environment in which they occur.

All these definitions and approaches are useful when discussing the life and works of Lord Byron. Byron's Orientalism is often praised, and used as a contrast with that of other "romantic" writers, because it was based on experience. While I do not deny the authenticity of his experience – feel, indeed, that it has been insuffiently examined – my argument will be that he also derived much of his knowledge of the orient from books. I think that at first he used the books – particularly travel books written by people more experienced than himself – to get his own ideas about the Orient in context. But as he got more sophisticated he used them more as factual sources, to give his later verse, in ottava rima, the convincing detail which he could now see that his early poems lacked.

∗∗∗

In medieval European epics and romances, written with the Crusades as background, and then in the sixteenth and seventeenth centuries, with the Turkish threat to Christian Europe hovering near, Islam was the enemy. In poetry, the dialogue between Islam and Christianity was, to put it mildly, simplistic. Here, from Pulci's *Morgante Maggiore* (the first book of which Byron translated), is Orlando speaking to the giant Marcovaldo, whom he has wounded fatally:

> Disse Orlando: – Da poi che tu mel chiedi
> per grazia, io userò mia cortesia:
> io sono Orlando; e questo che tu vedi,
> è mio scudier, ch'è meco in compagnia.
> Tu se' morto e dannato, s' tu non credi
> presto a Colui che nacque di Maria;
> battézati a Gesù, credi al Vangelò,

acciò che l'alam tue ne vadi in cielo.

Macometto t'aspetta nello 'nferno
cogli altri matti che van drieto a lui,
dove tu arderai nel foco etterno,
giù negli abissi dolorosi e bui. –
Disse il pagan: – Laudato in sempiterno
sia Gesù Cristo e tutti i santi sui!
Io voglio in ogni modo battezarmi,
e per tua mano, Orlando, cristian farmi.[4]

Orlando said, "Since you, from kindness, ask me to speak, I shall reply courteously. I am Orlando, and this whom you see is my squire [*Morgante, another giant*], who goes with me. You're dead and damned if you don't quickly believe in Him who was born of Mary; be baptized in Christ, believe in the Gospel, so that you can see your soul go to Heaven. / Mahomed, with all the other idiots who make up his train, is waiting for you in Hell, where you will burn in eternal fire, down there in the dark and miserable abyss." – The pagan said, "May Jesus and all his saints be praised eternally! I want to be baptised at once, and to be made a Christian, Orlando, by your hand".

This is so crude that one suspects a game is being played, and that the priests were right to look at Pulci askance. The Islamic viewpoint could not be entertained in these times, except perhaps as one side of a formal balance:

Poi che de l'arme la seconda eletta
si diè al campion del populo pagano,
duo sacerdoti, l'un de l'una setta,
l'altro de l'altra, uscir coi libri in mano.
In quel del nostro è la vita perfetta
scritta di Cristo; e l'altro è l'Alcorano.
Con quel de l'Evangelio si fe' inante
l'imperator, con l'altro il re Agramante.[5]

The pagan champion was given the second choice of weapons, then two priests stepped forth, one from either sect, book in hand. The book our priest held contained the unblemished life of Christ; the other's book was the Koran. With the priest of the gospel stepped forth the emperor [*Charlemagne*]; with the other, King Agramant.

4: Pulci, *Morgante Maggiore*, 12.63-4.
5: Ariosto, *Orlando Furioso,* 38.81; English translation by Guido Waldman, Oxford World's Classics, 1983, p.464.

Several of the protagonists of Ariosto, a poet whom Byron admired and imitated, seem, from their places of origin, to be Muslim (Ruggiero, Rodomonte, or Marfisa, for instance), but the fact worries Ariosto not a whit: they never threaten Jerusalem, never wash themselves ritually, and never pray towards Mecca. A Moslem warrior might be honoured for his or her courage, but he or she must be defeated, as is Rodomonte, or converted – as are Ruggiero and Marfisa.

The less light-hearted and more pious Tasso, whom Byron also studied, allows no real "Saracen" heroes, and his "Saracen" heroine, Clorinda, must convert before she dies. His Moslems, whose possession of Jerusalem is threatened, are likely to be called "Arabi predatori,"[6] "pagani," or even "palestini",[7] and to be described as worshipping "Macone" as often as "Maometto". Whether they adhere to Islam, or to the devil, or to what they adhere, is outside Tasso's field of interest. We can only be allowed to sympathise with them when they've been defeated. Tasso is unwilling sometimes even to give them coherent speech:

> Tacque; e 'l pagano, al sofferir poco uso,
> morde le labra e di furor si strugge.
> Risponder vuol, ma il suono esce confuso
> sí come strido d'animal che rugge;
> o come apre le nubi ond'egli è chiuso
> impetuoso il fulmine, e se 'n fugge,
> cosí pareva a forza ogni suo detto
> tonando uscir da l'infiammato petto.

This is rendered by Edward Fairfax as

> The Pagan patience never knew, nor used,
>   Trembling for ire, his sandy locks he tore,
> Out from his lips flew such a sound confused,
>   As lions make in deserts thick, which roar;
> Or as when clouds together crushed and bruised,
>   Pour down a tempest by the Caspian shore;
> So was his speech imperfect, stopped, and broken,
> He roared and thundered when he should have spoken.[8]

Detailed discussion of the differences between the two warring religions form no part of either writer's intention.

6: Tasso, *Gerusalemme Liberata.* 5.92,8.
7: Ibid, 3.29.1.
8: Tasso, *Ger.Lib.* 6.38. Translation by Edward Fairfax (1600).

However, by 1812, when *Childe Harold* II, the first of Byron's oriental poems, was published, the western perspective on the east had altered, at least in so far as academic studies were concerned. The threat to Europe from the Ottomans had long receded. In the late seventeenth century Barthélemy D'Herbelot, in the eighteenth Sir William Jones (see below), George Sale the translator of the Qu'ran, and John Richardson the translator of the Arabian Nights, had all demystified Islam to the extent that it was harder to regard it with the horror which made Dante deposit Mohammed in Hell,[9] and was necessary to be more explicit about what belief in Islam involved. Despite this increase in detailed understanding, there was no real increase in sympathy: instead of the cliché evil East of medieval tradition, a new cliché East emerged, which was still mysterious – full of houris, odalisques, eunuchs and djinns, crafty caliphs, oppressive sheikhs and flying carpets – only to an extent a surreal version of western society, but still much more commodifiable than its dark predecessor. A market was created which Robert Southey, Byron's most hated enemy, attempted to exploit, with little success, either artistic or monetary, with his epics *Thalaba the Destroyer* (1801), and *The Curse of Kehama* (1810). *Thalaba*, as Tim Fulford points out,[10] derives both from William Beckford's novel *Vathek* (1786), and from Walter Savage Landor's poem *Gebir* (1798). Byron, in his turn, borrowed, as we shall see, from *Vathek* (it was his favourite book), with greater success either than Southey, or Shelley, whose *The Revolt of Islam* appeared in 1817 – although Shelley, understating, admits that he does not make "much attempt at minute delineation of Mahometan manners".[11] Southey, Byron and Shelley all wrote in the pseudo-orientalist tradition which Beckford had developed from an earlier eighteenth-century one.[12] Shelley was in addition a fervent admirer of *Gebir*: Byron, in his preface to *The Vision of Judgement*, satirised it. Shelley, who loathed Christianity, could not be expected to admire Islam; Byron, who respected Christianity as long as it was divorced from English cant, was much more friendly to its fellow-monotheism.

9: Dante, *Inf.* 38.
10: Fulford at Pratt 3, p.viii.
11: *Letters of Percy Bysshe Shelley* (ed. Jones, Oxford 1964), I p.563 (letter of 13 Oct 1817, to an anknown publisher, perhaps Longman).
12: See Martha Pike Conant, *The Oriental Tale in England in the Eighteenth Century*, New York 1908.

The example of Sir William Jones

The great scholar William Jones (1746-94) set himself, while a student at Oxford, the task of translating (with assistance) *The Arabian Nights* from their French version back into Arabic. Nicknamed "Selim," his extraordinary achievements in Orientalism, made in part in India, may usefully be summarised here, as a way of getting Byron's initial amateurishness in the same subject into perspective. He thought that a thorough knowledge of Eastern culture would be a useful counterweight to Graeco-Roman traditions, a narrow adherence to which he found provincial and chauvinistic – as, of course, Byron did, or affected to do. His multitudinous translations, from Persian, Arabic, Turkish, and Sanscrit, were done with a view to achieving that end. It was through his work that Byron claimed to have became early familiar with such poets as Sa'di, Ferdausi and Hafiz. Jones combined encyclopaedic oriental knowledge with a radical domestic Whiggism closer to Cobbett's than to Byron's (though in India he favoured despotism). At the same time he was aware of the supposedly delicate sensibilities of his readers, "silently heterosexualised" some of the poems he translated (the phrase is Michael Franklin's: see below), and understated the traditional natures of such Hindu entities as Kali. His translation of the Sanscrit play *Sacontalà* went through six editions between 1790 and 1807. He was also an expert on Hindu and Islamic law.

Jones's work was much appreciated in India itself, where, as Michael Franklin writes,

Orientalism, through its retrieval of Sanskrit texts and its reconstruction of India's past, shaped the way Indians perceived themselves, ushering in the Bengali Renaissance ... Although a key member of the colonial administration, Jones's Enlightenment aspirations were ultimately to work in the service of Indian nationalism.[13]

Jawaharlal Nehru wrote in *The Discovery of India* that "... to Jones and many other European scholars, India owes a deep debt of gratitude for the rediscovery of her past literature".[14]

Byron knew Jones' labours well, having read Baron Teignmouth's *Life* (1799),[15] and, we may assume, the six-volume *Works* to which it was

13: Michael Franklin (ed.), *The European Discovery of India* (Ganesha 2001), Vol 3, p.xviii.
14: Jawaharlal Nehru, *The Discovery of India* (London: Meridian, 1945), p.266. I am grateful to Andrew Rudd for drawing my attention to this quotation.

attached. He expressed an initial desire to travel, not to the Eastern Mediterranean, but to India;[16] but was thwarted by officialdom. His scholarship pales into insignificance next to that of Jones; though clearly he had poetic talents much greater than Jones's. What no-one has said of his Orientalism is that it heightened, as Jones's did, a national sense of identity in the non-Christian countries he wrote about. Turkish and Arabic translations of his works have been few, and the Islamic critical response to his work has, in 2005, barely begun.[17]

***

Robert Southey was happy, in correspondence, to describe Indian language, in the most un-Jonesian way, as "a baboon jargon," as if there were only one.[18] He wrote *The Curse of Kehama* against a background of controversy over English Christian missionary work in India, which he came to support, with less and less toleration of the religions such work would, if successful, supplant.[19] Both imperialism and evangelism found a much more stalwart defender in Southey than in any of his orientalist rivals. "*Kehama*," writes its modern editor, "offers itself implicitly as an instrument of colonialist policy".[20]

Little of this strange material sold well, apart from Byron's. Of the orientalist works of Byron's contemporaries,[21] only Moore's *Lalla Rookh* was in commercial competition with him, and *Lalla Rookh* – though it's still, I'm told, very popular in India – does not seem to have stood the test of time in the West (see Allan Gregory's paper below).

On the other hand, Coleridge's *Kubla Khan*, (published at Byron's insistence, its subject influenced by Southey),[22] has stood the test of time

---

15: CMP, 5.

16: BLJ I, 175.

17: At *Sir William Jones and Literary Orientalism*, in C.C. Barfoot and Theo D'haen (eds.), *Oriental Prospects:Western Literature and the Lure of the East* (Amsterdam: Rodopi, 1998), pp.27-41, Garland Cannon writes about Jones's influence on the English romantic poets, but discovers no direct borrowings on Byron's part.

18: CSL II, 96-7, quoted Daniel Sanjiv Roberts at Pratt 4, p.x.

19: Traced by Roberts at ibid, x-xiv and Marilyn Butler, at *The Orientalism of Byron's Giaour,* in Beatty, Bernard and Vincent Newey, eds., *Byron and the Limits of Fiction*, Liverpool University Press 1988, pp.80-4.

20: Ibid, p.xiii.

21: For an examination of Blake's orientalism, see Edward Larrissy, *Blake's Orient*, in *Romanticism* 11:1, 2005, pp.1-13.

22: Fulford at Pratt 3, p.xiii.

with more success than much of Byron's: but is not an oriental narrative in quite the same way as his are; and is not Islamic.

Coleridge had been as far as Malta; but of all other the writers in this interrelated sequence, only Byron had visited any oriental countries. All the others wrote about an Orient which they knew only from books. Southey, especially, as Fulford writes,

> ... developed *Thalaba* as an imitation of 'Oriental' tales that were already tales made in Europe. His poem ... grew from western fantasies about the East and had at its root the desire to use the Orient as an exotic other – a stage on which the dilemmas produced in the west could be played out.[23]

The question is, does Byron do the same – dress up Occidental drama in Oriental clothing? Or are his tales more authentically Oriental? Are we naïve to look to his poems for an understanding of the East in his day – is he just playing a game with our gullibility? When, writing to Shelley in 1822, he called his earlier work "exaggerated nonsense which has corrupted the public taste,"[24] was he referring only to their style?

Landor and Southey invert the theme of *Vathek*: instead of charting with fixation and strange empathy the downward path of a ghastly, faintly comical transgressor, they celebrate the defeat of such a one at the hands of a pure hero. In so far as the theme of Shelley's *Revolt of Islam* is comprehensible, he follows them rather than Beckford. If we are looking for a Western subtext to their Eastern texts, anti-imperialist messages are implicit in the work of all three, with either Napoleonic or Tory imperialism as the foe.

But Byron celebrates the defeat of a hero – never a pure one – at the hands, either of a cruel establishment, as in *The Bride of Abydos*, or through the hero's own compromised politics, as in *The Siege of Corinth,* or through his compromised sexuality, as in *The Giaour,* or through a mixture of all three. His is a less easily bracketable version of orientalism.

***

In his 1807 reading list, Byron includes the following entry:

23: Fulford at Pratt 3, p.x.
24: BLJ IX, 161.

Arabia, Mahomet, whose Koran contains most sublime poetical passages
far surpassing European Poetry.[25]

This may be teenage posture (he was nineteen in 1807): or he may
have been reading George Sale's *Preliminary Discourse*:

> The style of the *Korân* is generally beautiful and fluent, especially
> where it imitates the prophetic manner, and scripture phrases. It is
> concise, and often obscure, adorned with bold figures after the eastern
> taste, enlivened with florid and sententious expressions, and in many
> places, especially where the majesty and attributes of GOD are
> described, sublime and magnificent … Very extraordinary effects are
> related of the power of words well chosen and artfully placed, which are
> no less powerful either to ravish or amaze than music itself …[26]

I have to confess that it's not clear to me that Byron read Sale's
translation of the Qu'ran. Jerome McGann finds echoes, but they are
doubtful;[27] and we never find Sale mentioned either in the Letters and
Journals,[28] or the sale catalogues. However, I have proceeded on the
charitable assumption that Byron at least knew Sale's *Preliminary
Discourse*.
Had he relied on such authorities as Voltaire (whom we know he
respected), he would have found the following, relative to the Qu'ran:

> Il est vrai que les contradictions, les absurdités, les anachronismes, sont
> répandus en foule dans ce livre. On y voit surtout une ignorance
> profonde de la physique la plus simple et la plus connue. C'est là la
> pierre de touche des livres que les fausses religions prétendent écrits par
> la Divinité, car Dieu n'est ni absurde, ni ignorant; mais le peuple, qui ne

---

25: CMP, 1.
26: Sale, pp.61 and 62.
27: See CPW III 419 and 420 (*Giaour*, B.'s notes to 488 and 748: McGann's
references are to Sale 59 and 101, women in paradise, and Eblis), and III 441,
(*BoA*, Byron's note to II 409, or 891: McGann's reference is to Sale sec I:
paradise). The page references do not tally with anything on those pages in Sale. In
fact McGann takes all three from the notes of Coleridge (see Coleridge III, 110,
121, and 197) and Coleridge uses the 1880 translation of E.H.Palmer, as well as an
1877 Sale, which McGann does not state.
28: "I hope you and Bland roll down the stream of Sale" (BLJ I, 241) refers to the
book market.

voit pas ces fautes, les adore, et les imans emploient un déluge de paroles pour les pallier.[29]

It is true that this book is crowded with contradictions, absurdities, and anachronisms. In it we see, above all, a deep ignorance about the simplest and most well-known aspects of physical science. It is the touchstone for all books which false religions claim to be written by the Divinity, for God is neither so absurd nor so ignorant; but the people, who do not see these faults, adore them, and the imams use a flood of words to make them acceptable.

Despite these worries about the second-hand nature of Byron's "Oriental" knowledge, Byron's supporters are confident about the depth of his eastern study. Mohammed Sharafuddin writes that "Even if Byron is exaggerating his precociousness, the range and depth of his [*oriental*] reading cannot be doubted".[30] Sharafuddin dwells at length, especially, on Byron's reading of the letters of Lady Mary Wortley Montagu. Abdur Raheem Kidwai praises Byron's "eye for detail, his meticulous accuracy, and his positive appreciation of the Orient".[31] Naji B. Oueijan goes further still:

Among his contemporaries Lord Byron was the only Englishman who truly experienced the Orient by assimilating himself into the culture … Unlike those who actually toured the East for merely political and/or religious propaganda and presented distorted images of the Eastern world and its peoples, or those who for purely academic reasons employed their time in recording their observations of its antiquities and archaeology, Byron spent his time in living, enjoying, and studying Oriental life and culture for its own wealth as well as for its existing exoticism.[32]

For more on these three critics, see below.

Nevertheless, in a letter to Murray of December 1814[33] Byron asks if it is Mecca or Medina that contains the "*holy* sepulchre"; and laments that, as "a good Mussulman," he doesn't know. His facetiousness may be crafted for the innocent publisher. Since he had no respect for the canting model of Christianity, and was a dabbler also in neo-Platonism and

---

29: Voltaire, *Essai sur les moeurs et l'esprit des nations*, chap. vii. — De l'alcoran, et de la loi musulmane.
30: Sharafuddin, p.215.
31: Kidwai, p.30.
32: Oueijan, p.18.
33: BLJ III, 191.

Zoroastrianism, both of which he eventually jettisoned too, we have no reason to think he held Islam in any regard in terms of his own salvation. But not to know that Mohammed is buried in Mdina is like wondering if St Peter's is in Rome or Venice.[34] Would Murray have been sufficiently sophisticated to see that? Is Byron trying it on, or is he really so ignorant? Just how careful he was with eastern material, in the face of a readership he despised, is an important point.

***

In his essay below, Seyed Mohammed Marandi makes some damaging points about the way Byron portrays Islamic society in *The Bride of Abydos*. Amongst other things he points out that Byron treats Islam as monolithic, speaking of Ottoman society as if there were no other kinds in Islam: that he is wrong about Islamic ideas of the female soul; wrong about women not being allowed near Islamic shrines: wrong about dowries: that he would have us believe that all Moslem fathers are tyrannical, that all young Moslem women harbour incestuous feelings, and that the only civic virtues in the Islamic world are ones which come fortuitously from one's having Greek blood (Greece being by convention a western society, despite the evidence).

If these points are upheld, then Byron was pulling the wool over his readers' eyes about his orientalist understanding, and has been ever since. He had, we know, a low opinion of most of his readers.

However, his seeming positive attitude to Islam would have been fostered and reinforced by *Vathek*, in which the sins of the protagonist are measured against Islamic, not Christian, moral standards. But is *Vathek's* orientalism any more than a huge camp gesture?

The Giaour, alone among Byron's tales, is told in part from an Islamic viewpoint (see especially lines 723-46): and Byron enters into the spirit of, and seems master of a Moslem's perspective. He knows enough to see that in killing Hassan, the Giaour has destroyed a fount of Islamic virtue, of which he, Byron, has had personal experience:

> I need hardly observe, that Charity and Hospitality are the first duties enjoined by Mahomet; and to say truth, very generally practised by his

---

34: Byron would have learned the place of Mohammed's burial from Sale, p.3 (and p.5n); or from Castellan's *Moeurs ... des Othmans*, I, p.42 (I, pp.xix-xxj in original French).

disciples. The first praise that can be bestowed on a chief, is a panegyric on his bounty; the next, on his valour.[35]

There needs no very profound or lasting knowledge of Islam to know these things; and in any case, it's not Mohammed who enjoins hospitality in the Qu'ran, but Allah, speaking through Mohammed. It's not as if charity and hospitality are frowned on in Christian countries, either. However, George Sale, in his *Preliminary Discourse*, underlines the idea:

> Hospitality was so habitual to them [*the pre-Mohammedan Arabs*], and so much esteemed, that the examples of this kind among them exceed whatever can be produced from other nations.[36]

Nevertheless, Byron's note wears its anti-occidental polemic with some self-consciousness.

Byron's eastern poems are famous for their "local colour" – in flaunting this they echo, as I think Byron meant them to, Scott's familiarity with archaic Scots words as shown in *The Lay of the Last Minstrel,* which is replete with "minivers" and "bartizans," "cleuchs" and "actons," "jennets," "cushat-doves" and "need-fires". Byron enjoyed using intriguingly similar oriental vocabulary, whose meaning only he could elucidate, via prose notes, thus emphasising his role as bold traveller, and expert in unknown areas that fascinated and thrilled. "Palampores" and "caïques", "tophaikes" and "djereeds", "ataghans" and "chaius's" litter *The Giaour* and *The Bride of Abydos* (though not *The Corsair* or *The Siege of Corinth*). My suspicion is that he saw Scott's game, and knew he could take the same game further afield. But displaying your knowledge of what djereeds and ataghans are, and claiming thereby an intimacy with Islamic culture, is like having your photo taken on the Rialto and saying how well you know Venice. Byron, via Shakespeare, later mocks people, including himself, who do the latter:

> *Motto. Rosalind.* – "Farewell, Monsieur Traveller; look you lisp and wear strange suits, disable all the benefits of your own country, be out of love with your nativity, and almost chide God for making you that countenance you are; or I will scarce think that you have swam in a gondola. – *As You Like It*, Act 4. Scene 1.[37]

35: *The Giaour*, Byron's note to line 35.
36: Sale, p.29.
37: *Beppo*, epigraph.

It could be addressed to Childe Harold. The earlier Byron is keen to know that he has "swam in a gondola," Islamic fashion: yet he sometimes displays the greatest ignorance. Here is *The Giaour*, 487-90:

> Oh! Who young Leila's glance could read
> And keep that portion of his creed,
> Which saith that woman is but dust,
> A soulless toy for tyrant's lust?   490

Next to these lines he places a note:

A vulgar error; the Koran allots at least a third of Paradise to well-behaved women; but by far the greatest number of Mussulmans interpret the text in their own way, and exclude their moieties from heaven. Being enemies to Platonics, they cannot discern "any fitness of things" in the souls of the other sex, conceiving them to be superseded by the Houris.

He has one good point, for Islamic theory and Islamic practise often differ; but has created an alternative "vulgar error" of his own, for the Qu'ran puts no limit on the proportion of women who may enter Paradise:

Verily the devout Moslems of either sex, and the true believers of either sex, and the devout men, and the devout women, and the men of veracity, and the women of veracity, and the patient *men*, and the patient *women*, and the humble *men* and the humble *women*, and the alms-givers of either sex, and the *men* who fast and the *women* who fast, and the chaste *men*, and the chaste *women*, and those of either sex who remember God frequently; for them hath God prepared forgiveness, and a great reward.[38]

I don't know where Byron got his "thirty-three percent only" idea from,[39] but I suspect from his own misogyny and uncontrollable desire to "hum". He would have found the following in Sale's *Preliminary Discourse*:

38: Sale, 1734, p.346. The verse is Q 33.35.
39: Harold Wiener (see below) sees a remote source in Sale's *Preliminary Discourse* to the Qu'ran; but the passage he quotes says nothing about "a third" of women. In their article *A Vulgar Error: Byron on Women and Paradise* (*Byron Journal* 21 1993, pp.87-8), A.R.Kidwai and Vincent Newey refer to Byron's note without assessing its accuracy.

… the same prophet [*Mohammed*] has also declared, that when he took a view of paradise, he saw the majority of its inhabitants to be the poor, and when he looked down into hell, he saw the greater part of the wretches confined there, to be women.[40]

But, to counterbalance this poor impression:

Before we quit this subject, it may not be improper to observe the falsehood of a vulgar imputation on the *Mohammedans*, who are by several writers reported to hold that women have no souls, or, if they have, that they will perish, like those of brute beasts, and will not be rewarded in the next life. But whatever may be the opinion of some ignorant people among them, it is certain that *Mohammed* had too great a respect for the fair sex to teach such a doctrine; and that there are several passages in the *Korân* which affirm that women, in the next life, will not only be punished for their evil actions, but will also receive the rewards for their good deeds, as well as the men, and that in this case GOD will make no distinction of sexes. [note: see *Kor.* c. 3 p. 58 c. 4 p. 76. And also c. 13, 16, 40, 48, 57 &c.] It is true, the general notion is, that they will not be admitted into the same abode as the men are, because their places will be supplied by the paradisiacal females, (tho' some allow that a man will there also have the company of those who were his wives in this world, or at least such of them as he shall desire;) but that good women will go into a separate place of happiness, where they will enjoy all sorts of delights; but whether one of those delights will be the enjoyment of agreeable paramours created for them, to compleat the œconomy of the Mohammedan system, is what I have no where found decided. One circumstance relating to these beatified females, conformable to what he had asserted of the men, he acquainted his followers with in the answer he returned to an old woman; who desiring him to intercede with GOD, that she might be admitted into paradise, he told her that no old woman would enter that place; which setting the poor woman a crying, he explained himself by saying, that GOD would make her young again.[41]

Lady Mary Wortley Montagu (whom Byron read and admired: see *DJ* V, 3, 8), has an impressive section on Islamic women and their chances of paradise:

As to your next enquiry, I assure you it is certainly false, though commonly believed in our parts of the world, that Mahomet excludes women from any share in a future happy state. He was too much a

---

40: Sale, p.98.
41: Sale, pp.102-3.

16 Peter Cochran

gentleman, and loved the fair sex so well, to use them so barbarously. On the contrary, he promises a very fine paradise to the Turkish women. He says, indeed, that this paradise will be a separate place from that of their husbands; but I fancy the most part of them won't like it the worse for that; and that the regret of this separation will not render their paradise the less agreeable. It remains to tell you, that the virtues that Mahomet requires of the women, to merit the enjoyment of future happiness, are not to live in such a manner as to become useless to the world, but to employ themselves, as much as possible, in making little Mussulmans. The virgins who die virgins, and the widows who marry not again, dying in mortal sin, are excluded out of paradise: for women, says he, not being capable to manage the affairs of state, nor to support the fatigues of war, God has not ordered them to govern or reform the world; but he has entrusted them with an office which is not less honourable, even that of multiplying the human race, and such as, out of malice or laziness, do not make it their business to bear or to breed children, fulfil not the duty of their vocation, and rebel against the commands of God. Here are maxims for you, prodigiously contrary to those of your convents. What will become of your St. Catharines, your St. Theresas, your St. Clares, and the whole bead-roll of your holy virgins and widows? who, if they are to be judged by this system of virtue, will be found to have been infamous creatures, that passed their whole lives in a most abominable libertinism.[42]

If therefore Byron's oriental women – in the ottava rima poems at least – appear more libidinous than his occidental ones, they could almost claim divine sanction for it. Donna Julia (part Moorish), Haidee (half Moorish), and Gulbeyaz (entirely Turkish) wouldn't have merely their genes to blame.

It would perhaps have pleased Byron (who was unhappy with the body), to read in Sale that in Mohammed's paradise the blessed will need neither "to ease themselves, nor even blow their noses, for that all superfluities will be discharged and carried off by perspiration, or a sweat as odoriferous as musk"[43] – but he never mentions it.

Byron's Islam is a *faux*-Islam, a marketable literary construct first and an authentic record and meditation some way second.

***

An author who denied any value to Eastern poetry, religion, or ethics, was Southey, who wrote poems about the East on behalf of the East, in

---

42: Lady Mary Wortley Montagu, *Letters* (two vols Paris 1803), II, pp.158-60.
43: Sale, p.99.

the imperialist conviction that it couldn't write them about itself; that it couldn't make sense at all, indeed, unless a westerner wrote about it. Byron had been engaging in covert dialogue with Southey about the East long before the two came into public contact, and before he thought of going on his own eastern journey. Southey had written *Thalaba* despite an innate literary distaste:

> It had been easy to have made Zeinab [*an early heroine in* Thalaba] speak from the Koran, if the tame language of the Koran could be remembered by the few who have toiled through its dull tautology.[44]

Byron had read *Thalaba* by 1807[45] when he wrote out his own juvenile reading list. In a later note by Southey to *Thalaba* Book 1, he would have found

> A waste of ornament and labour characterises all the work of the orientalists ... The little of their literature that has reached us is ... worthless. Our *barbarian* scholars have called Ferdusi the Oriental Homer ... To make this Iliad of the East, as they have sacrilegiously styled it, a good poem, would be realising the dreams of alchemy, and transmuting lead into gold.
> The Arabian Tales certainly abound with genius; they have lost their metaphorical rubbish in passing through the filter of a French translation.[46]

Southey ignores the question, "Is Homer an occidental or an oriental poet? The *Odyssey* centres on a Greek island, the *Iliad* on a city in Asia ..." and it's clear that he thought the poets of the east could only become great after having been re-written by western ones, and not always then: *Thalaba*, his "Islamic" poem, and *The Curse of Kehama*, his "Hindu" poem, must therefore be seen as gifts to the East, epics of which the indigenous poets were incapable (he planned a Zoroastrian epic, too).

Byron again disagreed. He listed further among his early reading:

> Ferdausi, author of the Shah Nameh the Persian Iliad, Sadi, and Hafiz, the immortal Hafiz the oriental Anacreon ...[47]

44: *Thalaba* Book 1, n: Pratt 3, p.193.
45: See letter to Elizabeth Pigot, BLJ I, p.127.
46: *Thalaba* Book 1, n: Pratt 3, p.194.
47: CMP, 1. The influence on him of Jones's translations is clear here: see BLJ III, 164.

The implication here is that he is fluent in Persian; few think he was.

The conflict which was erupt in 1820 over *A Vision* and *The Vision of Judgement* is to be seen in embryo in Byron's early clash with Southey over the value of eastern cultures.

The Islamic East in Byron's day

It won't help to imagine the Islamic world in 1809-24 as a mirror of today's. Oil was not important, and the Kingdom of Saudi Arabia did not exist. The Saud family ruled oasis villages. Neither did Israel exist. By far the most important state was Ottoman Turkey, and all roads led to Constantinople (not yet renamed Istanbul). Greece, Albania, Syria, Lebanon, Palestine, Iraq ("Mesopotamia"), and Egypt were all provinces of the Ottomans, as was most of what came to be called Yugoslavia. These were ruled with varying degrees of imperial strength and conviction: some pashas – such as Byron's friend Ali – were virtually independent. North African states such as Libya ("Tripoli"), Tunisia, and Algeria, were all powerless Turkish colonies, often dominated by pirates, and as often prey to massive internal division and constant regime-change: one wag had it that in Tripoli there were often eights Deys every week. Morocco was more stable (Haidee's mother was born in Fez). Despite occasional forays such as the abortive attack on Constantinople in February 1807, and the successful raid to free the European slaves in Algiers in August 1816, English imperialism was only interested in the area in so far as Bonapartist France was interested in it – as shown by the French invasion of Egypt in 1798, quickly neutralised by the English at the Battle of the Nile and the Siege of Acre, and the French occupation of the Ionian Islands, quickly overthrown by the English in 1809, with Byron's visit to Ali Pacha as a collateral event.

The Turks were supreme, and supremely arrogant, not just over Greeks and Bulgarians, but even – asserts Byron – over their fellow-Moslems: "The Turks abhor the Arabs (who return the compliment a hundred-fold) even more than they hate the Christians", he writes, in a note to *The Bride of Abydos*, line 144.

Threats to the hold Turkey had on her colonies, such as the one posed by the Greek War of Independence, were regarded with deep unease by the Tories who ruled England for most of Byron's life, as threats to Legitimacy in general. The Ottoman Empire had, after all, always been there, and was probably preferable to a French or Russian alternative. The Wahhabi fundamentalist movement, begun in the eighteenth century by the scholar Ibn Abd al-Wahhab and temporarily defeated by Sultan

Mahmoud II between 1812 and 1818, was noted, as a thing remote but interesting.

The Eastern Mediterranean – especially that part around Corfu and the other Ionians – was a gateway to India, in which the English were by contrast very interested; they had already thwarted French ambitions in India in the eighteenth century, and were now nervous, not about French encroachments towards it, but about Russian encroachments. Catherine the Great had christened her eldest son Constantine with a view to putting him on the ancient Byzantine throne, after having defeated the Ottomans (two ambitions in which she never succeeded). Russia's constant thrust towards Turkey – illustrated by the Siege of Ismail in *Don Juan* VI-VIII – was balanced by corresponding imperialist incursions into Ukraine and the Crimea, the invasions of the Caucasus, about which Pushkin and Lermontov wrote some of their most famous Byronic poetry and prose (chronicled by Svetlana Klimova in her paper below), and by the non-stop pressure which, still further eastwards, they kept up on Persia (Iran). Persia had experienced a considerable expansion under Nadir Shah (see *DJ* IX, st. 44), who conquered Afghanistan and India as far as Delhi, but who went crazy, and was assassinated. According to Byron (who may only have dragged him in for the sake of the rhyme, "trophy / Sophy / coffee"), he went mad from constipation. In fact Nadir Shah had, from whatever motives, attempted that much-to-be-desired thing, a synthesis of Sunni and Shia (a schism never mentioned by Byron), but his death put an end to the dream. For the second half of the eighteenth century, Persia had non-stop internal conflicts, only brought to a close in 1796. In March 1813 Byron entertained the idea of travelling to "Bagdad & Tahiran" with the Marquis of Sligo;[48] but nothing came of it.

Greece was not a nation, and few mainland Greeks had any idea of patriotism. That was an idea cultivated by people in the diaspora like Hobhouse's friend Adamatios Korais. Mainland Greeks owed their allegiance either to the Turks, or to their feudal leaders.

A tragic-comic spectacle was afforded by Venice, once a major imperialist power in the Eastern Mediterranean – as shown by Shakespeare in *Othello*, and by Byron in *The Siege of Corinth* – but now defeated, decayed, and prostituted by Napoleon to the Austrians, as implied in *Beppo*.

England's foe was, until 1815, Bonapartist France, and in so far as the parallel imperialisms of Turkey and Russia also saw France as a threat, Turkey and Russia were friends of England – Christian Russia especially, alarming though her ambitions were in a longer perspective. Turkey was

48: BLJ III, 27.

powerful, but so clearly disintegrating that she was held in contempt, even though she didn't disintegrate for another century.

Despite the amount of study to which the specialists had subjected it in the previous century, the Islamic faith was in general little known about in the west, and Byron's work added little to its profile. It was, then as now, a multifaceted and sophisticated system, varying in both practise and belief from country to country and from culture to culture. Byron – who despite his boasts and air of familiarity, never, I think, read the Qu'ran – still regarded Islam as monolithic, and was happier using its positive qualities as a stick with which to beat Christian cant, than as a thing worthy in itself. More of this below.

Byron's eastern travels

A question rarely if ever asked is, how many Moslems did Byron meet and converse with during his time in the east? He had a few Arabic lessons while on Malta,[49] but as he never travelled in any Arab countries, they would have done him little good – and we don't know whether he was learning spoken, or written Arabic. In Albania he met some Moslems – though it's rash to describe Ali Pacha, supposedly his friend, as a typical Moslem, or a typical Albanian, or a typical anything. Ali provided him with a bodyguard for the return journey to the Gulf of Corinth – but whether they were Moslems, Christians, or anything other than jovial, opportunist klephts (bandits), is not clear. It was not uncommon for Albanians to be Christians one day and Moslems the next, depending on what kind of government official was questioning them.

In Greece Byron mixed with Christians, who would have had a particular, and negative, attitude to Islam. There are gaps in our knowledge of his day-to-day itinerary, in the months between the parting with Hobhouse off Zea in mid-1810, and his arrival back in London in 1811. He seems, however, not to have left Greece in that time – but there were many Turks in Greece – the Greeks didn't kill them all until later – and Byron had a considerable network of friends among them.

These things are examined in greater detail below.

One thing is clear – wherever he went, Byron had no opportunities for meeting Moslem women, such as figure in at least two of the tales, and in

---

49: Peter Vassallo is the only scholar who has dared suggest who his teacher might have been: "His tutor was, in all probability, the Abbate Gioacchino Navarro who was librarian at the time and an Arabic scholar. Indeed Abbate Navarro was highly esteemed by most travellers who made his acquaintance while visiting the library" (*Byron and the Mediterranean*, ed. Vassallo, Malta 1986, p.23).

Don Juan. For his knowledge of them, he consulted Lady Mary Wortley Montagu and, later, after he had written the Turkish Tales but before he'd started *Don Juan*, the *Narrative of a Ten Years' Residence in Tripoli* by Richard Tully's sister-in-law. These two liberal-minded women had been privileged over any Christian males, and had been guests in areas where their husbands and brothers-in-law were never permitted.

***

I wish to look in detail at what we know of Byron's Eastern travels, and to try and deduce what experiences he might have had to qualify him as an orientalist. I shall divide the examination into two parts: those days when we have the diary of his travelling companion John Cam Hobhouse for assistance, and those after Hobhouse had left him and come home. I take Greece, a Turkish province in 1809-11, to have been an oriental place.

Byron travels with Hobhouse

Any examination of Byron's Orientalism must start with an examination of the audience for whom he was writing, their attitude to the Orient, and his attitude to them. His attitude to them was founded on a negative assessment which he derived from one important fact: that he had gone to Albania in October 1809 on the encouragement of English naval and diplomatic Intelligence on Malta, who wanted him (though naturally he didn't know this), to visit Ali Pacha as a toyboy present, what we would call a sweetener, while they took over the Ionian Islands from the French. Evidence from the Marquis of Sligo[50] suggests that Ali thought Byron was George III's nephew. Ali had himself coveted the Ionians for years, and the English had promised that he could have them – but then decided that Empire had priority over promises: so some sort of compensation was called for, and Byron was beautiful, and "of great family". This was argued by me in 1995,[51] and no-one has challenged the thesis so far.

The humiliation (as a result of which Byron does not, however, seem to have suffered either in physical, psychological, or public terms), was one about which he kept silent for ever, only dropping the faintest hints

---

50: Yale Beinecke, OSB MSS 74 Box 1, Folder 1, 2.
51: See Cochran, *Nature's Gentler Errors: Byron, Ali Pasha and the Ionian Islands, Byron Journal*, 1995, pp.22-35.

to people who could not possibly understand them.[52] But he wrote about
the East with a hidden agenda – and the agenda wasn't against the East, it
was against the British "rascals" who had first tried to prostitute him, and
then gobbled up the prostitute poetry he'd written out of the experience.

The best description of the way he and Hobhouse were received by
Ali Pacha is not from Hobhouse but from a letter from Byron to his
mother of November 12th 1810, from Prevesa, after they had returned to
Greece from Ali's Albanian territory:

> I shall never forget the singular scene on entering Tepaleen at five in the
> afternoon as the Sun was going down, it brought to my recollection
> (with some change of *dress* however) Scott's description of Branksome
> Castle in his lay, & the feudal system. – The Albanians in their dresses
> (the most magnificent in the world, consisting of a long *white kilt*, gold
> worked cloak, crimson velvet gold laced jacket & waistcoat, silver
> mounted pistols & daggers,) the Tartars with their high caps, the Turks
> in their vast pelises & turbans, the soldiers & black slaves with the
> horses, the former stretched in groupes in an immense open gallery in
> front of the palace, the latter placed in a kind of cloister below it, two
> hundred steeds ready caparisoned to move in a moment, couriers
> entering or passing out with dispatches, the kettle drums beating, boys
> calling the hour from the minaret of the mosque, altogether, with the
> singular appearance of the building itself, formed a new & delightful
> spectacle to a stranger. – I was conducted to a very handsome apartment
> & my health enquired after by the vizier's secretary "a la mode de
> Turque". – The next day I was introduced to Ali Pacha, I was dressed in
> a full suit of Staff uniform with a very magnificent sabre &c.– – The
> Vizier received me in a large room paved with marble, a fountain was
> playing in the centre, the apartment was surrounded by scarlet
> Ottomans, he received me *standing*, a wonderful compliment from a
> Mussulman, & made me sit down on his right hand. – I have a Greek
> interpreter for general use, but a Physician's of Ali's named [Seculario?]
> who understands Latin acted for me on this occasion. – His first
> question was why at so early an age I left my country? (the Turks have
> no idea of travelling for amusement) he then said the English Minister
> had told him I was of a great family, & desired his respects to my
> mother, which I now in the name of Ali Pacha present to you. He said
> he was certain I was a man of birth because I had small ears, curling
> hair, and little white hands, and expressed himself pleased with my
> appearance & garb. He told me to consider him as a father whilst I was
> in Turkey, & said he looked on me as his son. Indeed he treated me like

52: See this, to Mercer Elphinstone in May 1815, about his famous Albanian
costume: "… if you like the dress – keep it – I shall be very glad to get rid of it – as
it reminds me of one or two things I don't wish to remember" (BLJ IV, 111-12).

a child, sending me almonds & sugared sherbet, fruit & sweetmeats 20 times a day. – He begged me to visit him often, and at night when he was more at leisure ..."[53]

It's interesting that he describes an Albanian scene as though it's from Scott's *Marmion*. Even on the spot, his reaction and interpretation are in part literary. His liking for the idea that Ali Pacha, sadistic mass-murderer that he was, offered himself as a father-figure (Mrs Byron was flattered, and asked for her compliments to be returned), stayed with Byron for ever. On October 22 1820, Teresa Guiccioli wrote him a letter, with the following in the postscript:

Ali – Bassa – quel tuo Amico – Padre – quel cuore tenero – liberale – forse è morto – – è una perdita pel Mondo – pe'buoni patriotti – e per le finanze de'suoi domini – (perchè la popolazione si accrescerà), irreparabile. Ma davvero Amor mio si dispiace a te, dispiacerà anche a me la sua morte – – nulla però potrà farla dispiacere a Pierino! – in ogni modo però se fosse morte nella maniera che si dice sarebbe il punto più luminoso della Sua vita. – Ma perchè ti ho fatto queste ciarle? io non lo sò – – ma io credo *p* una magica potenza che non mi permette quando scrivo, o parlo a te, *di star ne'limiti della discrezione. Perdona Amor Mio!*

[Ali – Pasha – that Friend – Father of yours – that tender heart – liberal – perhaps he is dead – – it is a loss to the World – to good patriots – and to the finances of his domains (because the population will increase), irreparably. – But in truth, my Love, if it causes you sorrow, his death will be a cause of sorrow to me also – – nothing, however, can make it a cause of sorrow to Pierino! In any case, however, if he died in the manner that they say, it would be the most brilliant moment in his Life. – But why have I run on like this? I do not know – – but I think because of a magic power that does not permit me when write or speak to you *to remain within the limits of discretion. Pardon me my Love!*][54]

He was fully aware of the depths of Ali's barbarity; but never, it seems from Teresa's irony, lost a nostalgic affection for him.[55]

To proceed with some experiences which he did *not* use as poetic capital, and which would have upset the decorum of his style in the

---

53: BLJ I, 226-8.
54: *Shelley and his Circle* X (ed Reiman and Fischer) Harvard 2002, p.942.
55: See Cecil Y. Lang, *Narcissus Jilted: Byron, Don Juan, and the Biographical Imperative,* in *Historical Studies and Literary Criticism*, ed. McGann, Madison 1985, pp.143-79.

Turkish tales, perhaps affecting their market. On October 28th 1810 he
and Hobhouse attended a puppet show at Ioannina. Hobhouse writes:

> Went to a Turkish puppet-show at a coffee-house, this being the
> comedy exhibited during Ramadan. The show was in the corner of the
> room, the figures being shown on a piece of greased paper a yard or so
> in length and breadth. The hero of the presentation was a [*BLOT*]
> personage with an immense head and body tapering to the waist of a
> wasp, and from the regions of his breeches proceeded an enormous yard
> [*penis*], supported by a piece of visible string from his neck, which he
> seemed to wear *par excellence*, none of the other characters having this
> engine displayed. Towards the conclusion a certain *divertissement* was
> introduced between this man and a lady, which was highly to the taste of
> the audience, which consisted mostly of young boys. Nothing could be
> more beastly, but Lord Byron tells me that he has seen puppet-shows in
> England as bad, and that the morris dances in Nottinghamshire are
> worse. One of the most admired passages in the play was where the
> above important character held a soliloquy addressed to the appendage
> alluded to, which he then snubbed most soundly with his fist, which was
> a prelude to the devil descending and removing this engine from before
> and affixing it to his posteriors. To bed at twelve.

Hobhouse offers an occidental distaste: Byron counters with an anti-
occidental gloss. We in the twenty-first century do not put much sex into
our Morris-dancing, but evidently conventions have changed. Any idea
that Moslems preserved a grave and chaste public demeanour at all times
would have been hard to maintain for Byron from then on.

Three days after they see the puppet show, Hobhouse records Byron
as having started *Childe Harold*.

On Sunday March 11th 1810 at Smyrna, they witnessed a djereed
practice (a djereed is a short spear, for throwing), from which Byron
seems to have learned much, though Hobhouse seems in two minds about
it.

> Up half-past nine. Walked out to see the exercise of the *djerid*,[56] on a
> point of land to the north of the town. Childishness of this
> amusement, the Turks shouting "Olloh olloh!" – the Governor being

---

56: See *The Giaour* 251, and B.'s note: "Jerreed, or Djerrid, a blunted Turkish
javelin, which is darted from horseback with great force and precision. It is a
favourite exercise of the Mussulans; but I know not if it can called a *manly* one,
since the most expert in the art are the Black Eunuchs of Constantinople. – I think,
next to these, a Mamlouk at Smyrna was the most skilful that came within my own
observation" (CPW III, 417). See also *The Bride of Abydos*, I, line 238.

darted at impartially with the others. Fine-looking horses and expert performers – the horsemen, some of them, have a cane with a crook at the end, with which they pick up the *djerid*. A Greek murdered last night – murderer taken refuge with the French Consul, whose gate is surrounded with janissaries and crowds of friends and relations of the deceased. These latter likewise went in a body to the Governor on the djerid-ground.

Street violence was as common in London then as it is now; but I can think of no English sports which would have involved the main public spectator having lances hurled towards him.

In Constantinople they mixed largely with people from the British Embassy and factories – though they did meet the Capudan-Pasha, or Admiral of the Turkish fleet, observed Dervish rituals (one authentic, one *quasi* showbiz), and saw examples of Turkish brutality. Byron seems not to have learned much Turkish apart from a few greetings, or oaths – "saban hiresem saban serula,"[57] or "Ana seing siktim,"[58] for example.

Byron is anxious to stress the glory of certain parts of the East and the gloom of others. He would wish us to know that he witnessed a flight of eagles over Mount Parnassus, and heard jackals howling in the ruins of Ephesus, thereby stressing on the one hand the way poets are inspired, and on the other the way nature gloats over the decay of empires. But Hobhouse sees no eagles over Parnassus,[59] and what he hears at Ephesus are frogs.[60] Eagles are for the most part solitary anyway, and humbugging was something at which Byron was ever expert.

57: *The Giaour*, line 358, Byron's note.

58: See *D J*, IV, st.116, rough draft.

59: In a journal entry for March 20 1814 Byron records "I remember, in riding from Chrisso to Castri (Delphos), along the sides of Parnassus, I saw six eagles in the air. It is uncommon to see so many together; and it was the number – not the species, which is common enough – that excited my attention" (BLJ III, 253). Over seven years later, in the Ravenna Journal, he doubles the number of eagles, as Falstaff does his men in Kendal green: "Upon Parnassus going to the fountain of Delphi (Castri) in 1809 – I saw a flight of twelve Eagles – (Hobhouse says they are Vultures – at least in conversation) and I seized the Omen. – On the day before, I composed the lines to Parnassus – (in Childe Harold) and on beholding the birds – had a hope – that Apollo had accepted my homage" (BLJ IX, 41). In his diary Hobhouse doesn't mention a single eagle.

60: Hobhouse, in *A Journey through Albania* (hereafter *Journey*: second edition, II, pp.647-8) expands: "The whole country resounded with the croaking of the frogs, which was so loud, and in so different a tone from any we had ever heard before, that we were at first inclined to believe it proceeded from the packs of jackalls with which the mountains abound, and whose howling we had been told

In Constantinople Byron and Hobhouse witness, not violence, but the effects of violence:

> Monday May 14th 1810: Cold rainy bad weather. Left the frigate in the gig at twelve. Rowed round the first point. There were waiting fellows with rope lines, which they flung into the boat and towed her against the strong current under the walls of the Seraglio Gardens for more than a mile.
> Saw two dogs gnawing a body.

This sight is recollected by Byron some years later, at *The Siege of Corinth*, 409-12. A week later, on Monday May 21st 1810, they see something more horrible still:

> Went across the water to the Arsenal and thence to the Galeogis Wharf, where saw a dead man on his belly with his head off lying between his legs, face upwards. He had been executed yesterday on the same spot. The skin was off his legs and arms by bastinado or burning. He had been a Greek Cogia Bash and was from Toccala. His face was black and he seemed to have been dead a week at least.

---

we should hear upon our journey". Byron, as time passed, seems to have remembered the warning rather than the fact. See *Don Juan* IX 27, 2-3: "I've seen them [jackals] in the Ephesian ruins howl / By night". This is the fourth time in his works that he refers to jackals at Ephesus (which they don't reach until tomorrow). He does so in a note to 1024-5 of *The Siege of Corinth*, written 1812-15 ("The jackal's troop, in gathered cry, / Bayed from afar complainingly"): "I believe I have taken a poetical license to transfer the jackal from Asia. In Greece I never saw nor heard these animals; but among the ruins of Ephesus I have heard them by hundreds. They haunt ruins, and follow armies". At *CHP* IV, 153, 4-6, he writes:
> *I have beheld the Ephesian's miracle –*
> *Its columns strew the wilderness, and dwell*
> *The hyaena and the jackall in their shade ...*

See also his abuse of Hewson Clarke in the Preface to *Hints from Horace:* "I have been rambling upwards of two years and heard nothing like the voice of Hewson Clarke, except the yell of the jackalls in the ruins of Ephesus" (CPW I, 430). However, in a letter to Henry Drury of 3 May 1810 (BLJ I, 240) he mentions Ephesus without referring to any jackals; although in his journal on 23 Nov 1813 (BLJ III, 218: he is planning a trip to witness what he hopes will be a revolution in the Netherlands) he writes "I have heard hyænas and jackalls in the ruins of Asia; and bull-frogs in the marshes, – besides wolves and angry Mussulmans. Now, I should like to listen to the sound of a free Dutchman". Perhaps his memory played him tricks, or perhaps he was just anxious to emulate Richard Chandler, who records in the Ephesus section of his 1775 book *(Travels in Asia Minor,* p.113): "... a jackall cried mournfully, as if forsaken by its companion, on the mountain".

A Cogia Basha is an elder, or senior provincial governor. Accused of trafficking with the Russians, he had been the victim of the rapacity of the Capudan-Pasha, who coveted his wealth.[61] Beheading was a death more humiliating than strangulation, and to place the head between the legs was further humiliation: had he been Turkish it would have been placed under his arm. Public violence was thus a factor in Eastern life which they would have taken for granted, perhaps more horrible than the English kind, which was horrible enough, though corpses were not left exposed in this way at Newgate.

In Constantinope on June 26th 1810 they saw a more elaborate, and even more disgusting, entertainment than the puppet-show at Ioannina. This one disguised itself as an Islamic religious ritual. Here again is Hobhouse's description:

> Went out with Captain Bathurst and a party to see the howling Dervishes. [...] We were informed that this religious ceremony did not take place except when there was a sufficient audience collected. After staying some time in a little ante-court, hearing the singing and praying in the small room of ceremony, entered whilst there were a large party singing, or rather bawling, in a dirty deal apartment filled up at one end with several flags in the centre, axes, swords, small drums on one side, and a silk lettered cloth on the other, which they say is part of Mahomet's tent, the rest being at Vienna.
>
> Here were three principals kneeling and waving their heads sideways to the music, and in the right-hand corner a small, black, starving, thin fellow, kneeling also, and contorting himself in every horrid and ridiculous gesture, now and then becoming furious and knocking his arms and head violently against the ground, and at last opening his half-opened shirt below his navel and led off as a maniac. Then the principals advanced, the vulgar, not monks, forming three sides of the oblong and in the middle six persons sitting or squatting down. The singing began from those squatting, the whole keeping up chorus, which seemed to be the name of God. They continued waving backwards and forwards and sideways, all close together, howling and grunting, to a kind of tune that at last was lost in an exclamation: "Yullah Illah!", when they jumped and jogged themselves into that which appeared to me a sensual ecstasy, from certain symptoms in the youngest part of the performers (who are promiscuous, introducing themselves only by kissing the principal's hands, &c.)
>
> The principals only jogged their heads and moved on their heels and seemed half in joke – as many were – especially a person or mosque-reader, who accompanied us and joined in the jogging and howling to

---

61: *Journey*, II, p.905.

great effect, as I saw by his hiding his fork with his robe.[62] During this
time the chief entered. He looked a red-faced fellow and whispered as if
conducting a ceremony, with frequent "pishes" of anger. (I must
mention that before the violent howling and jogging began, an itchy
scabby friar came round, and reverently took away every man's turban,
and placed it under the banners on that side of the room.)

After the howling, &c., there was a prayer, and all dispersed, going
away to take pipes and coffee in an adjoining small chamber, to recruit
them.[63] They soon came back when a jug of water that the chief had
blown into was handed round, and afterwards a shirt, consecrated,
before or holy. Two little children were also at intervals brought in and
being laid on a mat before the chief, he stood first on their bellies and
then on their backs and they were supposed, after he taking them up had
breathed on them, to be cured of some complaint.

The howling and jogging then recommenced, then after some time
was a prayer by the chief. Then he took two men and ran needles, like
netting needles, with curious handles, through one cheek, and through
the thick skin above the windpipe. After a short time he pulled these out,
spitting on his fingers and wetting the wound and certainly nothing
appeared, for we were close, and the performers brought the fellows
near that we might see all fair. At last a black curly-haired Egyptian, on
the chief drawing out the needle, appeared to faint, fell down, stayed
some time till the chief recovered him by puffing or spitting in his
mouth, when he rose up, screaming out "Yollah!" in a convulsed
manner, but, ridiculously, recovered in a moment.

This boring ceremony was performed on several, the jogging and
crying still continuing. then the chief (who indeed only seemed chosen
for the occasion as head of the conjuring) took out an ataghan, having
first drawn several rusty swords – breathed on it – and gave it to a black
Arab, who stripped to his waist and, after crying out several times on the
name of God, applied [the sword] to the narrow of his belly as tight as
possible, working his belly and the sword about in a very frightful
manner, but without hurting himself, except leaving something like
bloody scratches. Whilst performing he cried out to us, "Bono? bono?"
Then another black Arab took the ataghan, did the same and lay down,
suffering the chief to stand on the knife when it was across his body.
The same fellow then took two sharp iron spikes with wooden globes
filled up with iron chains and knobs, and appeared to drive them
repeatedly (these also being breathed upon and blessed), so as almost to
meet into his lower abdomen. He seemed in a fury, and with an
enthusiastic coquetry could scarcely suffer the priests to take the spikes
from his hands.

62: For *fork,* see *Beppo* 92, line 3 (*"Is 't true they use their fingers for a fork?"*).
63: A subsidiary meaning of to "recruit" is to "refresh" or "reinvigorate".

Then followed half-a-dozen fellows, seemingly promiscuously chosen, holding red-hot irons (having licked them cooler), in their teeth – one fellow near us made dreadful faces and pulled the instrument out, but the others pretended that they were loath to part with them. Then one of the Arabs swallowed several pieces of glowing charcoal, and without a trick, the coals, as all the other instruments being first solemnly breathed upon by the chief.

[...]

Such a mixture of religion and jugglery was never seen. 'Twas very tedious, lasting from half-past one to half-past four. We paid fifteen shillings for our seats, and were afterwards followed by the two Arabs (one of whom spoke a little English) asking for an additional reward for their tricks. What is singular is that the dervishes appeared only directors of the ceremony, the principal performers being only common fellows.[64]

Dined at the Palace. Told long stories about s<ec>ts and heard no new ones.

It would be all too easy, if this were all they saw, for them to associate at least this (one of the more extreme forms of Islamic mysticism), with thinly-disguised, publicly-displayed sexual perversion, staged for money. With their talk of "sects" (meaning varieties of deviation), and their code-word for "homosexual" being already "Methodist," it would be only a short step from an anti-Christian leer to an anti-Islamic one. But such things as these, or the Ioannina puppets, would too offensive to put even in *Don Juan*: they would wreck the high but precarious decorum of *Childe Harold* or of the Turkish tales. Fortunately for Islam, the Howling Dervishes were not all they saw. On Friday May 10th 1810 they had already witnessed the Turning Dervishes. The primary meaning of "Dervish" is "poor man", which is the way Byron normally uses the word (minus the "h") at, for example, *The Giaour* 340, or *The Corsair* 49. Only at *Don Juan* III 29, 6-7 *(dancing / Like Dervises, who turned as on a pivot)* does he employ it as it is to be understood here. The Turning or Whirling Dervishes were Sufi mystics whose ecstatic dances brought them closer to communion with the Godhead. *Journey* (II, 925) identifies those seen here as monks from the Mevlevi monastery in Pera:

Up eleven. Went with a party to the Turning Dervishes. We were conducted into the room by a private door and were seated in the gallery of the room, which was octagonal with the interior part railed off, with a wood floor, highly polished. We waited some time, when the large door

---

64: They were "taken from the spectators" *(Journey* II, p.934).

opposite the red carpet placed for the Superior of the order was opened, and the Turks rushed in exactly like the mob into a playhouse, each however carefully taking off his shoes or slippers as he entered. The place outside the rails and the gallery was soon nearly filled. The Dervishes dropped in one by one, and as they entered the railed enclosure, most reverently, and most of them most gracefully, bowed to the Superior's seat. At last the Superior entered, better dressed than the rest, and with his feet not naked. With him was another man, better dressed, who seemed to officiate afterwards as clerk Other dervishes arrived, and went up into the gallery opposite the Superior, where were lying four small cymbal drums. The Superior now began praying for about ten minutes. Then a dervish stood up in the gallery and sang from a book for some time. Next the drums were beat, and a general song commenced in the gallery, four dervishes playing also on long yellow cane-pipes, to tunes by no means unpleasant and indeed something like an English air.

On some sudden note being struck, the dervishes all suddenly fell flat on their faces, clapping their hands all at once on the earth. Then the music ceased, and the Superior began again to pray. Then he rose and began to march slowly round the room, all the others following and bowing, each of them, on both sides of the Superior's cushion. They compassed the room three times, the Superior bowing also, but not to the cushion only – when he was half-way across it – then the Superior re-seated himself, prayed a short time, the music struck up, and the Dervishes stood up. Fourteen out of the twenty who were present let drop a long coloured petticoat and threw off their cloaks, then the clerk marched past the Superior and bowed, retiring into the middle of the room.

A Dervish followed, bowed and began to whirl, his long petticoat flying out. The rest all followed, and soon all were in a whirl, a circle round the room, and three or four in the middle – the arms of one man alone were held straight upwards, the rest had theirs extended horizontally, out full length, generally with the palm of one hand turned upwards, and of the other downward, the fingers close together. Two of them had their right arm crooked like a kettle spout.

Some of them turned with great speed – they revolved round the room imperceptibly – the clerk continued walking amongst them and the Superior waving his body gently sideways and smiling. They continued at this work for twenty-five minutes but with four short intervals. The last time they turned ten minutes, nor did any one seem affected by this strange exercise, though there was one boy about fifteen and another seventeen perhaps.

The clerk, after the turning and music ceased, prayed, and a man walking round threw his cloak upon each of the Dervishes as he was in his place bending to the earth. The Superior then prayed the last prayer and we left him in the midst of it.

These Dervishes are more liberal and learned (in Arabic) than any
men in Turkey &c., and the public is obliged to them for the
preservation the beauties of the Arabic, as all of them are instructed in
that tongue, and as they gather together collections of books in that
language.

"The Superior then prayed the last prayer and we left him in the midst
of it:" it seems they walked out in the middle of a reading from the
Qu'ran: the British were certainly not "assimilating themselves into the
culture," as Naji Oueijan, quoted above, has it. But, strange (un-Anglican)
as this ritual had been, it had at any rate given them an idea of the curious
dignity of eastern religion, and the Turning Dervishes had impressed them
as vehicles of learning, spirituality and tradition, rather as the Armenian
monks on San Lazzaro were to in 1816.
    They arrived in Constantinople a few months after two Sultans, Selim
III and Mustapha IV, had been assassinated. The unsuccessful reforming
ambitions of Selim, especially (he had aspired to be a Turkish Peter the
Great), struck them as tragic, and the two recent deaths impressed on them
the unease and violence which seemed to attend Turkish politics, to which
the low-key hypocrisy of dull George III's England presented a strong
contrast. On July 10th 1810 they attended an audience with the then
Sultan, Mahmoud II, a highly successful ruler, who later in his reign –
after Byron's death – would solve the problem of the Janissaries by killing
25,000 of them in a single day. This easily beats George IV, at the funeral-
procession of whose wife only two people were killed – "What monarch
hath so little done?" The ideals of Selim and the achievements of
Mahmoud represented a major effort at modernising the Ottoman Empire,
but Byron was too close to the sequence of events to understand them
fully.

Byron travels without Hobhouse[65]

In Turchia sicuramente non si fa l'amore così.
—*Il Turco in Italia*, Act II

Having left Hobhouse at Zea, Byron arrives back in Athens on July 18th
1810; he leaves for the Morea on July 21st. At an unspecifiable date in
August he meets Veli Pasha at Tripolitza (9), having been anticipated
there by the Marquis of Sligo, who is himself taken for Byron, who is
assumed, as I said, to be George III's nephew. By late August Byron is

---

65: Page-references in this section are to BLJ II.

back in Athens at the Capuchin Convent (11), leaving again for the
Morea in September: this is the expedition on which he is ill (14-15; 18-
19), and is nursed back to health by his two "Albanian" guards.

On October 2nd he tells his mother "I have now seen a good portion
of Turkey in Europe and Asia Minor" (17). He returns to Athens on
October 13th, having experienced the uncharacteristic failure of Turkish
hospitality which leads to the Bey of Corinth writing him a letter of
apology (40). This will appear as a fold-out supplement in *Childe Harold*
I and II. "I conceive that brutality will not be countenanced even by the
Turks, as we are taught that hospitality is a Barbarian's virtue," he writes
to Stratford Canning, *à propos* of this misadventure (24). On November
12th he calls upon "Mahomet" to witness that he won't sell Newstead
(26); however, as he also calls on Christ, Confucius and Zoroaster to the
same effect and in the same sentence, we can't take this as a pro-Islamic
gesture: and of course, he does at least try to sell Newstead.

He developed a large network of Moslem Turkish friends. He had, via
Sligo and Stratford Canning, the English ambassador in Constantinople, a
line of communication straight to the Sultan. Using this, he made the Bey
of Corinth apologise for his failure of hospitality, and the Caimacan of
the Morea apologise for the Bey of Corinth. His friend Suleiman Aga
sent a letter of recommendation for him to Ibrahim Effendi, the Turkish
Governor of Cairo; and he easily obtained a firman from Constantinople
allowing him free passage to Egypt, Jerusalem, and elsewhere – only lack
of funds made it impossible for him to use it. Other Turkish friends lent
him money, another argued with him about the relative levels of
oppression in Turkey and England; and one ordered a gold watch and an
expensive gun from him.[66]

On November 27th 1810, in a letter to Francis Hodgson, Byron
describes his Oriental social milieu thus:

> I am living alone in the Franciscan monastery with one Fri*ar* (a
> Capuchin of course) and one Fri*er* (a bandy legged Turkish cook) two
> Albanian savages, a Tartar, and a Dragoman, my only Englishman
> departs with this and other letters. – The day before yesterday, the
> Waywode (or Governor of Athens) with the Mufti of Thebes (a sort of
> Mussulman Bishop) supped here and made themselves beastly drunk
> with raw Rum, and the Padrè of the convent being as drunk as *we*, my
> *Attic* feast went off with great éclat … (27)

Notice that there are no Greeks in his party.

66: See Appendix.

The letter gives us evidence a-plenty that he became intimate with Islamic hypocrisy (alcohol being forbidden),[67] as well as mixing in the highest circles. He's proud of remaining in the East alone (the "Englishman" is Fletcher, who left because he couldn't take any more: 34, 49) and in a fine cross-section of non-western-European humanity – Moslem females excepted as ever, though not Turkish prostitutes, as we shall see. If a man couldn't become thoroughly adept in the customs and religions of the East in such society, where could he? Anxiety to humbug Hodgson, who was about to take orders (see below), should not, however, be ruled out:

> Talk of Galileeism? Show me the effects – are you better, wiser, kinder by your precepts? I will bring you ten Mussulmans shall shame you in all good-will towards men, prayer to God, and duty to their neighbours.[68]

Byron's contrary understanding, of Islamic hypocrisy as opposed to its real moral worth, would have been reinforced by the following, from the *Memoirs* of Baron de Tott. The Baron is here a guest of Khan Girey, later to figure as the protagonist of Pushkin's early Byronic poem, *The Fountain of Bakhchisarai*:

> Krim-Geuray, during the [*dramatic*] representation, asked me many questions about Moliere's plays, which he had heard spoken of. What I told him of the dramatic laws, and of the decency observed on our theatres, gave him a disgust for the farces with which the Turks are still obliged to be satisfied. He perceived himself, that the *Tartuffe* was preferable to *Pourceaugnac*; but he could not perceive how such a character as the *Bourgeois Gentilhomme* could exist in a society where the difference of rank is so perfectly understood, and so invariably established; and I rather chose to let him remain in ignorance, and imagine the poet was in the wrong, than to undertake his justification, by exposing the history of our irregularities. "But," added he, "if it be impossible to carry on the deception respecting *birth*, a man may easily impose upon the world by his character. Every country has its *Tartuffes*; (hypocrites) Tartary has hers; – and you will oblige me by getting this piece translated."[69]

67: "That wine is forbidden in Islam, and that some Muslims flout this rule, most probably came to Byron's notice during his stay in Turkey" – Kidwai, p.68.
68: BLJ II, 89 (letter to Hodgson, September 3rd 1811).
69: Baron de Tott, *Memoirs*, I, pp.424-5.

Byron's most famous oriental adventure is one for which we have to
rely on the words of the Marquis of Sligo:

> The new governor [*of Athens*], unaccustomed to have the same
> intercourse with the Christians as his predecessor, had, of course, the
> barbarous Turkish ideas with regard to women. In consequence, and in
> compliance with the strict letter of the Mohammedan law, he ordered
> this girl to be sewed up in a sack, and thrown into the sea – as, indeed,
> quite customary at Constantinople. As you were returning from bathing
> in the Piraeus, you met the procession going down to execute the
> sentence of the Waywode on this unhappy girl. Report continues to say,
> that on finding out what the object of their journey was, and who was
> the miserable sufferer, you immediately interfered; and on some delay
> in obeying your orders, you were obliged to inform the leader of the
> escort that force should make him comply; that, on further hesitation,
> you drew a pistol, and told him, that if he did not immediately obey
> your orders, and come back with you to the Aga's house, you would
> shoot him dead. On this the man turned about and went with you to the
> governor's house; here you succeeded, partly by personal threats, and
> partly by bribery and entreaty, in procuring her pardon, on condition of
> her leaving Athens. I was told that you then conveyed her in safety to
> the convent, and despatched her off at night to Thebes, where she found
> a safe asylum. Such is the story I heard, as nearly as I can recollect it.[70]

The tale is often told – it has been dramatised twice on television –
and is often cited as subtext to *The Giaour;* though this ignores the fact
that Leila, the Circassian heroine of *The Giaour*, *is* drowned; the
protagonist is unable to save her. Drowning adulterous women – or even
potentially, or reputedly, adulterous women – was not rare in the East in
Byron's day. The tale of Phrosyne and her companions, drowned by
Byron's friend Ali Pacha and referred to in the note to *The Giaour's* last
line, is still commemorated in modern Greece. In a letter to his Cambridge
friend Edward Daniel Clarke, Byron confirmed Sligo's story as "not very
far from the truth."[71]

One trip to Sunium apart, during which his party are *almost* ambushed
by banditti (30-1), he stays in Athens until he leaves on April 22 1811. At
the beginning of February he announces that he has obtained the firman
to travel to Egypt, Palestine and Syria (38-41) – but nothing comes of it.

A letter to his mother of January 14 1811 could not state more clearly
what he has learned:

70: CPW III, 414. Byron erased some lines in this, but he claims they were
unimportant – see BLJ III, 105, 156, and 200.
71: BLJ III, 200.

> ... I am so convinced of the advantages of looking at mankind instead of reading about them, and of the bitter effects of staying at home with all the narrow prejudices of an Islander, that I think there should be a law amongst us to set our young men abroad for a term among the few allies our wars have left us. – Here I see and have conversed with French, Italians, Germans, Danes, Greeks, Turks, Armenians, &c. &c. &c. and without losing sight of my own, I can judge of the countries and manners of others. – Where I see the superiority of England (which by the bye we are a good deal mistaken about in many things) I am pleased, and where I find her inferior I am at least enlightened (34-5).

It is not so much an Orientalist lesson to which he has subjected himself, as one enabling him to get his English Occidentalism in perspective. The adventure with Ali Pacha would not have diminished the lesson's effect. To Henry Drury he had already written:

> I see not much difference between ourselves & the Turks, save that we have foreskins and they none, that they have long dresses and we short, and that we talk much and they little. – In England the vices in fashion are whoring & drinking, in Turkey, Sodomy & smoking, we prefer a girl and a bottle, they a pipe and a pathic.[72]

It's not clear that he hadn't, while amongst the Turks, enjoyed the company of some pathics himself.

Between March 2 and 11 he drafts *Hints from Horace*, a poem devoid of oriental references (42, 43, 45, 49); he also writes most of *The Curse of Minerva*. He tells Hobhouse that he has "had a number of Greek and Turkish women," and has been clapped (46). He says he's still clapped after leaving Malta (48).

Byron is at Malta from April 30 to June 2, when he sets sail for home, and is back at Sheerness on July 14 1811. His earlier insistence on heterosexual transgression with adults may be modified when on July 18-19, he returns, and the following cryptic record appears in Hobhouse's diary: "none female nor under ten nor Turk".

Harold goes to Hell: the Orientalism of *Childe Harold's Pilgrimage*, Canto II

... j'ai deux fois vainqueur traversé l'Acheron ...

72: BLJ I, 238.

Manfred will visit Hell. Juan may end up there – or he may get married:
Byron isn't certain which punishment is worse. Both, if they stayed, would
deserve to do so. Childe Harold would like to go, too, but only for some
variety, out of boredom:

> And now Childe Harold was sore sick at heart,
> And from his fellow bacchanals would flee;
> 'Tis said, at times the sullen tear would start,
> But Pride congealed the drop within his ee:
> Apart he stalked in joyless reverie,   50
> And from his native land resolved to go,
> And visit scorching climes beyond the sea;
> With pleasure drugged he almost longed for woe,
> And e'en for change of scene would seek the shades below.

Odysseus visits Hell in *Odyssey* XI; so does Aeneas, in *Aeneid* VI: but
they come out again. Unlike them, Harold is no epic hero. He has no wife
to return to, and no city to found. Both those things would be outside his
remit. If he visited Hell, there'd be neither external nor internal pressure
on him to leave.

One possible entrance to Hell is via Acheron, whose name means
"river of woe". It is one of the rivers of the underworld; it flows through a
desert, and has the Acherusian lake at its end, across which the dead are
ferried by Charon. It vies in myth with Styx in claiming this terminal
function. The smaller rivers Pyriphlegethon (a river of lava) and Cocytus,
are two of its tributaries (see Hom. Od. X. 513). If you are lucky, your
soul may, after a trip down it, and a shorter or longer stay on the shore of
the Acherusian lake, be reborn. If you aren't (and Harold wouldn't want to
be reborn), you'll stay there ...

Herakles had, as one of his Labours, to drag Cerberus through the
cavern in which the Acherusian lake runs. The Acherusian lake is not a
happy place, and Acheron lacks the charm of the Cam or the Avon, as
Oberon and Puck know:

> Thou see'st these lovers seek a place to fight:
> Hie, therefore, Robin – overcast the night.
> The starry welkin cover thou anon
> With drooping fog, as black as Acheron ...
>
> (M.N.D. III ii 354-7)

Titus Andronicus, speaking of Revenge, swears:

> I'll dive into the burning lake below

And pull her out of Acheron by the heels. (T.A. IV iii 43-4)

Dante, "really, truly," experiences the place:

> E poi ch'a riguardar oltre mi diedi,
>> vidi genti a la riva d'un gran fiume;
>> per ch'io dissi: «Maestro, or mi concedi
> ch'i' sappia quali sono, e qual costume
>> le fa di trapassar parer sì pronte,
>> com'io discerno per lo fioco lume».
> Ed elli a me: «Le cose ti fier conte
>> quando noi fermerem li nostri passi
>> su la trista riviera d'Acheronte». (INF. III. 70-8)

[And then, directing my sight farther on, I saw people on the bank of a great river, so that I said, 'Master, now grant me to know who they are and what law makes them so eager for the crossing as they seem by what I discern through the dim light.' / And he said to me: 'These things will be plain to you when we stay our steps on the sad shore of Acheron.']

It also has the honour of being the last proper noun used by Ariosto in *Orlando Furioso*. It's the place to which the Christian Ruggiero's double dagger-thrust to the forehead of the Algerian king (and savage killer) Rodomonte, sends Rodomonte:

> Alle squalide ripe d'Acheronte,
> sciolta dal corpo più freddo che giaccio,
> bestemmiando fuggì l'alma sdegnosa,
> che fu sì altiera al mondo e sì orgogliosa.

[Released from its body, now ice-cold, the angry spirit which, among the living, had been so proud and insolent, fled cursing down to the dismal shores of Acheron.][73]

Harold has few Shakespearean or Ariostan experiences: his life isn't that interesting; there'd be no place for him at all in *Orlando Furioso*, and if ever he got into the Divine Comedy, he'd probably stay in Limbo, with the myriads of other people whom God doesn't find interesting enough either to save or damn. He has *one* Odyssyean experience before he arrives at his own Acheron:

73: Ariosto, *Orlando Furioso*, Canto 46, 140, 5-8 (the final lines of the poem). Translation by Guido Waldman, Oxford World's Classics 1983, p.573.

> But not in silence pass Calypso's isles, *
> The sister tenants of the middle deep;
> There for the weary still a haven smiles,   255
> Though the fair goddess long hath ceased to weep,
> And o'er her cliffs a fruitless watch to keep
> For him who dared prefer a mortal bride:
> Here, too, his boy essayed the dreadful leap
> Stern Mentor urged from high to yonder tide; 260
> While thus of both bereft, the nymph-queen doubly sighed.

> * Goza is said to have been the island of Calypso.

His Calypso seems to be Constance Spencer Smith, with whom Byron had his first important affair, at Malta. She's not his "mortal bride", not his Penelope: neither Harold nor he would want a Penelope – or a "boy", in the sense, that is, of a son, a Telemachus. Neither Harold nor Byron is a family man. Calypso has the advantage of being more chimerical than Penelope, too; she wouldn't do anything embarrassing, like be seen eating at table.

Spencer Smith / Calypso hadn't got to know Byron / Harold that well:

> Little knew she that seeming marble heart,
> Now masked in silence or withheld by pride, 290
> Was not unskilful in the spoiler's art,
> And spread its snares licentious far and wide;
> Nor from the base pursuit had turned aside,
> As long as aught was worthy to pursue:

> But Harold on such arts no more relied;   295
> And had he doated on those eyes so blue,
> Yet never would he join the lover's whining crew.

But it's a measure of the epic hero that he can fall in love, and with what Keats called "a real woman", not a goddess: what would Aeneas' stature be in our eyes, without his love for the material Dido?

Homer gives Ogygia, not Goza (in the Maltese archipelago) as the name of Calypso's island (see Od. VII. 244, 254); but Byron defies us to know this, or to check it. He will rack the ancient poems to fit his own Procrustean bed. He went off Spencer Smith after his first experience of Greece, and didn't renew the liaison. Liaisons, as both he and Harold knew, weren't worth it:

> 'Tis an old lesson; Time approves it true,
> And those who know it best, deplore it most;

> When all is won that all desire to woo,
> The paltry prize is hardly worth the cost: 310
> Youth wasted, minds degraded, honour lost,
> These are thy fruits, successful Passion! these!
> If, kindly, cruel, early Hope is crost,
> Still to the last it rankles, a disease,
> Not to be cured when Love itself forgets to please. 315

Both he and Harold, it's clear, value their youth, minds, and honour, too much to degrade them via a "Passion", even a "successful" one. Hell is a more dramatic destination.

***

To line 415 of Canto II Byron appends a note saying that the lake of Acheron is "According to Pouqueville the lake of Yanina; but Pouqueville is always out." François Charles Hugues Laurent Pouqueville was a career diplomat who had boldly gone where Harold was to still more boldly go (though he hadn't gone to Hell). By 1809 he was French Consul in Ioannina – rival to Byron's and Hobhouse's uncertain host, Captain William Martin Leake. Though the two young Englishmen passed through Ioannina, England and France were then at war, so they never met Pouqueville, who had in 1805 published *Voyages en Morée, à Constantinople, en Albanie et dans plusieurs autres parties de l'Empire Othoman*, a three-volume work which contains one of the first extended portraits of Ali Pacha. Here is the way Ali is introduced in the official version of *Childe Harold* II:

> In marble-paved pavilion, where a spring   550
> Of living water from the centre rose,
> Whose bubbling did a genial freshness fling,
> And soft voluptuous couches breathed repose,
> ALI reclined, a man of war and woes;
> Yet in his lineaments ye cannot trace,   555
> While Gentleness her milder radiance throws
> Along that aged venerable face,
> The deeds that lurk beneath, and stain him with disgrace.

No cruel underground river, but a "genial" spring, heralds him. It's deceptive, as was Ali himself.

Ioannina was the administrative headquarters of Ali's Greek dominions: it was nowhere near Acheron. As with Ogygia and Goza, the real Acheron is by tradition located elsewhere, further south in Epirus than

Ioannina, and therefore Pouqueville would indeed, in this case, be "out." Elizabeth Longford writes:

> Around, the rocks and forests; above, the bluest of skies after the storm; below, the grey village among its vines, and far below that, a waterfall with a drop into the River Kalamas, which Byron understood to be 'black Acheron', river of the underworld. (In fact, the River Kalamas was the ancient Thyamis, while the Acheron flows through the savage Suli country to the south-east; Byron was later to enter it in dramatic circumstances.) The vertiginous heights and roaring cataract gave to lovely Zitza that peculiar combination of opposites which 'shock yet please the soul'. To be at once shocked and pleased was Byron's idea of heaven.[74]

We find on reading Pouqueville that he doesn't actually say the lake of Ioannina and the Acherousian lake *are* the same. He merely compares the two:

> C'est dans cette presqu'ile, et hors de toute atteinte, qu'Ali pacha vit isolé de la ville et de ses sujets. Dans cette position, qui tiendrait encore après qu'un ennemi se serait rendu maître de Ianina, il vit au milieu d'une troupe d'élite a'Albanais, non point environné de terreurs, mais dans la sécurité que donne la bravoure et le courage. Il a réuni dans ce lieu ses munitions, ses trésors et ses femmes; en un mot, ce qu'il a de plus précieux. C'est là où il accumule des ressources que son prévoyant genie mettra en usage, s'il est jamais menacé. Il sortira comme un géant des bords de l'Achérusie, et l'étranger, assez imprudent pour se hasarder dans des gorges stériles, ne reverra plus le rivage qui l'aura vomi.[75]

> [It's on this peninsula, and away from all threat of attack, that Ali lives, isolated from the town and from his subjects. In this position, which he would have stayed in after an enemy had taken Ioannina, he lived in the midst of an élite troupe of Albanians, far from terrors, but in that security which gave him bravado and courage. He kept his munitions, his treasures, and his women in that place; in one word, everything that was most precious to him. There he accumulated the resources of which his prescient genius would make use if ever he were menaced. He would come out like a giant from the depths of Acherusia, and the foreigner who was imprudent enough to risk himself in the sterile mountain passes, would never again see the shore which had vomited him up.]

74: Elizabeth Longford, *Byron's Greece*, Weidenfeld and Nicholson, 1975, pp.16-17.
75: Pouqueville, *Voyages*, III, p.41.

But the knowledge that his despised French source is either speaking loosely, or is "out", does not prevent Byron from using the idea of the lake at Ioannina as Acherousia, at more than one point. Here is the first, which is stanzas 47-8:

> He passed bleak Pindus, Acherusia's lake, *   415
> And left the primal city of the land,
> And onwards did his further journey take
> To great Albania's chief, whose dread command †
> Is lawless law: for with a bloody hand
> He sways a nation, turbulent and bold: 420
> Yet here and there some daring mountain-band
> Disdain his power and from their rocky hold
> Hurl their defiance far, nor yield unless to gold.

* According to Pouqueville the lake of Yanina; but Pouqueville is always out.[76]
† The celebrated Ali Pacha. Of this extraordinary man there is an incorrect account in Pouqueville's Travels.[77]

> Monastic Zitza! From thy shady brow, *
> Thou small, but favoured spot of holy ground! 425
> Where'er we gaze around, above, below,
> What rainbow tints, what magic charms are found!
> Rock, river, forest, mountain, all abound,
> And bluest skies that harmonize the whole:
> Beneath, the distant torrent's rushing sound   430
> Tells where the volumed cataract doth roll
> Between those hanging rocks, that shock yet please the soul.

* The convent and village of Zitza are four hours journey from Joannina, or Yanina, the capital of the Pachalick. In the valley of the river Kalamas (once the Acheron) flows, and not far from Zitza forms a fine cataract. The situation is perhaps the finest in Greece, though the

---

76: Pouqueville's *Voyages en Morée* ... is a book with which Byron parades an acquaintance now, but which Hobhouse, at least, does not read until July 1811 (he may be re-reading it: the day after he finishes it, he begins his *Journey into some Provinces of Turkey*). Hobhouse writes in his diary for Oct 6, 1809: "Captain Leake told us that Pukeville had never been in Albania when he wrote his book." This is clear from the book, in which the Albanian section is stated as being second-hand.
77: A perfectly adequate sketch of the life (so far) of Ali appears at Pouqueville's *Voyages* III, pp.22-7; except for the sentence *sa stature est haut et athlétique* (p.24), which it wasn't.

approach to Delvinaki and parts of Acarnania and Ætolia may contest the palm. Delphi, Parnassus, and, in Attica, even Cape Colonna and Port Raphti, are very inferior; as also every scene in Ionia, or the Troad: I am almost inclined to add the approach to Constantinople; but from the different features of the last, a comparison can hardly be made.

"The finest in Greece" would suggest that Byron had been all over the country, instead of just sections of its southern and eastern areas.

Here is the second reference to Acheron, which is stanza 51:

> Dusky and huge, enlarging on the sight,
> Nature's volcanic amphitheatre, *
> Chimæra's alps, extend from left to right:
> Beneath, a living valley seems to stir;
> Flocks play, trees wave, streams flow, the mountain-fir 455
> Nodding above; behold black Acheron! †
> Once consecrated to the sepulchre.
> Pluto! If this be hell I look upon,
> Close shamed Elysium's gates, my shade shall seek for none.

* The Chimariot mountains appear to have been volcanic.

† Now called Kalamas.

Lines 454-6 remind me of *Kubla Khan* in the way they depict bodily organs and orifices:

> A savage place! as holy and enchanted
> As e'er beneath a waning moon was haunted
> By woman wailing for her demon-lover!
> And from this chasm, with ceaseless turmoil seething,
> As if this earth in fast thick pants were breathing,
> A mighty fountain momently was forced …

Hobhouse would have hated such an idea. For him, bodily orifices and organs were shameful necessities. His diary, in any case, contradicts his friend's poem, as it often does:

Monday October 9th 1809: Up ten. After breakfast, went out on the lake fowling. No good shooting. Mr Poukeville talks of the Acheronian lake, Mount Tomarus, the Elysian fields, and *le petit Pinde*. We were in the midst of these, but saw nothing of them except perhaps *le petit Pinde*.

But Byron went on bluffing. To Henry Drury he wrote, on July 7th 1811:

> The enclosed letter is from a friend of yours, a Surgeon Tucker whom I met with in Greece, & so on to Malta, where he administered to me for three complaints, viz. a *Gonorrhea* a *Tertian fever*, & the *Hemorrhoides*, *all* of which I literally had at once, though he assured me the *morbid* action of only one of these distempers could act at a time, which was a great comfort, though they relieved one another as regularly as Sentinels, & very nearly sent me back to Acheron, my old acquaintance which I left fine & flowing in Albania. [78]

Wherever the mythical Acherousian or Acheronian lake was (and who really knows?) the idea of Ali emerging giant-like to attack his enemies from Acheron was too good to turn down, as was the idea of Byron / Harold visiting him there, and experiencing its stirring valley and nodding firs for himself. So Byron covers his tracks by impugning Pouqueville's knowledge even while borrowing his idea. Byron (or is it Harold speaking?) finds Hell more attractive than Heaven, as he will in *The Vision of Judgement*. He's keen to "spread [*his*] snares licentious far and wide"; and, having tried doing so at home, and on Calypso's isle, why not try Hell?

***

If you wanted to experience Hell on earth, the dominions of Ali Pacha were a good place to start:

> A few days later a monk named Demetrios ... was taken prisoner and tortured: sharp laths were driven under his nails, a chaplet of knucklebones was drawn tight around his head, he was hung upside down over a slow fire, covered with a board which was jumped on in order to break his bones, and at last was walled up in a cell with only his head free. He took ten days to die.[79]

On December 1st 1809, after they've seen the last of Ali, Hobhouse and Byron hear a story of his treachery as well as his sadism, of which the following is a later French account:

78: BLJ II, 58.
79: William Plomer, *The Diamond of Jannina, Ali Pacha 1741-1822* (Jonathan Cape 1970) p.143.

L'adjutant-général *Rose* [*Hobhouse's diary has "Rosa"*] commandait à Corfou. Ali-Pacha lui écrit qu'ayant à l'entretenir sur des intérêts qui les touchait l'un et l'autre, il le priait de se rendre à un lieu de conférence qu'il lui indiquait. Le général n'ayant aucune défiance, traverse le canal, débarque, une voiture le transporte auprès d'Ali-Pacha, qui l'accueille avec les plus grands égards, les marques les plus touchantes d'amitié. Ils dînèrent ensemble, *Ali* paraissait extrêmement gai, *Rose* s'abandonnant à la joie que lui inspirait une telle réception, lui dit qu'il espérait que rien n'altérerait leur amitié: <<Je vais t'en donner une preuve nouvelle,>> lui répondait le Pacha, et il ordonna aux Albanais de s'emparer de la personne du général: on se jette sur lui, on le garrotte, on l'entraîne dans une pièce voisine, où pendant qu'il dînait, on avait préparé des tortures. Tandis que le malheureux officier français rélévait, au milieu des plus horribles supplices, la situation militaires des îles Ioniennes, Ali lui criait: <<Tu m'as parlé de l'amitié? il ne peut y avoir entre un Musulman comme moi et un chien de chrètien comme toi, que celle dont je te fais éprouver les suites en ce moment.>> Après l'avoir fait cruellement torturer, il le fit conduire sous bonne escorte à Constantinople, en dénonçant le général comme un espion qu'il avait surpris; l'infortuné mourut au bout d'un mois des suites de la torture. Rose n'a pas été vengé par les Français![80]

[Adjutant-General Rose commanded on Corfu. Ali Pacha wrote to him that, having things to discuss that concerned them both, he begged that he would come to a place of conference, which he named. The general, without suspicion, crossed the water, disembarked, and a carriage took him to Ali Pacha, who greeted him with the greatest endearments, and the most touching expressions of friendship. They dined together. *Ali* seemed very happy, *Rose*, giving himself up to the joy which such a reception had inspired in him, said to him that he hoped that nothing would change their friendship. "I'm going to give you a new proof of it," the Pacha answered, and he ordered the Albanians to take hold of the person of the general: they threw themselves upon him, bound him tightly, and dragged him into a nearby room, where, while he had been dining, they had prepared instruments of torture. While the unfortunate French officer revealed, under the most horrible sufferings, the military situation of the Ionian Islands, Ali shouted at him, "You have spoken to me of friendship? The only kind there can be between a Moslem like me and a Christian dog like you is the sort of which I am giving you evidence right now." After having cruelly tortured him, he had him conveyed with a large escort to Constantinople, denouncing the general as a spy whom he had caught.

80: Ibrahim-Manzur-Effendi, *Mémoires sur la Grèce et l'Albanie, pendant le gouvernement d'Ali-Pacha* (Paris 1827), pp.32-3.

The unhappy man died a month afterwards, of continuous torture. Rose
was not avenged by the French!]

Ali was devilish in his loves as well as his hates: a true Rodomonte if
ever there was one, except that Rodomonte only goes for women. Byron
had, in his original manuscript version of stanza 61, been franker about
this than his colleagues – Murray, Gifford, perhaps Hobhouse, and Dallas
– had permitted him to be in print. He wrote of Tepellene (not Ali's Greek
headquarters, but his Albanian one):

> Here woman's voice is never heard – apart,
> And scarce permitted guarded, veiled to rove,
> She yields to one her person and her heart,
> Tamed to her cage, nor feels a wish to move;
> For boyish minions of unhallowed love
> The shameless torch of wild desire is lit,
> Caressed, preferred even woman's self above,
> Whose forms for Nature's gentler errors fit
> All frailties mote excuse save that which they commit.[81]

It's not at all like Calypso's island. In stanza 63 he had originally been
franker still:

> It is not that yon hoary lengthening beard
> Delights to mingle with the lip of youth;   560
> Love conquers age – so Hafiz hath averred,
> So sings the Teian, and he sings in sooth –
> But crimes that scorn the tender voice of Ruth,
> Beseeming all men ill, but most the man
> In years, have marked him with a tyger's tooth; 565
> Blood follows blood, and through their mortal span,
> In bloodier acts conclude those who with blood began.

Line 560 was in the event swapped for its alternative manuscript
version, "Ill suits the passions which belong to youth". In what way Love
had conquered age in the relationship between Harold and Ali we are not
told; but with Hafiz the Islamic poet and Anacreon the classical poet ("the
Teian") for moral support, can we doubt that it had triumphed? Harold
seems pleased to have met with one who was as keen to "spread his snares

---

81: CHP II st. 61. Text edited from Erdman, David, and David Worall (eds.),
Byron VI: Childe Harold's Pilgrimage, A Critical, Composite Edition (Garland
1991), p.135.

licentious far and wide" as he was himself. Where better to spread them
than in Acheron, where the inhabitants would be well used to such things?

The problem is that neither Hafiz nor Anacreon give sinners of
differing ages, such as Harold and Ali, encouragement. Hafiz sometimes
seems to encourage lust in the elderly:

> Drink then, nor dread th'approach of age,
>   Nor let sad cares your mirth destroy:
> For, on this transitory stage,
>   Think not to taste perpetual joy.
>
> The spring of youth now disappears,
>   Why pluck you not life's only rose ...

But he then recommends a moral attitude as one approaches death.
The poem continues:

> With virtue mark your future years,
>   This earthly scene with honour close.
>
> With generous wine then fill the bowl,
>   Swift, swift to Jami, Zephyr, fly;
> Tell him that friendship's flow of soul,
>   While Hafez lives, shall never die.[82]

Byron's way with moral examples from poetry is one with his lack of
scruple in locating islands and underworld rivers. In Thomas Moore's two-
volume set of Anacreon's Odes, I find very few out of the seventy-nine
poems which may be read as saying that "Love conquers age". But here's
one:

> The women tell me every day
> That all my bloom has past away.
> "Behold," the pretty wantons cry,
> "Behold this mirror with a sigh,
> "The locks upon thy brow are few,
> "And, like the rest, they're withering too!"
> Whether decline has thinn'd my hair
> I'm sure I neither know nor care;
> But this I know, and this I feel,
> As onward to the tomb I steal,

82: *A Specimen of Persian Poetry, or Odes of Hafez*, translated from the German
of Baron Revizky by John Richardson, London 1801.

> That still as death approaches nearer,
> The joys of life are sweeter, dearer;
> And had I but an hour to live,
> That little hour to bliss I'd give![83]

Ali Pasha, I'm sure, would have had no need of either Hafiz or Anacreon, still less of Tom Moore, to justify the "gentler errors" of his private life. It may be a sign of Byron's and Harold's redeemability that they do feel the need for classical and literary precedents to justify theirs.

But it may not be, if they're as inaccurate as they seem with their classical sources and topography. More relevant to Ali Pacha's case (as it will be, by 1824, to Byron's), is the following – another Moore Anacreon translation:

> Golden hues of youth are fled;
> Hoary locks deform my head.
> Bloomy graces, dalliance gay,
> All the flowers of life decay.
> Withering age begins to trace
> Sad memorials o'er my face.
> Time has shed its sweetest bloom.
> All the future must be gloom!
> This awakes my hourly sighing;
> Dreary is the thought of dying!
> Pluto's is a dark abode,
> Sad the journey, sad the road:
> And, the glooming travel o'er,
> Ah! We can return no more![84]

Pluto dwells in Hades, not in Acheron; but it's comforting to be able to assert that the cul-de-sac of depravity down which you're journeying has already been described by such famous and distinguished pens.

Byron, Christianity, Islam, predestination, and sexism

Byron's motive in writing was often to shock or upset his reader. There is nothing wrong with such a motive; but the reader should be aware of it. On June 28 1811 Byron describes himself as "a man who hates bustle as he hates a bishop" (53); and this to his cousin, the Reverend R.C.Dallas. He was unable to accept the Atonement as morally logical or just:

83: Thomas Moore, *Odes of Anacreon* (1805), I, pp.54-6.
84: Ibid, II, pp.88-91.

... the basis of your religion is *injustice*; the *Son of God*, the *pure*, the *immaculate*, the *innocent*, is sacrificed for the *guilty*. This proves *His* heroism; but no more does away with *man's* guilt than a schoolboy's volunteering to be flogged for another would exculpate the dunce from negligence, or preserve him from the rod. You degrade the Creator, in the first place, by making Him a begetter of children; and in the next you convert Him into a tyrant over an immaculate and injured Being, who is sent into existence to suffer death for the benefit of some millions of scoundrels, who, after all, seem as likely to be damned as ever. [85]

This is from a letter to Francis Hodgson, written just before Hodgson took holy orders. It seems that Byron chose his readers with care when making anti-Christian remarks.

Islam will have no truck with the Incarnation, so Byron's ethical objections do not apply to it. However, neither he nor Hobhouse ever discuss the huge theological differences between Christianity and Islam. Neither do either of them show any awareness that there existed – as there still do – huge differences in Islamic practise between one Islamic country and one Islamic culture and another. As Seyed Mohammed Marandi writes in his essay below, the "Mussulman" world was in Byron's eyes a monolith.

It pleased Byron, when writing to some friends, to claim that he had been instructed in, and had learned to detest and reject, Calvinism, during his childhood in Aberdeen:

It was the comparative insignificance of ourselves & our world when placed in competition with the mighty whole of which it is an atom that first led me to imagine that our pretensions to eternity might be overrated. – – This – & being early disgusted with a Calvinistic Scotch School where I was cudgelled to Church for the first ten years of my life – afflicted me with this malady – for after all it is I believe a disease of the mind as much as other kinds of Hypochondria.[86]

I was bred in Scotland among Calvinists in the first part of my life – which gave me a dislike to that persuasion ...[87]

In fact, as Christine Kenyon Jones has discovered, he was humming. The religious teaching in Aberdeen was much more diverse:

85: BLJ II, 97.
86: BLJ III, 64 (letter to William Gifford, June 18 1813).
87: Ibid, 119 (letter to Annabella Milbanke, Sep 26 1813).

Far from being the recipient of a monocultural 'Calvinism' in Aberdeen
... Byron had by the time he left experienced several different types of
religious teaching and of national and theological vocabulary: each
associated with a different stratum of society.[88]

But he needed, with such innocent interlocutors as his wife, to paint
himself as one convinced of his own predestined damnation. It added to
the image he enjoyed projecting to her, of one doomed, helpless, and at
the mercy of things:

> [*He said*] that God was a malignant spirit, delighting in the sufferings of
> his creatures ... that he was himself created only to exist in torture, and
> foredoomed to evil. In this fatalism concerning himself personally, he
> was most anxious to believe –
>
> "And half mistook for fate, the acts of will."
>
> But he lamented to me once in London that he *could* not resign himself
> implicitly to that tenet as the Turks did. His gloomy creed of
> predestination had however an earlier origin in the Calvinistic doctrine
> of Election amongst the Scotch, and his was a pernicious bigotry which
> – by depriving God of his best attributes, those of a Benevolent Being –
> creates the wish to annul & the resolution to deny his existence ...
>
> He often spoke of a mysterious necessity for his return to the East,
> and vindicated the Turks with a spirit of Nationality, admiring above all
> their complete predestinarianism. He would say "The East – ah, there it
> is," ... and he has two or three times intimated to me that he abjured his
> religion there. In the autumn in London, he said with a shudder of
> conscious remembrance, "I was very near becoming a Mussulman." He
> preferred the Turkish opinions, manners, & dress in all respects to ours.
> This idea of his conversion to their faith having occurred to me at
> Halnaby, derived some confirmation from his composing at Seaham that
> part of the Siege of Corinth which relates to Alp's assumption of the
> Turban, and also from a paper which he then wrote as the
> commencement of a Critique upon Leake's work, afterwards reviewed
> in the Edinr. by Hobhouse.[89]

88: Christine Kenyon Jones, 'I was bred a moderate Presbyterian': Byron, Thomas
Chalmers and the Scottish religious heritage, in Hopps, Gavin, and Jane Stabler
(eds.), Romanticism and Religion from William Cowper to Wallace Stevens, The
Nineteenth Century Series, Ashgate, (Aldershot 2005/6).
89: Annabella Milbanke, quoted Malcolm Elwin, *Lord Byron's Wife* (Macdonald
1962), pp.270-1. The quotation is *Lara*, line 336.

He never writes or talks about such things to his more sophisticated correspondents, like Lady Melbourne: the pose is exclusively for Annabella, whom one can perhaps imagine staring at him and sighing, *"Really, truly?"*[90]

Such a habit of self-dramatisation would have indeed made Islam a useful backcloth for him; for, as George Sale writes,

> The sixth great point of faith ... is GOD's absolute decree, and predestination both of good and evil. For the orthodox doctrine is, that whatever hath or shall come to pass in this world, whether it be good, or whether it be bad, proceedeth entirely from the divine will, and is irrevocably fixed and recorded from all eternity in the *preserv'd table*; GOD having secretly predetermined not only the adverse and prosperous fortune of every person in this world, in the most minute particulars, but also his faith or fidelity, his obedience or disobedience, and consequently his everlasting happiness or misery after death; which fate or predestination it is not possible, by any foresight or wisdom, to avoid.[91]

In fact there are as many interpretations in Islam as to exactly what predestination involves as there are in Christianity. But neither Christian or Islamic theology was a discipline which Byron studied. In one of his earliest oriental adventures he had had, however, an excellent opportunity to see Islamic stoicism in the face of the inevitable. Hobhouse writes (not in his diary, but forty-two years after the event):

> When we dropped anchor under her the Spider, our commander ordered the Turks to be brought on board, and, having heard what had happened, requested me, as I spoke a little Italian, to tell the Turkish captain that he should be hanged in half an hour for firing on the British flag and killing an Englishman. I delivered the message with due solemnity, and, pointing to the yard-arm as being ready for the execution, asked him what he had to say in his behalf. I then had an opportunity of witnessing the tranquillity with which in general the Mussulman meets death. The Turk said, "I have before told you I mistook you for a pirate – I have nothing more to say: if I must die, I must die. God's will be done." The man spoke with the utmost composure, although he had every reason to believe he was about to die.[92]

90: *Beppo*, 92, 1; *The Vision of Judgement*, 80, 8.
91: Sale, p.103.
92: Lord Broughton (J.C.Hobhouse) *Travels in Albania,* John Murray, 1854, I 3 na.

Islam is often accused of misogyny, as is Christianity, and as is Byron. Byron seems often to take those points of Islam where either its teaching is ambiguous, or is at odds with its practice, and to emphasise them. As with predestination, so with misogyny: if either can be imputed to Islam, he imputes it. Thus, as I said, he gives us the idea that one-third of places in paradise are allotted by Islam to women (*Giaour*, 488n) – a ludicrous concept, the source for which no-one has ever tracked down. Thus he tells us, contrary to the evidence, that women are not permitted at Islamic shrines (*Bride*, 313-4); and quotes the Genesis account of Eve's part in the fall as if it were the one in the Qu'ran (*Bride*, 158-61). It looks as if he's carelessly confounding Islam with Christianity, where Eve was always credited with having brought mankind to sin.

Orientalism in the Turkish Tales: a brief guide
The Giaour

I am missing out *Parisina*, which, though excellent, and though related to the others in interesting ways, is a family drama set entirely in Italy.

The Giaour is a lament for lost oriental paradises – first the paradise of ancient Greek heroes, replaced by modern Greek depravity, next the paradise Hassan experienced in his serai, which the poem associates with his mother (310), and which is disfgured by the eruption into his life of the nameless Giaour. The Giaour himself has a "native valley" (1220) for which he is turn nostalgic. These three laments are paralleled by the monastery lament of the Giaour, who in turn blames Hassan for depriving him of the paradise he experienced with Leila,[93] and who has had to kill him in revenge. Where there was serenity, trust, and love, the Giaour brings discord and violence. The fact that the Giaour's not a Christian, but an "Apostate from his own vile faith" (616: see also 812), seems to make his offence against Islamic hospitality worse: Byron does not explore how he came to be a renegade – did he actually convert, as Beppo will? We are not told. At 807 the new monkish narrative voice says that "His faith and race" are "alike unknown". How he was allowed into a religious house is in the light of this statement a mystery. His bribe must have been enormous: but Byron's sneering note to 1207 shows how little sympathy he has for Christianity.

93: Nora Liassis describes Leila as "a stateless, two-timing concubine with no official claim to Islamic paradise". See Liassis, *Oriental Females in Byron's Verse Narratives* in Raizis, M. Byron (ed). *Byron and the Mediterranean World, Proceedings of the Twentieth International Byron Conference in the University of Athens 20-21 September 1995*, Athens 1995, p.84.

Thus an occidental (of sorts), ruins an oriental paradise, and an oriental ruins an occidental paradise, while all the while one is aware of an ancient heroic paradise which its modern denizens have lost and despoiled.

Lines 745-6 suggest that Hassan has died for Islam, and that he will see the true paradise, more than ample compensation for the loss of his earthly ones: but is death in a blood-feud death for Islam? We are told that such "tribal relics" as blood-feuding still disfigure the religion sometimes. But the Giaour, an ambiguously renegade Christian, is hardly a foe to the faith, though he is a foe to Hassan. I quote below Bernard Beatty's argument that in killing his Islamic enemy, he's killed himself – the severed hand is his, and the "parent limb" is firstly the body of Hassan, and secondly, his own. Confrontational orientalism is a form of self-multilation.

The tale itself is told from a number of viewpoints, and in such a way as to make it necessary to read it several times in order to piece it together. Only when one knows how badly the Giaour suffers in the monastery can one see the ambush of Hassan in its true light, and only when one returns to the description of Hassan's desolate hall can one judge the full weight of the drowning of Leila. The technique makes one constantly suspect that a piece may be missing, and that something may be being withheld which the overarching narrative cannot voice. Whether, by the end, one has the full story, is doubtful. How, for example, did Leila and the Giaour part, and how did she fall into Hassan's hands again? Was the Giaour that poor an escaper, and that inadequate a bodyguard? At 1057 he seems to take responsibility for Leila's death. The cryptic tale thus lingers long after it's been read over and over again.

None of the other tales operate in quite this manner, incomplete and full of apparent suppressions though some of them are.

The Bride of Abydos

The Bride of Abydos opens with a compressed statement of the binary paradisal theme we saw *The Giaour* – here in the East vultures "melt into sorrow", and doves "madden to crime" – everything, in the orient, contains within itself the potential for self-inversion. We may wonder whether it does not do so in the west also; but that would spoil Byron's effect.

The enemies are now not chance acquaintances, like Hassan and the Giaour, but uncle and nephew, the one a Turk, the other half a Greek. Uncle distrusts nephew because he appears not to be martial, and probably – such is the uncle's paranoia – harbours treasonous thoughts. In fact he does harbour treasonous thoughts, but not anti-Islamic ones: he does not want to help recapture Constantinople for the Russians (95-6), but merely wants to overthrow his uncle, because his uncle had killed his father, and then posed as his nephew's loving, adoptive father. The Shakespearean parallel ("Think of us as of a father")[94] is lightly stressed. "Think not I am what I appear" (381), sums up both Giaffir and Selim, or would if they were as interesting as Iago or Viola, of whom we must think that neither are what they *are*.[95]

Lines 392-9 seem to suggest incestuous feelings on the part of Zuleika, the heroine (see Seyd Mohammed Marandi's essay below); lines 633-972 suggest on the part of Selim a huge preference for words over action, which would, if Pandarus were present, inspire him to his famous line "Words pay no debts – give her deeds!"[96] That the speech is necessary as exposition is no excuse for a faultily-constructed narrative which necessitates an expository speech of this length. But Byron, if he is to be believed, wrote the poem in only four days.[97]

Lines 861-8 reassure Byron's Whig readers that Selim – now self-revealed as a quasi-revolutionary – is no Painite; he is no more driven by desperate dreams of equality than is his creator. Neither does his half-Greek nature seem to have inspired any thoughts in him antipathetic to the faith of his uncle-father and his sister-cousin: Islam is not his foe, nor even the Ottoman Empire. His foes are Islamic; but that's not the same. He's not a Christian, nor even a renegado like the Giaour. As Daniel P. Watkins argues,[98] Selim's environment works to oppress him as an individual; but if we think an anti-Islamic point is being made, we have only to glance at Zuleika, who would not be the beautiful person she is without her comboloio, her lute, and her Qu'ranic readings. "… many of the Turkish girls are highly accomplished," says Byron, in his note to 554, even though he'd met no Turkish girls of this class.

The Bride of Abydos will offend no-one except those who enjoy a rattling good tale. Them it lets down. The action, when it comes, is over quickly, like the ambush of Hassan in *The Giaour*, although the surrounding build-up and termination do not contextualise it in the riddling, intriguing way they do the violence in the previous poem. Selim's career as pirate and rebel is over almost – from what we see of it –

94: *Hamlet*, I ii 107-8.
95: See *Othello* I i 66, or *Twelfth Night* III i 137.
96: *Troilus and Cressida*, III ii 54.
97: BLJ IV, 77.
98: See Daniel P. Watkins, *Social Relations in Byron's Eastern Tales*, Rutherford, NJ: Fairleigh Dickinson University Press, 1987.

as soon as it has begun. We feel cheated. Byron should have worked at the
poem for a bit longer.

The Corsair and Lara

The heroine's hair changes colour:[99] that's the only factual inconsistency
which makes us pause before treating these two tales as one, and even then
no-one's certain.Whether they are a unit or not, what can't be denied is
that they are both less thoroughly oriental than the two tales which precede
them, or than *The Siege of Corinth* which follows them, though written
earler.[100] *The Corsair* only ventures occasionally into oriental territory
(unless all of the Aegean is taken to be oriental), and *Lara* is set entirely in
Spain, with the Eastern Mediterranean as a cloudy memory.

Conrad, the strange hero of *The Corsair*, is "...more than Moslem
when the cup appears" (430). The only reference to Islam in the poem's
first canto prepares us for the weird incident in the second canto, in which,
disguised as an Islamic holy man, he infiltrates the stronghold of the
Moslem patriarch / villain Seyd (a move dictated by no military need),[101]
and ostentatiously refuses to partake of the bread and salt offered to him.
Now we know already from Byron's prose note to *The Giaour* 343, that
"To partake of food – to break bread and salt with your host – insures the
safety of the guest, even though an enemy; his person from that moment is
sacred"; and we know already from *Vathek* that to abuse the offer of bread
and salt is to court danger:

> ... it cannot be denied, that thou hast violated, to admiration, the laws
> of hospitality by seducing the daughter of the emir, after having
> partaken of his bread and his salt. Such a conduct cannot but be
> delightful to the Giaour ...[102]

Conrad is thus a blasphemer against Islam in posing as a dervish, and
against Islamic hospitality in refusing the bread and salt. Are the woes
which follow a result of this? Is he, like the Giaour, accursed by his own

---

99: At *The Corsair* line 1008 Gulnare's hair is auburn; at *Lara* line 1154 Kaled's is
raven. The discrepancy was first pointed out by E.H.Coleridge, *Byron's Works,* III,
321.
100: See McGann's discussion at CPW III, 479-81.
101: "It has been observed, that Conrad's entering disguised as a spy is out of
nature," wrtes B. in his note to 654; but it's not just out of nature – it defies
commonsense. B.'s note refers to a spy who escaped.
102: *Vathek*, p.99.

unholy and needless decisions, and condemned to "writhe / Beneath avenging Monkir's scythe"? (*Giaour* 747-8). Or is he, as I have argued elsewhere, a prey to his own instinct for self-defeat, and does that self-defeat take the form of blatant, public offences against Islamic custom? It's true that Seyd "dares to quaff" "forbidden draughts" (636); but that he's an Islamic transgressor doesn't make him any less Islamic. Indeed, although he's not a considerate lover (869-71), and although Gulnare claims that his guard is "Ripe for revolt" (1480), Seyd seems, in contrast to the fratricidal and duplicitous Giaffir in *The Bride*, to be a straightforward Moslem governor, only anxious to do his job, part of which is to destroy pests like Conrad. His "dotage" on Gulnare (1130) is lightly stressed, perhaps to make her murdering him more acceptable.

The opening of the third canto, recycled from *The Curse of Minerva*, reminds us that there is more to the Orient (here including Greece) than can be contained in the narrative. Conrad's guilt (1609-10) at the thought that in order to free him, Seyd has had to be murdered, is a reflection either of his own need to be impaled – most horrible of Ottoman forms of excution – or of his renewed guilt, that the man whose bread and salt he turned down in the second canto is now dead, and for his (Conrad's) benefit. Both explanations are silly: and that's the challenge with which *The Corsair* presents us. Even Gulnare the homicide is so upset by what she's done that she apologises by saying "I am not what I seem," (1639), just as Selim had said, but from a different motive.

Conrad is the least piratical of pirates. Blackbeard, Sir Henry Morgan and Long John Silver, Jean Lafitte, Ann Bonny and Mary Read, Grace O'Malley (Sligo's ancestor), even Captain Hook, would all laugh at the foolish moral sensibility he displays. Neither is he a revolutionary against Ottoman imperialism, as Selim almost is (though Selim would deny it), or like Lambro Canzones/Canzani, the famous Greek sailor who had in the late eighteenth century combined the two roles of pirate and rebel without strain, and to whom Byron refers at *Bride* 862 and n. It's one thing to want to pillage a stronghold of tyranny in a criminal act, quite another to aim at replacing its authority with a native power which you feel deserves the place more.

***

Though, when unconscious, Lara speaks in "accents of another land" (232), we do not know which land it is; nor do we know in what "tongue, which seemed his own" (242), Kaled answers him. "... those climes afar / Where the soul glows beneath a brighter star" (512-13), in which Lara and

Kaled met, may be the Eastern Mediterranean: they may be Norwegian, though it seems unlikely, given Kaled's Arabic name.

In what language is the "foreign book" Kaled reads from (548)? Byron is teasing us with the possibility of a hidden orientalist agenda. The agony with which Kaled reacts to Ezzelin at the feast is another tease: what horror does Ezzelin evoke in him / her? We *never* know, and this failure even to hint at a resolution to the problems *Lara* provokes is reason enough for our frustration. Riddles with no answers are bores, even oriental ones (which may after all not even be oriental).

The Siege of Corinth

This poem has less of Byron's hitherto habitual oriental "colour" (that is, Greek and Turkish words requiring annotation) than its rivals, and yet it focuses on issues which his hitherto equivocal and woolly analyses have avoided. We know that its hero is a single-minded renegade, where the Giaour is only rumoured to be one. This makes him more thoroughly and consciously alienated than any of the previous protagonists. Its heroine can only speak from beyond the grave, and so Byron does not find it necessary to sentimentalise her – she is indeed a precursor or prototype of the frightening and cryptic Astarte in *Manfred*. The conflict the poem dramatises cannot be described as other than an imperialist one; it contains no pirates anywhere.

Siege is, last but not least, unique among the Turkish Tales in possessing a well-structured narrative, and a fine poetic organisation (see Robert McColl's essay below).

It starts – if you include the lines Byron cut – with an apostrophe to Byron's orient, parallel to but differing from the opening to the third canto of *The Corsair*: there it is the skies and the history he sings, here the company he kept when he was in Greece – who were, we notice, a mixture of Moslem and Christian.

The action proper starts with a thing unknown in Byron's work so far: the depiction of a full-scale Moslem army confident of victory. It makes a huge change from the amateur piratics of Conrad, and the overhasty assemblage of misfits led by Selim:

> The tent is pitched, the crescent shines   30
> Along the Moslem's leaguering lines;
> And the dusk Spahi's bands advance
> Beneath each bearded pasha's glance;
> And far and wide as eye can reach
> The turbaned cohorts throng the beach;   35

> And there the Arab's camel kneels,
> And there his steed the Tartar wheels;
> The Turcoman hath left his herd,
> The sabre round his loins to gird;
> And there the volleying thunders pour,   40
> Till waves grow smoother to the roar.

Our understanding that foremost among this army's leaders – leader of the van, in fact – is a *ci-devant* young buck from Venice, gives hitherto unknown weight to the opening idea of *Bride*: every entity, oriental or occidental, has its opposite within it, waiting to get out.

Alp is the least compromising of all the so-called Byronic heroes: though he is also a successful man of action, which none of them are. He is theoretically a Moslem, but does not anticipate a Moslem warrior's death, for he is still motivated by hatred of the west – his anti-Christian prejudice is fuelled by no corresponding allegiance to Islam, but purely by distaste for the hypocritical persecution which is all Christian society has given him: "What Venice made me, I must be" (626). At the same time, many and brave though his Islamic warriors are, none of them admire or like him, because to them he's still a Christian. He inhabits a Manfred-like no-mans-land, cut off from all possible sources of human companionship. The schematic binaries of Orientalism have, in Alp, finally been left behind: or rather, he has fallen down the chasm between them. As Nora Liassis puts it,

> Alp is the only Byronic hero to die in Eastern exile in a "final merging of the twin themes of self-expression and self-destruction."[103]

Byron seems to feel at last that he has created a protagonist, and a framework, in which large-scale action is appropriate, as opposed to a skirmish he needs to tack on even though neither the characters nor the tale really demand it. In consequence the battle at the poem's climax is one of his most successful sequences, like one from a Scott novel, or like the still better battle he is to write in *Don Juan*. There Christians assault a Moslem town, here Moslems assault a Christian one. Byron has already forgotten the contempt he expresses for warfare narrative at *Lara* 909-10: "What boots the oft-repeated tale of strife, / The feast of vultures, and the waste of life?"

103: Nora Liassis, *"The Crescent O'er the Cross": Byron and Apostasy*, in Martin Procházka, (ed.) *Byron: East and West / Proceedings of the 24th International Byron Conference / Charles University Prague*, Prague 2000, p. 132. The quotation is from Fevre, *Studies in Philosophy* (1952).

In the final church sections, East and West confront one another, Moslem fighters before a painting of the Virgin. Byron describes it from a gleeful Moslem perspective:

> The foe came on, and few remain
> To strive, and those must strive in vain –
> For lack of further lives, to slake
> The thirst of vengeance now awake,
> With barbarous blows they gash the dead,   945
> And lop the already lifeless head,
> And fell the statues from their niche,
> And spoil the shrine of offerings rich,
> And from each other's rude hands wrest
> The silver vessels saints had blessed.   950
> To the high altar on they go;
> Oh, but it made a glorious show!

… and so on. Then the Christian Minotti lights his fuse, and blows the lot sky-high. The animal kingdom, innocent of all distinctions between occidental and oriental, are the only winners.

The "Oriental" tradition

Byron was breaking no new ground in exploring supposedly oriental themes, and in setting his narratives in theoretically oriental countries. Rather, he was <u>exploiting</u>, without scruple, a familiar European tradition in verse, prose, and drama. Writers had been doing such things at least since Shakespeare's time, with dramas such as Massinger's *The Renegado* (edited in 1813 by Gifford),[104] in which the heroine, who lures an innocent Christian in from the Tunisian streets to satisfy her lust, was probably more of an inspiration to Byron than the eponymous protagonist, who re-converts with facility. Dryden's *Aureng-Zebe* (a "Mughal" play), or Aphra Behn's *Abdelazer, or the Moor's Revenge* (a "Spanish / Moorish" play), furnish more examples.[105] The Moslem-Christian dialectic is, however, advanced not an inch by any of them: when, for example, Huon, the hero of Wieland's *Oberon* (see below), tries to convert his Moslem beloved, Rezia, to Christianity, it's revealed that he knows nothing about the latter

---

104: *The Plays of Philip Massinger*, ed. William Gifford, 4 vols 1813, II, pp.121-234.
105: See Bridget Orr, *Empire on the English Stage 1660-1714* (Cambridge 2001), pp.109-115 and 171-3.

apart from his paternoster and his creed.[106] Religious and cultural distinctions, in so far as there are any, are smothered beneath caricature and melodrama. Local oriental colour is absent. Southey inherits this tradition much more happily than does Byron, who adds several dimensions to it.

Byron shows a detailed knowledge of Voltaire's 1732 oriental tragedy *Zaïre*. In his long note at the end of *Don Juan* V[107] he quotes an important line from the play ("Zaïre – tu pleures"), only to correct it in a letter to Murray to "Zaïre *vous pleurez*".[108] Zaïre is a Christian heroine who has converted to Islam from love of Orosmane, the Sultan of Jerusalem, but who has now, unhappily, re-converted under pressure from her father. The line shows Orosmane's realisation that, despite her re-apostasy, Zaire loves him still. Byron quotes it to show Voltaire's superiority to the "filthy trash" of those Lakers who malign him.

Orosmane was the earliest role played by William Betty, the Young Roscius (see below).

Voltaire's moral is that religious differences make human misery, one with which Byron would agree: but it does not prevent Voltaire from putting Christian exhortations in his characters' mouths of a kind we never find in Byron. Here the father (an old crusader), argues with his daughter, taking advantage of their oriental environment to give his words weight:

LUSIGNAN: Ton Dieu que tu trahis, ton Dieu que tu blasphèmes,
　　　　　Pour toi, pour l'univers, est mort dans ces lieux mêmes,
　　　　　En ces lieux où mon bras le servit tant de fois,
　　　　　En ces lieux où son sang te parle par ma voix.
　　　　　Vois ces murs, vois ce temple envahi par tes maîtres:
　　　　　Tout annonce le Dieu qu'ont vengé tes ancêtres.
　　　　　Tourne les yeux, sa tombe est près de ce palais:
　　　　　C'est ici la montagne où, lavant nos forfaits,
　　　　　Il voulut expirer sous les coups de l'impie;
　　　　　C'est là que de sa tombe il rappela sa vie.[109]

LUSIGNAN: Your God whom you betray, your God whom you blaspheme, died for you and for the universe in this very place. In this place where my arm so often served him, in this place where his blood speaks to you through my voice. See these walls, see this temple taken

---

106: *Oberon, a Poem, from the German of Wieland* (tr. William Sotheby, 1798), p.193 (VI st. xxiv).
107: CPW V, 712. For the context of the line, see *Voltaire, Zaïre*, ed. Eva Jacobs, (Hodder and Stoughton 1975), p.129 (line 1154).
108: BLJ VIII, 162. Letter to Murray of July 30, 1821.
109: Voltaire, *Zaïre*, ed. Jacobs, p.108 (lines 669-78).

over by your masters: everything proclaims the God whom your
ancestors avenged. Look around, his tomb is near to this palace: there is
the mount where, cleansing our sins, he sought death beneath the arms
of impiety; it is there where, from his tomb, he rose again to life.

Lusignan was one of Voltaire's own favourite roles.[110] Byron is not
interested in the Christian aspects of the Orient, and his few references to
and dramatisations of Christian apologetics are caricatured.[111] Voltaire, his
idol, might have taught him better. The Orient turns into its opposite. If
you go far enough East you find yourself at the heart of the West.
An important ur-text for *The Giaour* is Charlotte Dacre's 1800 poem
Moorish Combat, from which Byron borrows his triangulated love-
conflict:

> Say, did they rest between each fervent kiss?
> Ah! no; but while their flutt'ring sighs unite,
> No moisture e'er their glowing lips might cool,
> Swiftly dried up by passion's fierce delight.
>
> How vain to stem their rapture as it flow'd,
> Or whisper to their stagg'ring sense, beware!
> His eyes inebriate wander'd o'er her charms,
> While hers to earth were cast with chastened air.
>
> Lo! from a mountain's steep and shadowy side,
> O'er which obliquely yet the beams were thrown,
> The fierce Zampogni, vengeance in his eye,
> Shot like a flaming meteor swiftly down.
>
> And now he paus'd, and scowling fell around,
> His arm uplifted, and his breath restrain'd,
> The flow'rs and herbage wither'd in his gaze,
> While he from instant vengeance scarce refrain'd ... *and so on.*

A longer comparison would make interesting distinctions, not just
between the conventional style of Dacre and the more disturbing one of
Byron, but between Dacre's aggressive feminism and Byron's
determination to keep his heroine suppressed and silent.
A clear source for *The Bride of Abydos* is the then well-known
tragedy *Barbarossa*, by John Brown, a Cambridge D.D. who was friends
with Gray and Warburton. Garrick had acted in the 1754 premiere, and

---

110: Roger Pearson, *Voltaire Almighty* (Bloomsbury 2005), p.246.
111: See *Giaour*, 1207, Byron's note.

Byron could well have seen a revival in 1805[112] with William Betty, the Young Roscius, of whom we know him to have been an admirer.

Barbarossa is set in Algiers – but an Algiers devoid of mosques, mullahs, muftis, or even palm-trees. The evil protagonist (his opening line is "Valiant Othman, / Are these vile slaves impal'd?": 1st edn, 1755, p.13), has killed his predecessor and sent assassins out to murder his predecessor's son, whose name is Selim! John Brown writes an effectively-constructed piece of theatre of the rant-and-anguish sort, with *Macbeth, Richard III* and *Hamlet* as his sturdy subtexts: it's a better stage-holder than *Marino Faliero*, a criticism by which Byron would not be bothered one iota. The essence of it is that Selim arrives back in court, disguised as his own assassin, with the aims of saving the virtue of his mother, Zaphira, killing Barbarossa, and marrying his love, who has the Byzantine name of Irene, but who is Barbarossa's daughter, torn between love and duty in the classic manner. Though she doesn't betray Selim, she makes Barbarossa suspicious of him. Brown creates from Selim's imprisonment, Irene's anguished guilt, and Barbarossa's cruelty, all the dramatic incidents which Byron, in his rushed conclusion to *The Bride*, eschews. Our suspicion that Byron's Selim is a bit of a wimp is reinforced when in this, the ur-text, it is an associate who slays the tyrant, not the hero.

It's clear Byron remembered *Barbarossa* (the name of Selim's father, Abdallah, comes from it: 1755 edn, p.55), and that his rushed narrative in *The Bride* is a consequence of his negative reaction to its excesses – mild though they are within the dramatic conventions of the eighteenth century. His negative reaction was, however, not compensated for by any inventivess of his own. Only his decision to increase the Shakespearean weight of the characters by making Giaffir Selim's uncle, and his use of numerous Islamic details, change the emphasis – Brown's Irene would not be the same if she read the Qu'ran and played with her lute and comboloioo, as Byron's Zuleika does. All Brown allows his characters by way of religion are invocations to the multi-faith ideas of "Angels" and "Heav'n".

The excessive scruple Conrad the Corsair displays when offered escape from his dungeon by Gulnare in the second canto is a result of Byron borrowing the entire episode from William Sotheby's translation of Wieland's oriental epic *Oberon* (1798),[113] where the ethics are quite

---

112: See Megan Boyes, *My Amiable Mamma* (1991), p.107.
113: This plagiarism was first pointed out by Alaric Watts in *The Literary Gazette*; though see also E.H.Coleridge's Byron edition, III 263, and Elizabeth French

different. Almansaris, the Sultana of Tunis, has (Gulbeyaz-like),
conceived a wild lust for the blue-eyed, blond, knightly hero, Huon
(disguised as Hassan, the gardener): but Huon's thoughts are all for his
beloved, Rezia (now christened Amanda). One morning Alamansaris, lute
in hand, tries to seduce Huon in her grotto – but is interrupted by the
arrival of her husband, the Sultan Almansor! (pp.382-403). Crying "Alla
be prais'd!" she pretends that her seduction is an attempted rape by Huon,
and Huon is thrown into a dungeon to be burnt on the morrow, "When the
imam summons from the tower".

The echoes so far are less of *The Corsair*, and more of *Don Juan* V.
But here are stanzas 32-35 of *Oberon's* twelfth canto, where the echoes of
The Corsair are obvious:

> When half the world lay wrapt in sleepless night,
> A jarring sound the startled hero wakes:
> With grating keys the dungeon hoarsely shakes,
> The iron door expands: a paly light
> Gleams thro' the vaults, at distance dim descried:
> He hears a step draw near – in beauty's pride
> A female comes – wide floats her glistening gown,
> Her hand sustains a lamp, her head a crown:
> Lo! the sultana's self stands graceful at his side!
>
> The smiling queen her beauteous hand extends –
> "Wilt thou forgive that counterfeited part,
> "When dire necessity belied my part?
> "O thou belov'd! my life on thine depends!
> "Oh! let this act that transient ill atone!
> "Spite of thy struggles here I come alone,
> "From death to snatch thee from that flaming pyre,
> "Where the stern tyrant dooms thee to expire,
> "And raise thee to the height thou well deserv'st – a throne.
>
> "Arise! for thee the sunny paths expand
> "Of empire – love conducts thee – wake to fame!
> "Let glory to the world thy deeds proclaim.
> "Go, where love guides thee by this proffer'd hand.
> "The ruthless tyrant dies! his guards retreat!
> "His slaves, like dust, shall fall before thy feet –
> "The harem to my nod obedient yields:
> "Love opes thy prison, love thy bosom shields:
> "Go forth! What love has dar'd, heroic youth! complete."

Boyd, *Byron's Don Juan, A Critical Study* (Humanities, New York, 1958), pp.126-7.

'Desist, O queen! The plan thou deign'st propose,
'Barbs with new pangs the shaft of tort'ring pain.
'Ah! why against my will my soul constrain
'To scorn each gift that from thy bounty flows?
'No deed of guilt shall these vile fetters loose!' –
"Can folly thus," she cried, "thy soul abuse?
"Wretch! while destruction tow'rs before thy sight,
"And on yon pile death waves thy funeral light,
"Canst thou my proffer'd hand, and throne at once refuse?"[114]

Wieland's / Sotheby's hero thus has a much better reason for refusing to be rescued – he'd have to sleep with and even marry his rescuer, whose embraces he shuns. This (we realise with interest), is not an option even hinted at in *The Corsair*. Huon is much more attached to his beloved Rezia / Amanda than Conrad is to Medora, about whom, characteristically, he never thinks in his dungeon. Byron has stolen the situation, but changed its context, in such a way as to make the protagonist's motives far less clear. Conrad the pirate is given the feelings of Huon of Bordeaux, the Christian knight.

The situation is resolved when, at the pyre, Huon remembers his magic horn, one note from which sends all of Tunis into a crazy dance (cp. *The Magic Flute*), and the lovers are rapt away in a swan-winged chariot to the land of the fairies, and thence to Paris, where Huon lays his trophies – the beard and several teeth of the late Sultan of "Bagdad" – at the feet of the Emperor Charlemagne. Tommy Franks could not have done better at the White House.

It seems to me that Byron's abuse of Sotheby (a "bustling Botherby"), at *Beppo* stanzas 72-6, is motivated, not by anything Sotheby had done, said, or written, but as a bluff to camouflage what Byron had stolen from him. Byron here bites the hand that feeds him. He was, in *Don Juan*, to go on stealing from Sotheby.[115]

Byron's idiom rises well above the operatic tones of his ur-texts, and he transmutes their high-quality dross, if not into gold, at least into iron: but that should not blind us to how much he owes to the orientalist tradition in which he writes so happily.

114: *Oberon, a Poem, from the German of Wieland* (1798), pp.409-10.
115: *Oberon* also contains a storm at sea, in which lots are cast to determine who shall go overboard as a sacrifice (p.218), and an illicit idyll on a Mediterranean beach (p.227), from which the heroine emerges pregnant (p.251). Others who borrow from "Sotheby's Wieland's *Oberon*" are Keats in *The Eve of St Agnes* and Southey in *The Curse of Kehama*.

Vathek

William Beckford's brilliant, oriental-comic novel was first published in French in 1786, with copious notes by Samuel Henley. Its protagonist is not like any Byronic hero, apart perhaps from Manfred: with Manfred he shares a desire to be omniscient; but Manfred's career of discovery is over before the play starts, whereas Beckford's novel charts the course of Vathek's career from inception to catastrophe. Vathek is seduced, and is throughout most of the action at the mercy of, a Mephistophelean Indian monster (called a Giaour), who is intent on his damnation. Manfred is of course seduced by no-one, and is the careful pilot of his proper woe. Vathek is also bullied by his mother, an idea which would be out of place in *Manfred*.

Byron loved Beckford's book, and a copy was found in his effects at Missolonghi. When on May 18th 1818 he writes to Murray

> My foot slipped in getting into my Gondola to set out (owing to the accursed slippery steps of their palaces) and in I flounced like a Carp[116]

… he is quoting *Vathek*, whose protagonist "flounced from the water like a carp" when his mother breaks in upon his sexual activities in the bath.[117] The famous last three words of *The Corsair* ("a thousand crimes") are from the last paragraph of *Vathek*.

To line 598 of *The Siege of Corinth* he appends a note:

> I have been told that the idea expressed in this and the five following lines has been admired by those whose approbation is valuable. I am glad of it: but it is not original – at least not mine; it may be found much better expressed in pages 182-184 of the English version of "Vathek" (I forget the precise page of the French), a work to which I have before referred; and never recur to, or read, without a renewal of gratification.

Siege was published early in 1816, some time after the other four Turkish Tales. *Vathek* was, by coinicidence, reprinted later in the year, with its notes pruned. Byron's admission of regard came late, and was not full enough as a revelation of his indebtedness: for he, who elsewhere expressed his pride at always having been "on the spot,"[118] took so many of his oriental details from Beckford's book, with which he had been familiar since well before his first eastern journey, that one can only blink.

116: BLJ VI, 133.
117: *Vathek*, p.93.
118: See Stephen Cheeke, *Byron and Place* (Palgrave 2003).

He need only have had *Vathek* and its notes to consult in order to understand the following concepts and vocabulary: houris (*Giaour* 486, *Bride* 147); genii (*Giaour* 385); the Nightingale and the Rose (*Giaour* 22 and n); the word "Giaour" itself; the order of Moslem prayers (*Siege* 22); Istakhar (*Bride* 358 and n); derviches (*Giaour* 340, *Corsair* 670); peris (*Bride* 567); butterflies of Kashmeer (*Giaour* 385); Mejnoun and Leila (*Bride* 72 and n); gouls (*Giaour* 784); the carbuncle of Giamschid (*Giaour* 479); clapping of hands (*Bride* 232 and n); bread and salt (*Giaour* 343 and n); Azrael (*Bride* 233 and n); Monkir (*Giaour* 748); Al-Sirat, the bridge to paradise (*Giaour* 483); afrits (*Giaour* 784); and Eblis (*Giaour* 750 and n).

An excellent example of the style of his borrowing may be seen at his note to "Monkir" at *The Giaour*, 748. Here's Henley's note to *Vathek*, first edition (1786), p.141:

> Monker and Nakir] These are two black angels of a tremendous appearance, who examine the departed on the subject of his faith: by whom, if he give not a satisfactory account, he is sure to be cudgelled with maces of red-hot iron, and tormented more variously than words can describe.[119]

Here's what Byron makes of it:

> Monkir and Nekir are the inquisitors of the dead, before whom the corpse undergoes a slight noviciate and preparatory training for damnation. If the answers are none of the clearest, he is hauled up with a scythe and thumped down with a red hot mace till properly seasoned, with a variety of subsidiary probations. The office of these angels is no sinecure; there are but two; and the number of orthodox deceased being in a small proportion to the remainder, their hands are always full.[120]

Byron mixes up the names of the angels (as if defying pedants to care), but otherwise follows Beckford / Henley closely, adding a scythe, and a heavier sceptic's irony. His joke in the last sentence anticipates the one at stanza 3 of *The Vision of Judgement*.

This indebtedness extends into *Don Juan*: lamb and pistachios (III, 62, 2);[121] the sacred camel (VI, 102, 8);[122] Kaf (VI, 86, 8);[123] and the use of dwarves and mutes (V, stanzas 87-9)[124] are all to be found in *Vathek*.

119: William Beckford, *Vathek*, (1786), p.313; ed. Lonsdale, p.151, 79n2.
120: *The Giaour*, B.'s note to p.748.
121: *Vathek* (1786), p.230.
122: *Vathek* (1786), pp.314-15.
123: *Vathek* (1786), pp.253-4.

The contemporary reception of the Turkish Tales

Many reviews of poetry consisted in the early nineteenth century of plot paraphrases, and, in the absence of effective nationwide book-distribution, of very long quotations. The first reactions to the Tales were complimentary, in a guarded sort of way. None objected to an oriental milieu, but all accepted it at once, as if emirs and odalisques were familiar items of poetic and narrative furniture. It's clear from their reactions that the tradition in which Byron was writing was an old one. Only now and then did they descend to cliché:

> The whole passage forms a highly picturesque representation of the Turkish character, relentless in jealousy, calm in vengeance, and resigned, even to insensibility, in suffering.[125]

One critic seemed to lament that Byron had chosen an Eastern milieu, even though he had observed it accurately, because it militated against conventional romance:

> Among the greatest advantages of visiting foreign parts is that accurate acquaintance with their manners, which, when well maintained in literary composition, proves highly gratifying to correct judges. The intercourse of young persons of both sexes with each other is rather encouraged and promoted than repelled by the institutions of Europe. Parents view with pleasure that decorous attention which their children excite, among their equals in rank and age. Public assemblies now the most brilliant would lose their attractions, and sink into mere mummery, were the young and the blooming forbid to grace them.——— Not so in the East. There the young men never see the objects of their future connection; and the young women are confined, if not, strictly speaking, within the walls of their bed-chambers, yet to a degree of privacy intended to be the preservative of their manners, a privacy not known among us; not conceivable except by a few, versed in oriental languages and literature. In vain would a stranger hope for a "charming partner" at a ball: there are no balls. In vain would he wait for a favouring glance from a box at the theatre: there are no theatres. There are (for him) no churches; no indiscriminate admission of the sexes. This Lord Byron knew; and therefore he has made his lover the *supposed* brother of his Bride of Abydos. He knew that nothing but such a near affinity could be tolerated in passing the threshold of the Haram; and roaming amid the

---

124: *Vathek* (1786), pp.227-8 (mutes) and p.260 (dwarves who are also mutes and eunuchs).
125: *The Champion*, June 27th 1813; (*RR* II, p.521).

secluded recesses of the sacred thicket and grove. He knew that no lover is admitted to profess his love, and to warm that bosom, the chillness of which forms the incessant subject of (poetic) complaint. Even a brother grown to manhood, were rather regarded as a trespasser, than welcomed as an intimate. This, however, we willingly overlook.[126]

Another saw through the *verfremdungs-effekt* Byron intended when he called his first oriental poem *The Giaour*:

The title of the work before us is an innocent instance of his Lordship's disposition to be occasionally whimsical. No one, we are convinced, not even the author himself, can tell us why, instead of the good old English term Infidel, this Turkish tale is called by such an odd, outlandish epithet as *Giaour*, unless it be intended that *Giaour* should be received into the language, as expressive of the character which the Mahomedans apply to the Christians, and that *infidel* should continue to contain its ancient signification of the character which the Christians apply to the Mahomedans. In this case his Lordship may probably have really done some service to those, who afterwards write about the Turks, particularly to the fabricators of melo-dramas; for it is certainly a very shocking thing to hear a raging turbaned-turk in a play calling a Christian infidel.[127]

Other reactions were comically conservative:

We wish Lord Byron would employ his incomparable talents on some national subject. The eastern fictions may be consonant to the particular turns of his mind, as supplying it with images of and delicate and pleasing nature but the deeds of many or our heroes are yet unsung and we should wish to see them transmitted to posterity adorned with the poetic wreathes woven by the fancy of a Byron.[128]

For Byron's reaction to this suggestion, see *Don Juan* I, opening.

Although no reviewers objected to "oriental" subjects on religious or cultural grounds, there was *almost* a consensus that Byron's use of "oriental" words in *The Giaour* and *The Bride of Abydos* was excessive, particularly when idioms became mixed:

Our poet also sometimes errs in the use of poetical language. Whatever merit words may independently possess, we ought not to mingle those

---

126: *The Literary Panorama*, April 1814, p.371; (*RR* IV, p.1528).
127: *The New Review*, December 1813, p.674; (*RR* V, p.1933).
128: *The Tradesman*, January 1814; (*RR* V, Byron,).

together in the same poem which point to nations, times, climates, and
customs very wide-apart. Thus 'clan,' 'foeman,' 'paynim,' do not mix
well with the 'rhamazan,' the 'kiosk,' and the 'palampore.' Nor are we
sure that the largest extent of poetical liberty will quite justify such an
importation of exotic terms into our language as 'salam,' 'ataghan,'
'palampore,' 'caique,' 'serai,' and others.[129]

The Eclectic Review refused even to spell the polluting signifiers
correctly:

> … this custom of disfiguring his pages with words that are not English,
> seems growing upon Lord Byron. There was something of it in the
> Giaour, but there is hardly a page in the present poem [*Bride*], but forces
> us to the notes at the end, for the explication of two or three outlandish
> terms. A rose and a nightingale are now Gul and Bulbul; a sailor, a
> Galiongee; and a rosary a Colomboro [*sic*]; Musselim [*sic*], Ollah, and
> Tchocada are not, we suppose, more generally understood; and old
> Giaffir
>
> > 'Resign'd his gem-adorn'd *Chibouque*,
> > And mounting featly for the mead,
> > With *Maugrabee* – and Mamaluke –
> > His way amid his *Delis* took,
> > To witness many an active deed
> > With sabre keen – or blunt *jereed*.
> > The *Kislar* only and his Moors
> > Watch well the Haram's massy doors.' p.12.
>
> There is, however, no other passage so unintelligible.
> For many of these words the corresponding English might have
> been used; and for those for which it could not, it was part of the
> author's business to manage without.[130]

This unease with the idiom Byron had chosen – or the decorative
system he had indulged in – was seen also in private comments. Murray
reported John Hookham Frere as saying "that such words as Gul and
Bulbul, though not unpoetical in themselves, are in bad taste, and ought
not to receive the sanction of your Lordship's example".[131]
Lord Holland wrote regretting Byron's use of irregular measures, and
said he wished Byron would stick to Spenserian stanzas and heroic
couplets:

129: *The British Review*, October 1813, p.141; (*RR* I, p.413).
130: *The Eclectic Review*, February 1814, p.188 (*RR* II, p.716).
131: Samuel Smiles, *A Publisher and his Friends* (John Murray 1891) I, p.221.

... the grandeur of your verse & the richness of your expressions make me, I own, regret that you so seldom write in heroick verse or regular stanzas & that you should be in this last beautiful & interesting work have adopted the irregularity of Walter Scott ...

... the sound of some of your Turkish words is not calculated to remove my aversion to them – Wulwulhey is the devil of a word & even in reading your obliging note on my kinder opinions about the nightingale's song I could not help regretting that Philomena had so inharmonious a name in the East as *Bulbul* – You will think me very independent to criticize at this note I should not do so unless I could say as I can with perfect sincerity that I am delighted with the poem ...

He ended on a note of alternate acceptance and doubt:

I am delighted with the poem, The descriptions the thoughts the story the language the characters & the versification wherever your Moslem predilections allow you to adhere to a Christian metre –
do you mean Selim's turning round when he is wounded to be a last look at Zuleika – ? – The Costume (as the affected critics call it) of the East seems to me perfectly preserved but after all I know little of it but what you have told me[132] –

Byron took due note, put aside his "Moslem predilections," and cut down on the use of Turkish words in *The Corsair* and *The Siege of Corinth*; and he next wrote *The Corsair*, as if bowing to Holland's conservative judgement, in heroic couplets.

Studies of Byron's orientalism

The task of collating and scrutinising what Byron had read about things eastern was begun in 1940 by Harold Wiener in his essay *Byron and the East: Literary Sources of the Turkish Tales*.[133] This is, as it were, a prelapsarian text, for in 1940 the state of Israel did not exist, and neither it nor the oil crises of the 1970s had given Islam the cultural and political weight it has now. Edward Said was only five years old.

Wiener stresses the excellence Byron's recall and the width of his oriental reading, above all his admiration of *Vathek*, and his reliance both on it and on its notes. He then looks at how Byron used D'Herbelot's

---

132: BL.Add.Mss. 51639 (letter of Nov 16, 1813).
133: Wiener, H.S.L. *Byron and the East: Literary Sources of the Turkish Tales*, in *Nineteenth-Century Studies in Honor of C.S.Northup*, ed. Herbert Davis, Ithaca 1940, pp.89-129.

Bibliothèque Orientale, dwelling on the rarity of the name "Zuleika," which otherwise occurs once only, in Sir William Jones. Jones is discussed next, and Byron's detailed familiarity with his works is argued.[134] Of Byron's assertion that he knew Hafiz and Ferdausi, Wiener writes

> In all probability he had not read the poems themselves, but had read what Jones had to say about Eastern poetry and forthwith accepted the scholar's critiques as his own ... When we find him saying that he had perused some of the Asiatic works "either in the original or translations," we are free to substitute "none in the original and few in translation."[135]

Next Wiener deals with the "Koran" (which is apparently an "Arabian classic": 110), of which he says "It is unwise to assume that he [*Byron*] is speaking with first-hand acquaintance of the book" (110). He concludes, having noted some parallel passages, that Byron's knowledge of the Qu'ran is derived not from Sale's translation, but from Henley's notes to *Vathek*, (the "orientalism" of which novel is "spurious": 115). He concedes that Byron may have read Sale's *Preliminary Discourse*. For the *Arabian Nights*, he says, Byron read Jonathan Scott's translation, even though Byron never mentions Scott:

> This is thoroughly in keeping with his failure, save in one ore two instances, to allude to the books he had consulted.[136]

There are no narrative analogues for the Turkish Tales in the *Arabian Nights*, writes Wiener, but he finds several points where details have been borrowed from Scott's Introduction. The same goes for the histories of Knolles and Rycaut, where, though again no narrative analogues are to be discovered, "Byron's poetry is thoroughly consistent with the details of Turkish life and manners as recorded by" them (121). A particular correspondence is to be found in the story of the depradations and capture of the "old and subtle" pirate Georgio, related by Rycaut. Georgio seems to me as much a precursor of Lambro as of Conrad (which is what Wiener

---

134: Wiener makes an error when he writes (p.108) that "Hafiz had not [in Byron's day] been done into English at all". One book in which Byron might have gathered an indirect knowledge of Hafiz is *A Specimen of Persian Poetry, or Odes of Hafez*, translated from the German of Baron Revizky by John Richardson, London 1801.
135: Wiener, op. cit., p.109.
136: Ibid, p.114.

stresses),[137] but Wiener's article does not mention *Don Juan* except in footnotes.

Wiener next adduces numerous examples of Byron's familiarity with the book of Demetrius Cantemir, and with the anonymous *Compleat History of the Turks* of 1719, quoted in the preface to *The Siege of Corinth*. Then he examines the memoirs of Baron de Tott, and the Letters of Lady Mary Wortley Montagu; Montagu, as I've said, had had access to ladies' quarters in Turkey, which gave her a privilege denied all the other authors whom Wiener lists.[138]

In his last pages Wiener lists numerous miscellaneous volumes which Byron's notes, and the two sales catalogues, show him to have possessed. He concludes:

> At times he [*Byron*] used his sources carefully; elsewhere, the finished product merely suggests previous reading. Occasionally he credits another author with having inspired a passage in his poetry; at other moments he borrows materials without acknowledgement
>
> His passion for accuracy is more immediately noticeable, and facts which were generally unfamiliar are duly documented and supported. But, as he says, "I could not write upon anything, without some personal experience and foundation" (129).

Wiener's essay is an invaluable summing-up of the literary background to Byron's Orientalism, at least in the Turkish Tales; but, as I

137: Byron and Hobhouse may have met a pirate called Lambro. For Monday July 2nd 1810, Hobhouse records: "Dined at Palace – met Colonel Rooke, (called "Captain" by Adair) a singular fellow, an old grey-headed man who lives amongst the Islands, keeps a boat of a hundred tons, and has been here eight or nine years. As rattling and as incorrect as a boy called Lambro. Lambro Cazzoni!! Took up the cause of the Syriotes about Ferguson's ship beating the town about ... proposals for a squadron of small craft. Septinsulars and others in these seas under British flag, and command very useful – numbers of ships here with French flag". See Byron's note to *The Bride of Abydos* II, 380 (CPW III, 135 and 441): "Lambro Canzani, a Greek, famous for his efforts in 1789-90 for the independence of his country; abandoned by the Russians he became a pirate, and the Archipelago was the scene of his enterprizes. He is said to be still alive at Petersburg. He and Riga are the two most celebrated of the Greek revolutionists". Politically and socially he is model for his namesake, Haidée's father, in *Don Juan*.

138: "Our elegant countrywoman, with a most voluptuous and animated pencil, has transported her reader into the paradise of Mahomet, by her lively powers of imagination; has entered into competition with the Prophet himself, and endeavoured to convert our Christian men and women too, into true believers" – de Tott, *Memoirs*, translator's introduction, I p.vii.

said, he only deals with those poems, not with *Childe Harold* or *Don Juan*. He makes no reference to Byron's travels, or to Hobhouse's diary.

Being a man of his time, Wiener is not interested in the political-religious-moral dimension which post-colonialist guilt, the need to consume huge amounts of oil, and the need therefore to keep well in with the Arab world, have since 1940 added (or so academic discourse implies), to a purely bookish approach to such matters. There is no discussion of imperialism, "penetration," or even to "the binarism of self and other". The most telling phrase in this context is his description of the Qu'ran as an "Arabian classic," as though the Qu'ran were a kind of Arabic *Great Expectations*.

***

In 1948 William Borst published *Byron's First Pilgrimage*,[139] a factual, not a literary account of Byron's relationship with the East, and a book of immense erudition which has not been superseded. The only major text to which Borst does not have complete access is Hobhouse's diary, then only available in *Recollections of a Long Life*, its mutilation by Lady Dorchester.

Borst makes large, if conventional, claims for Byron's experiences among the Albanians:

> ... the rugged, warlike impulsive Albanians, attired in their picturesque native costume, many of them strikingly handsome, ever armed, came to stand in Byron's mind as an antithesis to the hypocrisy he all too frequently detected among his more "civilized" fellow Englishmen. The extremes and the striking contrasts in their natures, their restlessness, their furious likes and dislikes – these inevitably appealed to a temperament that was in some degree akin.[140]

He hints – all that could be done in 1948 – at a hidden homosexual agenda.[141] And he accepts Byron's twin tall tales about eagles over Parnassus[142] and jackals in the ruins of Ephesus.[143] This gullibility apart, Borst's is an incredibly thorough book, necessary reading for anyone interested in its subject. Like Wiener, he is not interested in Islam as a

139: William A. Borst, *Lord Byron's First Pilgrimage*, Yale 1948, rptd. Archon Books 1969.
140: Ibid, pp.83-4.
141: Ibid, p.84n.
142: Ibid, p.88.
143: Ibid, p.108.

specific area of Byronic study, as we are in today. He does not analyse the Turkish Tales in any detail, makes no political points about them, and his conclusion about them is standard:

> ... it was something more than the mere surface appeal of the subject matter that led Byron to write *The Giaour* and *The Bride of Abydos*, *The Corsair* and *The Siege of Corinth* in the years immediately following his return from the East. The sharp contrasts, the violence, and the melodrama in those tales were in a sense akin to his own nature ...[144]

One senses an awareness of some factor which in 1948 was hard to articulate. But he does make another vital point, which Wiener skirts:

> There is significance, too, in the fact that Byron's last major poem, and his greatest poem, is rich in reminiscences of his early travels; it is no accident that Don Juan sailed from Spain through the Mediterranean and eventually arrived at Constantinople.[145]

***

One of the most extraordinary essays on Byron and Orientalism appeared in 1974 (pre-Edward Said). *Byron and Islam: the Triple Eros* by Bernard Blackstone[146] makes the most extreme claims ever for Islam as an influence on the poet. It includes a long section on Paul Rycaut's 1668 book *The Present State of the Ottoman Empire*: "Rycaut, disapproving strongly as a Huguenot Christian, has been infected, as an historian, with the paederastic virus and sees it everywhere" (330). Blackstone makes even larger claims for another book, Stephen Weston's *Moral Aphorisms in Arabic* (1805) which "knits together and throws into another perspective the threads of love, wisdom and power" (the "Triple Eros" of the title) "which Byron had found dispersed and sensationalized in Rycaut". Unfortunately for the thesis, there is no record of this book anywhere in Byron's writing or catalogues. Later Blackstone makes an even larger conjecture – that Ali Pasha was "a member of the Bektashi order of dervishes," and "had recognized in Byron a man of 'spiritual' birth, a man fit for initiation". It's even more unfortunate for his thesis that he adduces no evidence for this, and that no other writer on Ali Pasha

---

144: Ibid, p.152.
145: Ibid, p.153.
146: *Byron and Islam: the Triple Eros* by Bernard Blackstone in *Journal of European Studies* (1974) 4, pp.325-63.

credits him with any religious feelings or qualifications at all apart from those inspired by political calculation.

***

In 1978, Edward Said's *Orientalism* was published, and nothing was ever the same again. Any writer who had written about any Orient, factual, verifiable, or fantastical, was revealed to have done so at his peril. For Said, see my essay below.

***

In *Romantics, Rebels and Reactionaries* (1981), Marilyn Butler added a Saidian historical-political dimension to her reaction to Byron, which otherwise was not very dissimilar from that of Borst thirty-three years previously. Her book is about romanticism in general, and this is from one of its brief Byron sections:

> In *Childe Harold, The Giaour, The Bride of Abydos, The Corsair* and *Lara* he [*Byron*] developed the Byronic hero from prototypes such as Schiller's Karl Moor and Scott's Marmion. Masterful, moody outlaws, haunted by some secret consciousness of guilt, these heroes act as a focus for contemporary fantasies. Not the least element of guilty complicity about them is that they echo the French cult of Napoleon: they are fictional equivalents of Géricault's handsome idealized portrait of the French emperor on a white charger surmounting the Alps. By this daring hint, and by translating the hero from Scott's historical setting to a present-day theatre of war, Byron implies the possibility of effective action in the real world. Even so, his rebellious Corsair is sanitized ...[147]

The idea that the supposed "secret consciousness of guilt" may be the awareness of being either bisexual, or even gay, is not stated.

Of the heroes Butler lists, only Childe Harold is placed in "a present-day theatre of war," and he plays no part in it. Of the rest named, only Lara is placed in a theatre of war at all; and Butler seems carefully to leave out Alp in *The Siege of Corinth*, who is placed in an early eighteenth-century theatre of war. This inaccuracy bodes ill for Butler's next foray into Byron criticism, *The Orientalism of Byron's Giaour*, published in

---

147: Marilyn Butler, *Romantics, Rebels and Reactionaries* (Oxford 1981), p.118.

1988.[148] When it appears, her historicist approach is fully-fledged. Byron's Orientalism must be placed, to be understood, in the history of imperialism, and of the controversies surrounding it in his own day.

Butler shows from her first paragraph that she has learned from Said how to write in large, impressive assertions that don't bear examination. Here is the second sentence:

> Much, even perhaps most, of the best poetry of Byron and Shelley is set between Greece and the Hindu Kush, a region which in their day signified the crumbling Ottoman empire and the insecure overland route to British India.

Now Byron's best poetry consists of *Beppo*, set in Venice, *The Vision of Judgement*, set at the gate of Heaven, and *Don Juan*, of whose sixteen-and-a-bit cantos, only eight are set in parts of the area Butler specifies. I take Shelley's best poems to be *The Mask of Anarchy* and *The Triumph of Life*, neither of which is "set" anywhere. "... between Greece and the Hindu Kush" there are many regions, including Russia and Iran (Persia), as well as Ottoman Turkey; and "the insecure overland route to British India" was so insecure that only travellers who enjoyed danger took it. The normal route to India from Britain was by sea via the Cape of Good Hope.

Butler attempts to interpret *The Giaour* against the background of the struggle with Napoleon and the attempt to Christianize India. In order to do so, she has to insist that the main theme of *Childe Harold* II is the Greek struggle for freedom, and that of Southey's *The Curse of Kehama*, the need to make India Christian. I think few readers will have taken these impressions away from either work. However, she points out with success the sympathetic attitude to Islam found in *The Giaour*:

> Mohammedanism [*sic*] performs at least two useful social functions, it seems: to console people and draw them together. But for the monk who later in the poem attends the deathbed of the Giaour there is no such fellow-feeling".[149]

> ... the poem has good Moslems but no good Christians. The poem's main villains are the two great monotheistic codes, Christianity and Islam, *comparable* instruments of personal control over the lives of men

---

148: Marilyn Butler, *The Orientalism of Byron's Giaour,* in Beatty, Bernard and Vincent Newey, eds., *Byron and the Limits of Fiction*, Liverpool University Press 1988.
149: Ibid, p.88.

and women, and potentially of political control by great powers over the
destiny of small nations.[150]

"Potentially" draws back from the desire to make *The Giaour* into the
crude anti-Southey, anti-imperialist polemic the earlier part of the essay
implies it to be.

Butler would wish the writers of whom she speaks to be popular,
ignoring the fact that *The Corsair* sold ten thousand copies on its first day
of publication: "It was only by chance and in a travestied form that any of
the Oriental tales made their way into English popular political
mythmaking".[151] This point is at once contradicted when Butler quotes
Denman's defence of the insurgent Jeremiah Brandreth at his trial in
Derby, where the Corsair with whom he's compared is the character in
Byron's original poem, not one from a travesty. Byron was much more
popular than Southey, or Isaac Nathan, both of whom, insists Butler,
composed in "folk" idioms.[152]

***

In 1992, in *British Romantic Writers and the East (Anxieties of Empire)*,
Nigel Leask boldly takes Said's historico-erotic thesis – that for Western
writers, the East was an Other to be penetrated – and reverses it, arguing
that conventional writers feared "the swamping of English propriety by
grotesque oriental forms,"[153] a paranoia of which the terror of such
"oriental" diseases as elephantiasis and syphilis was a symptom. The
paranoia developed a political edge in such things as Gillray's depiction of
Frenchmen as monkeys (and, we could add, Southey's reaction to Indian
languages, quoted above.) One's English sense of righteous self was under
threat.

Leask writes about many things other than Byron, and includes (108-
18) a very patient dissection of that strange fish, Shelley's *The Revolt of
Islam*. However, in his Byron section, he insists that the Turkish Tales …

> … formed part of a broader cultural engagement with the question of
> imperialism, productive of so much stimulation and anxiety in Regency
> Britain.[154]

150: Ibid, p.91.
151: Ibid, p.93.
152: Ibid, pp.82 and 92.
153: Nigel Leask, *British Romantic Writers and the East (Anxieties of Empire)*,
Cambridge 1992, p.4.
154: Ibid, p.13.

and that in them,   → quote

> Byron reduces the imperialistic Self to a level with its oriental Other;
> but in doing so he in effect perpetuates the prejudice of the East/West
> binary opposition whilst attacking the ideology of empire which it
> empowers.[155]

I've not actually found much evidence of this stimulation and
anxiety, or of this opposition and ideology, all relating to imperialism, in
the politics of the era. The main focus of the country's anxiety until 1815
was, either how to defeat Bonaparte, or how to come to terms with him.
After 1815, it was how to deal either with the threat of internal
insurrection, or the threat to liberty which the Tory government posed,
crazed as it appeared to be by the imagined threat of internal insurrection.
Events in the East were fascinating, but distant, and no-one bothered about
them too much. The guilts and anxieties of English imperialist success in
the East were remote; the danger of French imperialist success was just on
the other side of the Channel, until Napoleon was defeated; or, most
horrifyingly for "true patriots", in the imagined insurgencies "put down" at
Spa Fields, Peterloo, and Cato Street, *after* Napoleon was defeated.

Of "the aristocratic hauteur of Byron's heroes" in the earlier poems,
Leask writes that Byron was "Aware of its status as commodity, of the
impossibility of 'virtue' in the world of the cash nexus."[156] This fastidious
awareness, I'd add, might explain the lengths to which Byron went,
embarrassed by the way he'd commodified the East, to refuse payment for
his oriental poems; lengths which his generous publisher went still further
to circumvent. Byron needed the money the Turkish Tales made; was too
proud to accept it; but didn't return it when it appeared mysteriously in his
bank account.[157]

Leask seems often to be writing about poems and movements that he
wishes, for the sake of his thesis, that Byron had written and lived through,
rather than about poems and movements that Byron really did write and
write through: he makes great play with the idea of the Giaour as "a
Venetian rather than a Spanish freebooter," for instance (32), or of Leila
"as symbolic embodiment of the Hellenic values underlying European
civilization" (33). Exactly which Mediterranean country the Giaour comes
from seems to me quite irrelevant; and if Leila embodies Hellenic values,

---

155: Ibid, p.4.
156: Ibid, p.16.
157: See Cochran, *Did Byron take money for his early poems? Byron Journal*,
2003, pp.72-6.

they're not the ones I think of when I read Sophocles or Thucydides. It's true that she is, like them, "a beautiful corpse" (33); but they're much more instructive corpses than she is. And she is in any case Circassian.[158]

Was there such a dignified thing as "The aristocratic Whig defence of liberty against tyranny" which "turned on a classical republican notion of honour," as Leask contends in his discussion of *The Bride of Abydos*? (38) The Whigs of Byron's day – a two-faced, untrustworthy, smug, toadying, place-seeking and frustrated load of parasites, devoid of scruple – would have been delighted to know that they were going to be credited with such a thing two centuries later, and that this would be the way academe would teach them.

Does Selim's relationship with Zuleika in *The Bride* really "emblematize ... the honour ideal"? (40) I feel, reading his long speech (it goes from line 633 to line 972, that is, it takes up 339 lines in a poem 1204 lines long) that he's closer to Sir Epicure Mammon chatting-up Doll Common in *The Alchemist* – words are all he can work with, and he could have gone on forever, like Hamlet whom he resembles, postponing forever the moment when language must cease and activity take over. It's true that "the heroes of the *Tales* live in an existential and moral cul-de-sac" (40); but not because they're "compromised by a value-system inadequate to the exigencies of the modern world" (40); it's because they're intent on failure and death at whatever cost.

Here another problem arises: Leask, like so many critics, lumps all six tales together as though they're a homogeneous group. It seems to me that *Parisina,* with its defiant heterosexual hero, is quite a different thing from the rest, and that *The Siege of Corinth* (again, see Robert McColl's essay below), is far superior in economy, pace, and structure to its eastern siblings[159] (not that *Lara* – set entirely in Spain – is eastern at all). Leask speaks of *The Corsair* and *Lara* as "the two later tales" (45) as if there were no more. As, again, with many critics, one feels that whether the tales are any good as narrative poems is a question in which Leask isn't interested.

Conrad's "penetration of the Pasha's court disguised as a dervish" in *The Corsair* isn't just "strategically botched" (47-8), it's strategically pointless, for the stronghold has already been reconnoitred. I interpret it as a sign of Conrad's desire to be defeated, just as his later horror at Gulnare's killing of Seyd, and at her creation of a means of escape for him, is a symptom of his desire to be impaled (though see also my argument about *Oberon*, above). These Byronic heroes are far odder than

---

158: See *The Giaour*, 505.
159: Leask makes a brief reference to *Siege* at p.56, and to *Parisina* at p.62.

they're generally reckoned. Talk of Conrad's "heroic values" (50) and of his pirate band's "revolutionary politics" (51) are further examples of Leask taking the tale at its own self-evaluation, with fatal results for commonsense, like his assumption that the mainstream Whigs may be credited with a philosophy. What kind of "value-system" is it (52), firstly, that a pirate would possess anyway, and secondly, that wouldn't allow him to escape a horrible death when the cell door was unlocked? If characters and plot defy reality and logic, what price any ideological subtext the critic projects on to them?

Leask insists that "There is a danger of making too much of" Byron's later shame at the success of the Turkish Tales.[160] One seemingly contemptuous reference to "the jingling *ottava rima*" (16) is, however, followed by the following half-hearted concession:

> ... the most that Byron can hope to do in *Don Juan* is to transmute his spleen into laughter and ceaselessly unravel the illusions of his age by acknowledging 'the constellation of his own social determinants', to become 'the man who discovers his voice in a conscious and dialectical act of poetic ventriloquism' (63: the first quotation will be found at McGann, *Byron and Romanticism*, p.51).

This makes *Don Juan* sound quite interesting: but Leask – like most writers in this section – seems to lack the will to describe *Don Juan* in detail.

***

In 2000 Michael Franklin published a paper[161] about the influence on Byron of Sir William Jones. Jones gets short shrift from Edward Said, who describes him (*Orientalism* p.77) as having "closed large vistas down, codifying, tabulating, comparing". "Persian Jones," writes Franklin, who when at Harrow wore Persian garb, spoke and read twenty-eight of the seventy-two supposed languages of post-Babel civilisation. He was concerned with imaginative authenticity and exactitude in his work, providing both literal and stanzaically-exact translations of his parallel texts – though Franklin concedes that, being blissfully married, unlike Byron, he did "silently heterosexualise" much of what he found. He

---

160: Ibid., p.15.
161: Michael Franklin, *The Building of Empire and the Building of Babel: Sir William Jones, Byron, and their Productions the of Orient*, in Martin Procházka, (ed.) Byron: *East and West / Proceedings of the 24th International Byron Conference / Charles University Prague*, Prague 2000, pp.63-78.

enabled his readers, of whom Byron was one, to "assimilate the Asiatic," and his work is an important subtext for Byron's, whose concern is (in, for instrance, *The Giaour*), the radically un-Saidian one of "blurring the Eurocentric binarism of self and other", to see, as did Lady Mary Wortley Montagu, "English self in Asian otherness", and to employ, what Said has no time for at all, "a comic reflexivity and relativity" reflecting ironically on both East *and* West. This essay is a vital contribution to studies of Byron's orientalism.

***

After so many westerners had discussed Orientalism, it was time scholars from the orient had a go; and the last three books I'll examine are indeed by oriental scholars – from different backgrounds.

Mohammed Sharafuddin published *Islam and Romantic Orientalism; Literary Encounters with the Orient* in 1994. Sharafuddin has a surprisingly tolerant attitude to Southey:

> The idea of an affinity between the Bible and the Koran dominates *Thalaba* to such an extent that Southey came to believe that Islam and Christianity shared a common source, and that biblical ethics could combine with what he often called 'the morality of the Koran' into a single force for regenerating the moral order of the world.[162]

The Curse of Kehama, with its corresponding Hindu themes, is specifically excluded from Sharafuddin's discussion (48). He also skirts such points as Byron's note on "one third" of women's souls going to paradise, and his ignorance as to where the Prophet is buried (220-222), and praises "the local colour which Byron was able to apply with great effect as a result of his prolonged stay in the region" (224). He entertains, only to reject, the idea – deriving from Annabella, Isaac Disraeli and Blackstone – that Byron once almost converted to Islam (224-5), impressed perhaps by what he read as its "complete predestinarianism". He writes of the effect of the Mediterranean landscape on Byron, and of the density and conviction of what Byron termed his "costume" – his detailed knowledge of clothing, weaponry, rituals, and so on. He draws attention to the "irresistible femininity" of Byron's oriental heroines and to what he claims is the "incorrigible masculinity" of his oriental heroes (249).

162: Sharafuddin, p.129.

He concurs with Nigel Leask in identifying Leila with Greece (258), and describes Conrad as "the western liberal" – in all except his strange guilt (259). He stresses the alienation, both of Byron from his occidental context, and of his heroes from their oriental contexts, and is refreshing in the emphasis he places here on the centrality of Alp in *The Siege of Corinth*.

Sharafuddin's analyses are simplistic and conventional; but it is good to find Byron – if not Southey – written about so sympathetically, by a non-Christian.

His habit of centring all lines quoted, no matter what metre they're in, is annoying.

***

In 1995 Abdur Raheem Kidwai published *Orientalism in Byron's 'Turkish Tales': The Giaour (1813), The Bride of Abydos (1813), The Corsair (1814) and The Siege of Corinth (1816)*. He leaves out *Childe Harold* II and *Lara,* and has no space for the ottava rima satires. From the outset he proclaims an anti-Said inclination. *Beppo* and *Don Juan*, he writes,

> … seemed to me to point to a deviation from conventional western concepts of the Orient. Byron's Orientalism struck me as an alternative view, differing greatly from the dominant one, and his identification with a culture not his own tended to cut across the barriers of religious hostility and cultural blindness. (v-vi)

Despite this admiration, derived from the later satirical work, he doesn't deal with *Don Juan* or *Beppo*.

His book is, within its parameters, very thorough,[163] and is critical and sympathetic at the same time, in an understated way: of the often-referred-to *Vathek*, he writes, for example, that it "is not completely free from some misconceptions, though inadvertent ones, about Oriental beliefs and practices" (12). This is perhaps to take *Vathek* a bit too seriously. He's very good at pointing out editors' errors, where, for example, McGann has taken over a point from Coleridge without checking it. He decries Shelley's "dark, negative view of Islam," in, for example, *Hellas* (22). On the other hand, he thinks highly of Montagu and Jones (16-17; 14-15). He has perhaps too much respect for Marilyn Butler's idea of "a school of new powerful politicised poetry" in Southey, the Shelleys, and Thomas

---

163: Though full of misprints: for examples, *Syed* for *Seyed* (p.179, four times), *they* for *thy* (pp.68, 167, 176,), and *South* for *Southey* (p.201).

Moore (28, 200). He too thinks that, in *The Giaour*, "Leila's tragedy corresponds to the contemporary Greek liberation movement against the Ottomans" (162), even though Leila's role is entirely passive, which the Greeks certainly were not in their liberation movement, and even though when *The Giaour* was published, there was no such movement. He makes the same error in relation to Selim's revolt in *The Bride of Abydos* (178).

He points out, which no-one else has (69), that there is far less of Byron's vaunted oriental wardrobe in *The Siege of Corinth* than elsewhere – reason perhaps, though he doesn't say so, for its critical neglect. Of *Siege*, lines 221-2:

> As rose the Muezzin's voice in air
> In midnight call to wonted prayer;

… he writes,

> From a Muslim viewpoint, this passage is marred by inaccuracy: there is no 'midnight call' to prayer in Islam; Byron perhaps confuses the evening prayer with the midnight service (141).

Southey, he points out (206), makes the same mistake in *Thalaba*; but Southey is given no extenuating explanation. Sale's *Discourse* – available to both Byron and Southey – places the final prayer of the day "After the day is shut in, and before the first watch of the night".[164]

Kidwai's is a biased account of Byron – biased in his favour. When discussing Byron's ignorance about where Mohammed is buried, he points out how many writers – including Walter Scott – shared the ignorance, but still can't explain how Byron, the expert, would not know (39). He concedes that Byron's idea of one-third of the places in paradise being allotted to women is "fantastic" (53); but seems to forgive him for propagating it. In a note to *The Giaour*, 734, Byron writes

> "Alla Hu!" the concluding words of the Muezzin's call to prayer from the highest gallery on the exterior of the Minaret. On a still evening, when the Muezzin has a fine voice (which they frequently have) the effect is solemn and beautiful beyond all the bells in Christendom.

Now Kidwai points out (56), firstly that the words are in fact "Allahu Akbar" (God is great), and secondly that although they are a refrain in the muezzin's call, they are not its concluding words, which are "La ilaha il

---

164: Sale, p.107.

Allah" (there is no God but God). By this time we are starting to see how he approaches his theme, which is by saying that such elementary mistakes are all right if it's Byron who makes them. Presumably it's the anti-Christian context in which Byron often writes which redeems his Islamic ignorance – which has here made him do something like, in Christian terms, confuse an Amen with a Kyrie.

He provides, what Naji B. Oueijan later provides too, a compendium of Byron's oriental expressions, from "Ablutions" to "Wul-wellah" – the first time such a thing was attempted. Here he finds many accuracies, and apt borrowings, to stress.

He gives sympathetic critical accounts of Byron's Turkish Tales, contrasting them with Southey's work in a way which is quite unlike Sharafuddin's: "For him [*Southey*] the Western/Christian tradition is the norm and those outside it are perceived as utterly loathsome ... Southey simply cannot stand them" (229). Moore's attempt at the same territory, in *Lalla Rookh*, is, he writes, "conventional," and in some details blasphemous (237).

Kidwai's is an irreplaceable book, vital for anyone studying the subject: if anything, it places Byron on too high a pedestal.

***

In 1999 Naji B. Oueijan, who introduces himself as "a Christian Arab living in the East" (1), published *A Compendium of Eastern Elements in Byron's Oriental Tales*. Like Kidwai,[165] his position is anti-Said ("anti-Saidist"), though he finds fault with Kidwai:

> Kidwai's reduction of the Orient and Oriental to Islam and Islamic poses serious problems and reminds us of Said's reductionist claims (5).

Like Kidwai, however, he has a high opinion of "Byron's advanced Oriental scholarship" (12) as well as of other "genuine Oriental scholars" (13) such as Montagu, Beckford, and Goethe. His aim is to help the reader "identify true and false Oriental scholarship" (13); but he at once worries us by describing Blackstone's *Triple Eros* as "by all means the most illuminating and interesting of all the studies of Byron's Oriental reading" (19). He accepts the idea that Byron read Weston's *Moral Aphorisms in Arabic* (26), which is one of Blackstone's implausibles. Later he concurs with Blackstone's evaluation of Ali Pasha as a Dervish mystic. He believes that Byron "had ... a basic knowledge of ... Arabic and Persian"

165: Spelled "Kidawi" in Oueijan's bibliography (Oueijan p.186).

(27) despite Byron's own avowal that he never learned the former.[166] Byron writes in the same sentence that he never learned Armenian (beyond the alphabet), despite which Oueijan writes that he made "several translations" from Armenian, though he doesn't say where they're to be found.

Byron, he writes, spent four years "on his estate" (32); but doesn't say which years. Then, he writes, Byron went to the East:

> He sought the East which was powerful, wise, and organized but primitive, beautiful, and lively – a world of strong passions, romantic poetry, and true existence (33).

What he doesn't say is that if there hadn't been a war on the continent, Byron might have done the usual thing and travelled to France, Italy and Germany: Byron's orientalism is in fact a product of boring historical contingency (it's almost as if you mustn't say that). He also doesn't mention the fact that in order to go, Byron had to borrow £4,800 from Scrope Davies, thereby creating no small amount of stress for his friend. These important contexts for Byron's eastern travel are very rarely emphasised.

Oueijan tells us that

> Another incident Byron referred to in *The Bride* was seeing the body of a condemned man floating on the water with sea fowl hovering to devour the corpse. This event might have aroused Byron's disgust and provoked his second dramatic adventure which took place later in Athens (38).

The second adventure is the one with the woman in the sack, referred to above. Now Byron, while putting the incident of the dead man and the fowls into *The Bride* (see lines 1081-96), does not claim to have seen such a thing. Oueijan's omissions and errors of fact accumulate with such rapidity that when he speaks of the mass-murderer Ali Pacha "preferring to rule his native land and protect his countrymen" (39-40), we can imagine Ali's shade nodding quizzically up from Hell at the idea, and are not surprised, so sentimental – so romantic – is the portrait Oueijan paints. Evidence is not a consideration here, we can see – the book is prey to a polemical motivation as overt as anything by Edward Said. Ascertainable

---

166: BLJ IX, 31 (Detached Thought 55). Oueijan says that Byron "made contacts with the Rev. John Palmer, the Arabic Professor at Cambridge." In fact Byron tells his mother (BLJ I, 172) that he's asked a friend to try and contact Palmer, whom he doesn't name – but we hear no more.

reality is a barrier: the ideal is what needs serving. Of Byron's lodging in Athens, Oueijan writes

> His life with the Macri family in Athens reveals the genuineness of his participation with these peoples (43).

The facts point to something more mundane. The Macri household was short of money, and Hobhouse's diary records, for March 3, 1810:

> Teresa, twelve [*years*] old brought here to be deflowered, but Byron would not.

And on August 23 1810 Byron writes to Hobhouse, "... the old woman Teresa's mother was mad enough to imagine I was going to marry the girl."[167] On May 15 1811 he adds to the tale: "I was near bringing away Teresa but the mother asked *30 000* piastres!"[168] This would indeed show "the genuineness of his participation," but not in the warm style Oueijan wants us to believe in.

"In 1816 Byron left England for Switzerland and Italy," writes Oueijan (47), "and from there he went to Greece to bury his heart in the earth he loved". The seven years Byron spent between 1816 and his final departure for the East can form no part of Oueijan's tale. Neither can the amusing poetry he wrote during that time.

The main part of the book consists of the Compendium of the title, with sub-divisions into Settings, Architecture, and so on. These compliment Kidwai's third chapter in extremely useful ways, and include, as Oueijan promises, non-Islamic material. The excuse for Byron's ignorance about Mohammed's tomb is the feeblest yet, however: "Byron was not sure where the Prophet's Shrine was because he never visited Arabia" (85). Oueijan has no comment on the idea of the sequence of the muezzin's call, or of its occurring at midnight; and passes without comment the idea of one-third of places in paradise being reserved for women.

Oueijan's is another book which is very useful indeed for consultation, and is free of post-modern, post-imperialist jargon; but it goes even further than does Kidwai in idealising its subject.[169]

167: BLJ II, 13.
168: BLJ II, 46.
169: Another interesting essay by Oueijan is to be found in *Western Exoticism and Byron's Orientalism* in Procházka, Martin (ed.) *Byron: East and West, Proceedings of the 24th International Byron Conference*, Charles University

Byron's finances, and his state of mind, as he wrote and published *The Giaour*[170]

After him succeeds Mr Tibs, a very *useful hand*; he writes receipts
for the bite of a mad dog, and throws off an eastern tale to
perfection; he understands the *business* of an author as well as any
man; for no bookseller alive can resist him; you may distinguish
him by the peculiar clumsiness of his figure and the coarseness of
his coat: however, though it be coarse, (as he frequently tells the
company,) he has paid for it.[171]

Throughout 1813, when *The Giaour*, the first of the "Turkish Tales," was
written, Byron was in a very strange state of mind, not conducive to
sustained, self-critical creativity, but only to intense, manic bursts,
motivated by desperation, and insecurity about the direction in which his
life was, or was not, going. It was a state of mind which didn't really fade
away, but if anything got worse, until he left England in 1816. All the
Turkish Tales were written during this time.

The first edition of *The Giaour* was published on June 5, 1813.[172]
The Napoleonic Wars were still in progress: the climactic Battle of
Leipzig was still months ahead; no-one could travel safely on the continent
(though J.C.Hobhouse was travelling there, and having most interesting
adventures). Byron was determined to travel, but where to? He had, earlier
in the year, announced to Charles Hanson that "I go in May" (6); to Robert
Rushton he wrote on February 24 that "I have some intention of leaving
England in the Summer" (21); and the assertion echoes throughout the
year.[173] At one point he seems to think he's got Lady Oxford pregnant and

---

Prague, Prague 2000, pp.95-102. He distinguishes between exoticism, which is a
commodity, and orientalism, which is what Byron purveys, and which is more
authentic, even though Byron's consumers may think of it as exoticism. The twin
definitions imply greater discernment in Byron than in his readers.

170: Figures in brackets in this section are page-references to BLJ III.

171: Goldsmith, *A Citizen of the World*, Letter XXIX (Dent, 1900, p.141).

172: This is the relatively brief first edition, with 684 lines. Fifteen copies had
been circulated privately in late March.

173: See the following: page-references are to BLJ III, 22 ("almost immediately"),
23 ("in less than a fortnight"), 29 ("immediately"), 30 ("there is a world beyond
Rome"), 32 "(in June"), 33 ("in May"), 38 ("in May"), 39 ("forthwith"), 43 ("in
June"), 56 ("go I will … you shan't be troubled with me these ten years – if ever"),
59 ("next month"), 73 ("I am still in equipment for voyaging"), 74 ("our sailing
day is the 30th"), 81 ("almost immediately"), 82 ("I am quite equipped, and only
await a passage"), 84 ("We sail on board the Boyne"), 91 ("I have great hopes of
sailing soon"), 115 ("Gibraltar – or Minorca – or *Zante*").

to be planning to follow her and her husband abroad (40), with her encouragement (174). He appears to have despaired of the plan by August 25 (99).

He puts his money where his mouth is. Three days before *The Giaour's* publication, on June 2, he makes several purchases from William Pulsford, army equipment specialist, including the following: "A Green Spine Waterproof Camblet Horsmans Cloak with large Circular Cape, a smaller Cape to form Hood, Velvet Collar," for £9.9s.0d; and "A Mixt Waterproof Camblet Cloak … with Balloon & Sleeves, for £7.7s.0d". With sundries, the whole totals £25.1s.[174]

One month and thirteen days later, on July 15, after *The Giaour's* second edition has come out, he spends £395.8s.0d on twenty-six items from Bryant's, suppliers of military and camp equipage. They include £10.13s for a canteen; £53.11s for three patent bedsteads; £29.8s on four large solid leather trunks; £25.4s.6d on two "Handsome Military Saddles with Holsters Bare Skin Blouses & Bridles"; and £15.15s on five "Water Deeks & Circingles".[175]

I do not know what "water deeks and circingles" are, but the purchases indicate an intended expedition to savage foreign parts, of the kind where few if any hotels will be found, so that open-air living will be the norm: Greece, Albania, or Turkey, perhaps further afield – Egypt, Palestine, Persia, even India. On July 13, he writes to Moore: "I want to get away, but find difficulty in compassing a passage in a ship of war" (75).

On July 21 he buys, among much else, from H.W.Mortimer, gunmaker, two pairs of plain steel mounted pistols with goler & bolt locks; three pairs of small brass mounted pistols with goler and bolt locks (for six guineas); and a pair of best small pistols, well cleaned. The bill comes to £84.2s.

Next, on July 24, he buys, from Berger, manufacturer of optical instruments, six three-feet portable telescopes for £37.16.0; six sliding gold achromatic operas (opera-glasses), for £18.18.0; two silver hunting sprung compasses for £7.7.0; two telescopes in mahogany cases for £9.9.0; and two thermometers in varnished cases for £2.20. On the same date he runs up a bill for £113.16.6 at Standenmayer, manufacturer of guns and swords.

On August 4, his Hammersley's account book shows that he pays "W Thomas for / 9 Oz Doubloons / @ 109 / pr oz / (£)49 1(s) and Circular

---

174: John Murray Archive / National Library of Scotland.
175: Ibid.

Notes / & Stamps (£)3004 10(s)." These are the 1813 equivalent of our old traveller's cheques.

He is making detailed preparations for travel: but his destination is a problem, for with a war on one can't just book a passage in a civilian transport, but has to rely on the Navy. However, his leaning is towards the Orient:

> I am in the agonies of three different schemes – the first you know – the 2d. is Sligo's Persian plan – he wants me to wait till Septr. set off & winter at Athens (our old headquarters) & then in the Spring to Constantinople (as of old) & Baghdad & Tairan. – This has its charms too & recalls one's predilections for gadding, – then there is Hobhouse with a Muscovite & Eastern proposal also – so that I am worse off than ever Ass was before to which bundle of hay I shall address myself. – However I am going somewhere though my agents want me to stay where I am – an additional reason for wanting to get away (27-8; letter to Lady Melbourne, Mar 18).

By the start of August he's actually obtained a berth (84n): but still doesn't go – there's only space for himself and Fletcher, and "this would not do" (88); he needs more interesting companions. On August 18, after the third edition of *The Giaour* has been published, he writes to Moore again:

> Ld. S[ligo] is in town & we are much embarrassed with ye. plague which is it seems all over ye. Levant – but having been both at a prodigious expenditure in large trunks – small clothes – & small arms for ourselves – snuff boxes & Telescopes for the Mussulman gentry – & gewgaws for such of the Pagan women as may be inclined to give us trinkets in exchange – why – lest so much good preparation should be thrown away – we are determined to go – God knows where – for he is bewildered & so am I. (90)

On November 10 1813, the Hammersley account book shows that he cancels the order made on August 4 "for Cir^r Notes (£)3000". His plans for travel have been abandoned. Towards the end of the year, after Leipzig, he makes more plans for a trip to Holland – but that doesn't materialise either, though travelling is now much safer.

***

During 1813, Byron has no idea how much money he's worth. His outgoings for the whole year are £19,783.10s.6d, over an income of

£21,591.7s.1d, of which £15,000 is money from Thomas Claughton, who may or may not be purchasing Newstead Abbey from him, but who is at least able to put the fifteen thousand down in two £7,500 lots, on July 19th and 27th – a fortnight, and three weeks, respectively, after *The Giaour's* publication.[176] In fact Byron never knows, during this period, whether or not Claughton will pay the remainder of the price, and therefore doesn't know whether or not he owns Newstead. Early in 1813 he tells Lady Melbourne "I have been signing the N[ewstea]d contracts today, & that business is happily terminated" (3); but it never is. On January 3 he writes that "Newstead is in a sort of abeyance between sale and purchase" (7); on February 25 that "C[laughton] is a fool or is shuffling" (24).[177]

He has at least initiated the process of selling his ancestral seat, a statement of termination which few other English aristocrats were able to make, and without which he will be broke. Newstead was not a "settled" estate, as nearly all were. Owing to an error on the part of the "Wicked" Fifth Lord's lawyers in 1773, he had inherited it, not as a life tenant, as was usual, but as owner of the fee simple: that is, it was his absolute possession, his to dispose of, and he had run up massive debts using it, or a mortgage on it, as collateral – the only problem being that he is now unable either to sell or mortgage it.[178] Claughton's £15,000 is a deposit which will have no follow-up; but Byron doesn't know that.

He is not paid for *The Giaour* in 1813: at some point between 17th and 22nd November he writes in his journal:

> Mr Murray has offered me one thousand guineas for the "Giaour" and the "Bride of Abydos." I won't – it is too much, though I am strongly tempted, merely for the say of it. No bad price for a fortnight's (a week each) what? – the gods know – it was intended to be called Poetry ... (90)

Money to be made from the two Turkish Tales written so far forms no part of his consideration; and about their artistic success, as can be seen, he feels ambivalent ("the popularity of ... [*The Bride*] really surprised – & ... certainly did not raise my opinion of the public taste": 168). His assertion is often that Murray is publishing *The Giaour* against his – Byron's – inclination (62, 63). He is not paid for the poems until October 25 1815, when, with the bailiffs closing in, Murray sends him

---

176: Information from Hoare's Bank, Fleet Street, owners of Byron's bank account, to whom I'm grateful.
177: See also BLJ III, 25, 29, 30, 32, 77.
178: See John Beckett, *Byron and Newstead* (Associated University Press, 2001).

(unsolicited), £1,050 – a thousand guineas – for the copyrights of *The Giaour*, and of *The Bride of Abydos*, published on December 3 1813.

***

It is during this period that Byron sits for three of his most famous and pretentious portraits: the Cloak and the Albanian Costume portraits by Phillips, and the "Leaning-on-one-hand-gazing-off-left" portrait by Westall. The arrogance, the distance, the aloofness, the security in selfhood and the awareness of being gifted and set apart from ordinary mortals, with which the paintings credit him, all seem a very long way from the man we intuit from the letters and biography.

"… he is bewildered & so am I." Both Byron and his friend the Marquis of Sligo have personal reasons for getting out of the country. Byron's letter to Moore of August 18 continues:

> His [*Sligo's*] Balarina has presented him with a babe – & Malice says he divides the honours of paternity with the Editor of the Courier – who – I suppose – published his trial & tried his fortune with the Lady – much about the time that Sir Wm. Scott passed sentence of matrimony on his mother – He is going to part with her – & is right – those Opera house connections are not very creditable … (90)

Sligo had spent December 1812 to March 1813 in Newgate for abducting sailors in time of war, so he must have impregnated his "Balarina" while in "Hob's pound". His mother marries Sir William Scott, the Admiralty judge who had passed sentence on him, on April 10. This double embarrassment may have given him excellent motives for wanting to get away.

Byron's private life is, at the age of twenty-five, even shakier than Sligo's. He starts the year in the midst of an affair with one older woman (Lady Oxford, for whose young daughter he also has a soft spot: 36, 42), and carrying on a detailed and nervous correspondence with another older woman (Lady Melbourne) about another affair, just terminated, with yet a third older woman (Lady Caroline Lamb), who refuses to acknowledge it terminated. Later in the year – while he revising *The Giaour* – he amuses himself by hovering for some time on the brink of an affair with Frances Wedderburn Webster – a younger woman – as much to play games with her jealous husband as out of affection for her. It's during a lull in this business (for it's not really an affair), that he writes *The Bride of Abydos*. "I begin to believe," he tells Lady Melbourne in October, "that *danger* &

difficulty render these things more piquant to my taste" (142); it's a bit late in the day, but he's beginning to attain a measure of self-understanding.

This is not all. Of the two Turkish poems, he writes in his 1813-14 journal, with asterisked gaps which make us regret very much that the original manuscript is missing:

> I sent Lord Holland the proofs of the last "Giaour," and the "Bride of Abydos". He won't like the latter, and I don't think that I shall long. It was written in four nights to distract my dreams from * *. Were it not thus, it had never been composed; and had I not done something at that time, I must have gone mad, by eating my own heart,—bitter diet!— Hodgson likes it better than the Giaour, but nobody else will,—and he never liked the Fragment. I am sure, had it not been for Murray, *that* would never have been published, though the circumstances which are the ground-work make it * * * heighho! (208)

Some maintain that the first gap in the first quotation would have held something to signify "Augusta". Meanwhile, he is thinking about marrying Annabella Milbanke, despite her initial refusal (18, 78, 98, 103, 109, 118, 119, 159, 178); but that doesn't stop him from planning to take Augusta abroad with him too! (85, 89). He is only hesitant, as he claims, because she'd have to take one of her children, and he doesn't like children (93).

This financial insecurity, plus perhaps a sense that he is, by selling Newstead, betraying the class to which he only belongs precariously, as mere great-nephew of the previous lord, plus the awareness that, while embroiled in different ways with three other women, he is in love with his own half-sister, must give Byron a strange sense of not being the person whom society, represented here by the portraits, the Whig Lord Holland and the Anglican vicar Francis Hodgson, insist that he is. Is his frantic, ostentatious heterosexualising a pretence? A game – like his poems – to fill in the time? He expends, in his surviving correspondence at least, far more energy excoriating Caroline Lamb than expressing affection for either Lady Oxford or Augusta. That might be natural; but Madame de Staël tells him he "had no feeling, and was totally *in*sensible to *la belle passion*, and *had* been" all his life (76). One can see why he might want to leave the country, away from "that same morass … in which I am now chin-deep" (53).

It looks like the behaviour of one at the mercy of his own need to live dangerously, with every statement, and every poem, an act of bravado. But travel in the Orient will, he thinks, provide an escape from it all.

On November 29 1813 Augusta writes to him (the "+"s signifying physical affection):

I want to know dearest B + your plans – When you come + when you go
– … umph! when the writings travel – when ye Cake is to be cut – when
the Bells are to ring – &c – &c – &c – by the bye my visitors and
acquainted with *a* & did praise her to the skies – they say her health has
been hurt by *Studying* &c &c &c I have not a moment more my dearest
+ except to say ever thine [*scrawl*][179]

The italicised "*a* … praised to the skies" is Annabella, and the whole
business spirals out of control when, thirteen months after Augusta writes
this, Byron marries Milbanke, aware all the time that it's a colossal
mistake, and despite Augusta's encouragement. Sixteen months after that,
when the marriage fails, he feels it necessary to leave England for good – a
decision which he has actually made at the time of the publication of *The
Giaour*, and which has merely been delayed. It is during this disastrous
period that he also publishes *The Corsair* (February 1st 1814); *Lara*
(August 5th 1814); and *The Siege of Corinth* and *Parisina* (February 13th
1816).

However, there is one difference. By 1816 the war is over, sea-
passage is by civilian transport, and he has no need to go the Orient any
more. Instead he goes first to Belgium. "Baghdad & Tairan" are forgotten
as if they'd never been thought of. Later he writes to Moore:

I may say to you, what I would not say to every body, that the last two
were written, the Bride in four, and the Corsair in ten days, – which I
take to be a most humiliating confession, as it proves my own want of
judgement in publishing, and the public's in reading things, which
cannot have stamina for permanent attention. "So much for
Buckingham."[180]

Lalla Rookh makes Byron take stock

At the end of August and the start of September 1813 Byron recommends
a book to Thomas Moore. He does so at the end of the letter in which he
also advises Moore to …

… Stick to the East; – the oracle, Staël, told me it was the only poetical
policy. The North, South, and West, have all been exhausted; but from
the East, we have nothing but S<outhey>'s unsaleables, – and these he
has contrived to spoil, by adopting only their most outrageous fictions.

179: Michael and Melissa Bakewell, *Augusta Leigh* (Chatto and Windus 2000),
pp.141-2.
180: BLJ IV, 77.

His personages don't interest us, and yours will. You have no competitor; and, if you had, you ought to be glad of it. The little I have done in that way is merely a "voice in the wilderness" for you; and, if it has had any success, that will also prove that the public are orientalizing, and pave the path for you.[181]

That he should liken himself to John the Baptist may have caused the Catholic Moore's brow to wrinkle a little, given what that implied about *him*: we do not know. Here is the book Byron thinks Moore should consult:

If you want any more books, there is "Castellan's Moeurs des Ottomans," the best compendium of the kind I ever met with, in six small tomes ... I send you, begging your acceptance, Castellan, and three vols. on Turkish Literature, not yet looked into.[182]

Antoine Louis Castellan's *Mœurs, Usages, Costumes des Othmans, et abrégé de leur histoire* was published in Paris in 1812, and an English translation was brought out, entitled *Turkey*, as part of a series called *The World in Miniature,* in 1821. Both Oueijan and Kidwai refer to it in their indices and bibliographies, but never quote from it; Wiener makes no reference to it. It shows what Byron would have had available to him for the "oriental costume" of the Tales, had his memory failed him. The English translation is accurate, but free; it sometimes elevates notes into text, and sometimes adds its own notes.

Castellan starts with an outline of the foundation and spread of Islam, in the course of which he writes

Two of the tenets taught by Mahomet rendered his troops extremely formidable: that of predestination, according to which no man can avoid his destiny, or defer by any means the hour of his death, so that if the fatal moment is not arrived, a shower of arrows would be discharged at a person in vain; and by the second, the Prophet solemnly promises to those who shall die in battle with infidels the full remission of all sins committed by them, the palm of martyrdom, and admittance into a paradise of delights.[183]

Castellan leaves the nature of the delights to his reader's imagination.

181: BLJ III, 101.
182: BLJ III, 102, 104 (letters to Moore of 28 Aug and 1 Sep 1813).
183: Castellan, 1821 English translation, I, p.30; original, I, p.xij.

Volume II is a history of the Sultans, ending in three chapters about Selim III, Mustapha IV, and Mahmoud II, bringing the books thus right up to date for both the French original and its English translation. Of Selim's proposed reforms, Castellan writes,

> Whoever possesses the slightest knowledge of the character of the Turks will easily conceive with what an eye such innovations were viewed by all pious Musulmans: to resemble the Christians ever so little was in their opinion to infringe all laws human and divine, and to debase the dignity of the true believer.[184]

Volume III is about the Seraglio and its harem, and would have introduced Byron to the name "Gulbeyaz." Gulbeyaz was a favoured concubine of Sultan Mahomet IV (1649-87), and incurred the jealousy of his leading wife, Guneche. Her tale is told in the English translation at Castellan III 84-90 (original, III 79-84). Her name is analysed:

> The word [*Gulbeyaz*] signifies, white rose, being composed of *gul*, a rose, in Persian, and *beyaz* or *beyadh*, white, in Arabic.[185]

Various scandalous stories are related about the jealousies of concubines, wives, and even mothers; the varying roles of harem officials are described in detail, including those of eunuchs and dwarves. Volume IV is about politics, and defines the roles of such men as the Caïmacham-Pacha, or the Reïs-Effendi, with which Byron should have been familiar with from having met some of them, or at least been in their proximity, at Constantinople.[186] A section on arms refers to the "djeryd," but not to the ataghan, preferring the word "sabre" (the same word is used both in the original and the translation). Another section on the capitan-pacha – the Admiral of the Turkish fleet – gives a better impression of that person's naval competence than Byron would have received from his meeting with the real thing in 1810; for the capitan-pacha he met had had never been to sea.

The fifth volume is about law and religion, and contains what Byron would have recognised as a section (V 65-70; same pages in original) on the Howling Dervishes or roufays, here placed in a more correct religious context than Hobhouse allows them; and another on the Turning Dervishes or mevlevys (V 70-73; same pages in original). It's clear (V 104; 107 in

---

184: Ibid, II, p.210; original, II, pp.201-2.
185: Ibid, III, p.87n; original III, p.82n.
186: He had been in the presence of both the Caïmacam-Pacha (the Vice Grand Vizier), and the Reïs-Effendi (the Foreign Secretary), on 28 May, 1810.

original) that the final prayer of the day is at "an hour and a half after sunset," not at midnight. The muezzin's call is translated, not quoted in Arabic (V 119; original 117).

There are no references to how many women, if any, may enter paradise.

The sixth and last volume is about clothing, food, and trades. We look in vain for a symar or a palampore, a calpac or even a capote. Instead we have the benych, the feredjeh, and the hedjaz; none of which are in Byron.

The section on cuisine includes such things as this:

> They [*the Turks*] eat flesh-meat either boiled or roasted: they eat roast fowls and even whole lambs, stuffing them with minced meat and spices: but this dish can only be served up at the tables of the great. Their ordinary dish is pilau, which is made of rice or peeled wheat boiled in water: it is then drained and butter added to it. This is the real diet of the soldiers. It is good, light, easy of digestion and readily cooked (VI, 206-7 original VI 197).

Why did Byron recommend Castellan's six very useful volumes to Moore, when he himself had made absolutely no use of them at all, and would make none in the future, when writing his own early oriental verse? There is no *pilau* in any of the Tales, though there is a *pilaff* at *The Corsair* 635; however, it is not dwelt on, for the point of that episode is the way in which Conrad rejects both the Moslem meal and the polite Moslem conventions surrounding it – prior to revealing himself, and trying to destroy the palace in which the meal is being held. The Tales contain no Howling or Turning Dervishes; no tales of harem jealousy; no eunuchs; no dwarves; no Caïmachams or Reïs-Effendis; no references to Selim III or Mahmoud II; and Gulbeyaz, as we all know, is one of the heroines of *Don Juan,* a poem in which food figures prominently. Is Byron implying to Moore that now Moore is to embark on an oriental work, taking up the Byronic burden, it would be as well to rely not on a faulty memory and not on a gullible readership, but to try and make one's "costume" as accurate as a reliable source such as Castellan can make it?

With or without Castellan, Moore had already embarked upon his magnum opus, the long quadri-partite oriental poem *Lalla Rookh.* Its writing took him five years.

***

Lalla Rookh was published on May 22nd 1817; for more thoughts on it, see the essay below by Allan Gregory. Byron seems to have received it at the beginning of September; and his reaction seems to have been one of embarrassment at having been the encourager – the godfather – of such a thing. For the first few lines he tries (he's writing to Murray, not Moore, on September 15th), to avoid an evaluation of it at all: then he expresses admiration for Moore as a man (an evasive technique he later employs when avoiding comment on Shelley's verse): then sums up a very limited reaction in half a sentence: and finally launches into a diatribe against all contemporary poets, including himself.

It looks as if *Lalla Rookh* has fallen flat. Here is the relevant part of the letter:

> I have read "Lalla Rookh" – but not with sufficient attention yet – for I ride about – & lounge – & ponder & – two or three other things – so that my reading is very desultory & not so attentive as it used to be. – I am very glad to hear of its popularity – for Moore is a very noble fellow in all respects – & will enjoy it without any of the bad feelings which Success – good or evil – sometimes engenders in the men of rhyme. – Of the poem itself I will tell you my opinion when I have mastered it – I say of the *poem* – for I don't like the *prose* at all – at all – and in the mean time the "Fire-worshippers" is the best and the "Veiled Prophet" the worst, of the volume. – – With regard to poetry in general I am convinced the more I think of it – that he and *all* of us – Scott – Southey – Wordsworth – Moore – Cambell – I – are all in the wrong – one as much as another – that we are upon a wrong revolutionary poetical system – or systems – not worth a damn in itself – & from which none but Rogers and Crabbe are free – and that the present & next generations will finally be of this opinion. – I am the more confirmed in this – by having lately gone over some of our Classics – particularly *Pope* – whom I tried in this way – I took Moore's poems & my own & some others – & went over them side by side with Pope's – and I was really astonished (I ought not to have been so) and mortified – at the ineffable distance in point of sense – harmony – effect – and even *Imagination* Passion – & *Invention* – between the little Queen Anne's man – & us of the Lower Empire – depend upon it [it] is all Horace then, and Claudian now among us – and if I had to begin again – I would model myself accordingly – Crabbe's the man – but he has got a coarse and impracticable subject – & Rogers the Grandfather of living Poetry – is retired upon half-pay, (I don't mean as a Banker) –

> > Since pretty Miss Jaqueline
> > With her nose aquiline

and has done enough – unless he were to do as he did formerly. –[187]

He doesn't write to Moore again until February 2nd 1818,[188] when he sums up the above letter to Murray briefly, and refrains from mentioning *Lalla Rookh* until a P.S., when he congratulates Moore, not on it, but on its success.

It looks as if seeing Moore's attempt at an oriental poem has made Byron ashamed at the success of his own. Three years later, in 1820 he wrote, in *Some Observations upon an Article in Blackwood's Magazine*:

> I have thus expressed myself publicly upon the Poetry of the day the opinion I have long entertained and expressed of it to all who have asked it, and to some who would rather not have heard it. – – – As I told Moore not very long ago "we are all wrong except Rogers, Crabbe, and Campbell." Without being old in years, I am old in days, and do not feel the adequate Spirit within me to attempt a work which should show what was right in Poetry, and must content myself with having denounced what was wrong. There are I trust younger Spirits rising up in England who escaping the Contagion which has swept away Poetry from our literature, will recall it to their Country, such as it once was & may still be – – – – –
>
> In the mean time the best Sign of amendment will be repentance – and new and frequent Editions of Pope and Dryden.[189]

His memory plays him false. He had, so far as we know, never told Moore that "we are all wrong":[190] he had told Murray, and it was probably Murray who had told Moore. A year later he returned to the attack, in *A Letter to John Murray Esqre*. Speaking of nameless modern versifiers, he wrote that

> They have raised a Mosque by the side of a Grecian temple of the purest Architecture – and more barbarous than the Barbarians from whose practise I have borrowed the figure – they are not contented with their own grotesque edifice – unless they destroy the prior and beautiful fabric which preceded and shames them & their forever and ever. – – I shall be told that amongst these – I *have* been – (or it may be still *am*) conspicuous; – true – and I am ashamed of it; – I *have* been among the builders of this Babel attended by a confusion of tongues – but never

---

187: BLJ V, 265-6.
188: BLJ VI, 9-11.
189: CMP, 110.
190: In his letter to Moore of February 2nd 1818 (BLJ VI, 10) he almost says it, but not exactly.

amongst the envious destroyers of the classic temple of our Predecessor.
– – I have loved and honoured the fame and name of that illustrious and
unrivalled man – far more than my own paltry renown.[191]

That he should choose the image of a mosque beside a temple, and
refer to the builders of the mosque as barbarians, will probably not bear
the anti-Islamic interpretation which it seems to invite; but that he should
refer to the mosque as a grotesque edifice is slightly embarrassing, even
though, within the metaphor ("the figure"), he concedes that he was its
architect and builder. More central is the idea of a Babel, for his
ostentatious play with Turkish and other oriental vocabulary and myth is a
distinguishing feature of many of the Tales, for having written which he is
now apologising.

To return to the last passage but one: his claim that he is, though
young, too old to "feel the adequate Spirit within me to attempt a work
which should show what was right in Poetry" ignores the fact that he has,
since ceasing to write in his old manner, written *Beppo*, and the first
cantos of *Don Juan*.

Orientalism in Byron's ottava rima work (1): *Beppo*

The Turkish Tales are, above all, solemn, like *Lalla Rookh* – very
unShakespearean indeed. There's not a joke to be found in any of them
(except in the notes), and this is perhaps their biggest unacknowledged
weakness (though another is the indifferent plotting of at least three of
them). Byron may have read *Vathek* over and over, but he didn't care to
note that part of the charm of its orientalism lay in its brutal humour, often
bordering on farce:

> 'Fancy not,' said Vathek, 'that you can detain me. Your presents I
> condescend to accept; but beg you will let me be quiet; for I am not
> over- fond of resisting temptation. Retire, then:— Yet, as it is not
> decent, for personages so reverend, to return on foot; and, as you have
> not the appearance of expert riders, my eunuchs shall tie you on your
> asses with the precaution that your backs be not turned towards me: for,
> they understand etiquette." – In this deputation, were some high-
> stomached sheiks who, taking Vathek for a fool, scrupled not to speak
> their opinion. These, Bababalouk girded with double cords; and, having
> well disciplined their asses with nettles behind, they all started with a

---

191: CMP 148-9.

preternatural alertness; plunging, kicking, and running foul of each other in the most ludicrous manner imaginable.[192]

A scene which involved flogging asses' backsides with nettles would not sit well with the gravity Byron affects in *The Giaour*, or *The Siege of Corinth*. He enjoyed such jokes himself, but dared not put them in his poetry before 1817.

It was Goethe who wrote that "Jerusalem Delivered could be poisoned with a single line from Don Juan,"[193] and the same is true of the Tales. We enjoy *Romeo and Juliet* as much as we do *Pyramus and Thisby*, its parody, for there's humour in *Romeo and Juliet* already (see below); but few who write about the Turkish Tales write with equal enthusiasm of *Don Juan* and *Beppo:* they seem to feel self-conscious, as though they're aware that it's all a trap. Orientalism must be serious: academic careers are based upon its solemn analysis, and a writer who jokes about it makes us feel insecure, no matter how great his expertise. And in truth, it's hard to reconcile a taste for such poetry as this, from *The Corsair* ...

> He passed the portal, crossed the corridore,
> And reached the chamber as the strain gave o'er:
> "My own Medora! sure thy song is sad –"   365
>
> "In Conrad's absence wouldst thou have it glad?
> Without thine ear to listen to my lay,
> Still must my song my thoughts, my soul betray;
> Still must each action to my bosom suit,
> My heart unhushed, although my lips were mute!"   370

... with a taste with this, from *Beppo*:

> "Beppo! what's your Pagan name?   725
>   "Bless me! your beard is of amazing growth!
> "And how came you to be away so long?
> "Are you not sensible 'twas very wrong?
>
> "And are you *really, truly*, now a Turk?
>   "With any other women did you wive?   730
> "Is't true they use their fingers for a fork?
>   "Well, that's the prettiest Shawl – as I'm alive!

192: *Vathek*, p.102.
193: His words are, "mit einer einzigen Zeile des ‚Don Juan' könnte man das ganze ‚Bereifte Jerusalem' vergiften." Eckermann: *Goethes Gespräche mit Eckermann*, int. Franz Deibel, Leipzig (Insel, 1920?), I, p.32.

"Well, that's the prettiest Shawl – as I'm alive!
"You'll give it me? – they say you eat no pork –
"And how so many years did you contrive
"To – bless me! did I ever? No – I never   735
"Saw a Man grown so Yellow! How's your Liver?

Laura's speech is in normal conversational English, despite the
constraints of a verse-form three times more complex than that in which
The Corsair is written:[194] but of Medora's speech one can only say,
quoting the famous line from the cinema, "Nobody talks like that!" As
long as you don't juxtapose her idiom with Laura's, you accept her use of
pompous words like "lay," "soul," "bosom," and "heart," as a poetical
convention – but put the two poems side by side, and you find it hard to
read *The Corsair* at all. Its style stops being a convention, and becomes
just pretentious. You wonder how you ever took it seriously – why were
you so polite about it? Some of the squalid details about the East that
Byron and Hobhouse noticed are here in *Beppo* – from the real world, and
thus material which Byron couldn't include in his "Turkish" idiom. "And
are you *really, truly*, now a Turk?" means, "Have you been circumcised?"
– a pertinent question, coming from his wife. "Is't true they use their
fingers for a fork?" is only a question about table-etiquette on its primary
level. You have to choose between rhyming "fork" with "pork" and
rhyming it with "Turk;" and at first reading you take the second option.
Byron's rhyme-scheme leads you into gross, Elizabethan indelicacy.[195]

Beppo's seventy-seventh stanza is awash with facetiousness at
Byron's own expense, and at the expense of those who had read and
criticizsed his Turkish Tales. Referring to professional poets as *instructive,
pleasant people*, it builds on previous allusions to the lack of western-type
culture among Islamic ladies, and expresses the desire to convert them all
– if not to Christianity, at least to Christian grammar:

The poor dear Mussulwomen whom I mention
        Have none of these instructive, pleasant people,   610
And *One* would seem to them a new Invention,
        Unknown as bells within a Turkish Steeple;
I think 'twould almost be worth while to pension
        (Though best-sown projects very often reap ill)
A Missionary Author – just to preach   615

194: For an approach to the heroic couplets of *The Corsair*, see Susan Wolfson,
Couplets, Self, and The Corsair, Studies in Romanticism, Winter 1988, pp.491-
514.
195: For "firk," see Dekker, *The Shoemaker's Holiday*; or *Henry V*, IV iv.

Our Christian usage of the parts of Speech.

If such an idealistic scheme succeeded, Byron might actually find an oriental readership, and John Murray might find it worth while to open branches in Constantinople and Smyrna.[196]

Beppo's career, as "A Renegado of indifferent fame" (752), is sketched with far greater regard to realism than that of Conrad, or of Alp. We never know what sort of ship Conrad sails, nor what kind of merchandise he steals – indeed, the idea that Conrad is a thief would spoil the *The Corsair's* tone, for his "thousand crimes" must be kept nameless – they're more mysterious that way. But the ship Beppo sails home in is "a fine polacca, / Manned with twelve hands, and laden with tobacco" (759-60). The rhyme would not be possible in *The Corsair*, where ships are "barks," "craft," or "vessels."

We gather that The Giaour bribed his way into the monastery where he dies; that he,

> … not from piety, but pride,
> Gives wealth to walls that never heard
> Of his one holy vow nor word. (902-4)

It's so shocking that it has to be said discreetly. But the idiom of *Beppo* needs no such circumlocution:

> His wife received, the Patriarch re-baptized him,
> (He made the Church a present by the way) (777-8)

In ottava rima, religion may be purchased – it goes without saying.

Byron's intention in *Beppo* and *Don Juan* is just this: to make it impossible for anyone to take his earlier oriental poems seriously. His motive is to make "the rascals (i.e. the public)" who drank in "my Harrys and Larrys, Pilgrims and Pirates"[197] embarrassed at having done so – embarrassed at the poor critical faculties they displayed in buying and claiming to enjoy the stuff at all. And we could say the same about what his motive would be towards modern academics who write about the Tales as though they furnished serious evidence for their historico-political theories:

> Oh! that I had the art of easy writing

196: The first Greek translation of Byron, of *The Giaour*, by K. Lampryllos, was published in Smyrna (Izmir) in 1836; the first Turkish one, of *Sardanapalus*, by Mehmet Emisi, in 1934.
197: BLJ IV, 252-3.

> What should be easy reading! could I scale
> Parnassus, where the Muses sit inditing
>   Those pretty poems never known to fail!
> How quickly would I print (the world delighting)   405
>   A Grecian, Syrian, or *Ass*yrian tale,
> And sell you, mixed with Western Sentimentalism,
>   Some samples of the *finest Orientalism*. §

§: The *"finest Orientalism"*: a new phrase for a very common sort of poetry. For its meaning, consult Mercutio, *Romeo and Juliet*, Act 2 Scene 4:
      "The *What?*"
      Mercutio: "The pox of such antick, lisping, affecting fantasticoes – these new turners of accent – "By Jesu, a very good blade – a very tall man – a very fine whore."

Byron thus condemns his earlier self as a vulgar innovator – a "new tuner of accent" – and, by implication, condemns those who modelled themselves on him, and were with him "upon a wrong revolutionary poetical system"[198] (a thought which occurred to him about a month before he wrote *Beppo*.)

"The finest Orientalism" is a phrase used by the strangest coincidence by Jeffrey in the *Edinburgh Review* in November 1817, the month after *Beppo* was written, but three months before it was published:

There is a great deal of our recent poetry derived from the East: But this is the finest orientalism we have had yet. The land of the Sun has never shone out so brightly on the children of the North – nor the sweets of Asia been poured forth, nor her gorgeousness displayed so profusely to the delighted senses of Europe.[199]

This is the start of Jeffrey's review of *Lalla Rookh,* the poem written with Byron's encouragement. The phrase which Byron satirises one month, Jeffrey uses seriously the next. For Jeffrey (who *may* write with tongue in cheek), orientalism is a treasure to shine out, to be "poured forth", or to be "displayed ... profusely": for Byron, it's an easy-reading commodity to be sampled and sold. "Oh that I had the art ...!" is disingenuous, because he had it, not so very long ago, and the poems he wrote with it sold thousands of copies.

198: BLJ V, 265 (letter to Murray, 5 Sep 1817).
199: *Edinburgh Review*, November 1817, 1.

Orientalism in Byron's ottava rima work (2): *Don Juan*

Don Juan is a work of far greater ambition than *Beppo*, and its orientalist horizons are correspondingly wider. In *Beppo*, unless you take Venice to be an oriental location, the biggest "oriental section" comes at the end, when we heard of where and into what scrapes Beppo's wanderings have taken him. In *Don Juan*, all the cantos between the second and tenth partake of an orientalist dimension – if you count Russia as an Asiatic country with European pretensions, which seems fair enough, both then and now.

The eastern cantos divide into four parts: Juan's adventures on Haidee's isle (I-IV); in the Constantinople harem (V-VI); at the Siege of Ismail (VI-VIII); and at the court of Catherine the Great (IX-X). All parts, including the third, are dominated by a sexually predatory female, whose ambitions, though perhaps satisfied at first, are in the long run thwarted – Haidee's by death, Gulbayez by comic plot-twists, and Catherine's by the fact that the effort and distaste involved in satisfying her makes Juan ill. At once we see, not only that is there a much greater variety of subject in *Don Juan* than in the Tales, but that women have a much more central and active part. None of the heroines of the Tales, apart from Parisina, seems to have a sexual appetite at all – and *Parisina* is an exception in lots of other ways too: is, as I have said, not oriental. Gulnare may be assumed to have a sexual agenda in wishing to free Conrad, but she must not express it; and, if she is indeed Kaled in *Lara*, has to atone for her temerity by spending the rest of the time in drag. Lady Mary Wortley Montagu's idea, quoted above, that Islam encourages women to procreate, had clearly not registered with Byron – few of whose heroines procreate anyway. Of his couples, only Cain and Adah are happy parents.

[margin annotation: Brontë's idea Cleopatra in Vilette]

Juan's adventures on the island of Haidee and Lambro constitute Byron's most extended and explicit attempt at creating an oriental Eden – for more so than anything in the Turkish Tales. The fact that Juan's arrival on the island is nautically and geographically impossible, and the fact that he is passive throughout his stay, is what (I assume), prevents historicists and post-colonialists from interpreting it as an imperialist act. His sojourn on the island – which is either Ionian or Aegean depending on which line you read[200] – is more like a fantastical episode from *Orlando Furioso* than from Captain Bligh, or from Dalyell's *Shipwrecks and Disasters at Sea*.

Another striking difference between *Don Juan* and the Tales is that Byron, who in the Tales relied on his capacious but fallible memory and

---

200: See see *DJ* II 150,7 or III 56 2 for Ionian, II, 127, 2 or IV 72, 8 for the Aegean.

capacious but casual reading for his "diction" and "colour," here often has a reliable prose source open by his side constantly, which he versifies. This applies not just to the oriental passages, but to the shipwreck in Canto II, where his source is Dalyell's *Shipwrecks and Disasters at Sea*,[201] and to the battle sections in the Ismail cantos, where nearly all the military detail is from Castelnau's *Histoire de la Nouvelle Russie*.[202] As late as Canto XV he has open next to him, while writing, a cookery book, of all things, to add verisimilitude to the poem. It is *The French Cook, a system of fashionable, practical and economical Cookery, adapted to the use of English families* by Louis Eustache Ude: here Byron is looking not so much at the text, as at the illustrations and captions.

· His anxiety is perhaps to avoid such small errors as his reference to a midnight Moslem prayer, or to the wording of the Muezzin's call, pointed out above – though he never appears to have acknowledged that he got these things wrong. His major source for much of the "colour" in the Haidee cantos is the 1816 book *A Narrative of Ten Years' Residence at Tripoli in Africa*, which seems to be by the otherwise anonymous sister-in-law[203] of Richard Tully, who was English consul in Tripoli from 1783 to 1793. Byron's borrowing from this book is extensive,[204] but may been seen in these three stanzas from Canto III:

> Haidee and Juan **carpeted their feet**
>   **On Crimson Satin, bordered with pale blue;**   530
> **Their Sofa occupied three parts complete**
>   **Of the Apartment,** and appeared quite new;
> **The velvet Cushions** (for a throne more meet)
>   **Were Scarlet, from whose glowing Centre grew**
> **A Sun embossed in Gold, whose rays of Tissue,**   535
> Meridian-like, were seen all light to issue. –
>
> **Chrystal and Marble, Plate and Porcelain,**

201: See Cochran, Don Juan, *Canto II: A Reconsideration of some of Byron's Borrowings from his Shipwreck Sources, Byron Journal*, 1991, 1pp.41-5; also *Byron's* Don Juan *Canto II Stanza 94: a previously un-noted source in the Medusa Narrative, Notes and Queries*, June 1992, pp.172-3.
202: See Cochran, *Byron and Castelnau's* History of New Russia, *Keats-Shelley Review* October 1994, pp.48-70. I have yet to find a source for the story of the severed head at VIII, 84, pp.7-8. It is not in Castelnau.
203: The first edition has "sister".
204: See Cochran, *Byron and "Tully's Tripoli", Byron Journal*, 1992, pp.77-88. Stung by someone gloating over his unacknowledged borrowings from Dalyell, he acknowledges those from "Tully" (without saying that "Tully" is a woman), in a letter to Murray of 23 Aug, 1821 (BLJ VIII, 186).

     Had done their work of Splendour; **Indian Mats**
And Persian Carpets, which the heart bled to stain,
   Over the floors were spread; Gazelles and Cats, 540
And dwarfs and blacks, and such like things, that gain
   Their bread as Ministers and favourites (that's
To say by degradation) mingled there
As plentiful as in a Court or Fair. –

There was no want of lofty mirrors, and   545
  The tables, most of Ebony inlaid
With mother of pearl, or Ivory, stood at hand,
  Or were of Tortoise-shell or rare woods made,
Fretted with gold or silver; – by command
  The greater part of these were rarely spread 550
With viands and sherbets in ice – and wine –
Kept for all Comers, at all hours to dine.

Here are the passages from "Tully" which he is glancing at while writing:

"**The carpet was of crimson satin with a deep border of pale blue quilted; this is laid over Indian mats and other carpets. In the best part of the room the sofa is placed, which occupies three sides of an alcove, the floor of which is raised. The sofa and the cushions that lay around were of crimson velvet: the centre cushions being embroidered with a sun in gold of highly embossed work, the rest were of gold and silver tissue.** The curtains for the alcove were made to match those before the bed. **A number of looking-glasses and a profusion of fine china and chrystal** completed the ornaments and furniture of the room, in which there were neither tables nor chairs. **A small table, about six inches high, is brought in when refreshments are served; it is of ebony inlaid with mother-of-pearl, tortoiseshell, ivory, gold and silver, of choice woods,** or of plain mahogany, according to the circumstances of the proprietor." (Tully 135.)

"The sides of the door-way, and the entrance into the room, were **marble;** and according to the custom of furnishing here, **choice china and chrystal** encircled the room on a moulding near the ceiling. Close beneath these ornanents were placed **large looking-glasses** with frames of gold and silver; the floor was covered with curious matting and rich carpetting over it; loose mattresses and cushions placed on the ground, made up in the form of sophas, covered with velvet, and embroidered with gold and silver, served for seats, with Turkey carpets laid before them." (Tully 32.)

I don't think it's sexist to say that the observation in "Tully's Tripoli" betrays its author as a woman – few men would take in this amount relating to Islamic furniture, interior decoration, or crockery. The fact becomes still more obvious in Byron's later descriptions of Haidee's clothing, nearly all of which is from Tully's descriptions of North African women's dress. Byron is now borrowing a woman's eye to make his oriental descriptions more exact. We don't know, because he never confesses – but one could argue that he's intent on obtaining a more verifiable kind of oriental colour for his ottava rima work than he achieved in the Tales. Tully's sister-in-law, like Lady Mary Wortley Montagu, knows what she's talking about. Here is her description of the way Moslems, in Tripoli, speak of their faith:

> Though the Moors never say much concerning the religious ceremonies they perform at Mecca, yet for those they mention they express the highest veneration. They seldom speak to Christians on these topics, except to those in whom they have the greatest confidence, and then it is with circumspection. They dwell with religious zeal on the certainty of the Koran's having been delivered by angels to Mahomet verse by verse. They relate the miracle of Mahomet's tomb, at Medina, being suspended from the earth by an invisible power, and persuade themselves they have seen it in this extraordinary situation. They say, that the lamps have burned constantly round it ever since his death, without ever having been replenished at any time; that celestial spirits have been seen by the devout Mussulmans who visit with real holiness the Prophet's tomb, the brilliancy of which, without the aid of human art, never has, nor ever will be, in the least tarnished or faded in its appearance, and which, they profess, surpasses all that can be imagined. The Black Stone in the Temple of Mecca, placed there by Abraham the Patriarch, is called by the Prophet the Ruby of Paradise, and passes by that name in all descriptions given of it by the Mahomedans.
> The Mahomedans assemble at a mountain not far from Mecca, where they oblige all the Christians, Jews, or Pagans in their suite, to quit them, that they may not contaminate the Holy City of Mecca, to which the Mussulmen set out together in a religious procession from the foot of the mountain. Their pilgrimages are not so expensive as those of the Franks and Christians.[205]

The manner is grave, and the moments of scepticism are few and lightly accented ("[they] persuade themselves they have seen" the

---

205: *A Narrative of Ten Years' Residence at Tripoli in Africa* (1816), pp.198-9.

Prophet's tomb suspended);[206] one cannot say that Islam is being ironically treated, either from a Christian or from a rationalist standpoint. "Ms Tully's" open-mindedness is, for an Englishwoman of the 1780s, remarkable. She is, as I have written elsewhere, "no canting evangelical,"[207] and no cultural imperialist either. One can see why Byron found her congenial. Why, she even compares the relative costs of the different monotheistic pilgrimages.

The question of clothes is important, because the Tales contain few if any detailed descriptions of them, and Byron is now interested in the topic, for reasons that we shall discuss. Here is a description of Haidee at *Don Juan* II 121 (a pre-Tully passage):

> But with our damsel this was not the Case;
>   Her dress was many-coloured, finely spun;
> Her locks curled negligently round her face,
>   But through them Gold and Gems profusely shone;
> Her Girdle sparkled, and the richest lace   965
>   Flowed in her veil, and many a precious stone
> Flashed on her little hand; but, what was shocking,
> Her Small Snow feet had Slippers, but no Stocking.

Neither Leila in *The Giaour* nor Zuleika in *The Bride of Abydos* create an impression which is "shocking" – Byron is being satirical at the expense of his English readers, easily outraged at women with bare feet. But more importantly, "dress," "Girdle," "veil," and "slippers" show that in terms of vocabulary he's not moved on from his earlier, unsatisfactory idiom. The words are the equivalent of the unchallenging "barks" and "vessels" with "sails" and "masts" in *The Corsair*. Here is *Don Juan* III 70 (post-Tully):

> Of all the dresses I select Haidee's:
>   She wore **two jelicks** – one was of pale yellow;
> Of azure, pink, and white was her **Chemise** –   555
>   'Neath which her breast heaved like a little billow;
> With buttons formed of pearls as large as pease,
>   All gold and Crimson shone her jelick's fellow,
> And the **striped** white **gauze baracan** that bound her
> Like fleecy clouds about the Moon, flowed round her. –   560

206: See Kidwai, p.6 for this superstition: he quotes Southey's *Roderick* and Marlowe's *Tamburlaine* (I, i 137-42). See also Castellan V, p.187 (original V, p.183) where it is said to occur at Jerusalem.

207: See Cochran, *Byron and "Tully's Tripoli"*, *Byron Journal*, 1992, p.77.

Here is its source:

> "Lilla Aisha, the Bey's wife, is thought to be very sensible, though rather haughty. Her apartments were grand; and she herself was superbly habited. Her **chemise** was covered with gold embroidery at the neck: over it she wore **a gold and silver tissue jileck** [*sic*] or jacket, without sleeves; and over that **another** of purple velvet, richly laced with gold, with coral and pearl buttons, set quite close together down the front: it had short sleeves finished with a gold band not far below the shoulder; and it discovered a wide loose **chemise** of transparent gauze, ornamented with gold, silver, and ribband stripes. The drapery or **baracan** she wore over her dress was of the finest crimson transparent gauzes, between rich silk **stripes** of the same colour (Tully 32-3).

Don Juan is as we all know a very moral poem, and one of its targets is conspicuous consumption. This strand climaxes in the feast at Norman Abbey in Canto XV, where Byron is careful to use Ude's cookbook as source, to anchor his ethic epic in the real world. But the process began earlier, for Haidee and Juan are, in their innocence, as conspicuous consumers as Lilla Aisha, the Bey's haughty wife in Tully, or as Gulbeyaz the Grand Turk's haughty wife in the Harem cantos, or as the haughty Amundevilles in the English cantos. Here is *Don Juan* III 64:

> The hangings of the Room were Tapestry made   505
>   Of Velvet pannels, each of different hue,
> And thick with Damask flowers of Silk inlaid –
>   And round them ran a yellow Border too;
> The upper Border richly wrought displayed,
>   Embroidered delicately o'er with blue   510
> Soft Persian sentences in lilac letters –
> From poets, or the Moralists their Betters. –

All these details are from Tully, including

> "The apartment ... was hung with dark green velvet tapestry ornamented with coloured silk damask flowers; and sentences out of the Koran were cut in silk letters and neatly sewed on, forming a deep border at the top and bottom: below this, the apartment was finished with tiles forming landscapes." (Tully 31-2.)
> "The hangings of the room were of tapestry, made in pannels of different coloured velvets, thickly inlaid with flowers of silk damask: a yellow border, of about a foot in depth, finished the tapestry at top and bottom, the upper border being embroidered with Moorish sentences from the Koran in lilac letters." (Tully 135.)

We need to read Tully along with the poem. In the midst of luxury is the reminder of its moral questionability. As Byron writes, at *Don Juan* III 65:

> These Oriental Writings on the Wall,
>   Quite common in those Countries, are a kind
> Of Monitors adapted to recall,   515
>   Like Skulls at Memphian banquets, to the Mind
> The words which shook Belshazzar in his Hall,
>   And took his kingdom from him: You will find,
> Though Sages may pour out their Wisdom's treasure,
> There is no sterner Moralist than Pleasure. – –   520

This moral dimension (derived in part, it has to be admitted, from *Vathek,* whose protagonist is a very conspicuous consumer indeed), is absent from the Turkish Tales. Conrad is ascetic in diet; but it does him no good morally at all. Byron has moved on from the days when he would buy, on impulse, six three-feet portable telescopes for £37.16.0., for an expedition with no destination. He knew (for he had very poor digestion), that feasts bring their own punishment:

> Hath the news of the overwhelming *day of judgment* reached thee? The countenances *of some* on that day, *shall be* cast down; labouring *and* toiling; they shall be cast into scorching fire to be broiled; they shall be given to drink of a boiling fountain; they shall have no food, but of dry thorns and thistles; which shall not fatten, neither shall they satisfy hunger.[208]

Byron's version of the Slave-Market

It is necessary for Byron's scheme that Juan should experience actual slavery, because slavery is one metaphor for his condition throughout the poem, and he must learn about it in as many ways as possible, physical, emotional, social and moral. The stoic Jack Johnson (named, it is important to remember, neither in Canto V nor Canto VI) is with him as teacher:

> "You take things coolly, Sir," said Juan. "Why,"
>   Replied the other, "what can a Man do?
> "There still are many rainbows in your Sky,
>   "But mine have vanished; all, when life is new,

208: Sale, p.488-9. Verses 88, 1-7.

"Commence with feelings warm and prospects high;   165
    "But Time strips our illusions of their hue,
"And One by One in turn, some grand Mistake
"Casts off its bright skin yearly like the snake.

"'Tis true, it gets another bright and fresh,
    "Or fresher, brighter; but the year gone through,   170
"This Skin must go the way too of all flesh,
    "Or sometimes only wear a week or two; –
"Love's the first net which spreads its deadly Mesh;
    "Ambition, Avarice, Vengeance, Glory, glue
"The glittering lime-twigs of our latter days,   175
"Where still we flutter on for pence or praise."

"All this is very fine, and may be true,"
    Said Juan; "but I really don't see how
"It betters present times with me or you."
    "No?" quoth the other; "yet you will allow,   180
"By setting things in their right point of view,
    "Knowledge, at least, is gained; for instance, now
"We know what Slavery is, and our disasters
"May teach us better to behave when Masters."

"Would we were Masters now, if but to try   185
    "Their present lessons on our Pagan friends here,"
Said Juan, swallowing a heart-burning sigh;

    "Heaven help the Scholar whom his Fortune sends
here!"
"Perhaps we shall be one day, by and by,"
    Rejoined the other, "when our bad luck mends here;   190
"Meantime (yon old black Eunuch seems to eye us)
    "I wish to G-d that Somebody would buy us!"

It is a lesson far more effective for being taught in the field ("on the spot"): the last and most successful stage of Juan's education, so inauspiciously begun by his mother in the first Canto. However, in order to accommodate it in Canto V, some forcible things have to done to historical likelihood. When, at *Don Juan* V, 7, 1-2, Byron writes that

    A Crowd of shivering Slaves of every Nation,
        And Age, and Sex, were in the Market ranged ...   50

... he assumes easily that slaves were put up for auction in such mixed lots in the Constantinople market – and in the 1790s. He could not have been sure; although it had once been his ambition to be. On September 8th 1809, reports Leslie Marchand,

> "... Byron made a bet of 20 guineas with a Mr Wherry that he get into the female slave market at Constantinople."[209]

But he never did, and had to rely on other writers, some of whom had read previous writers, who might have done so. One of the most important of these is Thomas Thornton, who had spent fourteen years at Constantinople, and is described by Hobhouse as "the writer who ... has given the truest and most satisfactory account of the Turkish government":[210] Byron trusts him rather less on the Greeks.[211] Thornton writes, challengingly for Byron's intention:

> All, except Turks, are now not only excluded from the slave-market, but are prohibited from retaining slaves.[212]

However, at *Don Juan* V, 10, 1-2, Byron writes again, unconcerned by such considerations:

> Like a Backgammon board the place was dotted
> With whites and blacks, in groups on show for Sale ...

On the following two pages of his book, Thornton does relate the display of an eighteen-year-old Circassian girl to a German merchant: but the event occurs in the Crimea. F.C.H.L.Pouqeville reports seeing, in a few brief moments of trespass before he was ejected from the market, three hundred to four hundred women on display; but his slaves are not at all like Byron's:

> ... they seemed scarcely affected by it [*their condition*] for they were laughing and indulging in the most vehement loquacity ... some of them had flaxen hair and blue eyes, yet ... none of them [*were*] deserving the high reputations of the Georgians and Circassians ... they were for the most part corpulent women ... and their complexion was of a dead white.[213]

209: *Marchand* I, p.199.
210: *Journey*, II, p.919.
211: CPW II, 203.
212: Thornton, *The Present State of Turkey* (1807) II, p.288.
213: Pouqueville, *Voyages en Morée*, 1806: quoted by Thornton at II, pp.290-1n, and sneered at by Byron at CHP II, 47, 1n.

We find no references to the sale of male slaves in either Thornton, or in the letters of Lady Mary Wortley Montagu: although "Honest Tournefort," as Byron describes him at *The Giaour* 755n, perhaps with a glance at *Othello*,[214] probably writing before slave-ownership was restricted to Moslems, has seen men displayed:

> The Market for Slaves of both Sexes is not far off: here the poor Wretches sit in a melancholy Posture. Before they cheapen 'em, they turn 'em about from this side to that, survey 'em from top to bottom, put 'em to exercise whatever they have learnt; and this several times a Day, without ever coming to any Agreement. Such of 'em, both Men and Women, to whom Dame Nature has been niggardly of her Charms, are set apart for the vilest Services; but such Girls as have Youth and Beauty, pass their time well enough, only they often force 'em to turn *Mahometans*.[215]

Byron would, in depicting the sale of two obviously valuable Frankish men, appear implicitly to be engaging again in creative dialectic with Lady Mary Wortley Montagu:

> I heartily beg your ladyship's pardon; but I really could not forbear laughing heartily at your letter, and the commissions you are pleased to honour me with. You desire me to buy you a Greek slave, who is to be mistress of a thousand good qualities. The Greeks are subjects, and not slaves. Those who are to be bought in that manner, are either such as are taken in war, or stolen by the Tartars, from Russia, Circassia or Georgia, and are such miserable aukward poor wretches, you would not think any of them worthy to be your house-maids. 'Tis true that many thousands were taken in the Morea; but they have been most of them redeemed by the charitable contributions of the Christians, or ransomed by their own relations at Venice. The fine slaves, that wait upon the great ladies, or serve the pleasures of the great men, are all bought at the age of eight or nine years old, and educated with great care to accomplish them in singing, dancing, embroidery, etc. They are commonly Circassians, and their patron never sells them, except it is as a punishment for some very great fault. If ever they grow weary of them, they either present them to a friend, or give them their freedom. Those that are exposed to sale at the markets, are always either guilty of some crime, or so entirely worthless, that they are of no use at all. I am afraid you will doubt the truth of this account, which, I own, is very different from our common notions in England; but it is no less true for all that.[216]

214: CPW III, 420.
215: J.P.de Tournefort, in *A Voyage into the Levant* (1741) II, pp.198-9.
216: Letter to Lady —, June 17th 1717: 1803 Paris edition, I, pp.219-20.

Like Thornton and Pouqueville (though, admittedly, unlike Tournefort, closer to her own time), Lady Mary refers only to female slaves. In his diary entry for May 26, 1810, Hobhouse refers to the sight of some enslaved Russian prisoners of war, who obviously anticipate Johnson, captured at Widin (*Don Juan* V, 15, 7-8): but they are a work detail, and are not available for purchase. The writer whom Byron probably chose to remember here was the supremely authoritative Demetrius Cantemir, who had actually been educated in the Constantinople Seraglio, and was writing about a time even earlier than Montagu's:

> But of what esteem the *Chercassians* are with the *Turks*, may be guess'd from the Price which the Sellers put upon their Captives. They value them in the first place, because their Virgins are more beautiful than all others, better proportion'd in their Bodies, capable of Instruction, and of great modesty, and their young Men, as they think, more sharp in their Wit, and capable of making the best artificers. The next in their esteem are the *Polanders*, then the *Abazà*, then the *Russians* for the hardness of their Bodies and their enduring of Labour, which considerations often send them to row in the Grand Signior's Gallies, then the *Cossacks*, then the *Georgians*, and last of all the *Mengrelians*. The *Germans*, *Venetians*, and *Hungarians*, (whom they are wont to call by the same name of *Ifrenk*) are by them thought incapable of all drudgery, by reason of the softness of their Bodies, and the Women of giving pleasure proper to their Sex from the hardness of theirs. So that were Slaves produc'd in the Market out of all these Nations of the same age, strength or beauty, a *Chercassian*, Man or Woman, would be sold for 1000 Imperial Crowns, a *Polander* for 600, an *Abazà* for 500, a *Russ* or a *Cozac* for 400, a *Georgian* for 300, a *Mengrelian* for 250, a *German* or *Ifrenk* for still less.[217]

Juan and Johnson are both, technically, Ifrenks: but by now it should be clear that in depicting their sale in the way he does, Byron happily takes what he wants from whatever source will give it him.

Byron's version of the Eunuch

Baba, who buys Juan to serve Gulbeyaz's sexual fantasies, and buys Johnson for no clear reason other than narrative convenience, is not the only eunuch in *Don Juan*; Byron associates the two ideas of willing

---

217: Demetrius Cantemir, *The history of the growth and decay of the Othman Empire*, (English translation, 1734-5), p.129n.

subordination of self to Imperial priority, and of castration, from very
early on. Here are Stanzas 11, 14 and 15 of the poem's Dedication:

> Think'st thou, could he, the blind Old Man [*Milton*], arise
>   Like Samuel from the Grave, to freeze once more
> The blood of Monarchs with his Prophecies,
>   Or be alive again – again all hoar
> With time and trials, and those helpless eyes   85
>   And heartless daughters, worn, and pale, and poor,
> Would he adore a Sultan? he obey
> The intellectual Eunuch Castlereagh?

***

> A Bungler even in its disgusting trade,   105
>   And botching, patching, leaving still behind
> Something of which its Masters are afraid,
>   States to be curbed, and thoughts to be confined,
> Conspiracy or Congress to be made –
>   Cobbling at manacles for all mankind –   110
> A tinkering Slavemaker, who mends old chains,
> With God's and Man's abhorrence for its gains.

> If we may judge of matter by the mind,
>   Emasculated to the marrow, It
> Hath but two objects – how to serve, and bind,   115
>   Deeming the chain it wears even men may fit;
> Eutropius of its many masters – blind
>   To Worth as Freedom, Wisdom as to Wit –
> Fearless, because no Feeling dwells in Ice,
> Its very Courage stagnates to a Vice. –   120

When Baba makes his entrance, Byron allows him a more laconic
dignity than he affords either Castlereagh, or his tame, "dry-bobbing"
scribbler Southey; but it is (I offer the idea with some distaste) worth
bearing in mind what Byron knew of Turkish eunuchs, if we are to see
the full force of the sexual and political parallel. Thornton, who relies
heavily on others for much of his harem material, often debating with,
but on balance giving credence to, Lady Mary Wortley Montagu,
quotes[218] two authorities[219] to the fact that castration habitually involved
the removal of the penis as well as the scrotum. He treats the idea with

218: Thornton, op.cit., II p.293n.
219: Busbeq, *Epis.* iii p.122, and Rigaud, *Généalogie du grand Turc*, p.25.

with Anglo-Saxon disbelief, but Aubrey de la Motraye, himself acknowledged elsewhere by Thornton as a reliable witness, concurs:

> They are Slaves that are bought, and have all that Part cut from them in their Infancy, that distinguishes a Man from a Woman, without leaving them the least remainder of it; and the Operation is so dangerous, that very often out of a hundred, fifty don't escape; they are reduced to the Necessity of making Water thro' a little Pipe in the Shape of a Funnel, which they apply to the Passage from whence the Natural Organ has been cut off.[220]

It will be agreed that Southey's creative incapacity, his "dry-bobbing", is seen in a dramatic new perspective here: even if he had anything to deliver, he would still lack the means with which to deliver it. Baron de Tott, referred to often by Hobhouse as one who had had a hand in the fortification of the Bosphorus (see next section), and by Byron at *Don Juan* VI, 31, 5, makes a further relevant point, which Byron doubtless stored away:

> It appears from this description, that the Eunuchs were more at the command of the Sultana than disposed to thwart her. These beings are no other than an object of luxury in Turkey, displayed no where but in the Seraglio of the Grand Signior, and the Sultanas. The pride of the great, 'tis true, extends so far, but with moderation, and the richest of them have scarcely ever more than two or three black Eunuchs. The white ones, who are less deformed, are reserved for the Grand Signior, to form the guard for the outer-gates of his Seraglio [*Byron encountered one: see below*]; but they are not suffered to approach the women, nor obtain any employment, whilst the post of Kislar Aga, furnishes the black Eunuchs, at least, a motive to support and animate their ambition. Their character is always ferocious, and nature offended in their persons, seems perpetually to feel the reproach.[221]

Thornton[222] casts further explicit doubt on the version of the eunuch's duties and responsibilities given by Montesquieu, to whom I shall refer again later.

220: Motraye, *Travels* (1723) I, p.172.
221: de Tott, *Memoirs* (1785 edition), I, pp.104-5
222: Thornton, II, p.265.

Byron's own experience of the Seraglio

The Harem of the Sultan of Constantinople – that part of the Seraglio
where the women were sequestered – is as important to *Don Juan* as
Julia's bedroom, Haidee's cave, or Catherine's palace. "Entrance" to any
of these places as clear a sexual metaphor as one could wish: and there is
the added excitement that very few "real" men, occidental or oriental, had
ever "experienced its interior". To try and do so was to risk death.

The Harem has as its classical precedents the island of Circe in the
Odyssey X and XII, that of Alcina in *Orlando Furioso* VI-VIII, and that
of Armida in Tasso's *Gerusalemme Liberata* XVII – although each writer
plays different variations on the idea. Odysseus defeats Circe on her own
island, and Ruggiero and Rinaldo have to be shamed into leaving. Juan,
threatened with transformation (not into a pig but into a Moslem, a
eunuch, and finally a woman), defeats his enchantress, the Sultana of
Constantinople, partly because he resists her, and partly because farcical
chance comes to his aid – an idea borrowed, as I've said, from Wieland's
Oberon.

Legends grew up rapidly around *Don Juan* Canto V. An anonymous
writer in the *New Monthly Magazine* asserted that the real Sultan of
Constantinople, Mahmoud II, had indeed, when Byron was present at an
audience with him on July 10th 1810, taken him for a woman:

> His youthful and striking appearance, and the splendour of his dress,
> visible as it was by the looseness of the pelisse over it, attracted greatly
> the Sultan's attention, and seemed to have excited his curiosity. I have
> recently been assured at Constantinople, that when the Sultan was
> informed of an English Vizier [*Byron*] having joined the Greeks for the
> purpose of assisting them in their struggles against his authority, and
> was given to understand that this Vizier was the same individual who
> had made a conspicuous figure at Mr. Canning's audience, the Sultan
> would not believe in the identity, insisting that the person who had
> appeared before him on that occasion was a woman dressed in man's
> clothes.[223]

Two dates are, perhaps significantly, being confused here: Byron
would not attend Stratford Canning's audience on May 28 1810, which
Hobhouse did attend, supposedly because he was angry at having to
follow behind the normal members of the Embassy: and the Sultan was in
any case not present then. The second audience was on July 10, when Sir
Robert Adair, the out-going Ambassador for whom Canning had

223: *The New Monthly Magazine* 1827, XIX, p.147.

previously deputised (as First Secretary) took his leave. This Byron did attend – see his letter to Adair,[224] letters to his mother,[225] and to Scrope Davies.[226] Hobhouse's description of the audience, in *A Journey through some Provinces of Turkey*, is, I think, is worth extended commentary, because it is important for understanding some of Byron's intention when he writes of the Seraglio ten years later.

Briefly to digress: there is no doubt that Hobhouse saw *Journey* (published in January 1814 by Cawthorne, Byron's publisher for *English Bards*) as his own *Childe Harold*. On October 1st 1811 he writes to Byron:

> I only hope my child will succeed as well as yours which I believe is better off both as to father & god father than my bantling.[227]

Preparing the book for the press was made difficult by Sir Benjamin Hobhouse's insistence that his son join the militia and go to Ireland, from whence he had the fatigue of correcting the proofs, assessing lists of Albanian vocabulary, and selecting engravings; *Childe Harold I* and *II* was published (by Murray) a year ahead of *Journey*; but in it, Byron puffed him generously in advance:

> On Albania and its inhabitants I am unwilling to descant, because this will be done so much better by my fellow traveller, in a work which may probably precede this in publication, that I as little wish to follow as I would to anticipate him.[228]

The much-discussed mystery of why Byron wrote so little about his visit to Constantinople may readily be explained as much by his desire to give his friend's book every opportunity as by his sense that it had all been done before. On May 3 1810 he wrote to Henry Drury:

> But why should I say more of these things? are they not written in the Boke of Gell? and has not Hobby got a journal? I keep none as I have renounced scribbling.[229]

224: BLJ I, 256.
225: BLJ II, 3 and 8.
226: BLJ XI, 157.
227: *Byron's Bulldog*, ed. Peter Graham, Ohio 1984, p.83.
228: CPW II, 192.
229: BLJ I, 238.

A Journey through some Provinces of Turkey – two epistolary volumes, like the Montagu letters – did indeed achieve a second edition.

Now to paraphrase Hobhouse's account of the Seraglio visit: the Ambassador's expedition started at 4.30 in the morning, with a salute from the guns of the Salsette frigate. Twenty-four marines, bayonets fixed, accompanied the mounted column – perhaps with Lieutenant Ekenhead, Byron's companion in his swim across the Hellespont (*Don Juan* II 105, 8n) in charge. On arriving at the Seraglio they all entered through the Sublime Gate (the "Baba-Humayun" as Hobhouse calls it) which often had severed heads in niches to each side, and a dunghill to the right upon which the dead bodies corresponding were thrown (the executions were normally carried out by the Head Gardener). Through this gate they proceeded into the first square, which included the royal mint and the armory, previously the church of St. Irene.

Having dismounted, they went through the Gate of Health (the "Baba Salam") into a dark, dirty chamber which was in fact the executioner's lodge (de Tott calls it "the Hangman's Chamber").[230] Here "all our state vanished"[231] as they were forced to wait until four thousand Janissaries had been given their morning pilau. Thence they moved into the smaller second square, colonnaded on three sides, with a green space in the middle containing cypresses, the Seraglio kitchens to the right, and a fountain and the Hall of the Divan – administrative centre of the Ottoman Empire – on the left: the walls of the Divan Hall were of stucco, polished up to resemble pink variegated marble. Here the Grand Vizier sat on a raised seat, with a latticed casement behind through which the Sultan was said secretly to inspect the Divan's transactions. The English were forced to stay in the Hall till nine o'clock, witnessing the adjudication of a cause, and the payment of the Janissaries – an undignified scramble for money-bags, evidently designed to "captivate and astonish" the Franks with Ottoman wealth.[232] The Ambassador sat, while the rest stood. What Hobhouse does not mention, and perhaps did not know, was that this was the nearest they got to the Harem, out of sight behind the Divan Hall, on the west side of the Seraglio.

After witnessing an hour-long audience of Janissary officers, and having been provided with wooden spoons, they had dinner served to them on coarse cloth (although most had to stand). Hobhouse's diary is at this point more particular than his book:

230: De Tott, *Memoirs* I, p.59n.
231: *Journey*, II, p.993.
232: Ibid, p.995.

> Mr Canning, Captain Bathurst, Lord Byron and myself dined at a table with Chelik Effendi, who was some time in arranging us, and seemed out of temper objecting at first to my sitting on the bench next to him.[233]

There were twenty-two courses, into some of which they had scarcely dipped before the food was "borne off as if under the influence of Sancho's dread doctor and his wand".[234] Their train was here infiltrated by "several ragamuffins in the Frankish habit collected purposely to disgrace the embassy".[235] After this, word arrived that the Sultan would receive them, and they were conducted to the third gate, the Gate of Happiness (the "Baba Saadi") and into the Interior Palace, where they had to sit under a wooden shed at the right of the entrance. A stone seat was reserved for the Ambassador, and fur pelisses were distributed to seventeen or twenty of the rest of the company, for etiquette dictated that visitors be clothed by their Imperial host (Byron enquires ironically[236] if Captain Bathurst of the *Salsette* "was pleased with your garment of yesterday" after the May 28th audience). Swords had at this point to be relinquished.

They were next jostled through the third gate, those without pelisses were pushed away (Ekenhead among them)[237] and a white eunuch took Hobhouse "somewhat strictly" by the right arm (for "he had not forgotten the assassination of Amurath":[238] I think we must assume another eunuch held Byron) to a court open on two sides, and into the audience chamber. Here the Sultan received them:

> The chamber was small and dark, or rather illumined with a gloomy artificial light, reflected from the ornaments of silver, pearls, and other white brilliants, with which it is thickly studded on every side and on the roof. The throne, which is supposed to be the richest in the world, is like a four-posted bed, but of a dazzling splendour; the lower part formed of burnished silver and pearls, and the canopy and supporters encrusted with jewels. It is in an awkward position, being in one corner of the room, and close to a fire-place.[239]

233: B.L.Add.Mss. 56529 65r.
234: *Journey*, p.996.
235: Ibid, p.996.
236: BLJ I, 245.
237: B.L.Add. Mss. 56529 66r.
238: *Journey*, p.998.
239: Ibid, p.998.

The Sultan neither spoke to nor fixed his eyes on the Ambassador
for the entire audience, which lasted between twelve and fifteen minutes:
all words were passed between them via two intermediaries. Etiquette
forbade the Sultan ever to fix his eyes on anyone else either, which brings
into question the subsequent tale of his taking Byron for a woman. When
the audience concluded, the Sultan having given Adair a letter to George
III, Hobhouse's white eunuch pushed him gently out, and they all passed
back through the third and second gates, and had to sit on horse-back
under a baking sun – still wearing their fur pelisses – until mid-day, when
the Caimacan (the Vice-Vizier, and Governor of Constantinople) left too,
with his Janissaries – who appeared to Hobhouse to be "the very scum of
the city".[240]

Several things are worth noting. Firstly, and perhaps naively,
Hobhouse's book transliterates the Turkish word for gate as "Baba".
Secondly and more importantly – for we can safely assume that
Hobhouse's impressions and judgements would in this respect have been
Byron's too – the Seraglio seems to have been at once squalid,
claustrophobic, and designed to overwhelm, humiliate and belittle, not
only the English party, but almost everyone who lived and worked in it.
Thirdly, the style of its internal decor was a very odd combination of
overwhelming richness, coupled with dark, grim squalor, and what
seemed a complete absence of taste.

Re-reading Canto V in the light of *A Journey through some
Provinces of Turkey* is most interesting, for Byron is at first clearly
employing, and making variations upon, his own experience of the
Seraglio, which was, we may guess, close to the experience of Hobhouse.

Juan and Johnson are taken in – by a non-committal black eunuch
called Baba – not through the main gate, but via a small side-gate, the
access to which is by water. They are almost at once disorientated,
indeed, lost, in the silent,[241] serpentine windings of the place, and the

240: Ibid, p.1001.
241: A certain unadventurousness may be seen in what has become the usual note
to *Don Juan* V, Stanzas 53-4 ("Others in monosyllable talk chatted ... But no one
troubled him with conversation") where all editors – Wright, Coleridge, DJP and
CPW – quote, as if with one mind, J.P.de Tournefort: "Any body may enter the
first Court of the Seraglio: here the Domesticks and Slaves of the Bashaws and
Agas wait for their Masters returning, and look after their Horses; but every thing
is so still, the Motion of a Fly might be heard in a manner: and if any one should
presume to raise his Voice ever so little, or shew the least want of Respect to the
Mansion-Place of their Emperor, he would instantly have the Bastinado by the
Officers that go the rounds; nay, the very Horses seem to know where they are,

numerous halls, rooms, and corridors through which they are taken (the Harem has in fact over three hundred rooms). They are both very hungry, which, coupled with their disorientation, is exacerbated by the smell of cooking which they perceive ("stews, and roast-meats, and pilaus" – *Don Juan* V, 47, 2) and defeats any thoughts they may have of overcoming Baba and trying to escape. Baba's words upon their protesting are "What you may be, I neither know nor care ... but pray do as I desire" (*Don Juan* V, 74, 1-2) which aptly sums up the attitude of the whole Seraglio towards them.

Baba's activities include clothing them as Moslems, trying to convert them to Islam, and changing the outward sexual identity of one of them. The decor is at once impressive, and meaninglessly profuse, and becomes more so the further they get into that part of the building which few Franks had ever seen. Here are *Don Juan* Canto V, Stanzas 64 and 65:

> At last they reached a quarter most retired,
> > Where Echo woke as if from a long Slumber;
> Though full of all things which could be desired,
> > One wondered what to do with such a number
> Of articles which nobody required;
> > Here Wealth had done its utmost to encumber   510
> With furniture an exquisite apartment,
> Which puzzled Nature much to know what Art meant.

> It seemed, however, but to open on
> > A range or suite of further chambers, which
> Might lead to Heaven knows where, but in this one   515
> > The moveables were prodigally rich;
> Sofas 'twas half a Sin to sit upon,
> > So costly were they; Carpets every Stitch
> Of Workmanship so rare, they made you wish
> You could glide o'er them like a Golden fish.   520

Baba conducts them through three gates:[242] in Stanzas 41 ("a small iron door") 51 (simply "the gate") and 85, where "a Gigantic portal", guarded by two dwarves, is given an entire stanza of description. Many other gates are implied by the narrative, but not insisted on. None of the three stated gates accord with the Sublime Gate, nor with the Gates of

---

and no doubt they are taught to tread softer here than in the Streets." (*A Voyage into the Levant*, 1741 English translation, II, p.183.)

242: The mother-in-law and wife of Baron de Tott were also inducted into a harem – not that of the Grand Signior – via three gates: *Memoirs* I, p.99.

Health and Happiness, and the third, most impressive one, is not Turkish
but Roman, and accords with nothing in the Seraglio at all. Here are *Don
Juan* Canto V, Stanzas 85-90:

And thus they parted, each by separate doors;
    Baba led Juan onward room by room
Through glittering galleries, and o'er marble floors,   675
    Till a Gigantic portal through the gloom,
Haughty and huge, along the distance lowers;
    And wafted far arose a rich perfume;
It seemed as though they came upon a shrine,
For all was vast, still, fragrant, and divine. –   680

The Giant door was broad, and bright, and high,
    Of gilded bronze, and carved in curious guise;
Warriors thereon were battling furiously;
    Here stalks the Victor, there the vanquished lies;
There Captives led in triumph droop the eye,   685
    And in perspective many a Squadron flies;
It seems the work of times before the line
Of Rome transplanted fell with Constantine. –

This massy portal stood at the wide close
    Of a huge hall, and on its either side   690
Two little dwarfs, the least you could suppose,
    Were sate, like ugly imps, as if allied
In mockery to the enormous gate which rose
    O'er them in almost pyramidic pride;
The gate so splendid was in all its *features*,.   695
You never though about those little creatures,

Until you nearly trod on them, and then
    You started back in horror to survey
The wondrous hideousness of these small men,
    Whose colour was not black, nor white, nor grey,   700
But an extraneous mixture, which no pen
    Can trace, although perhaps the pencil may;
They were misshapen pigmies, deaf and dumb –
Monsters, who cost a no less monstrous sum.

Their duty was – for they were strong, and though   705
    They looked so little, did strong things at times –
To ope this door, which they could really do,
    The hinges being as smooth as Rogers' rhymes;
And now and then with tough strings of the bow,
    As is the Custom of those Eastern climes,   710

To give some rebel Pacha a Cravat;
For Mutes are generally used for that. –

They spoke by signs – that is, not spoke at all;
    And looking like two Incubi, they glared
As Baba with his fingers made them fall   715
    To heaving back the portal folds; it scared
Juan a moment, as this pair so small,
    With shrinking serpent optics on him stared;
It was as if their little looks could poison
Or fascinate whome'er they fixed their eyes on.   720

Byron is expanding his epic parameters here. The italicisation of
"features" at 695 is explained by a note in which Byron draws attention
to Thomas Moore's joke about a mixed metaphor of Castlereagh's –
proof of a determination to keep the reader's mind on what must now be
a fairly distant sub-text. And the identification of the door as Roman or
Byzantine (687-8) would give the experience into which Baba is now
inducting them a more inclusive pedigree – occidental as well as oriental.

By this sinister point the transition has occured between the Seraglio
and the Harem; between verifiability and non-verifiability, between what
Byron could have seen, and what he had to imagine, or to have read about
in books ("I have seen it all" at *Don Juan* VI, 51, 4 is hollow bluff). The
dwarves, whom, as far as we can tell, he neither saw nor heard about
while in Constantinople, come nevertheless from an apparently
authenticating tradition, both historical and literary, with which he was
very familiar. Line 704 ("Monsters, who cost a no less monstrous sum")
recalls Rycaut's *The Present State of the Ottoman Empire* (1668):[243]

The Dwarfs are called *Giugé*; these also have their quarters amongst
the Pages of the two Chambers, until they have learned with due
reverence and humility to stand in the Presence of the Grand Signior.
And if one of these have that benefit, as by Nature's fortunate error to
be both a Dwarf, and dumb, and afterwards by the help of Art to be
castrated and made a Eunuch, he is much more esteemed, than if Nature
and Art had concurr'd together to have made him the perfectest creature
in the world; one of this sort, was presented by a certain *Pasha*, to the
Grand Signior, who was so acceptable to him and the Queen Mother,
that he attired him immediately in Cloth of Gold, and gave him liberty
through all the Gates of the *Seraglio*.[244]

243: See CMP 3, 4, and 219-20.
244: Paul Rycaut, *The Present State of the Ottoman Empire* (1668), p.35.

Byron would have derived from this the sense that, in order to be valued for one's own sake in the Ottoman Empire, it was necessary in advance to have been treated almost as badly as possible, both by nature and by human art. To "succeed" in Constantinople, as Baba has, and as Castlereagh, Southey, and perhaps even Byron himself, had in London, one had to have lost most of what made one oneself – the kind of loss with which Juan is threatened in Cantos V and VI.

William Beckford – who kept a dwarf himself at Fonthill Abbey – has an important fictional pair in *Vathek*.[245] They are the pious ones ushered into Vathek's presence by the eunuch Bababalouk (himself another important echo in *Don Juan*) with an apparent message from Vathek's mother. Henley's note reads,

> Such unfortunate beings, as are thus "curtailed of fair proportion," have been, for ages, an appendage of Eastern grandeur. One part of their office consists in the instruction of the pages, but their principal duty is the amusement of their master. If a dwarf happens to be a mute, he is much esteemed; but if he be also an eunuch, he is regarded as a prodigy; and no pains or expense are spared to obtain him. Habesci's State of the Ottomam Empire p. 164 &c.[246]

Line 712 ("For Mutes are generally used for that") further recalls *Vathek*, where the protagonist's mother has a hundred and forty of his most loyal subjects strangled:

> It was a pity! for they beheld not the agreeable smile, with which the mutes and negresses adjusted the cord to their necks: these amiable personages rejoiced, however, no less at the scene. Never before had the ceremony of strangling been performed with such facility.[247]

A note by Beckford added in 1816 reads

> The mutes are also the secret instruments of his [*the sovereign's*] private vengeance, in carrying the fatal string.[248]

Byron's dwarves thus function not only artistically, as Freudian nightmare-figures, naturally foreshortened and surgically neutered, jealously guarding the gateway to power and (conceivably) fulfilment;

245: *Vathek*, pp.51-3.
246: Ibid, p.139.
247: Ibid, pp.34-5.
248: Ibid, p.129n.

but also as historical reminders, via Beckford and Rycaut, of the real threat to the manhood and / or life of anyone who dared pass into the territory of totalitarian privacy, and of totalitarian concupiscence – both male (in historical fact) and female (in fiction, at least). The symbolism is neat; and it is therefore with some disillusion that we read, again in Demetrius Cantemir, the one writer we are certain knew the Seraglio intimately:

> a mute] ... I find, that most of the *Europeans*, who give an account of the *Othman* court, affirm, that these persons are often employed to put those privately to death, whom the Sultan has a mind to dispatch; but I cannot so much as guess what has occasioned this mistake. For it was never heard in *Constantinople*, that *Mutes*, *Dwarfs*, and *Buffoons*, who are all upon the same foot in the palace, were ever employed about any serious business, or sent any where, but out of a jest.[249]

Anne Barton has written that

> The extraordinary thing about *Don Juan* ... is the way in which as a work of art it contrives to honour fact in its very structure, not simply in its material or in the social and moral judgements it makes.[250]

However, there are facts and facts, and different sets of contradictory facts may appear equally verifiable. This was an awkwardness of which Byron took full advantage.

"The Serai's impenetrable tower": Byron's Seraglio reading

Tracing Byron's inspiration and sources for the second part of Canto V – and of Canto VI – involves trips through many books. Semi-facetious references to such standard writers as "Cantemir or Knolles" (*DJ* V, 147, 7) or "Cantemir ... or de Tott" (*DJ* VI, 31, 5) are Byron's way of acknowledging the bookish nature of his muse, and the mock-travelogue nature of his poem. They also disguise his primary debt, which was to someone who had written much more recently, and much closer to home.

In the winter of 1807 his widely-travelled friend Edward Daniel Clarke – later Professor of Mineralogy at Cambridge – had been at

---

249: Cantemir, *Growth and Decay of the Othman Empire*, p.379n.
250: Barton, *Byron and the Mythology of Fact,* Nottingham Byron Lecture, 1968, p.18.

Constantinople, and met the Sultan's German gardener: this man, or another German gardener, had previously smuggled Pouqueville into the harem.[251] The German seems to have made a habit of this risky business, for Clarke reports that previously, with the secretary of the Swedish mission, he had hidden terrified in his hut, and watched through spy-holes as black eunuchs searched the gardens before the Sultan's principal women were allowed to stroll in them. Clarke and the gardener (who would instantly have been executed had they been discovered) actually saw the Sultan Mother and the four principal Sultanas "in high glee, romping and laughing with each other". The passage occurs in the third volume of Clarke's *Travels*, published in 1817, and is worth quoting in full:

> Three of the four were *Georgians*, having dark complexions, and very long dark hair; but the fourth was remarkably fair, and her hair, also of singular length and thickness, was of a flaxen colour: neither were their teeth dyed black, as those of *Turkish* females generally are ... He [*the Swedish secretary*] described their dresses as being rich beyond all that can be imagined. Long spangled robes, open in front, with pantaloons embroidered in gold and silver, and covered by a profusion of pearls and precious stones, displayed their persons to great advantage; but were so heavy, as actually to encumber their motion, and almost to impede their walking. Their hair hung in loose and very thick tresses, on each side of their cheeks; falling down to the waist, and entirely covering their shoulders. Those tresses were quite powdered with diamonds, not displayed according to any studied arrangement, but as if carelessly scattered, as if by handfuls, among their flowing locks. On the top of their heads, and rather leaning to one side, they wore, each of them, a small circular patch or diadem. Their faces, necks, and even their breasts, were quite exposed: not one of them having any veil.[252]

Byron must have writhed with envy at a Cambridge man other than himself getting so close as to interrogate one who had seen these prototype Gulbeyazes, Kattinkas and Dudùs: but worse was to come, for Clarke had himself, in the winter of 1807 – *only three years before Byron went to Constantinople!* – done a tour, not only of the deserted summer Harem, but of the entire private part of the Seraglio. He had made it with the help of and in the company of the same helpful and daring German gardener,

---

251: Castellan, op. cit., 1821 English translation, III, p.53; original, III, p.49n.
252: E.D.Clarke, *Travels in Various Countries of Europe, Asia and Africa*, 11 vols 1810-23: III (1817), pp.17-18.

... during the Season of Ramadan, (when the guards, being up all night, would be stupefied during the day with sleep and intoxication) ...[253]

Clarke knows, as well as Byron will three years later, the voyeuristic appetites to which his chapter on the Seraglio panders. His introduction is in the sensational tone of a Peepshow-man:

> We promise to conduct our readers not only within the retirement of the Seraglio, but into the *Charem* itself, and the most secluded haunts of the *Turkish* sovereign.[254]

... although few Peepshow-men would have risked their lives for their material in the way that he seems to have done. He and the gardener had entered the Seraglio gardens by the south-eastern gate, and examined them, with their fountains, trellis-work and gravel walks. They had then gone into the Sultan's summer kiosk, with the Sultan's apartments to one side and those of the attendant Sultanas on the other. In two chambers below they inspected the slaves' quarters. They were amused to find, as well as an English writing-box, clear evidence of alcohol consumption on the part of the Harem women, in the shape of neatly-cut-out labels from bottles – which they "carried off as trophies of our visit to the place, and distributed them among our friends".[255]

Clarke and his friend then really risked their necks by entering the Harem itself, their progress through which, from exterior to interior, from quasi-public areas to innermost private parts, closely resembles that taken by Juan, Johnson and Baba in Canto V. The first court was, mundanely enough,

> ... a small quadrangle, much resembling that of *Queen's College, Cambridge*, filled with weeds.[256]

They forced open a small window, and climbed through into the Harem. The first apartments they encountered were two sets of slaves' dormitories; then "a long matted passage" with "small apartments on the left for slaves of higher rank;"[257] then

---

253: Ibid, p.19.
254: Ibid, p.15.
255: Ibid, p.25.
256: Ibid, p.27.
257: Ibid, p.28.

... we at last entered the great *Chamber of Audience*, in which the *Sultan Mother* receives visits of ceremony from the *Sultanas*, and other distinguished ladies of the *Charem*. Nothing can be imagined better suited to theatrical representation than this chamber. It is exactly such an apartment as the best painters of scenic decoration would have selected, to afford a striking idea of the pomp, the seclusion, and the magnificence, of the *Ottoman court*.[258]

Next appears one aspect of the Harem to which Byron makes no reference:

The area below the latticed throne, or the front of the stage (according to the idea before proposed), is set apart for attendants, for the dancers, for actors, music, and whatsoever is brought into the *Charem* for the amusement of the court.[259]

Clarke next describes the Assembly Room of the Sultan, in language of which Byron took note:

It is surrounded by mirrors. The other ornaments display that strange mixture of magnificence and wretchedness, which characterize all the state-chambers of *Turkish* grandees.[260]

Compare *Don Juan* Canto V Stanzas 93 and 94:

With this encouragement, he led the way
    Into a room still nobler than the last;
A rich Confusion formed a disarray
    In such sort, that the Eye along it cast   740
Could hardly carry any thing away,
    Object on object flashed so bright and fast;
A dazzling Mass of Gems, and Gold, and Glitter,
Magnificently mingled in a litter.

Wealth had done wonders – Taste not much; such thin 745
    Occur in Orient palaces, and even
In the more chastened domes of Western kings
    (Of which I've also seen some six or seven)
Where I can't say or Gold or Diamond flings
    Great lustre, there is much to be forgiven;   750
Groupes of bad Statues, tables, chairs, and pictures,

258: Ibid, p.28.
259: Ibid, p.30.
260: Ibid, p.30.

On which I cannot pause to make my Strictures.

As climax,

> ... we at length reached, what might be called the *Sanctum Sanctorum* of this *Paphian* temple, the *Baths* of the *Sultan Mother* and the four principal *Sultanas*. These are small, but very elegant, constructed of white marble, and lighted by ground glass above. At the upper end is a raised sudatory and bath for the *Sultan Mother*, concealed by lattice-work from the rest of the apartment. Fountains play constantly into the floor of this *bath*, from all its sides; and every degree of refined luxury has been added to the work, which a people, of all others best versed in the ceremonies of the *bath*, have been capable of inventing or requiring.[261]

Having seen the Chamber of Repose, the chaotic state of which reminded him of an old lumber room, Clarke crossed the Harem courtyard, gave a cursory inspection to the apartments of the inferior ladies ... and found that he and his companion had been locked in! The noise of some greedy turkeys eating facilitated the forcing of the gate, however, and – undeterred by the narrowness of their escape – the two men then inspected the Sultan's own private apartments, through a window which looked out over the hyacinth garden. They saw his mechanical singing birds, his library (bound manuscripts only), his washing utensils, his boots and slippers placed upon the floor (which was covered with a Gobelin tapestry), and the arms which decorated his wall. Narrowly missing discovery by a Bostanghy, they crawled away on hands and knees, and left.

Only one volume of Clarke's *Travels* appears in the 1827 Sale Catalogue of Byron's library[262] and it is not this one. I guess someone close to Byron took the rest – probably Hobhouse.

At BLJ II, 61, Byron hopes vainly that Hobhouse will "anticipate" Clarke; but Hobhouse has – as had many a writer before him, other than Clarke – to confess defeat when faced with the duty of satisfying his readers' fascination with the Harem:

> The purchase of females was at one time permitted to the Christians: at present, none but Mahometans are allowed that privilege, or can even be present at the inspection of the slaves. Aurat-Bazar, the former female slave-market, was burnt down in the last rebellion [*that against*

261: Ibid, p.30-1.
262: CMP, 253.

Selim III: see next section]. The Imperial Odalisques, belonging to the Sultan's harem, are for the most part presents from the Pashas, procured from the merchants who trade in Circassia and Georgia.[263] They are the attendants of the Khâduns, or favourites of the Sultan, the household of each of whom is composed of 150 or 200 of these beauties. This is a more probable relation that that the whole of the Odalisques live and sleep in two large dormitories, as is commonly reported. It is amongst the secrets of the seraglio (the dévlet juréck, words never pronounced without respect by the Turks), which, in spite of all research, are even yet preserved ...[264]

Four years later Clarke was to prove him wrong.

At *DJ* V, 3, 8, occurs the only reference to a writer who, although she had not gained access to the Harem itself, had become intimate with more high-ranking Turkish women than any other European:

> The European with the Asian Shore
>   Sprinkled with palaces; the Ocean Stream
> Here and there studded with a Seventy-four;
>   Sophia's Cupola with golden gleam;   20
> The Cypress Groves; Olympus high and hoar;
>   The twelve Isles, and the more than I could dream,
> Far less describe, present the very view
> Which charmed the charming Mary Montagu.

The husband of Lady Mary Wortley Montagu (1689-1762) was the British Ambassador to Constantinople from 1716 to 1718. Her *Turkish Embassy Letters* are classics, and Byron (who read them when young),[265] had them with him on his own stay in Constantinople in 1810. We may see an affectation of misogynist disbelief about them in this rare comment on his Constantinople reading, from a letter to his mother, of June 28 1810:

> ... by the bye, her Ladyship, as far as I can judge, has lied, but not half so much as any other woman would have done, in the same situation.[266]

Byron appeared, at least, to be more interested in Lady Mary's subsequent relationship with Pope[267] but he read the Embassy letters

---

263: For a Circassian girl, see IV, 114, 2; Kattinka and Dudù are both Georgian – VI, 41, 2, and VI, 113, 1 – as is Leila in *The Giaour*.
264: *Journey*, II, p.852.
265: See CMP, 220.
266: BLJ I, 250: see also his querying her at BLJ I, 250-1.

carefully, and the letter to which he refers in Stanza 3 is identifiable. It is the one of April 10 1717, to Lady Bristol:

> ... for twenty miles together down the Bosphorus the most beautiful variety of prospects present themselves. The Asian side is covered with fruit trees, villages and the most delightful landscapes in nature. On the European side stands Constantinople, situate on seven hills. The unequal heights make it seem as large again as it is (though one of the largest cities in the world) showing an agreeable mixture of gardens, pine and cypress trees, palaces, mosques and public buildings, raised one above another with as much beauty and appearance of symmetry as your ladyship ever saw ...[268]

Lady Mary Wortley Montagu's friendship with Turkish ladies will be commented on below.

Three other writers are often quoted as having provided sources for the two Harem Cantos: Cervantes, le Sage and Casti. In Chapters 39-41 of Cervantes' *Don Quixote* (1605) a Spaniard escapes from Algiers with his adoring Moorish love Zoraida; in Chapter 15 of le Sage's *Le Diable Boîteux* (1707) two noble Spanish lovers, Don Juan and Donna Theodora, have a similar adventure; and in the first Canto of the *Poema Tartaro* of Giammbatista Casti (1793: much more important as a source for the Russian Cantos) the young Irish hero is assisted in escaping from the "Babylon" Seraglio by his resourceful love Zelmira, the Caliph's favourite concubine – just in time, for he is danger of being promoted to Chief Eunuch. Mention might be made also of two operas: Mozart's *Die Entführung aus dem Serail* and Rossini's *L'Italiana in Algeri*; we have no evidence of Byron's having seen the former, but he refers to the latter in his note to *Don Juan* IV, 80, 8. In all these works, however (except Casti's), the stress is on the courage and constancy displayed by the Christian protagonists: not so with Byron, who peripheralises the traditional plot, and is not finally interested in how the lovers escape, or even in precisely which female lovers do escape (see *DJ* VII, 60, 2-3).

The theme of an attractive young man introduced into the Harem *en travestie* is familiar from a number of sources. Part of the drama in Byron's version is expressed at *DJ* V, 115, 1-4:

> His youth and features favoured the disguise,
>   And, should you ask how She, a Sultan's bride,
> Could risk or compass such strange phantasies,   915

267: See CMP, 125-6 and 172.
268: Montagu, *Letters*, II, pp.29-30.

This I must leave Sultanas to decide ...

The idea that such a thing might be possible[269] is in part from "honest" Tournefort:

> The Husbands [*in Constantinople*], that they [*the wives*] may have no pretence for going abroad, have made 'em believe there's no Paradise for Women; or if there be one, they may attain it by saying their Prayers at home. To amuse 'em, they build Baths for 'em, and treat 'em with Coffee: but notwithstanding all this Precaution, a way is often found to introduce handsom young Fellows, disguised like Female Slaves, with Toys to sell.[270]

In part it is from an anecdote Byron may have heard at Lisbon:

> Lord Wellington was curious about visiting a convent near Lisbon, and the lady Abbess made no difficulty; [*Dan*] MacKinnon, hearing this, contrived to get cleanly within the sacred walls, and it was generally supposed that it was neither his first nor his second visit. At all events, when Lord Wellington arrived, Dan MacKinnon was to be seen among the nuns, dressed out in their sacred costume, with his head and whiskers shaved; and as he possessed good features, he was declared to be one of the best-looking among those chaste dames.[271]

Byron may also have remembered the *Mémoires* of the Maréchal de Richelieu (9 vols., 1790-3) which he and Hobhouse had read at Venice in late 1816. Here is Richelieu's way of obtaining access to his mistress, Mlle Fermet:

> ... comme Richelieu étoit encore jeune, d'une figure adolescente, & d'une taille fine & légère, il lui étoit aisé de prendre les habits de femme, & de profiter de la permission donnée à un autre dont il prenait le nom, pour entrer dans le couvent.[272]

269: DJP and CPW draw our attention to an article by Margaret E. McGring in *Modern Language Notes* (1940, pp.39-42) ascribing the episode of Juan's dressing-up and smuggling-in to Byron's reading of a single sentence in "Tully's Tripoli"; but with all the other possibilities listed, plus Byron's unaided inspiration (never a factor to be neglected) I think we may discount it.
270: J.P. de Tournefort, *A Voyage in the Levant* (1741), II, p.160.
271: *The Reminiscences of Captain Gronow*, I, p.62; quoted Borst, *Lord Byron's First Pilgrimage*, p.9n.
272: *Mémoires du Maréchal de Richelieu* (1790-3), II, pp.229-30.

["... as Richelieu was still young, of a youthful figure, and of a slim and light appearance, it was easy for him to put on women's clothing, and to profit from permission given to another whose name he had taken, in order to get into the convent."]

Another, and more sinister, confirmation for the idea is in Jonathan Scott's notes to his 1811 edition of *The Arabian Nights*:[273]

In the cities of Hindoostan many accounts are current and believed of youths having been introduced in female apparel into the apartments of the enshrined beauties, as Mr. Burke emphatically named the Indian begums. It is said, too, that these divinities, after having exhausted the powers of their unfortunate admirers, have caused them to be put to death in order to conceal their crimes.[274]

Gulbeyaz would indeed have Juan put to death, even though she has not even experienced him, let alone exhausted him. Baron de Tott gave Byron much more recent evidence, not of European men being introduced into the harem in drag, but of the kind of interest a neglected Turkish lady of rank might (distantly at first) take in a good-looking European man. In the following passage de Tott is perhaps too discreet to finish his tale – which continues with material Byron probably remembered when he wrote of the harem's "little jealousies" (*DJ* VI, 38, 1):

My brother-in-law had become very intimate with the Intendante of that Princess, in order to obtain her interest in favour of his friends, or for his own concerns. The chief of her Eunuchs was also well disposed towards him; the Sultana had seen him several times through her window-blinds; he had a handsome face, and every thing combined to procure him her good wishes. Deprived for a long time of her husband, by whom she had a son and a daughter, the Princess seemed to endeavour to console herself in his absence, and to have availed herself of that want of rank, which approach[ed] her condition to that of ordinary individuals, by adopting their manners. In fact, one saw that jealousy which reigns among the Turkish women display itself in lively colours around her person. The pains she took in dressing Madame de Tott's hair, whom she had desired to see, displeased the woman who was her principal favourite so much, as to make her faint away; and Madame de Tott returned home more struck with the particular remarks

---

273: See CMP, 232.
274: *Arabian Nights* IV, p.415.

of affection the Sultana had lavished on her, than with the excessive
magnificence that reigned in her palace, and amongst her slaves.[275]

The problem soon arises for Byron, how to describe what few from
Western Europe – few, indeed, from Eastern Europe, or even from
Constantinople itself – had ever seen:

> With this encouragement, he led the way
> Into a room still nobler than the last;
> A rich Confusion formed a disarray
> In such sort, that the Eye along it cast   740
> Could hardly carry any thing away,
> Object on object flashed so bright and fast;
> A dazzling Mass of Gems, and Gold, and Glitter,
> Magnificently mingled in a litter.
>
> Wealth had done wonders – Taste not much; such things   745
> Occur in Orient palaces, and even
> In the more chastened domes of Western kings
> (Of which I've also seen some six or seven)
> Where I can't say or Gold or Diamond flings
> Great lustre, there is much to be forgiven;   750
> Groups of bad Statues, tables, chairs, and pictures,
> On which I cannot pause to make my Strictures.

Aubrey de la Motraye, or Aubry de la Moutraye, in *Voyages en
Europe, Asie et Afrique*, (1723), is quoted by Thornton as giving giving
one of the eighteenth century's rare authentic descriptions of the Harem's
interior. Anticipating Clarke, he visited it in the company of an expatriate
Huguenot clock repairer, when the women were at the Summer Palace:

> The Eunuch conducted us into the Hall of the *Harem*, which seem'd
> to me the finest and most agreeable of any in the *Seraglio* ... This Room
> was incrusted over with fine China; and the Cieling, [*sic*] which adorn'd
> the Inside of a *Cupola*, as well as all the rest of the Roof, was the richest
> that could be with Gold and Azure; in the middle of the Hall, directly
> under the *Cupola*, was an Artificial Fountain, the Bason of which was of
> a precious Green Marble, which seem'd to me either Serpentine, or
> Jasper; it did not play then on account of the Women being absent ... we
> cross'd several fine Halls and Chambers, treading under Foot the rich
> *Persian* Carpets that were spread upon the Ground almost every where,
> and in sufficient Number for us to judge the rest; and I found my Head
> so full of the *Sopha's*, rich Cieling, and in one word, of the great

---

275: Baron de Tott, *Memoirs*, I, p.107-8.

Confusion of fine Things so irregularly disposed, that 'twou'd be very hard for me to give a clear Idea of them ...[276]

Hobhouse found Turkish women "unwieldy and flaccid"[277] (barely worth penetrating); but Byron's poem was not to be filled with his friend's mundanities, even supposing them to be accurate; and when Juan comes face to face with his would-be sexual Nemesis, the Sultana Gulbeyaz, it is on his own imagination that Byron relies for her depiction – assisted by Lady Mary Wortley Montagu, who would certainly not have agreed with Hobhouse. When at *DJ* V Stanza 97 Byron writes about the difficulty of describing Gulbeyaz:

> Her presence was as lofty as her State;
>> Her Beauty of that overpowering kind,   770
> Whose force Description only would abate:
>> I'd rather leave it much to your own mind,
> Than lessen it by what I could relate
>> Of forms and features; it would strike you blind
> Could I do justice to the full detail;   775
> So, luckily for both, my phrases fail.

... he is echoing Lady Mary's astonished account of her meeting, not with the Sultana, but with the next best thing, the wife of the Kahya, or Second Officer of the Ottoman Empire:

On a sofa raised three steps, and covered with fine Persian carpets, sat the Kahya's lady, leaning on cushions of white satin embroidered; and at her feet sat two young girls about twelve years old, lovely as angels, dressed perfectly rich, and almost covered with jewels. But they were hardly seen near the fair Fatima, (for that is her name) so much her beauty effaced every thing I have seen, nay, all that has been called lovely either in England or Germany. I must own, that I never saw any thing so gloriously beautiful, nor can I recollect a face that would have been taken notice of near her's ... I confess, though the Greek lady [*Lady Mary's interpreter*] had before given me a great opinion of her beauty, I was so struck with admiration, that I could not for some time, speak to her, being wholly taken up in gazing. That suprizing harmony of features! That charming result of the whole! That exact proportion of body! That lovely bloom of complexion unsullied by art! the unutterable

---

276: Aubrey de la Motraye (Aubry de la Moutraye), *Voyages en Europe, Asie et Afrique*, (1723), *Travels* (English translation), 1727, I, pp.172 and 173: the original French is quoted by Thornton at II, p.272n.
277: Ibid, II, p.851.

enchantment of her smile! – But her eyes! Large and black, with all the
soft languishment of the blue! Every turn of her face discovering some
new grace![278]

Unlike Byron (but like the author of "Tully's Tripoli") Lady Mary
gives an elaborate description of the woman's dress. Later, she does in
fact meet a Sultana – but a widowed one. When at 785-6 Byron further
writes of:

> ... her attendants, who   785
> Composed a Choir of Girls, ten or a dozen ...

... the picture is from the description by Lady Mary of the Kahya's
wife's ladies:

> Her fair maids were ranged below the sofa, to the number of twenty,
> and put me in mind of the pictures of the ancient nymphs. I did not think
> all nature could have furnished such a scene of beauty.[279]

Montesquieu's *Lettres Persanes* form an interesting subtext to this
Canto and the next, though we have no direct evidence of Byron's having
read it. While the protagonist, Usbek, sends letters home unwittingly
satirical of Western European manners and morals, the correspondence
from Persia paints an ugly picture of a harem ruled by suspicious and
brutal eunuchs, who are unable to quench the flames of concupiscence
which arise in the absence of the place's true master (compare the
opening of the *1,001 Nights*); by the end of the book the harem is awash
with blood.

Byron's reference at *DJ* V, 126, 8 to "a Sultana's sensual phantasy"
is given ample illustration by Montesquieu. What such a fantasy might
involve is a question readily answered by reference to *Lettre Persane* No
141, which tells the story of Zulema (called, after death, Anaïs). The tale
is a critique of Islamic and Jewish myths about women's inferiority (by
implication, of Christian myths too). It features a learned and
philosophical heroine, who, after being murdered by her brutal husband,
is transported to a paradise containing immaculate male houris, devoted
entirely to gratifying her. Montesquieu is answering, in fiction, not
theology, the question asked by George Sale: do women have celestial
paramours after death, as well as men? Zulema even persuades one of the

---

278: Montagu, *Letters*, I, pp.185-6.
279: Montagu, *Letters,* I, pp.188-9.

male houris to return to earth, impersonate her husband, expel his eunuchs, please his remaining wives, and banish him two thousand leagues. The husband returns some years later to find thirty-six children attributed to him.

Gulbeyaz is not the first Islamic heroine whom Juan has encountered, merely the most powerful. We may remember Donna Julia's antecedents, described at *DJ* I, Stanza 56:

> The darkness of her Oriental eye
> Accorded with her Moorish origin;
> (Her blood was not all Spanish, by the bye –
> In Spain, you know, this is a sort of Sin);
> When proud Grenada fell, and, forced to fly,   745
> Boabdil wept, of Donna Julia's kin
> Some went to Africa, Some staid in Spain,
> Her great great Grandmamma chose to remain.

At line 443 here the satire about Julia's fine Moorish blood is directed in part at the anti-Islamic tendency of Southey's epics *Thalaba the Destroyer* and *Roderick, Last of the Goths*. Francis Jeffrey had pointed out the vulgarity of Southey's prejudices in his review of *Roderick* (a poem which Byron claimed at first to admire) when he wrote of "the excessive horror and abuse with which the Mahometans are uniformly spoken of on account of their religion alone".[280] Byron, who, unlike Southey, had travelled among Moslems, felt equally strongly on the subject (both men had travelled in Spain, and Southey was an Hispanic specialist) and probably made Juan's first Spanish lover part-Moorish by way of riposte.[281]

By 1820 and 1822, the time of the writing of the Harem Cantos, Southey had ceased to be a merely literary foe, and had transmuted into a beast to be hunted down and destroyed – making him the super-addressee of *Don Juan* was one way of doing just that. Byron, who, like Shelley, read Southey obsessively, cannot have forgotten *Thalaba the Destroyer* (see introductory section, above) and his gleeful plunge into writing his own version of the Orient is all part of the creative vendetta.

Julia is not alone. Here, from *DJ* Cantos II and IV, are parts of Byron's description of Haidee, whose "Mother was a Moorish Maid from Fez" (*DJ* IV, 54, 7):

280: *Edinburgh Review*, June 1815, p.3.
281: I'm told that there's a macho Spanish myth whereby the more ancient Moorish blood there is in your veins, the more likely you are to be gay.

Her brow was overhung with Coins of Gold,
        That sparkled o'er the Auburn of her hair,
Her clustering hair, whose longer locks were rolled
        In braids behind, and though her Stature were
Even of the highest for a female mould,   925
        They nearly reached her Heel; and in her air
There was a Something which bespoke Command,
As One who was a Lady in the land.

Her hair, I said, was Auburn; but her eyes
        Were black as Death, their lashes the same hue,   930
Of downcast length, in whose Silk shadow lies
        Deepest Attraction, for when to the view
Forth from its raven fringe the full Glance flies,
        Ne'er with such force the swiftest arrow flew;
'Tis as the Snake late coiled, who pours his length,   935
And hurls at once his Venom and his Strength. –

                            ***

Afric is all the Sun's, and as her earth
        Her human Clay is kindled; full of power
For good or evil, burning from its birth,
        The Moorish blood partakes the planet's hour,
And like the Soil beneath it will bring forth: 445
        Beauty and love were Haidee's mother's dower;
But her large dark eye showed deep Passion's force
Though sleeping like a Lion by a Source.

Her daughter tempered with a milder ray
        Like Summer Clouds all silvery, smooth, and fair,   450
Till slowly charged with thunder they display
        Terror to earth, and tempest to the air,
Had held till now her soft and milky way;
        But overwrought with passion and despair,
The Fire burst forth from her Numidian veins,   455
Even as the Simoom sweeps the blasted plains. –

Thus, when Juan is left alone with Gulbeyaz, the phrasing and rhymes almost imply that his two previous love-affairs have been rehearsals:

When he was gone, there was a sudden change;
        I know not what might be the Lady's thought,
But o'er her bright brow flashed a tumult strange,
        And into her clear cheek the blood was brought,   860

Blood-red as Sunset Summer Clouds which range
　　The verge of Heaven; and in her large eyes wrought
A mixture of sensations might be scanned,
　　Of half-voluptuousness and half command.

Her form had all the softness of her Sex,   865
　　Her features all the sweetness of the Devil,
When he put on the Cherub to perplex
　　Eve, and paved (God knows how) the road to Evil,
The Sun himself was scarce more free from Specks
　　Than She from aught at which the Eye could cavil,   870
Yet, somehow, there was something somewhere wanting,
As if She rather ordered than was granting. –

In *Orientalism*, Edward Said writes:

> Woven through all of Flaubert's Oriental experiences, exciting or
> disappointing, is an almost uniform association between the Orient and
> sex. In making this association Flaubert was neither the first nor the
> most exaggerated instance of a remarkably persistent motif in Western
> attitudes to the Orient.[282]

As Said makes so few direct references to anything Byron actually
wrote (see my essay below), we can only guess whether or not he thinks
Byron one of the first instances; however, *Don Juan* being an ottava rima
poem, anti-climax rules, and "disappointing" sexual experiences triumph
over "exciting" ones. The consequence of Gulbeyaz's trying to "order"
Juan to make love to her are convoluted, and ultimately bathetic: tearful
at first, and proudly, Hispanically obdurate second, he is about to relent
as she weeps, as an alternative to "cutting his acquaintance"; as Itsuyo
Higashinaka points out,[283] she is here reduced to the level of Betty the
chambermaid from *Joseph Andrews*. However, at this point the Sultan
turns up and admires "Juanna", despite which he takes Gulbeyaz out,
leaving Juan with the other odalisques, with one of whom – Dudù – he is
ordered into bed, and makes love (very quietly, we must suppose) thereby
concluding those Harem adventures in which Byron is interested. In *Don
Juan*, the sexual conquest of the Orient, at least, is a thing one cannot
accomplish ostentatiously, or even on one's own initiative.

　　J.P.Donovan describes the Symplegades as

282: Edward Said, *Orientalism*, p.188.
283: Itsuyo Higashinaka, *Gulbeyaz and Joseph Andrews*, 1984 *Byron Journal*
p.74.

... the clashing rocks that guard the passage between the familiar and
the mysterious East, the barrier Byron had reached and climbed before
turning back.[284]

But the Symplegades do not merely guard the way east, they guard
the way north – the way to Russia, a country neither European nor
Oriental; and it is there, most humiliatingly, that Juan is next led.

***

In its Harem Cantos, *Don Juan* descends into sexual farce of the kind
Byron enjoyed in *Tom Jones*. We do not know when he planned the switch
from them to the horrible military farce of the Ismail cantos; but he needed
a transition – or something: for the Ismail cantos plunge the poem straight
into the *real* real world of recent oriental history, in a way that none of the
Tales do except *The Siege of Corinth,* and that is set a safe century ago.
The siege of the fortified Turkish city of Ismail, by the Russians under
Suvorov, had occurred in the winter of 1790-1 (Ismail is on the Danube,
on the border of modern Byelorus and modern Ukraine); and, as Suvorov
(or "Suwarrow," as Byron spells him, for it makes rhyming easier), was
undoubtedly a real person, there was a problem of Byron's own creation,
if the jolt into actual events was to work. Here is the introduction of the
Sultan of Constantinople, as set up in Canto V, with Byron's prose note
following at once:

> His Highness was a Man of solemn port,
>> Shawled to the nose, and bearded to the eyes;   1170
> Snatched from a prison to preside at court,
>> His lately bowstrung brother caused his rise;
> He was as good a Sovereign of the sort
>> As any mentioned in the histories
> Of Cantemir or Knolles, where few shine *   1175
> Save Solyman, the Glory of their line. –

* It may not be unworthy of remark that Bacon in his essay on "Empire" hints
that *Solyman* was the *last* of his line – on what authority I know not. – These
are his words. – "The destruction of Mustapha was so fatal to Solyman's line,
as the Succession of the Turks from Solyman until this day is suspected to be
untrue, and of strange blood; for that Solymus the Second was thought to be
supposititious." But Bacon in his historical authorities is often inaccurate – I
could give half a dozen instances from his apothegms only.

284: J.P. Donovan, *Don Juan in Constantinople: Watching and Waiting;* 1993
Byron Journal, p.23.

He went to Mosque in state, and said his prayers
    With more than "Oriental Scrupulosity;"
He left to his Vizier all State affairs,
    And showed but little royal curiosity;   1180
I know not if he had domestic cares –
No process proved connubial animosity –
    Four wives and twice five hundred maids unseen
Were ruled as calmly as a Christian Queen. –

If now and then there happened a slight slip,   1185
    Little was heard of criminal or crime;
The Story scarcely passed a single lip,
    The *Sack* and Sea had settled all in time,
From which the secret nobody could rip;
    The Public knew no more than does this rhyme;   1190
No Scandals made the daily press a curse;
Morals were better, and the fish no worse.

Byron appends here the longest prose note that *Don Juan* has: a list of ten of Francis Bacon's Apophthegms, with notes impugning their accuracy (John Murray, who was not in on the secret, didn't print the note in his first edition).

Impugning someone else's historical accuracy about the blood-line of the Sultans, in order to cover up an inaccuracy of your own on that very subject, may be a cheap trick; though, as no-one has seen fit to point out that this is what Byron's doing, it looks as if he has – until now – got away with it. His description of the Sultan does not fit, and is an offence against recent Turkish history, a subject which he knew well. The Sultan in 1790, when Catherine ordered the attack on Ismail, was Selim III; he was nephew to the previous Sultan, and devoted to his uncle's widow, Aimée Dubucq de Rivery, herself cousin to Joséphine Beauharnais, subsequently Napoleon's wife. No smug ignoramus, as the *Don Juan* Sultan is, he was a westernised and reforming sophisticate – he recognised the French Republic, which few other "legitimate" monarchs did. However, almost all his reforms failed, owing to the obscurantist conservatism pervasive in the Turkish Empire,[285] and he was bowstrung, in 1808, on the orders of his cousin Mustapha, whom he had released from prison, and in whose favour he had abdicated. Mustapha was imprisoned again, and later bowstrung himself, by his half-brother, Aimée's son, who ascended the throne as Sultan Mahmoud II, the one with whom Byron attended an audience.

285: See Stanford J. Shaw, *Between Old and New; the Ottoman Empire under Sultan Selim III, 1789-1807* (Harvard 1971).

Mahmoud became another reforming Sultan, but with more craft than Selim, and reigned until 1839.

The career and death of Selim III are the subject of pages 1009-47 of Hobhouse's *Journey through some Provinces of Turkey*. Our suspicion that, in his huge note on Bacon, Byron protests too much about Bacon's historical inaccuracy, and is veiling an obvious contemporary joke about King George's inability to rule Queen Caroline, is enhanced by these reflections. A sad, weak idealist, Selim had captured the imagination of Hobhouse and of Byron in Constantinople, and Byron may have put some of him into the figure of Sardanapalus (published late in 1821). In the last paragraph of his book, Hobhouse describes the ruins of Selim's occidental dreams:

> The schools of the arsenal, and the barracks of the bombadiers, are no less deserted than the exercising-grounds of Scutari and Levend Tchiftlik; nor can the pious alarms of the Ulema be now raised by the unhallowed encouragement of Christian refinements. The presses of Ters-Hane are without employ; the French language has ceased to be taught in the Seraglio; and the palace of Beshik-Tash is no longer enlivened by the ballets and operas which amused the leisure of the unfortunate Selim.[286]

And on 29 November 1813, Byron writes to Annabella:

> I never saw a Revolution transacting – or at least completed – but I arrived just after the last Turkish one – and the *effects* were visible – and had all the grandeur of desolation in their aspect – – Streets in ashes – immense barracks (of a very fine construction) in ruins – and above all Sultan Selim's favourite gardens round them in all the wildness of luxurient neglect – his fountains waterless – and his kiosks defaced but still glittering in their decay. – They lie between the city and Buyukdere on the hills above the Bosphorus – and the way to them is through a plain with the prettiest name in the world – "the Valley of Sweet Waters".[287]

If Hobhouse is to be believed, Selim had wanted to convert his oriental empire into an occidental one, with printing-presses, ballets and operas. Such sentimental reflections could never of course have been expressed in *Don Juan*, with its perspective from near the start, not from after the termination, of Selim's reign.

286: *Journey,* II, p.1046-7.
287: BLJ III, 180.

***

The Siege of Ismail

The theme of Christianity and Islam at war is a staple of Italian renaissance epic, particularly of Ariosto's *Orlando Furioso*, a poem on which *Don Juan* is partly modelled, and in which the Christians besiege and sack the city of Bizerta ("chi fu di tutta l'Africa regina"),[288] and of Pulci's *Morgante Maggiore*, in which they sack the Spanish Moslem city of Saragossa. Byron translated the first canto of the *Morgante*. The theme is central to Tasso's *Gerusalemme Liberata*, a poem with which *Don Juan* is in ideological contention, as Goethe pointed out. In his dialogues with these three great predecessors we see Byron's concern with Orientalism reach its latest and last point of focus.

Those who wish us to read Byron as an anti-imperialist writer should take on board that his most pointed delineament of imperialism is one not of western, but of Russian imperialism. Here there is no allegory, but a clear reliance on a prose source, to which he draws our attention.

Byron had announced to Murray on February 16 1821[289] that "I meant to take him [*Juan*] on the tour of Europe – with a proper mixture of siege – battle – and adventure ..." He wrote the Siege Cantos between January and August of the following year. His source for their military detail was Castelnau's *Histoire de la Nouvelle Russie*, a Russian expansionist apologia, chronicling Potemkin's take-over of the Ukraine and Crimea in the late eighteenth century.[290] As is not the case with "Tully," but as is the case with Dalyell, whose narratives can often bear a pro-Christian interpretation which *Don Juan* II refutes, Byron inverts the values of his source, writes – what many assert (with doubtful success) the Turkish Tales to be – an anti-imperialist poem: and paints a horrid picture of what happens when a Christian army besieges a Moslem town. It's *The Siege of Corinth*, inverted.

Among some material borrowed from Castelnau, one episode stands out which illuminates the contrast with Tasso, and provides a counter-episode. It is the death of the old Tartar Khan, who falls, surrounded by all his sons, at *Don Juan* VIII 104-119. Here is Castelnau:

288: Ariosto, *Orlando Furioso*, 40, 32, 8.
289: BLJ VIII, 78.
290: See Cochran, *Byron and Castelnau's* History of New Russia*, Keats-Shelley Review* October 1994, pp. 48-70.

Le sultan périt dans l'action en brave homme, digne d'un meilleur
destin; ce fut lui qui rallia les Turcs lorsque l'ennemi pénétra dans la
place; ce fut lui qui marcha contre les Russes trop avides du pillage, et
qui, dans vingt occasions différentes, combattit en héros: ce sultan,
d'une valeur éprouvée, surpassait en générosité les plus civilisés de sa
nation; cinq de ses fils combattaient à ses côtés, il les encourageait par
son exemple; tous cinq furent tués sous ses yeux; il ne cessait point de
se battre, répondit par des coups de sabre aux propositions de se rendre,
et ne fut atteint du coup mortel qu'après avoir abattu de sa main
beaucoup de Kozaks des plus acharnés à sa prise; le reste de sa troupe
fut massacré.[291]

[The sultan died in the action as a brave man, worthy of a better destiny;
it was he who rallied the Turks as the enemy entered the place; it was he
who marched against the Russians, who were too eager for pillage, and
he who, on twenty different occasions, fought like a hero: this sultan, of
approved valour, surpassed in generosity the most civilised of his
nation; five of his sons fought at his side, and he encouraged them by
his example; all five were killed before his eyes; he never ceased to
fight, replied by sabre-strokes to the offers of surrender, and did not
receive his death-blow until he had killed with his own hand many of
the Cossacks who were most eager to capture him; the remainder of his
company were massacred.]

This is a characteristic technique from chivalric romance – once you
have your Moslem hero cornered and on the verge of death, you can
concede to him all the heroism you want. All that I know of the Siege of
Ismail is from Byron and Castelnau. The thought that Castelnau invented
this episode, to give his chronicle weight, and to infuse Catherine the
Great's invasion of Turkish territory with epic, medieval, Christian
dignity, is one which might make us pause.

Byron would have been amazed at the way Castelnau showed real
history to be paralleling fiction; for there is a parallel episode in Tasso: it
is the death of the Christian Latinus,[292] and *his* five sons. I print the
original, with Edward Fairfax's 1620 translation opposite:

291: Castelnau, *Histoire de la Nouvelle Russie*, II, p.215.
292: Or "Catinus," as he's called at CPW V 734, note to line 830.

27 Fra color che mostraro il cor piú franco,
Latin, su 'l Tebro nato, allor si mosse,
a cui né le fatiche il corpo stanco,
né gli anni dome aveano ancor le posse.
Cinque suoi figli quasi eguali al fianco
gli erano sempre, ovunque in guerra ei fosse,
d'arme gravando, anzi il tor tempo molto,
le membra ancor crescenti e 'l molle volto.

27 Among the rest that strove to merit praise,
Was old Latinus, born by Tiber's bank,
To whose stout heart in fights and bloody
    frays,
For all his eild, base fear yet never sank;
Five sons he had, the comforts of his days,
That from his side in no adventure shrank,
But long before their time, in iron strong
They clad their members, tender, soft and
    young.

28 Ed eccitati dal paterno essempio
aguzzavano al sangue il ferro e l'ire.
Dice egli loro: "Andianne ove quell'empio
veggiam ne' fuggitivi insuperbire,
né già ritardi il sanguinoso scempio,
ch'ei fa de gli altri, in voi l'usato ardire,
però che quello, o figli, è vile onore
cui non adorni alcun passato orrore."

28 The bold ensample of their father's might
Their weapons whetted and their wrath
    increased,
"Come let us go," quoth he, "where yonder
    knight
Upon our soldiers makes his bloody feast,
Let not their slaughter once your hearts
    affright,
Where danger most appears, there fear it least,
For honor dwells in hard attempts, my sons,
And greatest praise, in greatest peril, wons."

29 Cosí feroce leonessa i figli,
cui dal collo la coma anco non pende
né con gli anni lor sono i feri artigli
cresciuti e l'arme de la bocca orrende,
mena seco a la preda ed a i perigli,
e con l'essempio a incrudelir gli accende
nel cacciator che le natie lor selve
turba e fuggir fa le men forti belve.

29 Her tender brood the forest's savage queen,
Ere on their crests their rugged manes appear,
Before their mouths by nature armed been,
Or paws have strength a silly lamb to tear,
So leadeth forth to prey, and makes them keen,
And learns by her ensample naught to fear
The hunter, in those desert woods that takes
The lesser beasts whereon his feast he makes.

30 Segue il buon genitor l'incauto stuolo
de' cinque, e Solimano assale e cinge;
e in un sol punto un sol consiglio, e un solo
spirito quasi, sei lunghe aste spinge.
Ma troppo audace il suo maggior figliuolo
l'asta abbandona e con quel fer si stringe,
e tenta in van con la pungente spada
che sotto il corridor morto gli cada.

30 The noble father and his hardy crew
Fierce Solyman on every side invade,
At once all six upon the Soldan flew,
With lances sharp, and strong encounters made,
His broken spear the eldest boy down threw,
And boldly, over-boldly, drew his blade,
Wherewith he strove, but strove therewith in
    vain,
The Pagan's steed, unmarked, to have slain.

31 Ma come a le procelle esposto monte,
che percosso da i flutti al mar sovraste,
sostien fermo in se stesso i tuoni e l'onte
del ciel irato e i venti e l'onde vaste,
così il fero Soldan l'audace fronte
tien salda incontra a i ferri e incontra a l'aste,

31 But as a mountain or a cape of land
Assailed with storms and seas on every side,
Doth unremoved, steadfast, still withstand
Storm, thunder, lightning, tempest, wind,
    and tide:
The Soldan so withstood Latinus' band,

293: Tasso, *Gerusalemme Liberata* IX, 27-39. Text from <<liber.liber.it/
biblioteca/tasso/gerusalemme_liberate/html/frames.html>>.

ed a colui che il suo destrier percote
tra i cigli parte il capo e tra le gote.

32 Aramante al fratel che giú ruina
porge pietoso il braccio, e lo sostiene.
Vana e folle pietà! ch'a la ruina
altrui la sua medesma a giunger viene,
ché 'l pagan su quel braccio il ferro inchina
ed atterra con lui chi lui s'attiene.
Caggiono entrambi, e l'un su l'altro langue
mescolando i sospiri ultimi e 'l sangue.

33 Quinci egli di Sabin l'asta recisa,
onde il fanciullo di lontan l'infesta,
gli urta il cavallo addosso e 'l coglie in guisa
che giú tremante il batte, indi il calpesta.
Dal giovenetto corpo uscí divisa
con gran contrasto l'alma, e lasciò mesta
l'aure soavi de la vita e i giorni
de la tenera età lieti ed adorni.

34 Rimanean vivi ancor Pico e Laurente,
onde arricchí un sol parto il genitore:
similissima coppia e che sovente
esser solea cagion di dolce errore.
Ma se lei fe' natura indifferente,
differente or la fa l'ostil furore:
dura distinzion ch'a l'un divide
dal busto il collo, a l'altro il petto incide.

35 Il padre, ah non piú padre! (ahi fera sorte,
ch'orbo di tanti figli a un punto il face!),
rimira in cinque morti or la sua morte
e de la stirpe sua che tutta giace.
Né so come vecchiezza abbia sí forte
ne l'atroci miserie e sí vivace
che spiri e pugni ancor; ma gli atti e i visi
non mirò forse de' figliuoli uccisi,

36 e di sí acerbo lutto a gli occhi sui
parte l'amiche tenebre celaro.

And unremoved did all their justs abide,
And of that hapless youth, who hurt his steed,
Down to the chin he cleft in twain the head.

32 Kind Aramante, who saw his brother slain,
To hold him up stretched forth his friendly
    arm,
Oh foolish kindness, and oh pity vain,
To add our proper loss, to other's harm!
The prince let fall his sword, and cut in twain
About his brother twined, the child's weak
    arm.
Down from their saddles both together slide,
Together mourned they, and together died.

33 That done, Sabino's lance with nimble force
He cut in twain, and 'gainst the stripling bold
He spurred his steed, that underneath his horse
The hardy infant tumbled on the mould,
Whose soul, out squeezed from his bruised
    corpse,
With ugly painfulness forsook her hold,
And deeply mourned that of so sweet a cage
She left the bliss, and joys of youthful age.

34 But Picus yet and Lawrence were on live,
Whom at one birth their mother fair brought
    out,
A pair whose likeness made the parents strive
Oft which was which, and joyed in their doubt:
But what their birth did undistinguished give,
The Soldan's rage made known, for Picus stout
Headless at one huge blow he laid in dust,
And through the breast his gentle brother
    thrust.

35 Their father, but no father now, alas!
When all his noble sons at once were slain,
In their five deaths so often murdered was,
I know not how his life could him sustain,
Except his heart were forged of steel or brass,
Yet still he lived, pardie, he saw not plain
Their dying looks, although their deaths he
    knows,
It is some ease not to behold our woes.

36 He wept not, for the night her curtain spread
Between his cause of weeping and his eyes,

Con tutto ciò nulla sarebbe a lui,
senza perder se stesso, il vincer caro.
Prodigo del suo sangue, e de l'altrui
avidissimamente è fatto avaro;
né si conosce ben qual suo desire
paia maggior, l'uccidere o 'l morire.

But still he mourned and on sharp vengeance
  fed,
And thinks he conquers, if revenged he dies;
He thirsts the Soldan's heathenish blood to
  shed,
And yet his own at less than naught doth prize,
Nor can he tell whether he liefer would,
Or die himself, or kill the Pagan bold.

37 Ma grida al suo nemico: "È dunque frale
sí questa mano, e in guisa ella si sprezza,
che con ogni suo sforzo ancor non vale
a provocar in me la tua fierezza?"
Tace, e percossa tira aspra e mortale
che le piastre e le maglie insieme spezza,
e su 'l fianco gli cala e vi fa grande
piaga onde il sangue tepido si spande.

37 At last, "Is this right hand," quoth he, "so
  weak,
That thou disdain'st gainst me to use thy
  might?
Can it naught do? can this tongue nothing
  speak
That may provoke thine ire, thy wrath and
  spite?"
With that he struck, his anger great to wreak,
A blow, that pierced the mail and metal bright,
And in his flank set ope a floodgate wide,
Whereat the blood out streamed from his side.

38 A quel grido, a quel colpo, in lui converse
il barbaro crudel la spada e l'ira.
Gli aprí l'usbergo, e pria lo scudo aperse
cui sette volte un duro cuoio aggira,
e 'l ferro ne le viscere gli immerse.
Il misero Latin singhiozza e spira,
e con vomito alterno or gli trabocca
il sangue per la piaga, or per la bocca.

38 Provoked with his cry, and with that blow,
The Turk upon him gan his blade discharge,
He cleft his breastplate, having first pierced
  through,
Lined with seven bulls' hides, his mighty targe,
And sheathed his weapons in his guts below;
Wretched Latinus at that issue large,
And at his mouth, poured out his vital blood,
And sprinkled with the same his murdered
  brood.

39 Come ne l'Appennin robusta pianta
che sprezzò d'Euro e d'Aquilon la guerra,
se turbo inusitato al fin la schianta,
gli alberi intorno ruinando atterra,
cosí cade egli, e la sua furia è tanta
che piú d'un seco tragge a cui s'afferra;
e ben d'uom sí feroce è degno fine
che faccia ancor morendo alte ruine.[293]

39 On Apennine like as a sturdy tree,
Against the winds that makes resistance stout,
If with a storm it overturned be,
Falls down and breaks the trees and plants
  about;
So Latine fell, and with him felled he
And slew the nearest of the Pagans' rout,
A worthy end, fit for a man of fame,
That dying, slew; and conquered, overcame.[294]

Now Old Latinus is a Christian, and the Tartar Khan a Moslem. Byron makes the most of this strange coincidence and opportunity, and gives his versified Khan, and the Khan's final son, an end which he thinks suitable for a Moslem, not a Christian, warrior. I quote the entire passage:

But to our Subject: a brave Tartar Khan,
    Or *"Sultan",* as the Author (to whose nod   830
In prose I bend my humble verse) doth call
The Chieftain – somehow would not yield at all,

But flanked by *five* brave Sons (such is Polygamy,
    That she spawns warriors by the score, where none
Are prosecuted for that false crime bigamy)   835
    He never would believe the city won
While Courage clung but to a single twig; am I
    Describing Priam's, Peleus', or Jove's Son?
Neither – but a good, plain, old, temperate Man,
Who fought with his five Children in the Van.   840

To *take* him was the point. The truly brave,
    When they behold the brave opprest with odds,
Are touched with a desire to shield and save;
    A mixture of Wild beasts and demi-gods
Are they – now furious as the sweeping wave,   845
    Now moved with pity – even as sometimes nods
The rugged tree unto the summer wind,
Compassion breathes along the savage Mind. –

But he would *not* be *taken,* and replied
    To all the propositions to surrender   850
By mowing Christians down on every side,
    As obstinate as Swedish Charles at Bender;
His five brave boys no less the foe defied,
    Whereon the Russian Pathos grew less tender,
As being a Virtue, like terrestrial Patience,   855
Apt to wear out on trifling provocations.

And spite of Johnson and of Juan, who
    Expended all their Eastern phraseology
In begging him – for Godsake, just to show
    So much less fight as might form an apology   860
For *them* in saving such a desperate foe,
    He hewed away, like doctors of Theology
When they dispute with Sceptics; and with curses
Struck at his friends, as Babies beat their Nurses.

Nay, he had wounded, though but slightly, both   865
    Juan and Johnson; whereupon they fell,
The first with sighs, the second with an oath,
    Upon his angry Sultanship, pell-mell,
And all around were grown exceeding wroth

At such a pertinacious Infidel,   870
And poured upon him and his Sons like Rain,
Which they resisted like a sandy Plain,

That drinks and still is dry; at last they perished –
    His second son was levelled by a shot;
His third was sabred, and the fourth, most cherished   875
    Of all the five, on bayonets met his lot;
The fifth, who, by a Christian mother nourished,
    Had been neglected, ill-used, and what not,
Because deformed, yet died all game and bottom,
To save a Sire, who blushed that he begot him.   880

The eldest was a true and tameless Tartar,
    As great a scorner of the Nazarene
As ever Mahomet picked out for a Martyr,
    Who only saw the black eyed girls in green,
That make the beds of those who won't take quarter   885
    On Earth, in Paradise; and when once seen,
Those Houris, like all other pretty creatures,
Do just whate'er they please, by dint of features.

And what they pleased to do with the young Khan
    In Heaven, I know not, nor pretend to guess;   890
But doubtless they prefer a fine young Man
    To tough old Heroes, and can do no less;
And that's the cause, no doubt why – if we scan
    A Field of Battle's ghastly Wilderness –
For one rough, weather-beaten Veteran body,   895
You'll find ten thousand handsome Coxcombs bloody.

Your Houris also have a natural pleasure
    In lopping off your lately married men,
Before the Bridal Hours have danced their measure,
    And the sad, second Moon grow dim again,   900
Or dull Repentance hath had dreary leisure
    To wish him back a bachelor now and then;
And thus your Houri (it may be) disputes
Of these brief blossoms the immediate fruits.

Thus the young Khan, with Houris in his sight,   905
    Thought not upon the charms of four young brides,
But bravely rushed on his first heavenly night;
    In short, howe'er *our* better Faith derides,
These black-eyed Virgins make the Moslems fight,
    As though there were one Heaven and none besides –   910

Whereas, if all be true we hear of Heaven
And Hell, there must at least be six or seven.

So fully flashed the Phantom on his eyes,
    That when the very lance was in his heart
He shouted "Allah!" and saw Paradise   915
    With all its Veil of Mystery drawn apart –
And bright Eternity without disguise
    On his Soul, like a ceaseless Sunrise, dart –
With Prophets – Houris – Angels – Saints – descried
In one voluptuous Blaze – and then he died,   920

And with a heavenly rapture on his face;
    The good old Khan, who long had ceased to see
Houris, or aught except his florid race,
    Who grew like Cedars round him gloriously,
When he beheld his latest hero grace   925
    The Earth, which he became like a felled tree,
Paused for a moment from the fight, and cast
A Glance on that slain Son, his first and last.

The Soldiers, who beheld him drop his point,
    Stopt, as if willing once more to concede   930
Quarter, in case he bade them not "Aroint!"
    As he before had done. He did not heed
Their pause nor signs; his heart was out of joint –
    And shook (till now unshaken) like a reed,
As he looked down upon his children gone,   935
And felt – though done with life – he was alone.

But 'twas a transient tremor – with a spring
    Upon the Russian Steel his breast he flung,
As carelessly as curls the Moth her wing
    Against the light wherein she dies; he clung   940
Closer, that all the deadlier they might wring,
    Unto the bayonets which had pierced his young,
And throwing back a dim look on his Sons,
In one wide wound poured forth his Soul at once.

    Byron's skill lies in the way in which he balances several perspectives
in one passage. It's obvious that, while conceding the attractiveness of –
and motivation provided by – the Islamic concept of paradise,[295] he will

---

295: See Qu'ran, 2:25; 4:57; 37:40-9; 38:52; 44:51-5; 52:17-20; 55:54-6, 71-2;
56:12-40; 76:12-22; and 78:33. Or see Sale, 96-7: "But all these glories will be
eclipsed by the resplendent and ravishing girls of paradise, called, from their large

concede no credibility at all either to it, or that of any other concept of paradise. "...*our* better faith" is not his better faith – while not sneering at his correct readers, he won't allow them anything other than a share in his own capacity for scepticism. He's no believer in the Christian heaven either – see *The Vision of Judgement*, written the previous year. To say that "there must at least be six or seven" paradises is the same as saying that there probably aren't any. Compare the narrative reflection on Hassan's death in *The Giaour*:

> Yet died he by a stranger's hand,   735
> And stranger in his native land –
> Yet died he as in arms he stood,
> And unavenged, at least in blood.
> But him the maids of Paradise
> Impatient to their halls invite,   740
> And the dark Heaven of Houris' eyes
> On him shall glance for ever bright;
> They come – their kerchiefs green they wave,
> And welcome with a kiss the brave!
> Who falls in battle 'gainst a Giaour,   745
> Is worthiest an immortal bower.[296]

Here there were no ironic glances at the hero's preference for houris over wives, and no reflections about the multitudinous varieties of paradises available to different believers. Ottava rima, perhaps via its insistence on multiple and deflationary rhyming, insists also on a wider variety of tones and perspectives. One-dimensional solemnity is out; irony is in.

The young Khan is mocked for his insatiable appetite: having "four young brides" should be enough for any man, implies Byron, for whom one had been one too many; but the young Khan longs for the seventy-plus self-renewing virgins which Paradise – in some Islamic interpretations – offers him. His death, in lines 915-20, is aptly orgasmic. Meanwhile his

---

black eyes, *Hûr al oyûn*, the enjoyment of whose company will be a principal felicity of the faithful. These, they say, are created, not of clay, as mortal women are, but of pure musk; being, as their prophet often affirms in his *Korân*, free from all natural impurities, defects, and inconveniences incident to the sex, of the strictest modesty, and secluded from public view in pavilions of hollow pearls, so large, that, as some traditions have it, one of them will be no less than four parasangs (or, as others say, sixty miles) long, and as many broad ... in order to qualify the blessed for a full enjoyment of them, GOD will give to every one the abilities of an hundred men".

296: Byron, *The Giaour*, 735-46.

father, too old, perhaps, for sexual thoughts, is given the same dignified
paternal status as is Latinus in Tasso, and the same horror and regret at
losing it. Whether your hero is a Moslem attacked by Christians, or a
Christian attacked by Moslems, the tragedy of age bereft, and the heroism
of age fighting on, are the same.

There was never such drama, or complex juggling of ideas like this, in
the Tales. There death was a sentimental thing, only interpretable in
Christian terms:

> Yet sense seemed left, though better were its loss;
> For when one near displayed the absolving cross,
> And proffered to his touch the holy bead,
> Of which his parting soul might own the need,
> He looked upon it with an eye profane,   1125
> And smiled – Heaven pardon! if 'twere with disdain;
> And Kaled, though he spoke not, nor withdrew
> From Lara's face his fixed despairing view,
> With brow repulsive, and with gesture swift,
> Flung back the hand which held the sacred gift,   1130
> As if such but disturbed the expiring man,
> Nor seemed to know his life but *then* began,
> The life immortal infinite, secure,
> To all for whom that cross hath made it sure![297]

Now if Lara smiles disdainfully at "the holy bead", what price his
"life immortal"? Byron is taking refuge behind a fallible narrator, not
because it's a subtle story-telling device, but because he knows his readers
will prefer the conventional perspective over his own, "defiant" anti-
Christian one, and he doesn't want to offend them. It's a two-facedness
similar to his attitude to the mutiny on the Bounty in *The Island* – he wants
to have the anarchic excitement of the event, but without appearing to
encourage naval insubordination. He's having it both ways, neither of
them interesting.

How different his ottava rima way of doing things. Here he entertains
several mutually incompatible viewpoints, Moslem, Christian, and
rationalist, and holds them (precariously, no doubt) in balance. Three of
his favourite literary sources – the Bible, the Qu'ran, Christ, and Voltaire –
co-exist in the same passage.

"Orientalism" has finally been transcended. We have come a long
way since Harold went to Hell.

297: Byron, *Lara,* 1121-34.

***

Epilogue: the example of Lady Anne Blunt

Byron's grand-daughter (1837-1917), was taught drawing by Ruskin and the violin by Joseph Joachim. She inherited Byron's soft, attractive voice. She was a skilled linguist, chess-player, and (as you would expect), mathematician; and her sketches are breathtaking. But her real qualities were best revealed in the Near East, the remotest hinterlands of which she and her husband scoured with a thoroughness and an adventurousness which puts her grandfather's gestures in perspective. She was admittedly assisted by an income of £3,000 a year, which increased when her husband came into his own to £21,000 a year. In 1875-6 the Blunts toured Egypt, Sinai and Jerusalem, once nearly dying of thirst. They both learned Arabic. In 1877-8 they went to Syria, returning with six Arab horses from which nearly all Arab horses currently in the U.K. stem. In 1878 they traversed the Arabian peninsula into Mesopotamia (Iraq); she was the first European woman ever to go to these places, and only three men had gone before. She crossed the Tigris and Euphrates either on goatskin rafts, or clinging to her horse as it swam. Once she dislocated her knee and rode for days on her camel without medical help – asceticism was another quality she inherited from Byron.

Her tragedy was that she miscarried constantly, and only one child survived.

The Blunts purchased a house and garden near the Pyramids. Anne's Arabic became so perfect that she claimed she thought and dreamed in it. At the age of seventy-seven she could still vault into the saddle unassisted. Here is an example of her writing, one strange word in which we may recognise:

> The Bedouin never uses a bit or bridle of any sort, but instead, a halter with a fine chain passing round the nose. With this he controls his mare easily and effectually. He rides on a pad of cotton, fastened on the mare's back by a surcingle, and uses no stirrups. This pad is the most uncomfortable and insecure seat imaginable, but fortunately the animals are nearly always gentle and without vice. I have never seen either violent plunging, rearing, or indeed any serious attempt made to throw the rider. Whether the Bedouin would be able to sit a bare-backed

unbroken four-year old colt, as the gauchos of South America do, is
exceedingly doubtful.[298]

What Byron had only dreamed of, his grand-daughter achieved. She
wrote verse, too – but it never took on in the way his did.

298: Lady Anne Blunt, ed. W.S.Blunt, *Bedouin Tribes of the Euphrates,* 1879,
Chapter xxviii, *On Horses.*

BYRON AND THE ORIENT: APPROPRIATION OR SPECULATION?

RICHARD A.CARDWELL

On the July 2nd, 1809, after several delays, Byron set off for the "Orient" (Greece, Albania and Turkey) from Falmouth on the Lisbon Packet, the *Princess Elizabeth*. He was to be absent from England for two years. Four and a half days later he landed in Lisbon. Then on, across a war-ravaged Portugal and Spain, to Seville and Cádiz on horseback, and on again to British Gibraltar and by sea to Sardinia and Malta. From there, on a British warship, the *Spider*, he sailed into the channel between Cephalonia and Zante on the morning of September 23rd 1809, where he had his first sight of Greece. After a brief landing in Patras the *Spider* sailed up the western coast of the Morea towards Albania, landing at Previsa on September 29th. Byron travelled through Albania to a meeting with Ali Pasha and then he and Hobhouse rode south to Messalonghi and on to Athens, arriving late on Christmas Day 1809. The weeks in Athens were followed by the much-longed-for visit to Turkey. The two friends sailed from Athens on the British sloop of war, the *Pylades*, on March 5th 1810 landing in Smyrna and thence, again by sea, to Constantinople, arriving on May 13th 1810. This encounter with the Orient (with the caveat that Greece, though ruled by the Ottomans and their Muslim clients, was clearly not a true "Orient") left Byron overwhelmed. In the "Additional Note on the Turks", appended to *Childe Harold's Pilgrimage,* Byron is clearly at variance with the Philhellenic tone of Canto II. This latter, arguably, was inspired in the traditional and prejudiced view of the Ottoman Empire set out in Richard Knolles's *The Generall Historie of the Turks* (London, 1603) and William Eton's *A Survey of the Turkish Empire* (London 1789) which, as the standard textbooks for the traveller, had almost certainly been consulted by the poet. In this note Byron was to argue, at variance with many Western observers and travellers, that "the Ottomans, with all their defects, are not a people to be despised." He noted their high educational standards, their honest system of economic exchange and barter, the sophistication of their culture, the high standard of living and housing, and the superb craftsmanship of their manufactured products. In all ways, Byron thought, they were the equals of Europeans. Indeed, the Turkish "Orient" made such an impression that, in letters to his mother and others, we witness Byron's high regard and admiration rather than any symptoms of appropriation or restructuring. In a letter to Annabella Milbanke on November 10th 1810, he wrote: "I can't empty my head of the East". In another later letter he avowed that the East was "the greenest island of my imagination after Venice."[1] Yet any assessment of Byron's knowledge of the Islamic Orient would show that he had a poor grasp of the reality of daily Islamic practice and that he failed to recognise that Islam was neither a universal nor a single faith. For all his approval of the Qu'ran it would also appear that he had a poor grasp of that too.[2]

So how are we to read Byron's reflections as he left the Porte on July 14th 1810 bearing the manuscript of the early part of *Childe Harold's Pilgrimage*? After all, the often overlooked facsimile letter of apology from the Bey of Corinth, printed at the end of the Appendix to *Childe Harold* I and II, with its exotic and exquisite calligraphy, as much as the reproduction of Greek (Romaic) lists of authors, a war song, extracts, phrase lists, passages from the Gospels, inscriptions, etc., was intended to strike a contrast between East and West, to support the case for a nascent Greek culture on the one hand and to allay anti-Ottoman prejudices in his readers on the other.[3] The Appendix, nevertheless, sends out mixed messages.

The question of Byron's Orientalism has occupied the attention of many critics: Blackstone, Butler, Demata, Franklin, Kidwai, Leask, Makdisi, Melikian, Oueijan, Sharafuddin, Wiener, among others.[4] Of course, "Orientalism" had a very different meaning in Byron's lifetime from present day definitions of the word. In recent times, especially after the work of Edward Said,[5] the Orient becomes an Other which the subject desires to "possess", where one can redefine one's "self". Or, as Frederick Garber argues, "Byronic Orientalism involves a pitting of self against

---

1: BLJ V, 219.
2: See Peter Cochran"s Introduction, *passim.*
3: For an analysis of this aspect see Roger Poole, "What Constitutes, and What is External to, the Real Text of Byron's *Childe Harold's Pilgrimage, A Romaunt and Other Poems* (1812)?", in Richard A. Cardwell (ed.), *Lord Byron the European. Essays from the International Byron Society,* The Edwin Mellen Press, Lewiston/Queenston/Lampeter, 1997, pp.149-207.
4: See Bibliography.
5: Edward Said, *Orientalism*, Penguin, 1991. First published in 1978.

self".[6] Arguably, as we shall see, the Orient might be less a question of "encountering" (Said), or "pit[ting] ourselves for definition" (Garber), than a locus in which Byron could argue out with himself his divided loyalties, his self-made contradictions and give expression to his response to other earlier "Oriental" writers, especially Southey, Beckford, Moore, Dacre and Brown, among others.[7]

But what of Byron's reactions to the Ottoman Orient? Many critics argue that Byron's version of the Orient, based as some of his poetry was on a real and lived experience, is somehow truer than those writers who had not shared the same contact.[8] Leslie Marchand, with Borst and Elizabeth Longford,[9] argues, for example, that Byron disliked Constantinople. But, it seems more likely that Byron's observations were shaped by the reading of previous travellers and that, later, with first hand experience, he was able to colour in his verses with more realistic detail. In a letter to Francis Hodgson (May 15th 1810) he cites Gibbon and, nine days later, to his mother, he wrote: "of Constantinople you have of course read fifty descriptions of sundry travellers, which are in general so correct that I have nothing to add on the subject".[10] This seems to suggest that Byron and his mother shared the preliminary reading for his "pilgrimage". In other letters to John Hanson and Catherine Gordon Byron we find similar sentiments. A familiarity with William Jones' *Works* (1799), the *Letters* (1803) of Lady Wortley Montagu, George Sale's *Preliminary Discourse* (1734) and Pouqueville's *Voyage en Morée, à Constantinople, en Albanie et dans plusieurs autres parties de l'Empire Othoman* (1805)

6: Frederick Garber, *Self, Text, and Romantic Irony: The Example of Byron*, Princeton University Press, Princeton, 1988, p.82.
7: Robert Southey, *Thalaba* (1801); William Beckford, *Vathek* (1786); Thomas Moore, *Odes of Anacreon* (1805); Charlotte Dacre, *Moorish Combat* (1800); John Brown, *Barbarossa* (1754); Christoph Wieland, *Oberon* (tr. Sotheby, 1798).
8: "Among his contemporaries Lord Byron was the only Englishman who truly experienced the Orient by assimilating himself into the culture. [...] Unlike those who actually toured the East for merely political and/or religious propaganda and presented distorted images of the eastern world and its peoples, or those who for purely academic reasons employed their time in recording their observations of its antiquities and archaeology, Byron spent his time in living, enjoying and studying Oriental life and culture for its own wealth as well as for its existing exoticism" Oueijan, p.18.
9: Leslie A. Marchand, *Byron: A Biography*, 3 vols, John Murray, London, 1957; William A. Borst, *Byron's First Pilgrimage*, Yale University Press, New Haven, CT, 1948; Elizabeth Longford, *Byron's Greece*, Weidenfeld & Nicholson, London, 1975.
10: BLJ III, 191.

would have furnished the poet with more than sufficient detail for his Oriental Tales even without his first hand experience. Later, as Peter Cochran has argued, Byron read Miss Tully's *Narrative of a Ten Years Residence in Tripoli* (1817) which furnished further information on domestic details of the East, especially for the oriental sections of *Don Juan*.[11] Yet, as Massimiliano Demata has recently argued,[12] Byron's reading of the city was also through history. Santa Sophia, Byron writes, "is undoubtedly the most interesting from its immense antiquity" and the succession of rulers who had attended it.[13] Such an observation, among many, suggests a profound respect for Ottoman culture and an engagement with it.

Edward Said's celebrated (and slanted) *Orientalism*[14] argues that Western writers are unable to come to terms with the "real" Orient, preferring instead to create a space of representation in which the Orient is incorporated into Western hegemonic aspirations. Writers, argues Said, "restructured the Orient by their art and made its colors, lights and people visible through their images, rhythms and motifs. At most, the real Orient provoked a writer to his vision: it very rarely guided it".[15] Thus Byron, whom Said includes in his catalogue, is deemed part of a general project which aims at violating the real nature of the East by falsifying and, ultimately, domesticating it.[16] Even Marilyn Butler holds that English Romantic Orientalism allows the West to assert its own hegemony. Mohammed Sharafuddin's *Islam and Romantic Orientalism* would counter Said's rather partisan view with his theory of "realistic Orientalism" where European writers constantly checked their facts against former preconceptions and prejudices. Witness Byron's specific and apparently diligent (or perhaps deliberately mischievous?) query to John Murray, while preparing *The Bride of Abydos* for publication, as to the location of the Prophet's tomb. "Is it *Medina* or *Mecca* that contains the *holy* sepulchre? – don't make me blaspheme by your negligence – I have no

---

11: Peter Cochran, "Byron and "Tully's Tripoli", *Byron Journal*, 1992, pp.77-90.
12: For details see Demata, Massimiliano. *Byron, Turkey and the Orient*, in Cardwell, Richard A. (ed.) *The Reception of Byron in Europe* (Thoemmes Continuum, 2 vols, 2005), pp.441-5.
13: BLJ I, 251.
14: Edward Said, *Orientalism*, Penguin, London, 1991.
15: Said, p.22. For a critical assessment of Said's approach see Peter Cochran's essay in this volume. Cochran properly asks: "What's the difference between having been "provoked" into creativity by an environment, and being "guided" by it? Don't provocation and guidance go hand in hand in such circumstances?"
16: For a critical overview of this position see Peter Cochran's article in this volume.

book of reference or I would save you the trouble. I *blush* as a good Mussulman to have confused the point".[17] As Naji Oueijan demonstrates in *Compendium of Eastern Elements in Byron's Oriental Tales* (1999), Byron was intensely aware of the problems he faced in presenting the Oriental "Other", always striving to redress false Western notions of Islam and Turkish culture and religion. In the many notes appended to the Oriental Tales it is clear that Byron was at pains to be accurate in the details he supplies.[18] His travels in Turkey acquainted him with a first-hand knowledge of places and peoples. His reading of the earlier struggle of the Venetians with the Turks and the recent history of the Ottomans and the struggle with Russia and Greek insurgency, and Byron's use of stories he had collected on the way, together with his witness of actual events incorporated in the Tales all confirm Oueijan's thesis. Byron's reading of the Qu'ran in 1807 left him with the opinion that it "contains the most sublime poetical passages far surpassing European poetry" (CMP, 1). Thus *Childe Harold's Pilgrimage*, the Tales and Oriental sections of *Don Juan* seem to reveal Byron as a "true" rather than a hegemonic Orientalist in spite of the radical Philhellenic discourses that are expressed in his works.

Yet for all this, I want to suggest that Byron used the Orient in a different way. Said's inclusion of Byron in the Western project to incorporate the Orient and Oueijan's picture of Byron as a "realistic" Orientalist may have misled the reader and obscured other intentions. For all their arguments there remain two problems. The first, the locale or setting of the Tales; for the most part they are set in the Morea or in the islands of Greece. The second problem is the way in which the central protagonists are delineated and the world view and/or religion they express. Not one of the central male characters of the Oriental or Turkish Tales written after 1812 is what might be called a "true" Oriental let alone a Muslim. Childe Harold is an Englishman of doubtful religious allegiance. The Giaour is a Greek and a lapsed Christian. Selim is born of a Christian Greek mother ("Greek in soul if not in creed": *BoA*, 87) and only a Muslim through his adopted family. Conrad has no perceptible religious faith and is an enemy of the Muslim Seyd. Lara belongs to the Christian community of the Morea but remains outside its congregation. Alp, "the Adrian renegade" (*SoC*, 69), while fighting as a senior officer in

---

17: BLJ III, 191.
18: Peter Cochran has suggested that the idea for addition of notes to the Oriental Tales came from Walter Scott's *The Lay of the Last Minstrel* (1805) and *Marmion* (1808) which also have extensive footnotes. Indeed, such were the obvious echoes of Scott that Byron's friend and political patron Lord Holland objected, and Byron used fewer notes in his later works.

the Ottoman forces, has never actually become an apostate even though he hates his fellow Christians with an unallayed passion. So what is particularly "Oriental" about these extraordinary men? Do they in any way express a Muslim view of the world or sentiments that might be related to Qu'ranic scriptures? The answer must be "No". If not Muslim do they profess Christianity? And if not, what world view do they express?

Childe Harold's Pilgrimage Cantos I -III

Childe Harold is quickly delineated as wanting in virtue and a gross sinner who, sated with debauchery, seeks solitude in a pilgrimage (an ironic term for this journey of self-discovery given the absence of any form of epiphany or revelation). He flees from himself and from an unhappy emotional past. He "loved but one, /And that loved one, alas, could ne'er be his" (*CHP* I, 5, 3-4). He conceals his inner anguish from public view, a personal sorrow rooted in some undisclosed source: "a hidden feud" and "a disappointed passion". Childe Harold is re-introduced in Canto III, but only after Byron's own meditation on himself as narrator. What is striking is the singularly similar way character and author resemble one another, as if mirrored. It is an aspect to which I shall return. Byron the author/narrator of Canto III is now also an exile and separated emotionally; like his hero he has "grown aged in this world of woe, / In deeds, not years, piercing the depths of life, / So that no wonder waits him; nor below / Can love or sorrow, fame, ambition, strife, / Cut to his heart again with the keen knife / Of silent, sharp endurance" (*CHP* III, 5, 1-6). Byron's Childe, like his creator, is older and wiser, yet still restless, his restlessness a symptom of inner retreat from a world that offers no comforting illusions nor abiding values. Indeed, the close correspondence of the vital trajectories of the Childe and Byron himself between 1810 and 1816 gives the lie to his disclaimer in the "Preface to the First and Second Cantos" that his hero is "a real personage". Despite his insistence on the fictitious nature of the Childe, the mood of the narrator and the outlook of the Childe and their several emotional experiences are remarkably coincident. In the series of Tales which followed the early cantos the *Childe Harold* we find example after example of the same personality and vital outlook. This seems to suggest that Byron was employing his verses as a form of therapy, a means to argue out his feelings and thoughts, a mirror to his innermost spiritual distress.

The Giaour

In *The Giaour* (1813), set in the recent past of the Morea, the Giaour mysteriously appears and disappears under cover of darkness which seems to suggest a mystery at the level of narrative as much as at the level of meaning. After all, the narrative viewpoint shifts at various points in the poem and certain essential details are withheld from the reader. The Giaour has led "a life of pain, an age of crime" (details are left unexplained, as with the Childe); he endures "guilty woes" and "inward pain", likewise unexplained, the result of "some dark deed he will not name" (*Giaour*, 800). Since we know that he has killed Hassan in an ambush the "unnamed deed" cannot be the murder of his erstwhile friend. There has to be another reason, another "deed" that remains "unnamed". The effect is that we cannot judge him and we are led to believe that he may be "guilty without guilt"; that is, he experiences a gnawing sense of sin for some unspecified deed, perhaps for being a mortal, for still being alive. It is a motif Byron is to explore in later works. Indeed, two years before the publication of the Tale Byron had written to his friend Francis Hodgson expressing his inability to accept Christian teaching as morally just, let alone reasonable or rational, the typical struggle of Byron, the man of the Age of Reason, and Byron, the man of the new age of scepticism and doubt, an age of which he was to become a major spokesman. We note that Byron cleaves, not to faith, but to justice as his absolute benchmark of ultimate value.

> [T]he basis of your religion is *injustice*, the *Son of God*, the *pure*, the *immaculate*, the *innocent*, is sacrificed for the *guilty*. This proves *His* heroism, but no more does away with *man's* guilt than a schoolboy's volunteering to be flogged for another would exculpate the dunce from negligence, or preserve him from the rod. You degrade the Creator, in the first place, by making Him a begetter of children; and in the next you convert Him into a tyrant over an immaculate and injured Being, who is sent into existence to suffer death for the benefit of some millions of scoundrels, who, after all, seem as likely to be damned as ever.[19]

And this to a friend about to be inducted into holy orders! Such a comment is less the Calvinist sense of predestination he absorbed in his childhood and clearly not the Islamic acceptance of fate as God's will. Rather, I suggest, it is Byron's growing sense of a blind force operating in the world which amounts to a form of cosmic injustice, a sense of

---

19: BLJ II, 97.

metaphysical imprisonment and a rejection of any notion of a Benevolent Providence.

Byron seems to imply that the Giaour's inner anguish arises from the revenge he takes upon Hassan who, in turn, has destroyed the Giaour's own emotional serenity. Each of the two loses a fixed point in their inner being: Hassan his serai (associated with his mother) and the Giaour his "valley". Yet the revenge is exacted because Hassan has deprived the Giaour of love which, as we shall see, is a second absolute which can bring solace and emotional comfort. The narrator observes a Christian crest on the Giaour's helmet. Nevertheless, we later learn that he is "an Apostate from his own vile faith" (*Giaour*, 616), though we never discover whether he remains as such or whether he embraces Islam which would compound his ambush of Hassan as a vile breach of the Qu'ranic injunction on human relationships. His sorrow will not permit a single smile; yet he remains a "noble soul, and lineage high", a "mind not all degraded", a man of "lofty gifts" (*Giaour*, 869, 864, 873). He dwells apart (why or how we know not), in a Christian monastery longing "for rest", his "joys long dead" with the curse of Cain on his brow. Yet given that "his faith and race are alike unknown" (*Giaour*, 807), it is difficult to square the Giaour's presence in a Christian monastery. Nor can he accept the consolations of religion offered him: "I'd rather be the thing that crawls / Most noxious o'er a dungeon's walls, / Than pass my dull, unvarying days, / Condemn'd to meditate and gaze. / Yet lurks a wish within my breast / For rest – but none to feel 'tis rest" (*Giaour*, 990-5). It is as if he, like Manfred later, had been cursed by some cosmic agency to suffer, to long for some abiding principle or value, without success, to find some absolute of faith that would console and ease his anguish. Clearly such a belief is not to be found. He is fated to suffer with no absolute vital principle to which he might have recourse to find the "rest" for which he longs. Religion, glory, valour, renown, friendship, a return to his "valley", even the "quiet of death" are denied him. In the lonely meditations on his fate, in a clear anticipation of the scene of Manfred on the mountain edge, he recalls the vengeful murder by drowning of his Circassian beloved and the death of his erstwhile companion, Hassan, who killed her (*Giaour*, 822-31). But the death of Hassan, as with the death of the mysterious Astarte in *Manfred*, marks the onset of a gnawing guilt and an inner death in his very being. Byron seems uncertain whether Hassan has achieved his Islamic Paradise while at the same time the poet seems to recognise (especially in the section where he describes Hassan's empty hall) that an Oriental earthly paradise has been lost. His Turkish (Oriental) friend becomes his enemy, yet remains a "parent limb" (*Giaour*, 829). Given the textual ambiguities of the poem there may be a hint of "the love that dare not speak its name" in the Giaour's distress at the death of the man who had been a bosom friend which, in turn, may point to an underlying subtext of unconscious self-revelation as Byron himself struggles with his own sexuality and weighs the claims of his homosexual inclinations against the more acceptable and "Romantic" portrayal of heterosexual love. Just as Byron is divided so, too, the poem is divided in its intentions. Even the evocation of this prejudiced Oriental love idyll is also fraught with ambiguity. Given the fact that Byron had no opportunity to meet, let alone converse with, Muslim women, he is at a disadvantage in his portrayal of Leila. His only available source would have been, in 1812, the *Letters* of Lady Mary Wortley Montagu. It was inevitable that the love relationship would take on an Occidental cast. At the same time, as Byron's note to line 35 informs the reader, he is telling the story from an Islamic perspective. In killing Hassan the Giaour has violated one of the central tenets of the Qu'ran: the duty to offer charity and hospitality.[20] The mixed emphases and allegiances are symptomatic of an underlying psychological conflict. The Giaour, in effect, has destroyed his other half, a prominent theme in Byron's work before the Venice sojourn and a manifest of Byron's inner demons. Yet one value remains: love. The account of his beloved's fate and his revenge for her murder dominates the final part of the poem. But for all the stirring tale of revenge and bloodshed and loss it is the theme of love which dominates the finale and the way in which Byron describes this emotion gives a clue to his underlying thoughts. And, moreover, in a specifically Christian way. The Giaour has been "blessed" by Leila's love; "she was a form of life and light". "Yes", the Giaour continues, "Love indeed is light from heaven: / A spark of that immortal fire / With angels shared. /... / Devotion wafts the mind above, / But heaven itself descends in love; / A feeling from the Godhead caught .../ A Ray of Him who form'd the whole; / A Glory circling round the soul!" Leila was his "life's unerring light!". "Earth holds no other like to thee, / ... / thou art / the cherished madness of my heart" (*Giaour*, 1131-40, 1145, 1191). In this exchange between the old friar and the Giaour there lies the key to Byron's world-view in 1812-1813. In this conversation and confession Byron can explore the contending claims of Christian faith and the desire for an alternative. Yet the alternative is not Islam. The Giaour, like Manfred and Cain later,

---

20: "I need hardly observe, that Charity and Hospitality are the first duties enjoined by Mohamet; and to say truth, very generally practised by his disciples. The first praise that can be bestowed on a chief, is a panegyric on his bounty; the next, on his valour" (Byron's note to line 35).

cannot accept the consolations of Christianity, forgiveness and redemption, nor can he accept the religion of his erstwhile friend, Hassan. Rather Byron offers an alternative, a displaced theology. In the capitalised nouns and in the overall expression love is attributed all the epithets of orthodox religious devotion: "life and light", "light from heaven", "a feeling from the Godhead caught", "Ray of Him", "Glory", etc.. Love has become a surrogate religion, the last possible absolute to which the Giaour can cleave. But Leila is dead and even his revenge on Hassan can bring no emotional serenity, quite the reverse. So he rejects the absolution offered by the friar and goes in death to an unmarked grave, the ultimate state of existential solitude and nihilism. For all the apparent "Oriental" and Islamic background and subject Byron seems to be playing out his own personal drama, a Romantic Occidental drama, in an Oriental décor.

The Bride of Abydos

The Bride of Abydos (1813) sets out a similar pattern of contending values. Selim, too, has no real religious adherence. He is a Muslim since he has been brought up one. He expresses no specific Muslim sentiments and his behaviour is decidedly un-Islamic. He strives against his fratricidal Muslim uncle but not against his adopted faith. If anything he remains "Greek in soul if not in creed" (*BoA*, 87). The story line is tricked out with both Classical Greek and Oriental references as well as to the Old Testament (acceptable to both faiths). The initial story of apparently impossible, because incestuous, love is revealed to be untrue so that Zuleika and Selim can reveal their mutual affections. Once more Selim expresses Byron's Christian displaced theologies of faith to his Zuleika: "But be the star that guides the wanderer. Thou! / Thou, my Zuleika! Share and bless my bark; / The Dove of peace and promise to mine ark!" begs Selim. She is to be his "rainbow to the storms of life! / The evening beam that smiles the clouds away / And tints tomorrow with prophetic ray!" (*BoA*, 877 … 883). The overt references to God's Covenant to man after the Flood are evidence enough of Byron's manipulation of the discourses of Christian Judaic faith transferred to human affections. And so lovers part for the last time: "One kiss, Zuleika – 'tis my last!" (*BoA*, 996). Zuleika represents for Selim "thy hope – thy joy – thy love – thine all" (*BoA*, 1118), and, with his death, like a clock with a broken spring, she dies of a broken heart. The poem, too, seems to wind down all too readily as if it, too, lacked energy. And if Selim is less mysterious and less fate-bedevilled than other of Byron's heroes, with Conrad Byron returns in

1813-1814 to the rootless wanderer burdened by some dreadful past, to a reprise of his earlier archetype.

The Corsair

The Corsair stands beyond the rules of accepted human conduct, beyond the norms of self-preservation and fear. Like the Childe and the Giaour he is a "man of loneliness and mystery" (*Corsair*, 173); he is "warped by the world in Disappointment's school" (*Corsair*, 253), cursing common human virtues as shallow, a criminal wanting in guilt since the "rest [are] no better than the thing he seem'd" (*Corsair*, 266). Yet, for all his misanthropy, one value remains: "None are all evil; quickening round his heart,/ One softer feeling would not yet depart: ... the name of Love." "Yes, it was love", Byron goes on, " – unchangeable – unchanged, / Felt but for one / From whom he never ranged", despite the presence of "fairest captives" and "many a beauty", all enslaved, seductive, available. "Yes – it was love – if thoughts of tenderness, / Tried in temptation, strengthen'd by distress, / Unmoved by absence, firm in every clime, / And yet – o, more than all! – untired by time" (*Corsair*, 281-96). Love, for Conrad, is the last absolute value, "all virtues gone" as Byron informs his reader. So Conrad sets off on his (probably unnecessary) punitive expedition against Medora's wishes and the lovers part for what is to be the final time. Thus, when Gulnare secures Conrad's freedom at terrible personal risk, he cannot requite her love. He must return to his tower and Medora. And when he finds her dead, again of a broken heart, he does not take up with the beautiful and willing Gulnare. Rather he seeks a lonely and despairing death in the waves, his mortal remains never to be found. A nihilistic conclusion.

If there is any protective device against inner despair in this poem there lies, in Conrad's temperament, a psychological reaction which Byron has hinted at in *Childe Harold's Pilgrimage* and will explore more eloquently in *Don Juan*: the mocking laugh and black humour. Byron's reference to "the sad truth" and "romantic" in the quotation which follows from Canto IV, stanzas 3-4 of *Don Juan* refer to that sense of fallen values and lost absolutes that are common to his early work up to *Manfred* and *Cain*. Explored in later poems from *Beppo* onwards, the reaction is less one of despair but a special kind of humour:

> And the sad truth which hovers o'er my desk
> Turns what was once romantic to burlesque.
>
> And if I laugh at mortal thing,

> 'Tis that I may not weep; and if I weep,
> 'Tis that our nature cannot always bring
> Itself to apathy, for we must steep
> Our hearts first in the depths of Lethe's spring
> Ere what we least wish to behold will sleep. (*DJ* IV, 3-4)

Conrad, in chains in Seyd's tower, does not, as would ordinary mortals, give way to despair. Rather he "smiled in self-derision of his grief" (*Corsair*, 984). And Byron expands on the theme:

> Strange though it seem – yet with extremest grief
> Is link'd a mirth – it doth not bring relief –
> That playfullness of Sorrow ne'er beguiles,
> And smiles in bitterness – but still smiles;
> And sometimes with the wisest and the best,
> Till even the scaffold echoes with their jest!
> Yet not the joy to which it seems akin –
> It may deceive all hearts, save that within. (*Corsair*, 1051-8)

It is a panacea not a cure for metaphysical ills. This blackest of humours, Byron calls it "laughing wildness" (*Corsair*, 1060), is another means to escape, if only temporarily, from the toils of inevitable fate, a means of self-protection from total despair, a stoic pose only possessed by the strongest of wills. As if to emphasise the point Byron offers a footnote on those who, faced with execution, express "some *mot* as a legacy", a mocking laugh in the face of certain extinction. Nor will Conrad demean himself to bargain for his life: "I have no thought to mock his throne with prayer / Wrung from the coward crouching in despair; / It is enough – I breathe – and I can bear" (*Corsair*, 1087). His indomitable will, with sword and ship now gone, is sustained by this mocking laugh but, principally, by love: "my love – / For her in sooth my voice would mount above: / Oh! She is all that still to earth can bind!" (*Corsair*, 1090-2). But Medora is dead:

> It was enough – she died – what reck'd it how?
> The love of youth, the hope of better years,
> The source of softest wishes, tenderest fears,
> The only living thing he could not hate,
> Was reft at once – (*Corsair*, 1792-6)

We note the large emotional abstractions, the appeal of emotive nouns and adjectives and the presence of an existential emptiness at their disappearance. Also the unstated presence of some sinister and inimical power that has "reft" Medora from him. The world view of Byron's so-called "Oriental" heroes grows darker. And the more so since Conrad breaks the rules of Islam in masquerading as a holy man as well as in his refusal of the bread and salt of his host. While Seyd is less than a fastidious Muslim, he is, nevertheless, a more than typical Ottoman governor, comparing favourably with the rulers Byron had met in his travels in Albania, Greece and Turkey, and, moreover, a hospitable one. Conrad in his rejection, stands outside any form of social community; he also rejects both faiths.

Lara

The eponymous hero of *Lara* (1814) is another mystery. As Lara lies unconscious he utters "accents of another land" (*Lara*, 232). Byron does not tell us where that land is nor the language in which he speaks; nor, either, the language in which Kaled speaks. While Kaled's name suggests an Eastern language, we are no further forward. An air of mystery pervades the means of communication as much as the locale of the action merely defined as "those climes afar/ Where the soul glows beneath a brighter star" (*Lara*, 512-13), suggesting, in its turn, a lost paradise. If anything Lara belongs to a Christian community rather than an Islamic one. He also shares the same characteristics as the other protagonists of the Oriental Tales. He is a man of mysterious origins, "a stranger in this breathing world,/ An erring spirit from another hurled" (*Lara*, 315-16). He flees some terrible fate, soars above ordinary men in his humane amorality, a fighter for justice and freedom and for his own personal honour. Lara copes with his existential insights through action and revenge rather than through love or any form of displaced religion. Action and deeds become the vital lie that sustains Lara, a symptom of his flight from his inner self and his inner doubts.

The Siege of Corinth

The final work in the sequence of Oriental or Turkish Tales is *The Siege of Corinth* (1816). The poem, oddly, for a such a Tale, is, again, set in Greece and begins with a lamentation for the destruction of Corinth at the hands of the Muslim Ottomans. The city, a Venetian trading outpost, was reduced in the Prime Vizier's campaign of 1715, nearly one hundred years before Byron's visit. For all the city's ruination and Muslim occupation the citadel, nevertheless, Byron reminds the reader, remains "a fortress form'd to Freedom's hands .../ The keystone of a land which still, /

Though fall'n looks proudly on that hill" (*SoC*, 3-8). It symbolises, Byron goes on, a pattern of historical resistance, and a story of the former glories of the personal sacrifice of Timoleon and the Greek defenders of the city against the Persian hordes of Darius and Xerxes, as much as the heroic resistance of the Christian Venetians in Minotti's final heroic and self-immolating stand against the Turks in 1715. In other words, as Byron contemplates the ruins of the city, he rejects the earlier idea of the civilising power of Ottoman Islam and portrays the ruined city as a mirror to his own longings. It becomes a present symbol of potential Freedom and Liberty, the dream that "Greece might still be free". Byron seems to be evoking another lost paradise, one similar to that of ancient Greek heroes in *The Giaour*. The same theme of a contended and devastated Greece recurs in stanza IX of the *Siege* when Byron refers to Minotti's governorship of the Morea in a period "while yet the pitying eye of Peace / Smiled o'er her long-forgotten Greece" (*SoC*, 175-6). That is, Greece momentarily had, and yet could enjoy, "Peace" under a Christian ruler. She could be "freed from the unchristian yoke" (*SoC*, 178). A return of Greece to Christian control, Byron seems to suggest, would restore Peace, Liberty and Freedom. While the Ottoman yoke remains there can be no such Freedom. In effect, Byron projects here the dream that, in part, inspired his first visit to the East in 1809-1810 and the ideal of an heroic struggle for Greece's Freedom which, ultimately, was to lead to his untimely death at Messolonghi in 1824. But there remains a problem: Venice, like the Turk now, was an occupying power in Corinth in the eighteenth century. And, if *The Siege* forms part of the cycle of Oriental or Turkish Tales is it not strange that Minotti, the sworn enemy of Alp, Byron's "Oriental" hero, should become the central figure of an heroic final self-destructive stand the telling of which occupies the final six stanzas of the poem, roughly one fifth of the Tale itself? His Herostratic act, at the powerful climax of the poem relegates the story of the apparent hero, the "Adrian renegade", to what seems, in hindsight, a walk-on part. As Alp meets his arch-enemy face to face and he learns that Francesca has died the night before when she revealed herself to him as a spiritual presence on the shore in her attempt to save his Christian soul, he is shot by a hidden sniper and falls dead with no time to shrive nor make amends for his sins, "Without a hope for mercy's aid, – / To the last a Renegade" (*SoC*, 850-1). The attention now given in the poem to Minotti seems to shift the balance of sympathies across the Tale. And more. Byron deliberately alters the account of the siege he found in the *History of the Turks* which he quotes as a preface to the poem. The explosion of the magazine originally took place in the Ottoman camp and not in the fortress. This significant alteration of historical events enables Byron to give space to the Christian and Venetian governor and to depict him as a hero and martyr to his faith.

Let us consider how Byron's Christian allegiances are unconsciously revealed in the evocation of the final scene where Minotti stands "darkly, sternly, and all alone .../ o'er the altar stone" (*SoC*, 902-3), awaiting the onslaught of his Muslim enemies. First we notice the positive substantives: "heavenly hues", "eyes of light and looks of love" and the complicit and involving "our" of "our thoughts" (both reader and narrator), the traces which reveal Byron's unconscious allegiances and sympathies. Minotti is protected by the image of the Madonna and child, who fix "our thoughts on things divine" and smile "sweetly on each prayer/ To heaven" (*SoC*, 908-11). The Madonna smiles: "Still she smiles; even now she smiles" – even as the "Mussulman" comes in "slaughter" with "steel and flame" (*SoC*, 918). Byron seems to be enjoying the Ottoman onslaught at this point in the poem even though the sympathies suddenly shift in the description of Minotti's penultimate act, when seizing the torch, he makes "the sign of the cross with a sigh" (*SoC*, 916). And in the final immolation of Christian and Muslim alike, significantly as the enemy seize the consecrated chalice from the altar itself, the building erupts in a "wild roar" and the profaning Turks as well as the heroic Christians are blown into shattered pieces. Only the ravens, the dogs and the jackals profit. But Byron concludes by claiming a moral victory, that "Corinth was lost and won" (SoC, final line). Minotti has won a spiritual battle if not a physical one. In the final analysis Byron's underlying sympathies are clearly for the Venetian, the Greek and Christian cause despite the Ottoman success at reducing Corinth. After all, Byron tells us in stanza II, the city is surrounded by "the Infidel". The ruins stand, then, for Byron's longed for ideals: Freedom, Liberty and Peace in the lands of the Hellenes, and a Christian Hellenes at that.

For all this underlying, arguably unconscious, idealism and sympathy with what Corinth symbolises, Alp stands in stark contrast in his personal world view. Strikingly he is neither a Turk nor a Muslim. Rather, he is an "Adrian renegade", an epithet Byron repeats to make his point clear. He is also the commander in the Ottoman besieging army. Yet, in spite of his much-admired bravery before the enemy, his fairness in the division of the spoils of war, his skill in leadership, he does not belong to the armies of Islam and he is suspect: "he stood alone among the host... / But still his Christian origin / With them was little less than sin" (*SoC*, 251, 270-1). In effect, for all his talents, he remains an outsider, outside the Christian congregation of Venice and outside the faith of Islam. His troops feel mixed bewilderment and envy at the fame that he, a renegade Christian, has gained under Muslim banners; neither can they understand how his personal pride could allow such an alliance and service. What they do not know is his mysterious past: "They did not know how hate can burn / In hearts once changed from soft to stern; / Nor all the false and fatal zeal / The convert of revenge can feel" (*SoC*, 277-80). Alp, as with other protagonists of the Tales, is the perpetrator and, at the same moment, the victim of some unmentionable crime which has made him the enemy of his kith and kin and of the city of his birth, Venice, and of the Venetian citadel of Corinth. We find the now-familiar theme of a man who bears "the memory of a thousand wrongs". He is the apparent victim of "unnatural accusers", of a secret denunciation offered by the public box through which the Venetians could identify enemies of their state. Yet the charge against Alp is "a charge uneffaced". Arguably, Alp is to offer the germ of an idea which Byron is to elaborate later in the Venetian plays and in *Manfred* just as the spiritual presence of the beloved seems to prefigure the haunting presence of Astarte. Yet, since no details are provided of Alp's "crimes", as with other "Oriental" and later heroes, we are unable to assess, even less judge, his actions. His "crimes" remain a mystery, mere traces of Byron's own inner thoughts. They symbolise a metaphysical conundrum which Byron poses elsewhere: the question of "guilty without guilt" and, thus, the question of the workings of earthly and divine authority and justice. It is a theme which is to echo down the next two centuries in the work of Vigny, Espronceda, Dostoevsky, Kafka, Betti, Alberti, Malraux and Camus, among others. We can discover but one reason for his enmity against his erstwhile community but, again, it refers to an age before his "fall": a moment "in happier mood, and earlier time", when "unimpeached for traitorous crime" (*SoC*, 143-4). Again the familiar Byronic and negative and sceptical Romantic contrast of past illusion and present reality, of past happiness and present despair. And that moment of a "happier mood" was not so much the period of innocence and carefree humour before Alp's sinister, anonymous and clandestine denunciation, even betrayal, but the time "When Alp, beneath his Christian name,/ Her [Francesca's] virgin hand aspired to claim, / In happier mood, and earlier time, / While unimpeached for traitorous crime" (*SoC*, 140-4). This promised union is cruelly denied by her father, Minotti. Thus, when Lanciotto (aka Alp), consumed with the idea of revenge, sets sail into exile for infidel shores as a *condottiero,* Francesca visibly sinks into unhappiness and withdrawal from company. Like earlier female lovers, with the absence of love Francesca slowly fades away, even when taken to Corinth whence her father, Minotti, has been appointed governor by the

Council of Venice. Alp's response is vital action: the path of revenge through the military power of the Ottoman Porte. Renegade Christianity is joined with Islam in an unholy and purely personal alliance.

On the eve of the final assault on Corinth Alp, unlike his troops, cannot sleep. He is beset by thoughts which afflict other of Byron's early protagonists: "but within his soul / The thoughts like troubled waters roll. / He stood alone among the host" (*SoC*, 249-51). He suffers from an existential loneliness brought about by his unjustified sufferings. He gains no pleasure from his service to the Ottomans, he has no desire to "plant the Crescent o'er the Cross" (*SoC*, 253), nor to enter the *jihadun* paradise of *houris* and immortal love. He is alone not for his inability to embrace the faith of his paymasters, nor so much for his desire to be avenged through the campaign on the power of Venice which has unjustly cast him out. While he might exult in the promise of that revenge and the achievement of glory which the forthcoming onslaught will bring, his mood is, nevertheless, tempered by the vision of broken corpses under the walls devoured by dogs and carrion birds. In reality he is alone and distraught because of his separation from the object of his affections, Francesca, the daughter of Minotti, who, he believes, is within the citadel. As he stands in the moonlight beneath the walls in the silence of the night he turns – "is he sure of sight?" – and sees before him a female figure. "There sat a lady, youthful and bright" (*SoC*, 487), that trope of the visionary female form so common in Romantic literature – consider Shelley's *Alastor* or Espronceda's *El estudiante de Salamanca* – a figure who, for the moment, offers Alp the emotional and spiritual sustenance he needs. Yet she is hardly the Francesca of the Venetian interlude and of their early passion. She is drained of energy, of warmth, of animation, even of corporeal presence: "Once she raised her hand on high; / It was so wan and transparent of hue, / You might have seen the moon shine through" (*SoC*, 516-17). She is, in effect, a projection of Alp's imagination and of his inner conflicts as much as the still earth-bound spirit of the recently-dead (as we later learn) Francesca. Once more lovers meet for the last time never to meet again, a topos (even cliché) of sceptical Romantic writing and symptom of irrevocable loss, metaphysical anguish and the removal of the last remaining existential support. She speaks to Alp, not of love but of repentance (suggesting that she is used as a means to project Alp's inner conflicts between former faith and its moral codes and his sense of injury and consequent desire for revenge). In the end, for justice. The price of a return to his youthful love is a return to his former faith and a rejection of his service to Islam. "But dash that turban to earth, and sign / The sign of the cross, and for ever be mine. / Wring the black drop from thy heart, /

And to-morrow unites us no more to part" (*SoC*, 532-5). But Alp can only think of his revenge on his native city: "Of Venice; and her hated race / ... those / Who vice and envy made my foes" (*SoC*, 246-9). The death-in-life figure of Francesca offers Alp a stark choice: forgive and spare the city and the sons of Venice and gain her love and that of Heaven or forever lose all hope of salvation and redemption and emotional fulfilment. Alp, in his pride, his sense of an absolute right of justice, of a wrong which must be righted, cannot accept her pleas and promises even at the offered reward of restored love and divine forgiveness. And Byron emphasises the point here by italicising the "he"s; he underlines Alp's sense of wrong, of social (even political) injustice, even the cosmic injustice of a malign Providence. Byron's hero has passed the stage of believing in love as the final existential support which, when lost, precipitates despair and loss of faith in life. The final metaphysical absolute to which he now cleaves is his own "self" and in his sense of outrage at a scheme of things, secular and divine, which have led to his loss of love, his separation from the beloved and his home, his exile and of his being made to suffer the sense of being "guilty without guilt" for unspecified and unstated crimes. Alp can only now find purpose in vital action, in the assault on Corinth and an heroic death on the walls of the fortress. He does not fight for the Ottomans; he fights for himself and his personal grudge. He chooses to be in the front line of the conflict because he wants to be the architect of his final moments, not because he owes allegiance to any cause, nor because he might submit to earthly or divine laws. And so he dies by an anonymous hand in a confrontation with his sworn enemy, architect of all his misery. Neither party has the satisfaction of the other's death in a hand-to-hand struggle. Alp's death is sudden, unbidden, secretly executed, anonymously inflicted, mysterious: an enigma, inexplicable and senseless. What Byron would later term "the fatal truth" of a universe without meaning and purpose.

From the early heroes who place love at the centre of their existential view Alp marks a significant shift in direction and it is an aspect which Byron is to explore further in *Manfred* and *Cain*. The story of the siege of Corinth is, in reality, a pretext to explore the new theme of the existential rebel, the solitary individual who, unable to discover any faith or trust in human or divine ideals must stand alone rejecting any form of revealed existential support other than the "self" itself. Yet, at the end of this Tale Byron seems undecided between the new insight which Alp portrays and the heroic Christian example of self-sacrifice in the name of Christ and the Madonna which Minotti displays.

Manfred and *Cain*

In a sense, all these characters and attitudes or philosophical positions are a prelude to two of Byron's most compellingly negative visions. I speak of *Manfred* (1817) and *Cain* (1821). The common characteristics of the Tales – the mysterious origins, the lost love, the defiance of malevolent forces, the rejection of Christian faith in the debate with a divine or with Lucifer, all find their consummate expression in these two dramas. What these poems express is a set of psychological and existential symptoms that signify one specific reaction: retreat. Retreat from life, from reality, from a point of view or a set of tenets held in youth which, suddenly, have become untenable. They mark the presence of a much deeper malaise. They express a metaphysical viewpoint, one that perceives no abiding values, no system of absolute truths, be they orthodox or heterodox, that can sustain any set of comforting beliefs. Only love, in the Tales, offers any meaningful vital or emotional support and it is snatched away. Lovers part for the last time never to meet again, even in death. No amount of rationalisation or spiritual fortitude can remedy the loss. Byron's heroes have no roots, no real home, they are exiles in the communities in which they dwell; they are existential outsiders. They are of uncertain birth or have lost their parents and their patrimony for reasons which remain a mystery but which retain the sense of some terrible crime; they have no circle of friends, no society. The live in a vital aporia. They are metaphysical abstractions. Even their love is interiorised; they put on a dissembling face to the world. They are enigmas. "Behold –", writes Byron in *The Corsair*, "but who hath seen, or e'er shall see, / Man as himself – the secret spirit free?" (*Corsair*, 248).

Conclusion

And so to speculation. We have speculated on what constitutes the "secret spirit free". Now to speculation in its original sense of "mirroring": *speculum*. Even as early as 1831 in his review of Thomas Moore's *Life of Byron*, Macaulay noted the similarity of Byron the man and his literary heroes. "He was himself", he wrote in the *Edinburgh Review* in June 1831, "the beginning, the middle, and the end of all his own poetry, the hero of every tale, the chief object of every landscape." Fiona MacCarthy's recent biography[21] notes, as an insistent theme, Byron's capacity not only to affect the celebrated (and apparently devastating) pose and studied upward

---

21: Fiona MacCarthy, *Byron. Life and Legend*. London, John Murray, 2002.

look, a part of a personal masquerade he adopted in the salons of his society at home and abroad, but also the fact that, despite his denials, his work formed a mirror to his own intimate concerns and to the picture of himself he wished to present to the world. The autobiographical element in *Childe Harold's Pilgrimage* is clear enough, even down to the close physical resemblance of Byron author/narrator and the Childe himself as I have noted. Large parts, especially the English section, of *Don Juan*, are specifically based on Byron's own experiences and mirror his view of himself as he had been (or imagined he had been), and reflect his own views and soured prejudices of his homeland and the English aristocracy. In *The Corsair* we find one of the nearest physical self-portraits of the entire works. In Canto I, stanzas ix-xxii, his hero's "dark eyebrow shades a glance of fire". His physique is "Robust but not Herculean – [...] forehead high and pale / The sable curls in wide profusion veil" (*Corsair*, 197 ... 204). And so on. The description tallies closely with the iconic representation of the poet cultivated for his public and the many portraits and engravings he permitted for publication, especially the two portraits (one in Albanian costume) by Phillips and the stylised leaning portrait of Westall. Even the admission that Conrad "knew himself a villain, but he deem'd / The rest no better than the thing he seem'd; / And scorned the best as hypocrites who hid / Those deeds which bolder spirits plainly did" (*Corsair*, 265-8) chimes with Byron's attitude to his fellow Englishmen in the early period of his exile. Conrad's rejection of social etiquettes and the hypocrisies of social intercourse, his ability to dissemble and bear adversities with a smile again rhyme with what we know of the poet himself. It is Alp, especially, who so violently rejects his homeland, its injustices and its hypocrisy, and who feels betrayed and isolated, who rejects love and seeks only revenge, who best chimes with Byron's mood at the time of the poem's composition. Byron, like his protagonists, is a man divided in himself. It is clear from Byron's letters and journals that the poet was far from the image the portraits suggest. Indeed, Byron was bedevilled with self doubt, with inner conflict, with the effects of his many affairs with younger and older women (especially the scandalous affair with Lady Caroline Lamb), with financial insecurity, with secret male affairs, immersed in the "morass" he mentions in his journals. The hinted incestuous love between Selim and Zuleika (happily untrue) may also be an unconscious *lapsus calami* that refers to his own relationship with Augusta. Byron's emotional life, like his heroes, is fraught with danger and problems. And the Tales were conceived and composed in this period. The disastrous marriage (which Byron never really desired) with Annabella Milbanke, which lasted less than a year and a half, may well have resulted in the desire for an escape into an exotic and distant world where the normal laws of conduct no longer obtain and where love becomes an emotional abstraction and a metaphysical abstraction, an escape from the realities of life in England. The only real and sensible escape was to leave England but, significantly, not for the Orient.

Thus, Byron's heroes are, like their creator, rootless, exiles, outsiders. The personae and the outlook they express, of which Byron is the supreme creator, was to capture the imagination of Romantic Europe and to be taken up, imitated and re-worked by his many admirers. This, of course, forms yet another hall of mirrors with Byronic images reflected and distorted across authors, translations, versions and countries in Europe as my recent edited study demonstrates.[22]

We must return, then, to the question of Byron's Orientalism. Does Byron "appropriate" the Orient as a Western hegemonist? Does he, as Said argues, "prefer instead to create a space of representation in which the Orient is incorporated into Western hegemonic aspirations"? (Said, 1991: 22). Certainly Byron's vision is not guided by the Orient, despite his admiration for Ottoman achievements. At the same time I can find no appropriation of the Orient either in the narrative or in characterisation. His heroes and the lives Byron recounts belong to the tradition of the medieval romance and of Walter Scott (which Byron knew well) rather than that of Turkish Tales. They are European in essence and, of course, entirely Byronic. The Orient, I suggest, was a convenient "Other" to frame the mirrors he creates to himself and make them more exotic, more theatrical, more saleable given the fame of *Childe Harold's Pilgrimage* (Cantos I and II) and the growing vogue for things Oriental of the period. The Orient is not "appropriated in a space of representation". For all the detailed notes to the text and the careful research that informs them, his heroes do not think or behave in an "Oriental" or "Islamic" way. Byron had seen enough of human cruelty in Spain and Portugal to know of man's depravity and cruelty without recourse to images or clichés of a supposed Ottoman savagery. For all the so-called Oriental wild extremes in the Tales, (readily found in many a European novel of the period), his heroes all share a common sense of justice that should belong to all men, a feeling for individual liberty rather than any sense if mindless cruelty and fanaticism, one of the many archetypal images of the Oriental temperament. To be a Muslim means that you accept the behest of Allah: "Inshallah". You accept Islam which means "acceptance" or "submission". You fight for Allah and the one true faith as revealed by God's last

22: See Richard A. Cardwell (ed.), *The Reception of Byron in Europe*, 2 vols, London-New York, Thoemmes-Continuum, 2005.

prophet, Muhammed, against those that would deny that Muhammed was the final messenger: *ashedu an la illa rasulu Allah.* The true Muslim is a *mujeheddin*, a fighter for a holy war, *jihad*. Byron, who had read and admired the Qu'ran, knew that. While it also true that he understood that the Ottoman rulers were also decisive politicians, even to the fact that the incoming ruler would often begin his reign with the murder of his siblings to ensure his throne, none of his so-called Oriental heroes expresses sentiments that smack of Islam or of the injunctions of the Qu'ran. His heroes desire a personal freedom freed from the shackles of convention. They desire to right personal wrongs, to redress injustices practised upon themselves rather than others. They desire to express a sense of personal justice freed from creeds and rulers. It is the spirit of the French Revolution rather than of Islam which underlies their mindsets. At the same time they also threaten that revolutionary, collective and libertarian spirit of popular protest against injustice. Rather they protest and rage mentally and physically against insult upon their personal sense of justice, against personal insult, against personal deprivation of honour, home, the beloved. They do not work for the collective but for themselves. They strive to restore what has been lost: birthright, status, name, freedom, love. In the case of Conrad it is hard to understand why he wages his war against Seyd; he seems to act for the sake of acting. His struggle would appear to be a vitalist action for its own sake, as a therapy for the tedium of life. Better the adrenalin of danger and the threat of death than the threat of internalised melancholy and *ataraxia*. Their longings coincide with those of their creator: abstract notions of longed for personal absolutes of justice, liberty and love. They are mirrors to their creator's personal concerns.

I find no "violations" or "falsifications" or "domestication" of the Orient in Byron's work. Rather, I suggest, the Orient served as a convenient (if recently experienced and vividly recollected), theatrical backdrop or screen or mirror on to which he projected his injured personal feelings and his maturing vision that revealed a world of cosmic injustice, a world bereft of any abiding value, emotional, spiritual or rational, the very vision he was soon, in Venice, to outline in one of his finest and bleakest poems, *Manfred.*

THOMAS MOORE'S ORIENTALISM

ALLAN GREGORY

Francis Jeffrey, in the *Edinburgh Review* of November, 1817, was lavish in his praise for Thomas Moore's *Lalla Rookh*:

> There is a great deal of our recent poetry derived from the East: But this is the finest orientalism we have had yet ... The beauteous forms, the dazzling splendours, the breathing odours of the East, seem at last to have found a kindred poet in that Green Isle of the West ... It is amazing, indeed, how much at home Mr. Moore seems to be in India, Persia, and Arabia; and how purely and strictly Asiatic all the colouring and imagery of his book appears.[1]

This was a glowing review from the so-called "self-constituted judge of poesy," and in sharp contrast to the same editor's review, in July, 1806, of Moore's *Epistles, Odes and Other Poems,* when the entire publication was given over to a rising torrent of invective. Longman's paid Moore the enormous sum of £3,000 for *Lalla Rookh*. Having read Jeffrey's review, one could be forgiven for thinking that Moore, in his extensive research, also discovered the ubiquitous oriental expectation of "baksheesh".

Academically, Moore was no stranger to the Orient. In his final year at Trinity College, Dublin, he worked on his translations from the Greek of the *Odes of Anacreon,* and was encouraged by the Provost to complete the task. These were published in 1800, with a dedication to the Prince Regent.

The first edition of *Irish Melodies* was published in April 1808 in two volumes. Their success was immediate, and despite the underlying intimations of Irish nationalism, the melodies were whistled and sung across the British Isles and beyond. "Melody Moore" had arrived.

But Moore was not content to rest on his laurels and be remembered only for his lyrics. Determined to jump on the oriental band-wagon, he wrote to Mary Godfrey on September 11th 1811:

1: *Edinburgh Review*, November 1817, p.1.

> I shall now take to my poem, and do something, I hope, that will place
> me above the vulgar herd both of wordlings and of critics; but you shall
> hear from me again, when I get among the maids of Cashmere, the
> sparkling springs of Rochabad, and the fragrant banquets of the Peris.[2]

The work he was referring to, of course, was *Lalla Rookh*. Moore had
the reputation of being a slow, fastidious writer; and in this case he was
nervously aware he was not writing out of experience of Eastern manners
or scenery, but from an idea of the Orient delved out of countless books;
an exercise that would prove fatal to the poem's vitality and realism. The
first draft shows he began writing on November 11th 1811.

On August 28th 1813, three months after Byron's success with his
first oriental poem, *The Giaour*, he encouraged Moore to proceed with his
plans for a work in similar mode.

> Stick to the East; – the oracle, [Madame de] Stael, told me it was the
> only poetical policy. The North, South and West, have all been
> exhausted; but from the East we have nothing but S[outhey]'s
> unsaleables …The little I have done in that way is merely a "voice in the
> wilderness" for you; and, if it has had any success, that also will prove
> that the public are orientalizing, and pave the path for you.[3]

Moore knew that his oriental poem, when it appeared, would
inevitably be compared to Byron's. Byron, "the oriental poet," became a
palpable presence to Moore during the years up to 1817, when *Lalla
Rookh* would finally appear in print. Byron published *The Bride of
Abydos*, which he wrote in one week, and the *Corsair*, which he wrote in
ten days. With each new appearance of Byron's oriental tales, Moore felt
more dejected and fearful for the prospects of his own poem. Amazed at
Byron's rapidity of composition and frustrated by his own lack of
progress, he found it increasingly difficult to concentrate on the work in
hand. Byron was conscious of this and so dedicated the *Corsair* to his
friend:

> … I trust truly, that you are engaged in the composition of a poem
> whose scene will be laid in the East; none can do those scenes so much
> justice. The wrongs of your own country, the magnificent and fiery
> spirit of her sons, the beauty and feeling of her daughters, may there be
> found; …Your imagination will create a warmer sun, and less clouded
> sky; but wildness, tenderness and originality, are part of your national

---

2: Moore Letters, I, 160.
3: BLJ III, 101.

claim of oriental descent, to which you have already thus far proved your title more clearly than the most zealous of your country's antiquarians.[4]

There is no doubt this dedication encouraged Moore greatly; he was ashamedly self-conscious of his lack of personal experience in Eastern culture; Byron made him consider his own cultural background and how the religious and political problems facing his own countrymen could be incorporated into his bookish orientalism.

***

Lalla Rookh, an Oriental Romance was finally published on the May 22nd 1817, six years after it was begun. In its final form it consisted of a prose narrative linking four poems: *The Veiled prophet of Khorassan, Paradise and the Peri, The Fire-Worshippers*, and *The Light of the Haram*. The linking narrative tells of the journey from Delhi to Cashmere of Lalla Rookh, daughter of the Emperor of Bucharia, who is being taken in ceremonial procession to marry the newly-ascended young emperor of Persia, whom she has never seen. On the way, she and her train are diverted by four verse tales told by Feramorz, a young Cashmere poet, with whom she falls in love and who turns out to be her intended husband. The "critical and fastidious" eunuch Fadladeen, chamberlain of the harem, also accompanies Lalla Rookh and, since he is ignorant of Feramorz's true identity, severely criticizes each of Feramorz's tales in the style of the afore-mentioned Francis Jeffrey of the *Edinburgh Review*. This was Moore's way of anticipating and simultaneously dismissing criticism of *Lalla Rookh*.

The *Veiled Prophet of Khorassan* and *The Fire-Worshippers* are protracted, bloody and tragic poems and are closest to Byronic mode in subject, tone and versification. Both poems have violent revolution as their main theme and both are, at least partly, intended as political allegories. *The Veiled Prophet* concerns itself with the French Revolution while *The Fire-Worshippers* is based on the struggles of Ireland against British Colonialism, especially with regard to the unsuccessful Irish uprising of 1798, and its disastrous aftermath. Both poems exhibit how Moore is able to use Islamic material to define and express his views. The text is littered with copious notes, explanations and extracts from numerous works as diverse as D'Herbelot, Gibbon, Knolles' *History of the Turks*, the translations of Sir William Jones, Pitts's *Account of the Mahometans*,

---

4: CPW III, 148-9.

Sale's Koran ... the list goes on and on, indicating the extent of Moore's exhaustive research.

The "veiled prophet" of the title is Hakim Ibn Hisham, known in Islamic history by the name of "Al Mokanna" of Khorassan, from a veil he wore ("mokanna" in Arabic meaning "veiled"). This veil, which masks his hideous repulsiveness, is required to protect his subjects from the dazzling brilliance of his countenance. He represents for Moore the power of despotism, which in Mokanna's case depends on systematic mystification for its effects. Like all despots, he possesses an air of supreme authority. This is how Moore presents him at the beginning of the poem:

> There on that throne, to which the blind belief
> Of millions rais'd him, sat the Prophet-Chief,
> The Great MOKANNA. O'er his features hung
> The Veil, the Silver Veil, which he had flung
> In mercy there, to hide from mortal sight
> His dazzling brow, till man could bear its light.[5]

But, as the poem develops, this dramatic portrait of Mokanna is revealed by Moore as merely a disguise hiding a monstrous reality:

> Upon that mocking Fiend, whose Veil, now rais'd,
> Show'd them, as in death's agony they gazed,
> Not the long promis'd light, the brow, whose beaming
> Was to come forth, all conquering, all redeeming,
> But features horribler than Hell e'er trac'd
> On its own brood; – no Demon of the Waste,
> No church-yard Ghole, caught lingering in the light
> Of the blest sun, e'er blasted human sight
> With lineaments so foul, so fierce as those
> The Impostor now, in grinning mockery, shows ...[6]

Mokanna's character, as interpreted in his chilling and ferocious speeches about the folly of mankind, is akin to the cynicism and misanthropy of a Byronic antihero. He mirrors Milton's Satan, as, although venomous, he is portrayed as audacious, defiant and supreme exploiter of the evils of humanity. Mohammed Sharafuddin in *Islam and Romantic Orientalism* notes that Moore's depiction of Mokanna "has several levels, from the moral to the political, from the psychological to the religious. These strata are not conducive to simplicity and directness of

5: LR pp.9-10.
6: LR p.114.

judgement."[7] He writes that in this tale Moore attempts to put the emphasis on the tyrant, whereas, in *The Fire-Worshippers*, the emphasis is on the tyrannized. While many commentators, including Sharafuddin, have insisted that Mokanna represents the figure of Napoleon, this interpretation is at best ambiguous, given that Moore, like Byron, was an ardent admirer of Napoleon. Moore's continuing admiration for Bonaparte overflowed into his *Fudge Family in Paris* which he published in 1818, the year after *Lalla Rookh*. Jeffrey Vail, however, in *The Literary Relationship of Lord Byron and Thomas Moore,* suggests that "Mokanna's crusade certainly represents an incarnation of the revolutionary French cause, but Mokanna himself is fundamentally motivated by hatred for mankind ..."[8] a form of evil that Moore would no more attribute to Napoleon than would Byron. Mokanna, according to Vail, "is more accurately seen as a personification of the most radical form of uprooting, demagogic Jacobinism, beautiful in theory but secretly animated by greed, lust, and the desire for vengeance."[9] Greed, lust, the desire for vengeance – somehow these words and phrases are so "out-of-character" with Moore, that one could be reading Milton, Blake, or indeed Byron himself.

The story of *The Veiled Prophet* is simple. Mokanna's success in his rebellion against the Islamic state of the Calif Al Mahdi results in a following which includes many young people who are attracted by his slogan "Freedom for the World". Azim, a Muslim officer, together with his beloved Zelica, join Mokanna's revolution only to discover that Mokanna has been using his rebellion to fortify a perverted lust for power and domination. The innocent, pious Zelica, having been appointed "Priestess of the Faith," has signed a contract to become Mokanna's bride in hope of a place in paradise. Azim is unable to convince her to flee with him from Mokanna's influence. In despair, he joins the army of the Calif Al Mahdi in an effort to overthrow Mokanna. At the end of a fierce battle, the defeated Mokanna flees to his palace in Neksheb, where he jumps into a bath of liquid fire. Azim breaks into the palace where he is met by a figure wearing Mokanna's veil. The figure throws itself onto his lance, and reveals itself to be his beloved Zelica. Azim spends the rest of his life in prayer at Zelica's grave, where eventually he is blessed by a vision in which angels tell him God has forgiven her.

Moore's acutely imaginative commitment to his orientalism results in a story full of ambiguities. His interest in oriental revolt and tyranny for its own sake safeguards him from European analogues such as the

---

7: Sharafuddin pp.140-1.
8: Vail p.121.
9: Vail p.121.

Napoleonic conquests and the French Revolution. Sharafuddin suggests that these ambiguities allowed Moore to "define a nuanced and subtle judgement, relatively free from the political prejudices of his readers or the political pressure of recent events".[10] However, the influences on Moore are many and varied. Voltaire, for example, can be detected here. Particularly the Voltaire of the play *Mahomet*, where he uses the character of the Muslim prophet to satirize religious fanaticism as a form of tyranny, showing how the emotional devotion of the prophet's followers could be misused for personal despotism. If Voltaire's Mahomet was a religious imposter, Moore goes further in portraying Mokanna in a double role – as false prophet and political dictator; the first role representing the religious and emotional side of tyranny and the second, the political and materialistic side. In both cases, the figures of Napoleon and George III come to mind, the latter being considered a tyrant to Ireland in his repression of Moore's countrymen, and particularly his stance on Catholic Emancipation. This is Moore's link between political and religious despotism.

Certain instances here mirror moments from Byron's tales. For example, Azim's reunion with his beloved begins with a mournful four-quatrain song sung by Zelica; in Byron's *Corsair* Medora sings a similarly sad four-quatrain song at the beginning of her reunion with Conrad. Zelica's grief over the loss of Azim and over her own sexual degradation drives her to a state of Ophelia-like insanity similar to that of the heroine in *Parisina,* who goes mad because of her incest and the death of her lover Hugo.

Moore's poem finishes with a coda in which the aged Azim is praying for the rest of his life over Zelica's grave; similarly, *The Giaour* concludes with its repentant hero spending the rest of his days pining over the dead Leila.

In the *Veiled Prophet of Khorassan* Moore explores the nature and origin of Mokanna's tyranny. In *The Fire-Worshippers,* the tyrant conqueror is scarcely mentioned directly; the force of his influence being portrayed on the reaction of the people he persecutes. In other words, the *Veiled Prophet* deals with the causes while *The Fire-Worshippers* deals with the effects. The story of *The Fire-Worshippers* is set in Persia, or Iran, in the seventh century, when that country was overwhelmed by the Arabs. Iran is ruthlessly dominated by the Emir Al Hassan, who has a beautiful daughter named Hinda. The Iranian resistance is led by a passionately idealistic young man called Hafed. While on a mission to

---

10: Sharafuddin pp.141-2.

assassinate the Muslim Emir, Hafed encounters Hinda and they fall in love, their love surviving the disclosure of each other's identity. Hafed's mountain retreat is betrayed to the Arabs by a treacherous member of the Persian guerillas; the Emir, in preparation for a final onslaught on the mountain retreat, sends Hinda back to Arabia by sea. Her ship is captured by Hafed, who takes her to his fortress, where she warns him of the impending attack and pleads for him to abandon his mission of madness and flee with her to safety. Hafed refuses, sending her back to her homeland so that he may seek martyrdom in a final battle for freedom. When Hafed's band is overwhelmed and massacred, he immolates himself on a funeral pyre, while Hinda, witnessing his death from her ship, in turn, casts herself into the sea.

Thus Al Hassan is the all-conquering, quintessential political and military colonialist. His actions produce a dark, sinister form of tyranny in which an entire nation is condemned to suffering and degradation. Moore's advocacy of the rights of the Persians against the colonizing Moslems is an allegorical defense of the Irish Catholics against the colonizing English. As Jeffrey Vail points out, "If Byron had good reasons for writing oriental tales that problematized colonialism, Moore had still better: Moore was an actual member of a people who had been colonized by the British, and whose religion had been proclaimed by the state to be barbaric and fraudulent. There are no Christians in Moore's two Byronian tales, but by strong and unmistakable implication, establishment Christianity, the state power it upholds, and the colonizing ideology it legitimizes are all criticized and finally condemned."[11]

Moore had befriended Robert Emmett at Trinity College, Dublin, and refused to collaborate in an enquiry which resulted in Emmett being expelled on suspicion of subversive activities. Following the United Irishmen's unsuccessful insurrection of 1798, Emmett went to France hoping to gain French assistance for a plan which included the seizure of Dublin Castle and other strategic targets, to be followed by what he hoped would be a largely spontaneous popular uprising. The planned insurrection, spearheaded on July 23rd 1802, was a disaster, resulting in the deaths of about fifty men, including Lord Kilwarden, the popular Lord Chief Justice, who was piked to death with his nephew when his coach was surrounded by insurgents. As his plans unravelled, Emmet went on the run to the Wicklow mountains, but remained close to the city because of his protective anxiety for his lover, Sarah Curran, daughter of the Whig M.P. and Master of the Rolls, John Philpot Curran. For the Romantic

11: Vail p.130.

poets, Emmet achieved heroic definition, not only by the tragic consequences of his failed conspiracy, but by his speech from the dock, which has become a classic in Irish nationalist literature. Although he defended his involvement and motives, he spoke in full and clear knowledge of his fate. The next day he was hanged and then beheaded; his head was exhibited on a stockade in Thomas Street near to where Lord Kilwarden and his nephew had been piked to death. Emmet achieved his martyrdom. His place of burial and the whereabouts of his body remain uncertain to this day.

These events touched Moore deeply. While he did not involve himself in Irish politics, his patriotic convictions were never in doubt, and he continually expressed his feelings in the best way he knew how – his melodies and poetry. Of Robert Emmet he writes:

> Oh breathe not his name, let it sleep in the shade,
> Where cold and unhonour'd his relics are laid;
> Sad, silent and dark, be the tears that we shed,
> As the night-dew that falls on the grass o'er his head.[12]

Of Hafed's renown in *The Fire-Worshippers*, Moore writes:

> Such were the tales, that won belief,
>   And such the colouring fancy gave
> To a young, warm and dauntless Chief, –
>   One who, no more than mortal brave,
> Fought for the land his soul ador'd,
>   For happy homes and altars free,
> His only talisman, the sword, –
>   His only spell-word, Liberty![13]

And on Sarah Curran, who was forced into exile:

> She is far from the land where her young hero sleeps,
>   And lovers are round her, sighing:
> But coldly she turns from their gaze, and weeps,
>   For her heart in his grave is lying.[14]

And on Hinda:

12: Moore Works p.144.
13: LR p.206.
14: Moore Works p.155.

And still she goes, at midnight hour,
To weep alone in that high bower,
And watch, and look upon the deep
For him whose smiles first made her weep; –
But watching, weeping, all was vain,
She never saw his bark again.[15]

This is not great poetry but it does show how much Moore was more "at home" with his melodies, than with his oriental poems. However, the comparisons are clear. In the notes to the first edition of *Lalla Rookh*, Moore hinted at his analogy when he wrote: "Voltaire tells us in his Tragedy "Les Guebres", he was generally supposed to have alluded to the Jansenists. I should not be surprised if this story of *The Fire-Worshippers* were found capable of a similar doubleness of application".[16] And so Moore gave us *Ali Baba and the Forty Thieves* on the one hand and *Robert Emmet and the United Irishmen* on the other.

Paradise and the Peri and *The Light of the Harem* are much shorter and lighter in tone and allow Moore exhibit his outstanding lyrical talents for which he was renowned. By balancing two tales of revolution and bloodshed with two tales of love and devotion, he was trying to please everyone.

Lalla Rookh was a bestseller when published in 1817, requiring a second edition within three days and a sixth by the end of the year. Longman's never regretted a penny of the £3,000 paid to Moore, and immediately recognized the poem's illustrative potential inspiring the romantic imaginations of artists, dramatists and composers alike with its combination of drama, poetry, romance, pathos, fantasy, horror and exoticism. Praise was lavish. Jeffrey referred to Moore as "The Rising of a sun which will never set".[17] The work was translated into several languages, including Persian, and was famously referred to as a miniature *Arabian Knights*, a comparison which prompted Henry Luttrell, the elected wit of Holland House, to write:

I'm told, dear Moore, your lays are sung.
(Can it be true, you lucky man?)
By moonlight in the Persian tongue,
Along the streets of Ispahan.[18]

15: LR p.218.
16: LR p.384.
17: White, Terence de Vere, *Thomas Moore The Irish Poet* (Hamish Hamilton 1977), p.131.
18: Quoted ibid, p.131.

Today, *Lalla Rookh* is forgotten. Parts of the poem can be fairly described as turgid reading. One of Moore's recent biographers, Terence De Vere White, even goes so far as to describe the work as "almost unreadable".[19]

Moore, however, accepted praise and criticism alike; his self-appraisal was always cool and well judged. On November 23rd 1837, twenty years after the publication of *Lalla Rookh*, he wrote to Thomas Longman, anticipating the verdict of posterity:

> "Dear Tom,
> With respect to what you say about 'Lalla Rookh' being 'the cream of the copyrights,' perhaps it may in a *property* sense; but I am strongly inclined to think that, in a race into future times (if anything of mine could pretend to such a run), those little ponies, the 'Melodies,' will beat the mare, Lalla, hollow."[20]

Trust an Irishman to indulge his analogy in horses.

***

Imagine, though, Moore's reaction when he learned that *The Bride of Abydos – A Romantic Drama in Three Acts*, adapted by William Dimond, would be staged at Drury Lane Theatre, with Edmund Kean playing Selim.

Byron's reaction to reading *Lalla Rookh* is dealt with by Peter Cochran in his introduction to this volume.

Byron, to his credit, continued to encourage Moore. In Moore's letter to Samuel Rogers on October 29th 1814, revealing the extent of his insecurity about *Lalla Rookh*, he states that the work was now destined to be a group of four tales rather than one extensive narrative. By March 1817, Murray mentioned to Byron that Moore had decided on *Lalla Rookh* as a title. Byron wrote to Moore:

> I am glad of it, – first that we are to have it at last, and next, I like a tough title myself – witness the Giaour and Childe Harold, which choked half the Blues at starting ... I wish you had not called it a "Persian Tale". I am very sorry I called some of my own things "Tales", because I think they are something better. Besides, we have had Arabian, and Hindoo, and Turkish, and Assyrian Tales. ...Really I want

---

19: Quoted ibid, p.131.
20: Moore Letters, II, 821.

you to make a great hit, if only out of self-love, because we happen to be old cronies…[21]

In Moore's case, Byron never allowed his critical doubts to outweigh his social loyalty.

21: BLJ V 186-87.

EDWARD SAID'S FAILURE
WITH (*INTER ALIA*) BYRON

PETER COCHRAN

[Quotations from *Orientalism* ("O."), are from the Penguin edition, 1991; from *Culture and Imperialism*, ("C."), the Vintage edition, 1993.]

> In 1998, to mark the 20th anniversary of the publication of *Orientalism*, the Middle East Studies Association (MESA) invited Said to address a plenary panel at its annual conference. As Said ascended the dais, his admirers leaped to their feet in an enthusiastic ovation. Then, somewhat hesitantly at first, the rest of the audience stood and began to applaud. Fixed in my seat, I surveyed the ballroom, watching scholars whom I had heard privately damn *Orientalism* for its libel against their field now rising sheepishly and casting sideways glances to see who might behold their gesture of submission.[1]

The theme of our conference is "Byron, the Orient, and Orientalism"; and it's on the most famous writer on those last two things – Edward Said – that I wish to concentrate. Said has come in for much criticism: Mohammed Sharafuddin writes of the way in which his approach

> ... suffers from a disease not unlike the one it seeks to diagnose, which may be called 'anti-Orientalism'. For Said the West is so systematically prejudiced that it distorts everything ... [Said] has cast the shadow of his own skepticism, both political and spiritual, over the possibility that some conscientious and high-minded writers may be born out of a society that has been defined as imperial.[2]

Nigel Leask writes that although

1: Martin Kramer, review of Robert Irwin's *Dangerous Knowledge*, *Commentary*, March 2007; from <<<http://www.campus-watch.org/article/id/3082>>>.
2: Sharafuddin, pp.xvi-xvii and ix.

Said is right in asserting the links between knowledge of the East ... and the history of colonial power, he is wrong in denominating it 'a closed system' ... the internal and external pressures determining and undermining such representations [of the East] are more various than Said's thesis will allow.[3]

Despite such statements, Said's name and views remain highly respected (especially now he's dead), in a way which I feel he doesn't deserve, and I think they still need countering. A noted critic said he thought our theme smacked of "yesterday's breakfast"; although I think I know what he meant in literary / critical terms, given what the West – especially the U.S.A – is still doing to countries who haven't succumbed to its blandishments, I feel that, in terms of current politics, today's breakfast is the same as yesterday's. We need to change the menu.

***

Referring to the French Oriental scholar Silvestre de Sacy, Edward Said writes

> The effect of Sacy's tone is to form a circle sealing off him and his audience from the world at large, the way a teacher and his pupils together in a closed classroom also form a sealed space. (O.125)

I know nothing of Sacy other than what Said writes, and thus can't tell if this strange definition of class-work is one with which Sacy would agree. It *is* the effect of reading Said's books – the teacher must only allow so much of the world to impinge as suits his agenda. For preference, he must exclude the world altogether – it's a form of paranoia.

Eventually you see what Said's doing – *Orientalism* is self-reflexive. He's talking about himself. When he writes of Ernest Renan that he ...

> ... set up a complex affiliation between Orientalism and its putative subject matter that is based finally on power and not really on disinterested objectivity. (O.148)

... you can only protest, "No – that's what you, Said, want to do! For all your gestures towards balance, you are a slave to your own polemic, and mustn't let too much reality intrude, or you know your game will be spoiled."

3: Leask, p.2.

This glum thought – that in describing the thing he despises (a reductivist Orientalism), Said describes himself – occurs throughout a reading of his book. The thought is reinforced when reading the introduction to his other work, *Culture and Imperialism* (1993). Here he counters one group of Western works – Conrad's novel *Nostromo*, and the very different movies *Salvador* (Oliver Stone), *Apocalypse Now* (Francis Ford Coppola), and *Missing* (Costa-Gavras) with one of his characteristic lists:

> … whereas Conrad wrote *Nostromo* during a period of Europe's largely uncontested imperialist enthusiasm, contemporary novelists and film-makers who have learned his ironies so well have done their work *after* decolonization, *after* the massive intellectual, moral and imaginative overhaul and deconstruction of Western representation of the non-Western world, *after* the work of Frantz Fanon, Amilcar Cabral, C.L.R.James, Walter Rodney, after the novels and plays of Chinua Achebe, Ngugi wa Thiongo, Wole Soyinka, Salman Rushdie, Gabriel García Márquez, and many others. (C.xxii)

His intention here is to put all his eggs into one basket and make a very large omelette in it with them. No writer or film-maker will survive being put in an Edward Said list with their individuality intact. Such big gestures are those of a critic who doesn't want his subjects to have any existence outside his own books. They must obey his listings – again, paranoia.

***

I find no evidence in *Orientalism* that Edward Said has read any Byron. He knows that Byron was an important "Orientalist" writer, who must be mentioned in a work of such ambition as his, so he mentions him – in lists, like the following:

> … William Beckford, Byron, Goethe, and Hugo restructured the Orient by their art and made its colors, lights and people visible through their images, rhythms and motifs. At most, the "real" Orient provoked a writer to his vision; it very rarely guided it. (O.22)

This is to undercut your own best points and to split hairs. Said wants to dislike the four writers, but knows he can't if he's to be a conscientious critic. What's the difference between being "provoked" into creativity by an environment, and being "guided" by it? Don't provocation and guidance go hand in hand in such circumstances? "… very rarely guided it" is in any case a gap through which several coaches and fours might be driven. There are huge distinctions to be made between Beckford, Goethe, and Hugo on the one hand – none of them travelled in the Orient – and Byron on the other. He did. It's like putting Stone, Coppola, and Costa-Gavras in the same sentence.

Consider the following (it is the next reference to Byron in the book):

> The choice of "Oriental" was canonical; it had been employed by Chaucer and Mandeville, by Shakespeare, Dryden, Pope, and Byron (O.31).

The word "oriental" occurs nowhere in Shakespeare.

Similar lists, all including Byron, so wide-ranging as to be meaningless, and the massive generalizations that Said wants to think they enable him to make, occur on pages 99, 101, 118, 167, and 192 of the Penguin edition. In fact, Said only ever includes Byron as one item in a list. He never mentions him as an individual writer, and only refers to one work – *The Giaour*, which he shows no sign of having read. Actually he calls it 'the "Giaour"'.

Said is addicted to lists. Lists at once hypnotise and threaten. Rarely does a page of *Orientalism* go by without at least three of them. Here is a paragraph, not from *Orientalism*, but from Said's *Orientalism 25 Years Later*, published in 2003:

> As a humanist whose field is literature, I am old enough to have been trained forty years ago in the field of comparative literature, whose leading ideas go back to Germany in the late eighteenth and early nineteenth centuries [*AS THOUGH THAT WERE A RECOMMENDATION!*]. Before that I must mention the supremely creative contribution of Giambattista Vico, the Neopolitan [*sic*] philosopher and philologist whose ideas anticipate those of German thinkers such as Herder and Wolf, later to be followed by Goethe, Humboldt, Dilthey, Nietzsche, Gadamer, and finally the great 20th Century Romance philologists Erich Auerbach, Leo Spitzer, and Ernst Robert Curtius. (http://www.counterpunch.org/said08052003.html)

It's either hopelessly pseud, or the transparent tactic of an intellectual bully, or both. Lists are also uncheckable. Who will muster the nerve, and have the time, to take such assertions as this to pieces, and make all the necessary distinctions they invite, even though they must be made, since Said fails to make them? Such an apparently distinguished group of models and teachers (Said is very keen on "method" and "training" – O.326-7) should have taught Said that to ignore a major writer such as Byron – whom it's clear he knows in outline, as is the case with several others – will blow his thesis apart and lay him wide open to the charge of bad faith. Said pretends to acknowledge the difficulty (at least I think he does):

> How then to recognize individuality and to reconcile it with its intelligent, and by no means passive or merely dictatorial, general and hegemonic context? (O.9)

But individuality is not what Said is interested in. The promise in this last quotation (insofar as one can be understood) is not honoured.

Said concedes that there would be an alternative way of conducting his investigation:

> Perhaps the most important task of all would be to undertake studies in contemporary alternatives to Orientalism, to ask how one can study other cultures and peoples from a libertarian, or a nonrepressive and nonmanipulative, perspective. But then one would have to rethink the whole complex problem of knowledge and power. These are all tasks left embarrassingly incomplete in this study (O.24).

His embarrassment, however, doesn't prevent him from writing the study in the way he's preconceived it. He sees much good in the work of many European writers and artists who dealt with the Orient. He seems a great admirer of Richard Burton, for instance, of I.A.Richards, and of the "towering Orientalist scholars" Louis Massignon and Sir Hamilton Gibb (O.195-6, 254, 255-6, and 258). And take George Sale's eighteenth-century translation of the Qu'ran. Said writes of his approach:

> Unlike his predecessors, Sale tried to deal with history in terms of Arab sources; moreover, he let Muslim commentators on the sacred text speak for themselves (O.117).

But instead of focusing on this unprejudiced, non-Christian-imperialist way of treating things eastern, he lets it go by without further comment. No new perspective must cloud his central assertion (contradicted by much that he writes), which is that "... every European, in what he could say about the Orient, was ... a racist, an imperialist, and almost totally ethnocentric" (O.204). Even Massignon and Gibb are brushed aside finally: in them, he writes, things Oriental "... have been subordinated ... to the linear prose authority of discursive analysis" (O.284) – oblivious to the fact that that's the medium in which his book is written, too.

What should be a balanced dialectic is in his hands an irresponsible polemic which ignores many of its own best insights. What he writes of Gibb applies equally to Byron (except that Byron wrote poetry, whereas Gibb wrote "quietly heedless but profoundly sequential prose" – O.284):

> For Gibb, the West has need of the Orient as something to be studied because it releases the spirit from sterile specialization, it eases the affliction of excessive parochial and nationalistic self-centredness, it increases one's grasp of the really central issues in the study of culture (O.257).

The closest he gets to Byron is the following:

> Later in the nineteenth century in the works of Delacroix and literally dozens of other French and British painters, the Oriental genre tableau carried representation into visual expression and a life of its own (which this book unfortunately must scant). Sensuality, promise, terror, sublimity, idyllic pleasure, intense energy: the Orient as a figure in the pre-Romantic, pretechnical Orientalist imagination of late-eighteenth-century Europe was really a chameleonlike quality called (adjectivally) "Oriental" (O.118-19).

Sounds good, despite "('adjectivally')" – how would you call something something, if not with an adjective? – and despite the way in which he makes the eighteenth century follow on from the nineteenth, and appears to put Delacroix in the eighteenth. He won't, however, allow such work as a lasting, positive achievement:

> But this free-floating Orient would be severely curtailed with the advent of academic Orientalism (O.119).

… which ignores his previous statement that academic orientalism started with the *Bibliothèque orientale* in the 1690s.

For Said, *all* systematic study is, it appears, objectionable: "All the *Bibliothèque orientale* did was to represent the Orient more fully and more clearly" (O.63). Later he writes, with seeming disapproval, "the Orient belongs to Orientalism, just as it is assumed that there is pertinent information belonging to (or about) the Orient" (O.239). Is there, then, *no* such information?

Said's aim throughout his very confused book is to make his western readers feel guilty about the way their writers wrote about the Orient, just as he expects them to feel guilty about what their governments, armies and commercial appetites took from it, and, very obviously in 2006, are still taking from it – and trying to impose on it. Western Orientalist writing is for Said a branch of western imperialism: "... *in general* [my italics] it was the West that moved upon the East, not vice versa," he writes on page 73, ignoring what he's written about the Arab conquest of North Africa and Spain in the ninth century, and the Ottoman threat to Eastern Europe in the seventeenth century, on page 59. The facts of Arab and Ottoman imperialism must be swept under the carpet. Only Westerners can be cast as bad guys.

British and Belgian imperialism are themes which Said rings dry in his essay on *Heart of Darkness* in *Culture and Imperialism*: "Conrad could probably never have used Marlow to present anything other than an imperialist world-view, given what was available for either Conrad or Marlow to see of the non-European at the time," he writes (C.26). By his "probably" I take him to mean that there were few educated or articulate Africans around in 1902. If there were so few, there were plenty of suffering Africans about, and Conrad, though he doesn't exactly articulate their viewpoint, leaves us in no doubt as to the extent of their suffering. Said's account of the novel is so blinkered and partial it wouldn't get him an 'A' level: "by the end of the narrative," he writes, "the heart of darkness has reappeared in England; outside the group of Marlow's listeners lies an undefined and unclear world" (C.32). No, we protest – the ebb tide, "the best of" which they've lost in the book's last paragraph, will take them back to the City of London, itself "the heart of an immense darkness," the commercial centre of an imperialism bigger than the Belgian one that the book describes (later he does give a better reading). Said uses an ironical passage from *Heart of Darkness* as his epigraph:[4] reading his chapter on the novel, we may wonder if he really understood the passage when he chose it. He has, we notice, little time for irony and humour: perhaps this was one reason why he was antipathetic to Byron.

He would even wish to make us imperialists ashamed of having created the Suez Canal (O.89); even though de Lesseps was "an entrepreneurial visionary ... whose plan was to liberate the Orient and the Occident from their geographical bonds" (O.219). In *Culture and Imperialism* he goes further, and tries to make us feel guilty about

---

4: "The conquest of the earth, which mostly means the taking it away from those who have a different complexion or slightly flatter noses than ourselves, is not a pretty thing when you look into it too much. What redeems it is the idea only. An idea at the back of it; not a sentimental pretence but an idea; and an unselfish belief in the idea – something you can set, and bow down before, and offer a sacrifice to ... *Heart of Darkness*, quoted Said, C., epigraph.

enjoying Verdi's *Aida*, which was written for the opening of the Cairo opera house, an elitist institution of little interest to the great majority of Egyptians, few of whom would have had access to it anyway. Now *Aida* is about the clash between ancient Egypt and ancient Ethiopia, two civilisations with which no-one living when the opera was written – in the late 1860s – could claim any connection. Neither country wins: all the principals end up either dead or miserable. Said tries to draw a parallel between the opera's action and England's alternate encouragement and discouragement of Khedive Ismail's expansion towards the Red Sea (C.151); but he soon gives up. Later he drags in Matthew Arnold's support for English massacres in Jamaica, (C.157) which occurred at the same time as the opera, and then has a paragraph on the first Gulf War (C.158). The action of the opera, the anguish of Aida, Amneris and Radames, and Verdi's problems in writing them, are sketched in, and one can sense Said trying hard to make the two themes of his essay, the political and the music-theatrical, cohere – but by the end he's given up. What the opera is about is as irrelevant to his polemic as the problems of Mr Kurtz and Charlie Marlow.

Any writer who, like Byron, treats the Orient "as lived in, exploited aesthetically and as a roomy place full of possibility" (O.181), has to be peripheralised into lists.[5] This is Said's way also with William Beckford, whose *Vathek* is conveniently left out of account, and with another of Byron's own favourite "Orientalist" writers, Lady Mary Wortley Montagu. Said makes no reference at all to her, any more than he does to the great unsung heroine of Byron studies – Miss Tully, either sister or sister-in-law to Richard Tully, Our Man in North Africa, a lady whose book *Narrative of a Ten Years Residence in Tripoli* is a vital subtext to *Don Juan* III and IV, and who, like Montagu at Constantinople, treats Tripoli with the same mixture of sympathy and skepticism with which she might treat Brighton, or Lyme Regis. Her attention to detail spared Byron an awful lot of research when he took upon himself the job of describing Oriental interiors, food, and clothing. Here is part of her book which Byron may have remembered as early as 1817 – the year of publication, for the *Tripoli* narrative, and of writing, for *Beppo*. Some Moorish ladies are being taken on a private tour of the English Residence. It's the first time they've seen the interior of a Christian house:

5: "As I discovered in writing *Orientalism*, you cannot grasp historical experience by lists or catalogues and, no matter how much you provide by way of coverage, some books, articles, and authors are going to be left out" (C.p.xxiv).

It was very entertaining to us, to see the curiosity and surprize every thing through the house excited in our visitors: they beheld in every second article something quite novel. They admired very much the books that were lying about, as they are only accustomed to see, or rather hear of manuscripts, and they seemed hardly to credit that ladies sat down to read the books they saw. On the apartments being shewn to them which were allotted for officers and gentlemen to sleep in occasionally, some of them manifested no less surprize, at male visitors being permitted to sleep in the same part of the house where the ladies of the family were ...[6]

Note the way in which, while conveying the comedy (to western eyes) of the Moorish women's reactions, Tully never lets us forget the Islamic values from which those reactions spring.

"Tully's Tripoli" deserves a modern reprint, and some research done on its author.

The model for Ms Tully's epistolary book is the letters of Lady Mary Wortley Montagu. Finding London fascinating and risible by turns, Montagu had been to Constantinople – and had found it, too, fascinating and risible by turns. Her destination may have spoiled her chances for Said, because Constantinople is not a location in which Arabs are to be found in any great quantity, and Said measures "Orientalism" purely in Arab terms. Writers who like Byron travel to and write about Turkey (to say nothing of more obscure places such as India, like E.M.Forster, or China, like Lord Macartney, or Japan, like Lafcadio Hearn much later), stand little chance of having justice done them by him (he gets them all out of the way in a single paragraph on page 17, and does so again in a single sentence on page 285).

Sir William Jones also gets short shrift from Said, who describes him (O.77) as having "closed large vistas down, codifying, tabulating, comparing". Codification, tabulation and comparison are liberating, clarifying techniques, not vista-closing ones (Said carefully leaves out "translating," into which Jones also put much energy). They prepare the ground for later visitors and scholars, who are always free to disagree with them. Jones's work is another important subtext for Byron, whose concern is the radically un-Saidian one of (to quote Michael Franklin), "blurring the Eurocentric binarism of self and other," to see, as did Montagu, "English self in Asian otherness," and to employ, what the unsmiling Said has no time for at all, "a comic reflexivity and relativity"

6: "Tully's Tripoli" (second edition, 1817) p.153.

reflecting ironically on both East *and* West.[7] Not for Jones the proselytisings of the loathed Southey, who, commenting on the "dull tautology" of the Qu'ran, wrote (I apologise at Nottingham for this next bit), his interminable epics *Thalaba the Destroyer* and *The Curse of Kehama* with a view to providing the allegedly savage cultures of Islam and Hinduism with the epics they were, he asserted, unable to provide for themselves.

To examine either Byron or Southey would be to break a taboo which Said observes throughout the book. "A literary text speaks more or less directly of a living reality. Its force is not that it is Arab, or French, or English; its force is in the power and vitality of words ..." (O.291). This is why, Said claims with amazing lack of self-awareness, modern American Orientalists don't write about literary texts: but it's clear by this point in the book that he doesn't, either, and for the same reason. He pays very little attention to the detail of the texts he writes about in *Culture and Imperialism*, either.

I often wonder if Said doesn't feel angry because he can produce no active Oriental writers about the passive Occident. He writes, "it has been estimated that around 60,000 books dealing with the Near Orient were written between 1800 and 1950; there is no remotely comparable figure for Oriental books about the West" (O.204); and "it is sobering to find ... that while there are dozens of organizations in the United States for studying the Arab and Islamic Orient, there are none in the Orient itself for studying the United States" (O.324: this was 1978 – things may have changed now).

Southey doesn't merit a single mention from Said: one suspects he's never heard of him. But Byron, as we know, had, and he'd have been familiar with such stuff as the following, which is a note from *Thalaba*:

> A waste of ornament and labour characterises all the work of the Orientalists. I have seen illuminated Persian manuscripts that must each have been the toil of many years, every page painted, not with representations of life and manners, but usually like the curves and lines of a Turkey carpet, conveying no idea whatever, as absurd to the eye as nonsense-verses to the ear. The little of their literature that has reached us is equally worthless. Our *barbarian* scholars have called Ferdusi the Oriental Homer. Mr. Champion has published a specimen of his poem; the translation is said to be bad and must certainly be unfaithful, for it is in rhyme; but the vilest copy of a picture at least represents the subject

---

7: See Michael Franklyn, *The Building of Empire and the Building of Babel: Sir William Jones, Byron, and their Productions of the Orient*, in Martin Procházka, (ed.) *Byron: East and West*, Charles University, Prague, 2000, pp.63-78.

and the composition. To make this Iliad of the East, as they have sacrilegiously styled it, a good poem, would be realizing the dreams of alchemy, and transmuting lead into gold.

The Arabian Tales certainly abound with genius; they have lost their metaphorical rubbish in passing through the filter of a French translation.[8]

To wish to "possess" and "penetrate" the Orient (one of Said's voyeuristic preoccupations)[9] is one thing: to devalue it, as Southey does here, is to try and make it impossible for anyone to wish to "possess" and "penetrate" it. Southey's implicit assertion – that *Thalaba* and *Kehama* make up for the inadequacy of Persian and Arabic poetry by providing readers with English poems on similar themes which are much better – provoked Byron's satire.[10] In his own ideological tract against Christianity – *Manfred* – he uses Zoroastrian ideas and figures, which he derives from Sir John Malcolm's *History of Persia*, another book to which Said makes no reference; and uses Zoroastrian ideas until well into *Don Juan*.

The little-studied facsimile letter printed with *Childe Harold* I and II (see Appendix) was intended by Byron to reverse the anti-Turkish feelings of his audience. Its beautiful calligraphy was, he asserted, evidence that Turks were civilized. They were artists and writers, not manufacturers of flying carpets. Turks were to be respected – like Scotsmen or Irishmen.

For such writers as Southey, and their readers, brought up on the *1,001 Nights*, all eastern carpets were flying carpets – items of the exotic Orient to be "possessed". Such Exoticism implies the superiority of the Occident over the Orient, an Orient which, in the best Saidian (or "Saidist") manner, one might own without loving, and praise without knowing. But Byron, Montagu, Tully and Jones loved, praised, and participated: theirs was what Said terms "an actual encounter with the real Orient" (O.80): it was their blinkered contemporary and subsequent Victorian readership which could not follow them. Byron's occidental heroes and oriental heroines make love with a natural eagerness which other "orientalist" writers eschew – compare the passionate Juan and

---

8: Southey, *Thalaba*, note: Works, 1850, p.215.
9: For "penetrate," "penetration," "penetrability," "impenetrable," and "pénétration," see *Orientalism*, pp.44, 179, 206, 210 twice, 211 twice, 213, 219, 224, 245, 250, 267, 270, 309); for "possess" and "possession" see pp.69, 86, 92, 244, and 245).
10: For an alternative view of *Thalaba*, at least, see Sharafuddin, Chapter 2.

Haidee (whose mother was "a Moorish maid from Fez" – this idea is from Ms Tully), published in mid-1819, with the frigid Ivanhoe and Rebecca, published later in 1819, as if by way of corrective Christian riposte. The Oriental maiden, implies Scott, must be admired from a distance only: get into bed with her, he warns (or indeed, of course, with any maiden before marriage), and your European (i.e. British) self is disfigured and contaminated.

It's not just a satirical bent that Byron indulges when depicting the Orient, though another paper could be given on why Sardanapalus has more in common with George IV than he has with Ashurbanipal IV, and what the Sultan in *Don Juan* V has in common with that obese British monarch:

> He went to Mosque in state, and said his prayers
>   With more than "Oriental Scrupulosity;"
> He left to his Vizier all State affairs,
>   And showed but little royal curiosity;   1180
> I know not if he had domestic cares –
>   No process proved connubial animosity –
> Four wives and twice five hundred maids unseen
> Were ruled as calmly as a Christian Queen. –

(This at the time of the "trial" of Queen Caroline).

> If now and then there happened a slight slip,   1185
>   Little was heard of criminal or crime;
> The Story scarcely passed a single lip,
>   The *Sack* and Sea had settled all in time,
> From which the secret nobody could rip;
>   The Public knew no more than does this rhyme;   1190
> No Scandals made the daily press a curse;
> Morals were better, and the fish no worse.

Confusing the Sultan in the Seraglio with George IV at Carlton House is an excellent way of "blurring the Eurocentric binarism of self and other," and more examples could be cited. But Byron was concerned to build bridges, not to raise barriers, and the chief bent of his Orientalism was a tragic one.

Why, in *The Giaour* (the one Byron poem which Said honours by naming, even though, as I said, he calls it "the 'Giaour'"), does the occidental protagonist, having killed his Turkish enemy, for having killed his Circassian beloved, retire to a monastery and die of self-neglect and misery, refusing all Christian consolation?

> "... Much in his visions mutters he
> Of maiden 'whelmed beneath the sea;
> Of sabres clashing – foemen flying,
> Wrongs avenged – and Moslem dying.   825
> On cliff he hath been known to stand,
> And rave as to some bloody hand
> Fresh severed from its parent limb,
> Invisible to all but him,
> Which beckons onward to his grave,   830
> And lures to leap into the wave."

Surely it's because his Turkish enemy was also his Turkish friend, and because, as Bernard Beatty argues,[11] in killing his enemy he's killed himself – the severed hand is his, and the "parent limb" is firstly the body of Hassan, and secondly, his. It's like Hamlet, who has to wait until his enemy has almost killed him before he returns the favour, because they must die together, being one and the same. The idea that, as with Ahab and Moby Dick, your enemy is yourself, is, Said would assert, unOccidental – Western writers don't identify enough with oriental characters. But it's the idea on which much of Byron's oriental writing rests.

Our ultimate answer to Said's attempt at ignoring Byron is *Don Juan* cantos VI to VIII: the Siege of Ismail, in which a Christian army besieges, captures and sacks an Islamic city. Here, from Canto VIII, is the death of a Moslem warrior, the last of his father's sons to die in the assault:

> So fully flashed the Phantom on his eyes,
>   That when the very lance was in his heart
> He shouted "Allah!" and saw Paradise   915
>   With all its Veil of Mystery drawn apart –
> And bright Eternity without disguise
>   On his Soul, like a ceaseless Sunrise, dart –
> With Prophets – Houris – Angels – Saints – descried
> In one voluptuous Blaze – and then he died,   920
>
> And with a heavenly rapture on his face;
>   The good old Khan, who long had ceased to see
> Houris, or aught except his florid race,
>   Who grew like Cedars round him gloriously,
> When he beheld his latest hero grace   925

11: See Beatty, *Calvin in Islam: A Reading of* Lara *and* The Giaour, in Procházka (ed.), *Byron: East and West*, Prague 200, p.83.

The Earth, which he became like a felled tree,
Paused for a moment from the fight, and cast
A Glance on that slain Son, his first and last.

The tale of the Khan and his five sons is derived not merely from
Byron's source, Castelnau's *Histoire de la Nouvelle Russie*, but from the
story of Latinus and his sons at Stanzas 27-39 of Tasso's *Gerusalemme
Liberata* (Canto IX). But Latinus is a Christian knight besieging a
(temporarily) Moslem town. Byron has changed the religion, and kept the
drama. In the Moslem, one sees the Christian; in the Christian, one sees
the Moslem. What better way of showing that East and West are one and
the same? By taking a Christian epic episode and making it into an
Islamic epic episode, he's demonstrated the interchangeability of both
traditions – even the fact that, in his judgement, both traditions are one.
The old Occidental / Oriental binarism of self and other, against the
exploitation of which Said fulminates so blindly, is exploded for good,
and Said's own proclaimed goal, "the common enterprise of promoting
human community" (O.328) advanced.

Said, a Palestinian Arab born in Egypt, who worked in America and
had many Jewish friends, who was sometimes feted in Israel and banned
(temporarily) by Yasser Arafat, should have recognized in Byron a man
who was, like him, a citizen of the world, and yet a citizen of nowhere.
"Ever since I can remember, I have felt that I belonged to both worlds,
without being completely *of* either one or the other," he writes (C.xxx).
But he didn't recognize Byron at all.

Above all, Said does not demonstrate how the East *might* be depicted
by a western artist, leading us to guess either that he doesn't want it to be
depicted at all, or that he just hasn't thought about that angle. As Javed
Majeed has written, Said aimed "… to unmask and dispel illusion, and
yet he does not specify what to replace this illusion with".[12]

I find Said's *Orientalism* dated: so much of its polemic has sunk in
over twenty-seven years, and metamorphosed into political correctness. I
do not think a Princeton reunion class would in 2005 consist of a fancy-
dress parade all pretending to be Arabs surrendering, as Said reports
happening in 1967 (O.285) – or would it? The fact that *Orientalism* is
such a blinkered, dogmatic book puts most political correctness,
however, into an even more annoying perspective than usual. At a time

---

12: Javed Majeed, *Ungoverned Imaginings: James Mill's The History of British
India and Orientalism* (Oxford: Clarendon Press, 1992), p. 198. I am grateful to
Andrew Rudd for bringing this quotation to my attention.

when Western imperialist intention towards the Arab world may be seen, in present-day Iraq, at its most stupid and naked, this is a disadvantage.

JEWISH TUNES, OR *HEBREW MELODIES*: BYRON AND THE BIBLICAL ORIENT

JEREMY DAVIES

I

THE *EDINBURGH REVIEW*'S NOTICE of Thomas Moore's collection of *Sacred Songs* in January 1819 began in high excitement: "SAUL among the prophets!!!"[1] The reference is to 1 Samuel 10:9-13. The Saul who accedes suddenly to spiritual wisdom here is a "choice young man," a head taller than his peers. The description is perhaps better suited to Byron, whose own slightly earlier collections of "sacred" lyrics included a submerged lyric sequence casting Saul as a Byronic hero,[2] than to his plump friend. The leading reviewers of Byron's *Hebrew Melodies* of 1815 and 1816, however, figured him as a Jew in a different way. Indeed, they made hay with the fact that his collection included several dramatic lyrics spoken in the voices of ancient Hebrews and modern-day Jews. The comparisons to Lord George Gordon, the insurrectionist demagogue and notoriously eccentric convert to Judaism, were probably inevitable.[3] The *British Critic* coined the memorable phrase "poet laureat to the synagogue," while the *British Review* thought that "a young Lord is seldom the better for meddling with Jews." To the *Eclectic Review*, the collection was "as *Jewish*, in opposition to every thing *Christian*, as [Isaac] Nathan and [John] Braham," the Jewish musicians with whom Byron worked, "could have desired." Crystallizing all this, the *Monthly Review* made reference to these "Jewish Tunes, or Hebrew Melodies, (as they are now styled)."[4] Byron had anticipated it all in a letter to Annabella Milbanke. It is odd that

---

1: *Edinburgh Monthly Review* I (January 1819), p.41.
2: Burwick and Douglass, p.15.
3: *British Critic (New series)* III (June 1815), p.603: *RR* 257.
4: Ibid.; *British Review* VI (August 1815), p.201: *RR* 424; *Eclectic Review (2nd series)* IV (July 1815), p.95: *RR* 731; *Monthly Review (2nd series)* LXXVIII (September 1815), p.41: *RR* 1760.

he, a supposed infidel, should be publishing Hebrew Melodies: "Augusta says 'they will call me a Jew next.'"[5]

This fascination with the racial status of Byron's text brings together the reviewers' two major concerns about the *Hebrew Melodies*. The first is religious. They believe that the word "Hebrew" denotes inescapably an intention to enter a poetic tradition "altogether dependent on scriptural authority,"[6] so they judge the *Melodies* as would-be sacred versification. That parts of the collection are not directly religious, and that many of its religious parts are unconventional in tone, are failures illustrating the inadequacy of Byron's piety. The second concern is Orientalist. The magazines find that Byron has failed to represent "Judæan scenery" properly; where, asks the *Christian Observer*, are the "vines and olives, and cedars ... streams bordered by date-trees ... richness and luxurious lassitude"?[7] This failure is seen as continuous with Byron's failure to express truly the orient's most ancient, remote and intoxicatingly mysterious quality of all. He cannot reproduce the passionate intensity of the spiritual life that its primitive peoples experience, either because he fails to move beyond the pedestrian and temperate or because in doing so he violates the mode of representation that his race and cultural location demand. Comparing the *Song of Songs*, "an oriental poem," to Byron's alleged intermingling of the sacred and the fervid, the *British Review* concludes that "Among the oriental nations these ardent strains were too much a language of course to produce any improper excitement in the minds of Asiatics. But it does not follow that such a practice is a fit subject for imitation ... [by] a Briton."[8] Thus, whether too occidental or too zealous, the meaning of the *Hebrew Melodies* is inflected decisively for its reviewers by the collection's ventriloquial relationship to the Orientalism of sacred poetry's origins. A strange side-effect of their perverse racializations of the poems, and of their equally ill-founded idealization of the concept of sacred verse, is a pattern of insight into the importance of Byron's manipulation of Biblical and Jewish cultural conventions that has largely been lost in subsequent interpretation of the *Melodies*. Reconstituting the reviewers' hostile account of a disputable, unfixed religious identity within the *Melodies* makes it possible to explore more sympathetically than they the ways in which Byron gives voice to specifically religious anxieties and resolutions about place, song and self-understanding.

5: BLJ IV, 220.
6: *Monthly Review*, p.42: *RR* 1760.
7: *Christian Observer* XIV (August 1815), p.544: *RR* 592.
8: *British Review*, p.207: *RR* 427.

In 1952, a sparkling essay by Joseph Slater began a new tradition in *Hebrew Melodies* criticism. Slater set out to rescue Byron's lyric collection from neglect not by an appeal to its immanent merit (the poems, he says, have little to offer "anthologists") but by a strategic recontextualisation. The *Melodies* may interest the "literary historian" who understands their relationship to "romantic nationalism," which is that they "clearly belong ... [in] the "national melodies' tradition,"[9] a short-lived vogue in songwriting inspired by the success of primitivist publications like *Ossian*. The first "national melodies" were George Thomson's *Scottish Airs* of 1793, and the tradition always consisted mainly of unthreatening, quasi-nationalistic Celtic sentimentalism; its exemplary achievement, commercially and artistically, was Thomas Moore's series of *Irish Melodies*. Byron's collaboration with the Jewish musicologist and composer Isaac Nathan produced a text "more ancient and exotic than had yet been seen,"[10] but the geographically transplanted signifiers still signified a collection wholly contained by the parameters of the "national melody": whimsical laments and love-songs for bourgeois drawing-room performance. Slater's recontextualisation required a tendentious assessment of the *Melodies'* contents. He described the poems as prominently nationalistic, proto-Zionist and even millennial, but virtually secular:[11] by proposing that Byron privileged the nationhood of the Jews above the Judaic religion he made the Hebrews a displacement of the Celts, co-partners in romantically antique oppression – Lebanon an analogue for the Highlands.[12]

Siting the *Melodies* solely within the "'national melodies' tradition," then, paradoxically effaces the nation to which they ostensibly refer. The genre's inherent inadequacies make this possible: as Tom Mole puts it, a "national melody" is typically "a self-enfolded discourse ... generic ... making no contact with the realities of national identity,"[13] where splashes of ersatz local colour barely disguise a uniform repertoire of conventions. Slater's contextualisation has had a pervasive influence on subsequent

---

9: Joseph Slater, "Byron's Hebrew Melodies," in *Studies in Philology* 49:1 (1952), p.75.
10: Ibid., p.77.
11: Ibid., pp.86, 91.
12: A fanciful ethnographic tradition of the period did indeed postulate a common ancestry for Celts and Hebrews. This putative connection, however, was likely to clarify, rather than overrule, the contemporary reviewers' anxiety to keep sacred poetic forms separate from secular ones.
13: Tom Mole, "The Handling of *Hebrew Melodies*," in *Romanticism* 8.1 (2002), p.25.

readings of the poems (Jeffery Vail cites him as his authority three times in a fairly brief 2001 discussion of them, for instance),[14] and one result of this is that again and again we find vague, essentialist formulations about Byron's Jews presented as praise for his universality or devil-may-care wilfulness: "the ... Jews ... are symbolic of man," a "metaphor serving the higher cause of Promethean liberty," "a symbolic cause in the time of the breaking of nations," or a way to express devotion "without a thought about how [the title *Hebrew Melodies*] befit[s] a lord of the Anglican realm."[15]

While Mole argues instead that Byron's "choosing the national melodies genre" prevented him from writing "a reformed poetry,"[16] he too is convinced that the poems all belong in "the "national melodies" tradition." Like many recent critics, his interpretation focuses strongly upon the circumstances of the poems' composition. Nathan's initial advertisement for the collection (stressing his tunes' authentic antiquity), the poems' publication in an edition much like those of the *Scottish Airs*, and Moore's jealously territorial response to them[17] demonstrate that the poems were expected to have a market appeal congruent with that of "national melodies" collections. Mole, like others, deduces that the *Melodies*' meaning is largely governed by this "national" status, narrowly conceived. Although the genre is largely unremarkable, Byron's entry into it is typically believed to have given his lyrics a substantial place in his poetic career, by freeing him from the yoke of hymnody. Unhampered by conventional pieties, it is argued, he finds in Jewish history a fertile but not overwhelming backdrop for his usual poetic preoccupations. Mole – through a selective reading of the contemporary critical response to the poems – goes on to suggest that Byron's reviewers in the London periodicals of 1815 and 1816 also saw his volume primarily as a national-melodies exercise.

However, a fuller survey of these reviews suggests that the Hebraism of the *Melodies* does not bind them securely within this self-enfolded songwriting practice, but commits Byron to producing an aberration from the genre that Nathan apparently invited him to take part in. Indeed, the

---

14: Vail, pp.89, 93, 98.
15: Robert F. Gleckner, *Byron and the Ruins of Paradise* (Baltimore: Johns Hopkins Press, 1967), p.207; Ashton, p.74; Gordon Thomas, "The Forging of an Enthusiasm: Byron and the *Hebrew Melodies*," in *Neophilologus* 75.4 (1991), p.630; Stuart Curran, *Poetic Form and British Romanticism* (Oxford: Oxford University Press, 1986), p.58.
16: Mole, "The Handling of *Hebrew Melodies*," p.22.
17: See Burwick and Douglass, pp.7-10.

Melodies anticipate their being read as sacred verse, and gain much of their interest from the way they frustrate without rendering irrelevant the expectations of such reading. Of the fifteen notices Donald Reiman records of Nathan's two numbers (April 1815 and April 1816) and John Murray's first edition (May 1815), about as many are favourable as hostile, but the favourable ones are mostly very brief pieces in society magazines – selections of the poems, garnished with commendatory epithets for their still-fashionable author. (The only positive verdicts of any length are the *Critical Review*'s of August 1815, and the *Augustan Review*'s, padded out with fatuous little maxims.)[18] The six most substantial notices, in a later *Critical Review*[19] and the *British Critic*, *British Review*, *Christian Observer*, *Eclectic Review* and *Monthly Review*, are all resoundingly disapproving, and all are centrally concerned with the inadequacy of the lightweight poet to the mighty devotional task they believe him to have undertaken. With varying degrees of wit and anti-semitism but uniform self-importance, they admonish Byron's flushed concubine of a muse for leaving her "couch of roses"[20] for the sanctum of holy men. Like the post-Slaterian critics, they recognise that fewer of the *Melodies* are explicitly religious than one would expect. Unlike them, they do not see this as a strategic preference for ill-defined nationalism above devotion; because they understand the religious meaning of the term "Hebrew" to be inescapable[21] they take both the sacred and the non-sacred poems to illustrate Byron's relationship to the sacredness that he cannot fully achieve. Whereas later critics claim to expect some religiousness in the *Melodies* but to find hardly any, the reviewers are disappointed that many rather than all of the poems have a religious bearing.

Four of the six notices are of Murray's edition, in physical appearance a straightforward book of verse; it is probably because he is the only one to review Nathan's first number, a songbook, that the *British Review*'s William Roberts associates Byron's *Melodies* with "national melodies" more readily than his colleagues do. He describes the tradition in excitable terms, however, as a vehicle for smuggling "prurient imagery" to impressionable girls, and considers the chief virtue of Byron's work to be that it will not "deprave the minds of the young"; the main thrust even of his review is that Byron desires foolishly to be a "modern Moses,"[22] and

18: *Critical Review (5th series)* II (August 1815) 166-71: *RR* 640-2; *Augustan Review* I (July 1815) 209-15: *RR* 57-60.
19: *Critical Review (5th series)* III (April 1816) pp.357-66: *RR* 647-52.
20: *British Review*, p.203: *RR* 425.
21: *Christian Observer*, p.543: *RR* 592.
22: *British Review*, pp.200, 207, 204: *RR* 424, 427, 426.

that such versifying of the Bible should proceed from the "devotional" spirit of "holy men" rather than being aimed like this at "the ears of amateurs."[23] Elsewhere, comparisons with Moore[24] suggest that the poems are being read in the light of *Irish Melodies*, but it is the specific personal association between Byron and Moore, a unique pair of high-society lyricists and satirists, that is uppermost in the reviewers' minds here.[25] "The Hebrew minstrelsy affords ... infinitely richer materials" than do the subjects of Scott's *Border Minstrelsy*, writes the *Christian Observer*,[26] indicating both Byron's connection to the "national melodies" tradition and his fundamental separation from it.

For these writers the sacred tradition is not quite the rigid-sounding "sacred model" that Byron refers to with evasive irony in the letter to Annabella cited above. Rather, it is an art definable less by its formal expression – incorporating scriptural versification, hymnody, and more meditative expressions of faith – than by what that form transmits. The reviewers' conception of the genre depends very overtly on a theistic faith in the possibility of the unmediated presence of the mind or soul in language: they hold that devout writings, more than all others, express nakedly the nature of the writer's mind to the receptive reader. "[M]ere ... poets" have no capacity for them, because religious subjects are not 'susceptible of ornament"; rather, the writer must be "emphatically a Christian."[27] Only "humble believer[s]" can attain a "scriptural elevation of mind,"[28] the supra-poetic achievement of high moral dignity that is the precondition for authentic participation in this tradition, for achieving "genuine pathos, which can never be represented but where it is felt, and can never be felt, except where God himself is enthroned in the affections."[29] And just as no meretricious talent can disguise insincerity from a reader not warped by cynicism, no homeliness of style can cancel out the value of "a soul impressed with the dignity ... of its holy task."[30] Because sacred versification is always an act of transparent self-revelation, and predominantly a means to a didactic end, verdicts about poetic achievement are necessarily subsidiary to judgment upon the humanity of the poet. This is why Byron is found lacking.

23: Ibid., p.202: *RR* 425.
24: *Eclectic Review*, p. 94: *RR* 731; *Critical Review*, p.358: *RR* 648.
25: Vail, pp.6-9.
26: *Christian Observer*, p.548: *RR* 594.
27: *Eclectic Review*, p.96: *RR* 732.
28: *British Review*, p.204: *RR* 426.
29: Ibid., p.202: 425.
30: *British Critic*, p.610: *RR* 261.

Reading the poems as would-be sacred melodies has a determining effect on all judgments about them: the *British Critic* concludes that "The hill of Zion alone is forbidden ground" to "the noble Lord"; the *Critical Review* that his "fervour" fails to compensate for his lack of "true poetical feeling"; the *Christian Observer* that Byron has "rather played than grappled" with the task of writing "on sacred ... subjects"; and both the *British Review* and the *Eclectic Review* that Byron's ability has withered upon touching the Ark.[31] Whatever the degree of suspicion in their response to Byron's new direction, however, all these critics are convinced that this really *is* a startlingly new direction, a switch not just from narrative to lyric, but from secular aestheticism (high and sublime in *Childe Harold*, gradually degenerate thereafter) to an engagement with or exploitation of the profundities of religion; indeed, Byron is "the first modern poet of note" to try "this species of sacred composition."[32] Above all, it must be stressed that even when the reviewers thought that the *Melodies'* cues to the geography of the Holy Land failed to provide a convincingly particularised account of the region, they did not respond to them as instances of interchangeable local detail but as markers of specifically religious intent. The collection's "national" poems, therefore, were organically connected to its contemplative ones like *If that High World, They Say that Hope*, and *When Coldness Wraps*,[33] but the secular lyrics were non-sequiturs included in error.[34] This is how racializations like the *Eclectic Review*'s, reading the poems as only minimally Hebrew, but intensely "Jewish, in opposition to every thing *Christian*," can develop: the *Melodies'* Orientalism is not just surface colour, but a semantic framework that changes radically the meaning of the poems contained within it.

The main reason that the reviewers' understanding of the *Melodies* as a transgressive religious text has consistently been evaded in modern times is probably its dependence upon an instinctive and often vicious racism. It is a mark of how subtle and elusive Christianity's relationship to Judaism is, however, that such racism can complicate rather than simplify thinking about it. An elaborate, cavilling introductory passage in the *British Critic*'s thunderously bigoted review[35] epitomises the strange contortions that

31: *British Critic*, p.611: *RR* 261; *Critical Review* III, p.357: *RR* 647; *Christian Observer*, pp.548, 543: *RR* 594, 592; *British Review*, p.202: 424; *Eclectic Review*, p.96: *RR* 732.
32: *Theatrical Inquisitor* VIII (June 1816), p.444: *RR* 2262.
33: *Christian Observer*, p.547: *RR* 594.
34: *Monthly Review*, p.42: *RR* 1760.
35: *British Critic*, p.604: *RR* 258.

Romantic-era anti-semitism undergoes in this delicate situation. To explain why Byron's retelling of Old Testament stories is unchristian, this reviewer describes at length how Christians should respond to the tragic narratives of the Old Testament, how they should "feel them as Christians not as Jews." He begins with a seemingly insoluble paradox. Byron shows himself either to "entertain a … ridiculous … attachment to the Jewish cause" or to "feign … affection towards a sacred object, to which his heart is … a stranger": because two antipathetic religions cohabit in the same holy symbols, the Jewish cause, which one should disdain, is indistinguishable from the sacred object to which devotion is required. The Christian "weeps with those who wept by the streams of Babylon" and "trace[s]…the analogy" between Judaic and Christian history, but must do so without "capricious fantasy" – without sympathy for the Jews as a race, but with "rational" emotion and "judicious piety," with calculated grief for the necessary sufferings wreaked on them by God's "dispensations." Hearing the Old Testament in church, he must "becom[e] a party" to the Jews' crimes and "sorrows," but only because this is how one learns with "precision" how God's "redeeming mercy" operates. Feeling must be channelled through and beyond the "Jewish cause" to reach the 'sacred object" that it reveals and defines but does not partake of. (To put it another way: "curiosity … in the Jews and their fate is prompted … exclusively by a desire to … interpret them not for their own sake but in terms of their meaning for Christianity.")[36] All this, the reviewer sniffs, is "perfectly foreign" to Byron.[37] Not true, of course: while his empathetic, instinctual response to Judaism in 1815 did not depend upon this kind of thinking, the passage illuminates the elaborate negotiations that the *Hebrew Melodies* were taking part in – negotiations about those very qualities of empathy and the painfully divided ways in which Christians were compelled both to offer tragic pity to Biblical Jews and to withhold it; negotiations that disappear if one pigeonholes the collection with the "national melodies."

The *British Critic*'s example shows us that the reviewers' proposal of a sacred-poetry context for the *Melodies* can teach us a great deal about the foibles and prejudices of their own era, but might also suggest that the collection's tendentious title conditioned their response so powerfully, making so great a degree of misreading inevitable, that it cannot be expected to advance our understanding of the poems in the way that Slater's national-melodies context has been employed to do. There might

---

36: Frank Felsenstein, *Anti-Semitic Stereotypes 1660-1830* (Baltimore: Johns Hopkins University Press, 1995), pp.3-4.
37: *British Critic*, p.605: *RR* 258.

therefore seem no good reason to reabsorb the reviewers' baffled hostility into *Hebrew Melodies* criticism. I suggest, though, that it is neither advisable nor especially easy to keep the earliest tradition of interpretation completely separate from the more recent. Concerns that still dominate criticism of the collection – about the extent and nature of its coherence, the semantic interrelationship of Byron's poetry and Nathan's music, and Byron's self-positioning in the marketplace – are all explored with provocative vigour in 1815 and 1816, sometimes in ways that will be repeated long afterwards. Leslie Marchand's complaints that Byron "could not resist inserting other [secular, inappropriate] lyrics" into the collection[38] show that his understanding of the *Melodies*" integrity and proper subject matter is, for better or worse, that of Byron's contemporaries. More tellingly, Kurt Heinzelman gives a very skilful account of how Byron's efforts towards "writing the Byronic out of the ... *Hebrew Melodies*"[39] make the collection's Hebrewness the site of a double gesture of self-recollection (his "remembering of his own lyric practice")[40] and self-effacement, which registers in a different way exactly the tension that the reviewers found between the imperative towards authorial transparency in carrying out this "holy task" and the ineradicability of Byron's degenerate, feminine presence in the text.

We have seen that the argument defining the poems as "national melodies" by reference to their positioning in the marketplace is undermined by the critical response of that marketplace, which received the poems as something other than "national," and that suggestions the poems were meant to impress Annabella by making public Byron's piety should acknowledge that any such attempt backfired spectacularly. More fundamentally, the general project of the reviewers can usefully be seen as a critical manoeuvre parallel to Slater's own: an attempt to rescue the *Melodies* from an ephemeral, non-literary wilderness and position them inside a definite tradition, enabling more informed and consequential readings. Equivalent to the historically uninformed misunderstanding that Slater identifies is the reading of the *Melodies* by what the reviewers take to be its major commercial audience, the fashionable "young ladies ... and their mammas"[41] who adore Byron's sumptuousness and are heedless of the risk that his sensual travesty of piety might, if left unexamined, pose to

---

38: Leslie A. Marchand, *Byron's Poetry. A Critical Introduction* (London: John Murray, 1965), p.133.
39: Kurt Heinzelman, "Politics, Memory and the Lyric: Collaboration as Style in Byron's *Hebrew Melodies*," in *Studies in Romanticism* 27:4 (1988), p.526.
40: Ibid., p.516.
41: *British Review*, p.201: *RR* 424.

their religious sensibilities. The ideals of liberal humanist scholarship, implicit in Slater's belief that literary historians should read the *Melodies* better, parallel the moralistic principles explicit in the reviewers' determination to expose with clarity and probity Byron's irreverent toying with Judaeo-Christian mythologies.

The essential difference, then, is that whereas the first move of the national-melodies theory is to try to show how neatly the collection fits within its own conventions, the earlier approach describes the *Melodies* as a failure of conformity, as transgressive and unconventional, above all as dangerously soliciting misreading. The reviewers, who fantasise an unmediatedly Christian poetry, find that in Byron's case the Christian fables best suited to versification are mediated through the Jewish race in such a way as to leave no room between God-denier and Jew-sympathiser, producing parodies of Christian purity. Slater, however, returns in part to their original fantasy when he postulates infinitely portable "national" signifiers, transparent and transposable symbols of nationhood. The de-Orientalizing national-melodies theory is a rejection of the earlier discovery that markers of Hebrewness are more typically perceived as endlessly infectious and contaminating. For the reviewers, the texts of this intensely mythologized and stereotyped race attach irresistibly to those who borrow from them – even down to the transformation of Byron's name into a ludicrous reminder of Lord George Gordon.

II

DR JOHNSON EXCEPTED, ROBERT LOWTH'S *Lectures on the Sacred Poetry of the Hebrews* (1753, English translation 1787) were "Britain's most important ... discussion of poetry" in the eighteenth century,[42] their epochal achievement being to show "that the prophetic books [of the Bible] were poetical, and should be regarded as literary expression."[43] The *Lectures'* greatest literary-historical importance is as a foundational text of two central proto-Romantic concepts: oriental primitivism, and a revolutionary psychology of composition. The most sublime of all poets, it asserts, are the most ancient, the Biblical poets who are attuned to divinity with unique immediacy,[44] and the single crucial characteristic of the

---

42: Howard D. Weinbrot, *Britannia's Issue. The Rise of British Literature from Dryden to Ossian* (Cambridge: Cambridge University Press, 1993), p.407.
43: Jonathan Culler, *Framing the Sign. Criticism and its Institutions* (Oxford: Basil Blackwell, 1988), p.80.
44: Robert Lowth, *Lectures on the Sacred Poetry of the Hebrews*, trans. G Gregory, 2 vols (London: J Johnson, 1787; facsim. rpt. London: Routledge /

language of poetry is that it is "one in which we are all primitives continually creating the world."[45] The primitive sublime, understood broadly as the outpouring of the essential emotions of mankind, is the measure and resting-place of all true poetry. As one of the great influences on the late eighteenth-century fascination with antiquarian nationhood, Lowth should figure in any account of the "national melodies" tradition, but the effect of his Biblical scholarship on conceptions of sacred versification is still greater. He offered persuasive new accounts of both the form of Biblical poetry – above all, his theory of "parallelism" in its construction[46] – and the way it should be read, with a radically historicized empathy for its pastoral and egalitarian roots seen as essential to grasping its virtues.[47] Indeed, "[a]fter the appearance of the [Lectures], no one could write [on Hebraic poetry] without considering Lowth's work."[48]

The *Hebrew Melodies'* reviewers illustrate the truth of this: their hostility was not just based on reactionary neoclassicism, but developed from a theoretical position substantially involved with the proto-Romantic ideas systematised by Lowth. This involvement goes much further than the *British Review* citing his conclusion that the ancient Hebrews' music has been lost,[49] the *Monthly Review* advising its readers to consult his work for an understanding of Hebrew poetry's "character and leading features,"[50] or even Lowth's intriguing pre-empting of the *British Critic's* maxim that "we feel [Hebrew poetry] as Christians not as Jews," his suggestion that the reader "is to feel them as a Hebrew, hearing ... the same words, at the same time."[51] For Lowth, the "function of art ... [is] the impression of the self-contemplating mind observing itself":[52] the determining characteristic of "poetical language" is to "exhibit ... the true and express image of a mind," its "interior recesses" and "inmost conceptions";[53] in sacred poetry especially, "the secret feelings of the author" are laid "open to public view," and the "emotions of the soul ... conspicuously displayed."[54]

Thoemmes Press, 1995), (hereafter "Lowth"), I, pp.359-62.
45: Brian Hepworth, *Robert Lowth* (Boston: Twayne Publishers, 1978), p.97.
46: Lowth, II, pp.25-33.
47: Ibid., I, pp.112-13.
48: David A. Reibel, "Introduction" to Robert Lowth, *De Sacra Poesi Hebræorum* (London: Routledge / Thoemmes Press, 1995), p.v.
49: *British Review*, p.202: *RR* 425.
50: *Monthly Review*, p.42: *RR* 1760.
51: Lowth, I, p.114.
52: Hepworth, *Robert Lowth*, p.89.
53: Lowth, I, p.79.
54: Ibid., p.312.

Lowth "is notable," then, "for conceiving the poem as a mirror which ... reflects the very penetralia of the poet's secret mind."[55]

If we conclude that the ideal – virtually consistent among the hostile reviewers of the *Melodies* – of the poet's inevitable self-revelation in sacred poetry evolves from this Lowthian notion that religious poetry is inherently primitivist, inducing in the poet the passionate and impulsive creative state of the first man, such evolution evidently consists of a restriction of the linguistic field open to the poet. Rather than the completeness of self-display following on from the completeness of his freedom of expression, it now comes from the rigour of the highly privileged form into which he has presumed to admit himself. The problem of ventriloquism emerges when the reviewers calibrate whether Byron has "injudiciously put [himself]" too closely "into competition with the ... model of all poetry,"[56] or equally unwisely strayed too far from it:[57] the meaning of his poetic practice is altered in an extremely elusive manner by the ways it rewrites the general heritage of Biblical verse. This compulsion to adopt an alien voice is precisely what is seen by more recent writers to be lacking in the "national melodies" tradition: the "self-enfolded discourse" that Mole describes would see all poetic figures returning swiftly to their point of origin in the poet-as-himself, rather than being conditioned by the specificity of their attachment to the Biblical orient.

The Wild Gazelle, for instance, looks at first like an almost completely secular poem, and as such connected to the orient only by a few proper nouns. We seem to be among the archetypes of the national-melodies tradition when the "temple" is paired with the "throne" as a symbol of nationhood[58] and when the loss of "Judah's statelier maids" is mourned [12]: the *British Review* notes the obvious, that the women are "wanderers as their lovers are,"[59] but the point is that they are no longer *state*ly, that the loss of their nationhood is congruent with the loss of their human dignity. Describing lost masculinity, palm trees – rooted, static, "blest" [13] in their inability to survive transportation – are contrasted with the speakers, who "wander witheringly" [19], perpetually intermediate, lacking the native death that would confirm their selfhood and their manhood. It seems that the palm trees, their identity deriving from the soil

---

55: M.H.Abrams, *The Mirror and the Lamp. Romantic Theory and the Critical Tradition* (Oxford: Oxford University Press. 1953), p.77.
56: *Critical Review*, p.362: *RR* 650.
57: *Eclectic Review*, p.94: *RR* 731.
58: Burwick and Douglass, *The Wild Gazelle*, ll.23-4.
59: *British Review*, p.206: *RR* 427.

they occupy, symbolise the men who desire to be buried in the same soil as their fathers, and that this desire is itself a symbol or abstraction of the desire to preserve a homeland that links the generations, that validates the identity of each generation by matching it geographically to its predecessors and successors. Not so. A specifically Hebrew thematic in the key lines

> where our fathers' ashes be
> Our own may never lie [21-22]

disrupts or even reverses this system. Byron had very probably read Robert Southey's *Letters from England* by now,[60] and from there at least would have known the legend that Jews "wherever buried, can rise again ... nowhere except in the Promised Land," and if buried elsewhere "will have to make their way there through the caverns of the earth."[61] The desire to be buried among the "fathers' ashes," then, is not allegorical but literal, something sought for its own sake and for unique religious reasons. The "blest ... palm[s]" are less a metaphor than a God-given model, an originary ideal to which the speakers" burials must aspire. The priority of the roots laid down by the trees and the fathers does not come from the seeking of historical continuity, but from a religious imperative overpowering history.

The ideal of Hebrew masculinity and fidelity, however, is produced negatively, by the fact that the palms "cannot ... will not live in other earth" [17-18]; Byron's poem takes part in the same process as Southey's prose, of marking Judaism as irreducibly separate at the moment of death and predicated upon a necessarily incomplete presence in the "other lands" [20] of the Diaspora, where even burial is partial, illusory, and temporary. But whereas Southey takes the burial myth as an example of wretched superstition and self-interest in the context of a violent attack upon these characteristics among the Jewish community, *The Wild Gazelle* replays the experience as tragic. Semi-covertly particularised in its final stanza from a general national-melodies account of ethnic upheaval into a specifically Jewish concern with the place and form of death, it becomes both precisely "Hebrew" and universal in its concern with the difficulty of reproducing an authentic paternity. The shifting valence of its allusion is

---

60: Peter W. Graham, *Don Juan and Regency England* (Charlottesville: University Press of Virginia, 1990), pp.43-4.
61: Robert Southey, *Letters From England*, ed. Jack Simmons (London: The Cresset Press, 1951), p.396; cf. Alan Unterman, *Dictionary of Jewish Lore and Legend* (London: Thames and Hudson, 1991), p.98.

comparable to that in the penultimate line of *Oh Weep for Those*: the *Monthly Review*[62] was offended by the echo of Jesus' words (Matthew 8:20) in "The wild-dove hath her nest – the fox his cave," but Byron's intention was to claim for the Jewish experience of exile the ability to exemplify a wider human condition. Byron's Jews are not just "symbolic of man." It is by representing them as themselves that the poems ascribe to them a larger significance as well.

Here as elsewhere Byron's engagement with Judaeo-Biblical legacies is not a facile thematic starting-point but a poetic reserve that he draws upon with thoughtfulness and skill. What, then, of Slater's verdict that the *Melodies* are "almost as secular as *The Bride of Abydos*,"[63] and its many repetitions in different forms since then? By my count, seventeen of the twenty-five *Melodies* published in Byron's lifetime include to a prominent degree the characteristics of sacred verse: sacredness is by far the chief characteristic to distinguish and link the collection. At the very least, to take at face value Byron's claim in April 1814 not to have written fifty lines "touching upon religion"[64] and suggest that "The Hebrew Melodies added little to this figure"[65] is wrongheaded.

Most of the non-religious, non-oriental *Melodies* were written before Byron took up Nathan's project in September 1814. Byron must therefore have felt them to be still more alien to a narrowly "Hebrew" theme than did the reviewers. Yet he placed *She Walks in Beauty* first in the first number, ending that number with three secular poems; the second number concluded with *Francisca* and *Sun of the Sleepless*, following ten sacred poems. These last two were obviously "thrown in ... as make-weights," deduced one reviewer:[66] too obviously, for if they had embarrassed Byron or Nathan they would surely have been buried in the middle or just not published; nor would *Francisca* have received two settings. A more sympathetic reader would see an opening out of the possibilities of Hebrewness. Just after *From the Last Hill* (*On the Day of the Destruction of Jerusalem by Titus*), where ancient Jewish history culminates in flames and a vow to reserve "Our worship ... for [God]" [20], come a very private love-drama and a self-absorbed meditation upon moonlight. They might seem like a falling-off from the vow that precedes them, but their speakers preserve the fidelity and reflectiveness seen in *From the Last Hill*: a tone established as "Jewish" ceases to be bound in by Hebrew

62: *Monthly Review*, p.43: *RR* 1761.
63: Slater, "Byron's Hebrew Melodies," p.86.
64: BLJ IV, 82.
65: Ashton, p.66.
66: *Critical Review*, p.364: *RR* 651.

themes, and the blurring of the devout into the secular that so troubled the reviewers becomes a manifest strategy of the way the collection is organised.

Neither Jewish nor gentile, neither oriental nor occidental, the closing poems link the collection to Byron's literary practice outside the *Melodies* (*Francisca* is extracted from *Parisina*) but are not incompatible with the text of which they are a part. The meaning of these "secular" poems, then, lies in the way the reader relates them to the religious poems around them: they are not an area of the text closed off from sacred meaning, but placed so as to maximise their engagement with the debatable sacredness of the volume. *On Jordan's Banks*, in the centre of the first number, describes God's terrible silence in an age of blasphemy; the critical scarcity of sacred speech that is thematized here is enacted in the collection's shortage of reliably sacred texts. Byron's sympathetic treatment of the Jewish cause, its people scattered, lapsarian and compulsively elegised, is at its most subtle and even tender in its problematic assemblage of inadequately devotional poems that still seem to have some affinity with their sufferings: *Oh Snatched Away in Beauty's Bloom*, mourning the loss of innocence; *Thy Days are Done*, an elegy for Byron's friend Peter Parker or Napoleon or Saul,[67] or perhaps all three; and *It is the Hour*, closing the first number in rapt but unfulfilled expectation.

In warning Byron that he risks being called a Jew, Augusta recognises a spectrum of fears about the power that Jewishness wields, and shows how Christianity's vast historical embarrassment, whereby it traces its ancestry through a bloodline that it declares to be illegitimate, has been converted into a system for patrolling its borders. The Old Testament narratives that Byron relates are worthy of solemn respect, because they are Hebrew; to fail in this reverence would make them, and him, merely Jewish; but in these circumstances the Hebrew and the Jewish are so completely intermingled that determining which is which is a purely local, subjective matter, and the distinction can be mobilised in any direction at any time, to exclude texts from or incorporate them into Christianity at a moment's notice. Dividing its ancestry into Hebrew and Jewish recreates Christianity's formative self-contradictions as an ideally flexible guard against self-contradiction, which in this case identifies Byron's poetry as "Jewish Tunes" rather than "Hebrew Melodies," obscurely allying them with petty theft and usury against contemplative sublimity. The Hebrew/Jewish distinction has no recourse to reason, so it is the feel of the poems that makes them "Jewish," and this can be accounted for as easily by Byron's notoriety as by the contents of his collection; nevertheless,

---

67: Burwick and Douglass, p.19.

comparing the *Melodies* with the work that re-made Moore as a "Saul among the prophets" may shed light upon this strange judgment, and define more clearly the place of the orient in Byron's collection.

Like the *Melodies*, Moore's *Sacred Songs* are "something quite new,"[68] a radical shift to the Judaic "instrument of sublimer inspiration,"[69] and so, again, poetic quality is created only by supra-poetic value, by "chastened ... imagination," "preparatory discipline" and the "fervour of piety," but the general verdict on the *Songs*, unlike the *Melodies*, is favourable. These were poems written with "genuine feelings of reverence and piety,"[70] sincere "offering[s] at the shrine of devotion,"[71] that were "often sung as hymns in church."[72] Such differences in the reception of these symbiotic intertexts, emerging from extremely similar cultural moments, are highly revealing. Moore's first number, planned from 1812, was published in 1816, two months after Nathan's second.[73] Six of its sixteen poems are Hebraic, compared to six of twelve in Byron's first offering; the authors' poetic (and indeed moral) reputations and lyric techniques were so similar that several of the *Songs'* reviewers believed they were clearly planned to rival "the *Hebrew Melodies* of Lord Byron."[74] Moore's lyrics are now typically considered the worst of his three song-series, uninspiring hymns expressing his "vague romantic religious feeling."[75] Perhaps, then, they are especially useful as an answer to his notorious question, "Was there ever any thing so bad as the Hebrew Melodies?"[76] – the banal religiosity of this *bona fide* minor poetry establishes a context that makes sense of the counterintuitive notion that Byron's work was devotionally and formally eccentric. There is, however, more to be said about the reasons Moore's poems were considered an illumination rather than a Byron-like corruption of the word of God.

The most celebrated of all Moore's *Irish Melodies*, *The Harp that Once Through Tara's Halls*, unmistakably provided the model for Byron's *The Harp the Monarch Minstrel Swept*. The second number of Moore's *Songs* in turn rewrote Byron's meditation on David's harp with *Like*

68: *Blackwood's Edinburgh Monthly Magazine* I: vi (September 1817), p.631.
69: *Monthly Review (2nd series)* XC (December 1819), p.413.
70: Ibid.
71: *Blackwood's*, p.631.
72: Miriam Allen DeFord, *Thomas Moore* (New York: Twayne Publishers, 1967), p.38.
73: Ashton, pp.32-3.
74: *Critical Review (5th series)* III (June 1816), p.611.
75: DeFord, *Thomas Moore*, pp.37-8.
76: Quoted at Ashton, p.48.

Morning, When Her Early Breeze.[77] The royal harp seen as a locus of national and spiritual identity undergoes a three-part, sixteen-year lyric journey. In ways that exemplify Byron's treatment of his "sacred" verse, the middle part of that journey renders problematic the national harp as a symbol by complicating its relationship to the song's representation of its own musical identity. Moore's first poem is an elegy for *The Harp of Tara* [10],[78] which no longer "shed[s]" upon Ireland the 'soul of music" [2]: it is "as mute ... As if that soul were fled" [3-4]. Its silence represents the stilling of past "glory" [6]: the story of the Irish harp is that of the destruction of a particular national music, and the "soul of music," its underlying, essential being, is mourned because it has departed to other nations. The "soul" or purpose of the song that mourns it arises from the displacement of music's soul.

Byron's responding poem is traditionally read as a self-affirming, celebratory account of the affective power of song, as a declaration of "the power of music to transcend earth's limitations"[79] central to his lyric project. It is seen to match *The Harp that Once* as a poem that re-establishes in itself a lost ideal music. More precisely, however, the meaning and form of Byron's poem are governed by an ontological distinction between ordinary "national" music and uniquely Hebraic music: the latter, the Davidian harp, is constructed as the locus of *all* spiritual power within music, so *The Harp the Monarch Minstrel Swept* records itself as a product not of the exile of the Moorean "soul of music," but of its absolute disappearance. Indeed, that which the harp creates is called "tones," "chords," "sound" and "sounds," but the only use of the word "Music" has a different meaning. "The harp"...

> Which Music hallowed while she wept
> O'er tones her heart of hearts had giv'n –
> Redoubled be her tears – its chords are riv'n! [3-5]

So "Music" is prior to Davidian "tones," and remains in the lyric present after the latter are riven (or risen). Her "tears" are understood to represent musical creations (compare *In the Valley of Waters*), so the present song describes itself as part of the excess ("Redoubled") produced by the lapsarian separation between "Music" and her "heart of hearts,"

77: Vail, pp.93-4, 100.

78: Thomas Moore, *Poetical Works*, ed. A.D. Godley (London, 1910). Further references abbreviated [in square brackets] in the text.

79: Frederick Shilstone, *Byron and the Myth of Tradition* (Lincoln: University of Nebraska Press, 1988), p.107.

between the practice of music and the Davidian ideal. In conformity with King David's overwhelming presence in the sacred tradition as the pre-eminent musician of humankind, Byron describes his reign as not just a golden age of affective piety but also the time of a special mediation between God and man through music. David's harp gives men new "virtues," and is a political instrument of divinity "mightier than his throne" [7-10]; it brings "glory" to God and "mountains nod" before it [12-15]; removed to heaven, it becomes that to which "Devotion" directs humanity's "dreams" [17-20]. Here, the soul of music is not just transmitted locally by the royal harp, as in *The Harp that Once*, but identified with it, with the sacred oriental "lyre" through which God becomes present in music. The poem's identity is split: it is one of Music's tears, a feminine lament that her transcendent affective centre has been lost in apotheosis, but equally it is spoken by one of David's mythic subjects from a desire to fire men's souls [8-9] as the harp once did, to reproduce the harp in the lyric moment where description is never demarcated from reproduction.

Moore's *Like Morning* contains obvious echoes of his friend's lines. Here, David's "touch" upon the harp-strings [9] once paralleled God's "touch" upon the "soul" [13-14]; while he played "Ev'n Angels," so presumably men as well, 'stoop'd" to listen [12]; and the "breath" of the "chord" rises to "the skies" [14-16] just as Byron's "chords ... aspired to heaven." This account of music, then, shares the divinity, political efficacy and ascending airiness described in Byron's poem, and both conclude by celebrating the harp-music's preservation in less tangible forms. However, in Moore's treatment the possibility that the Davidian harp might be Music's "heart of hearts," a constituting presence or absence throughout all music, is eradicated. Although David's touch upon the harp is still forever unmatchable, the thrust of Moore's poem is that souls continue to be "wak'd" by God with all the perfection of which his musicianship was just a reflection. The theme of a unique period when music carried God's essence is not relevant here because interaction between God and man is not seen to need mediation through music or any other sign-system.

Although one of Moore's poems is nationalist and one is emphatically religious, in both cases the subject remains insulated from its handling, resistant to the possibility of meta-poetic reflection. In contrast, Byron's lyrics repeatedly, but always with local and varying effects, make their sacred qualities, their concern with specifically Davidian lyres, a fundamental part of the way they are put together. This is why the reviewers' readings of the poems as sacred versification, for all their inaccuracies, still have more than curiosity value today. Their grumpy double recognition that the *Melodies* are inextricably bound up with the conventions of sacred verse, and that their relationship with those conventions is unsettled and fragmentary, forms a valuable counterpoint to the approach that fits Byron's work too neatly into a "national melodies" category and so represses the particularity of its concern with the Biblical orient. Reading the *Hebrew Melodies* as sacred poetry implies a respect for Byron's ability to manipulate a sympathetic description of Judaism into a poetic form that shadows unnervingly the "sacred model" he claimed to have followed. The semi-sacredness that he achieves operates simultaneously in individual poems and in the collection as a whole, underlying and politicising his melodic project.

THE BRIDE OF THE EAST

SEYED MOHAMMED MARANDI

Byron's contemporary critics, as well as many modern day ones, generally regard *The Bride of Abydos* as an authentic representation of the Moslem East. A study of the poem alongside the observations of literary scholars and critics can help one to further understand both the discursive landscape of his age, and that of more contemporary critics.

There is an almost unanimous conception among critics that the work presents the Orient as it truly was or even still is. Kidwai explains[1] that Byron is at his best in recreating an Oriental atmosphere specifically when Giaffir claps his hands for servants or when he is shown enjoying "jerreed" and "mimic slaughter," as a diversion in the company of the homogeneous "Maughrabee, Mamaluke, the Kislar and Moors", as well as when he exclaims "Ollahs" in the javelin–throwing.[2] Byron is also said to show an "astute understanding" of the Orient when he refers to the "horse tails"[3] and explains that this is the standard of a Pasha. Other critics, like Bagabas, stress that to a large extent the authenticity of *The Bride* is suggested by Byron's reference to Eastern myths, Oriental literary fashion, Oriental vocabulary, and other authentic material.[4]

It is difficult to understand how these critics can conclude that people with different languages, cultures, ideologies as well as geographical backgrounds, can be authentically represented, through references to horse tails or a particular ceremony. If so, this implies that the Oriental mind is both shallow and monolithic, and that with a limited amount of knowledge one can fully comprehend and judge it.

Sections of this essay appeared in the *Byron Journal* 33:2 (2005) and are reproduced here with the permission of the Academic Editor. The essay should be read alongside the same writer's *Byron's Infidel and the Muslim Fisherman*, 2006 *Keats-Shelley Review* pp.133-55.
1: Kidwai, p.167.
2: Byron, *The Bride of Abydos* (*BoA*), 1, 231-251.
3: *BoA* 2, 232.
4: Bagabas, p.262.

In the eyes of these critics, it is not necessary for Byron to be able to converse in these Oriental languages in order for him to understand these people and to develop an objective picture of the typical Oriental. Hence, one should not be surprised when Watkins claims, without providing evidence, that Byron has "shown" how Islam endorses "the spread of violence and exercise of power" even though he can not speak in any of these Eastern languages.[5]

Oueijan responds to the problematic issue of the poet's authenticity, by claiming that Byron probably knew Arabic and even Persian. He claims that since Byron stayed in Malta for about twenty days, he was able to learn some basic Arabic.[6] Although, there is no reason to believe that Byron knew either Turkish, Arabic, or Persian, Blackstone too, insists that this must be the case.[7] It seems that it would be necessary for him to be able to converse fluently in these languages, for Oueijan to claim that Byron presents the "sensuous" and "primitive" Oriental through "genuine" and "advanced Oriental scholarship".[8] However, in the eyes of these critics it seems is enough to learn a few words of one of the numerous Eastern languages. This, of course, implies that Orientals lack a sophisticated civilization and are culturally impoverished.

In general, when critics argue in support of the authenticity of *The Bride*, usually their reasoning falls into two categories. They lay stress upon Byron's personal experience of the Orient, through which scholars such as Webb claim that he gained extensive knowledge of it and its political realities. Also, they point out that he studied the works of Orientalists and Eastern travellers, which, generally speaking, Byron himself viewed as reliable.

While supporting Byron's credibility, as an observer of the Orient, Garber quotes John Ruskin who informs the reader that the poet, "spoke only of what he had seen and known and spoke without exaggeration, without mystery, without enmity, and without mercy".[9] According to Byron, the first part of the poem "was drawn from observations of mine". Elsewhere, he also says, "I had a living character on my eye for *Zuleika*".[10] Also in a letter to Murray on *The Bride*, Byron states, "I don't care a lump of Sugar for my *poetry* – but for my *costume* and my *correctness* I will

---

5: See Watkins, p.60.
6: Oueijan, p.29.
7: Blackstone, *Triple Eros*, pp.327-8.
8: Oueijan, p.12.
9: Frederick Garber, *Self, Text, and Romantic Irony* (Princeton 1988), p.81.
10: BLJ III, 195.

combat lustily".[11] Sharafuddin concludes from this that "the tale was inspired by personal adventure in the East".[12]

However, equally important, is the other reason Byron gives for writing *The Bride*:

> It was written in four nights to distract my dreams from ** [...] and had I not done something at the time, I must have gone mad [...]. I am much more indebted to the tale than I can ever be to the most partial reader; as it wrung my thoughts from reality to imagination – from selfish regrets to vivid recollections – and recalled me to a country replete with the *brightest* and *darkest*, but always most *lively* colours of my memory.[13]

This quotation shows that a great deal more about Byron's own state of mind can be learned from this Oriental tale perhaps than about the Orient itself. However, critics still see him as reliable and the proof lies in his journal where he refers to Zuleika, while quoting Virgil in Latin, that *The Bride* deals with actual events, "quæque ipse ...... vidi, / Et quorum pars magna fui."[14] (I myself saw these things ... and I bore great part in them). According to McGann it was statements such as this which "led to the idea that B[yron] actually witnessed certain events in the Levant which more or less correspond to the narrative of *Bride*. This supposition may be true [...]".[15] As John Keats puts it, Byron "describes what he sees".[16]

Few question how the work could possibly have been inspired by some personal adventure of Byron's in the Ottoman Empire. It is not seen as necessary to question how, in the barbaric world that Byron describes, where women are locked up, could a hated foreign giaour gain such intimate access into the personal lives of its Muslim inhabitants. Giaffir himself warns, "Woe to the head whose eye behold / My child Zuleika's face unveiled".[17] While Caroline Franklin observes that Byron, among other things, brings the reader's attention to the extensive restrictions placed on the freedom of movement of women, this does not seem to contradict Byron's claims to personal knowledge about Oriental women in general and someone like Zuleika in particular. Many scholars take it for granted that reality is being presented and it is of little significance that the poet's claims are often self-contradictory.

11: BLJ III, 165.
12: Sharafuddin, p.223.
13: BLJ III, 208, 212.
14: BLJ III, 205.
15: CPW III, 435.
16: H.E.Rollins (ed.), *The Letters of John Keats* (Harvard 1958), II p.200.
17: *BoA* 1, 39-40.

Another reason usually given to confirm Byron's authenticity is, as previously mentioned, his early and profuse reading of the works of Orientalists. Late in his life he says:

> The Turkish history [*Rycaut and Knolles*] was one of the first books that gave me pleasure when a child; and I believe it had much influence on my subsequent wishes to visit the Levant, and gave, perhaps, the oriental colouring which is observed in my poetry.[18]

However, this "oriental colouring" may be more closely related to Rycaut's personality and his sensual desires than to the Orient and it should be conceivable that it is a colouring that not all Orientals would recognize. Byron's statement also implies that not only were the works of Western Orientalists authentic, but also that it is not really necessary to have personal experience to know the Orient, because his own "oriental colouring" comes from these works.

Also, in a letter to Moore regarding *Lallah Rookh*, Byron states, "You have caught the colours as if you had been in the rainbow, and the tone of the East is perfectly preserved ..."[19] Regardless of the fact that Moore's Oriental constructions are even further from the truth than Byron's, one can conclude that in the eyes of Byron it is not necessary to see the East in order to construct it authentically. Interesting too is the fact that Byron sees himself as an authority on the regions that are the settings of Moore's work, as he implies that he has himself been in the "rainbow". However, Byron has never visited Persia or the Indian subcontinent, and the only way he can see himself as an authority is if he views the Orient as a monolithic entity.

Alongside the works of Orientalists, Byron informs his audience that he uses Oriental texts as well to authenticate his works. He claims that *The Bride* "is thoroughly Eastern – and partly from the Koran"[20] and that "the characters & the costume & the tale itself [...] are Mussulman".[21] Not only does he see himself as an authority on the Muslim mentality and culture, but he also appoints himself as an authority on their ideology as well. According to Watson he is "a crusader and a hero, a fighter in the cause of truth and justice".[22] His authority is often respected without question and

---

18: Pietro Gamba, *Lord Byron's Last Journey to Greece* (John Murray 1825), p.149.
19: BLJ V, 249-50.
20: BLJ III, 169.
21: BLJ III, 175.
22: J.R.Watson, *English Poetry of the Romantic Period 1789-1830* (Longman 1992), p.262.

he does not need to have command of the Arabic language to gain such a status (nor do some critics). That is why in his critical study of the work Gleckner can conclude[23] that the Qu'ran is an instrument of destruction, without producing, or feeling the need to produce, any textual evidence to substantiate this claim.

Among examples cited by contemporary scholars when discussing Byron's obsession with facts are his letters to Murray. For example, he once wrote to Murray asking about the Holy Prophet's burial place, which he intended to refer to in *The Bride*. He says, "Look out in the Encyclopaedia article *Mecca* whether it is there or at *Medina* the Prophet is entombed".[24] In a subsequent correspondence he asks:

> Did you look out? Is it *Medina* or *Mecca* that contains the *holy* sepulchure? – don't make me blaspheme by your negligence – I have no book of reference or I would save you the trouble I *blush* as a good Mussulman to have confused the point.[25]

Using such examples, Oueijan can vouch that through "pure scholarly interests", an obsession with authenticity, along with actual experience, Byron creates a work where, "one lives the Orient rather than learns about it".[26] However, the fact is that Byron's question is one which anyone with even a minimal amount of knowledge on Islam would be able to answer.

However, according to Blackstone, "The Tales attracted, and still attract, by their authenticity".[27] According to Marchand, *The Bride* is considered as an "objective Oriental tale with authentic background of Muslim customs",[28] as Byron knew the Eastern culture from personal experience. In the words of Blackstone and Rutherford, *The Bride* informs the reader "without rhetoric" about "another faith and culture" and real life Eastern "passion" and "adventure".[29] Such scholars also see the East as a monolithic entity that does not change with the passage of time, as distinctions between the supposed East at the time of Byron's travels and the East today are rarely made.

23: Gleckner, Robert F. *Byron and the Ruins of Paradise* (Johns Hopkins 1967), p.130.
24: BLJ III, 190.
25: BLJ III, 191.
26: Oueijan, p.12.
27: Blackstone, *Survey*, p.118.
28: Leslie Marchand, *Byron's Poetry A Critical Introduction* (John Murray 1966), p.63.
29: Blackstone, *Survey*, p.119; Rutherford, Andrew, *Byron, A Critical Study* (Oliver and Boyd, 1962), p.37.

The poem begins, as in *The Giaour*, with a lament for the fallen state of Greece as a theme, even though the events take place in an area that is predominantly Turkish and Muslim. This paradise, according to Francis Jeffrey, is populated and ruled by passionate savages. That is why it is in the Orient that, according to Oueijan, one witnesses "the most brutal actions committed by man".[30] Yet, ironically the *Tales* owed a great deal of their public appeal to the portrayal of these breathtaking acts of savagery in exotic settings.

This attitude towards Orientals continues in the next stanza where typical Eastern stereotypes are displayed. Oriental men are divided into two categories; despots and their "brave" and "gallant" slaves who mindlessly await their "Lord's behest".[31] Giaffir's face is typically Muslim. "Not oft betrays to standers by / the mind within, well skill'd to hide / All but unconquerable pride".[32] Muslims hide their true thoughts from others, a feature which makes them unknowable, mysterious, and untrustworthy. Bagabas goes further and claims that Muslims are skilled in hiding their "true nature".[33] Yet, according to *The Bride*, there is one thing that Muslims cannot hide and that is their pride and arrogance and those characteristics which can be hidden from other Orientals or "standers by",[34] cannot escape the scrutiny of the Western eye. In the eyes of McGann:

> What B[yron] knew from personal experience was the Eastern culture which lent verisimilitude to the plot of *Bride*, a number of specific incidents and scenes, and much local colouring.[35]

Byron's notes to the work confirm this. He states that the story of Giaffir is based upon historical reality that was even more horrible than what exists in the poem.

According to the poem, all Muslims are despots who even treat their own sons as slaves. The "son of Moslem must expire, / Ere dare to sit before his sire".[36] This is a point echoed by Bagabas who believes that in *The Bride*, Byron's observation of Turkish haughtiness, rudeness, arrogance, reticence, and pride is well reflected.[37] Even more astonishing

---

30: Oueijan, p.74.
31: *BoA* 1, 22.
32: *BoA* 1, 27-9.
33: Bagabas, p.271.
34: *BoA* 1, 27.
35: CPW III, 435.
36: *BoA* 1, 51-2.
37: Bagabas, p.268.

is the explanation offered by Oueijan regarding these two lines. Not only does this critic authenticate Byron's claims, but he goes further and explains that this behaviour is directly linked to Islam and Eastern ideology. He claims that in the Orient, blind obedience is viewed as a virtue:

> To obey father and mother is no less important than to obey a caliph, which in turn is equivalent to obeying the Prophet and Allah. Thus, at all stages and levels obedience or disobedience is always perceived as obedience or disobedience to Allah.[38]

According to this claim, Oriental obedience is not accompanied by legitimacy, justice, or rationalism, rather it is blind obedience. Neither of the two verses that Oueijan refers to as proof state anything to support the claims that he makes. Q 4:80 says, "He who obeys the Messenger / He is indeed obeying Allah [...]" and Q 47:34 says, "O you believers, do obey / God and obey the Messenger [...]". Indeed, the Qu'ran repeatedly speaks of justice and struggling against oppression.[39] Nevertheless, many literary scholars claim that Giaffir symbolizes the Oriental male, even though the particular Turkish-Muslim despot that Giaffir represents (Ali Pasha), was neither Turkish nor a practicing Muslim.

After discovering that Giaffir is a typical Muslim, the reader get more insight of what a Muslim is like. He orders a slave to lead his daughter from the tower. The language he uses here is, according to Franklin,[40] language reminiscent of punishment or execution. Giaffir then informs his daughter Zuleika that he has determined her fate and that she is to be married. After her marriage, it is made clear, absolute authority over her will be transferred to her husband, whom she has never met. This, Oueijan claims, is basically what "any Eastern father" would have done as Eastern women had absolutely no freedom of choice at all.[41] Bagabas, whose explanation of Islamic law is not accompanied with evidence from Islamic texts, puts it even more bluntly. He claims that in Eastern countries, asking the opinion of children regarding their own marriages, "is no more than a charade" and that this is the truth of an "Islamic marriage".[42]

38: Oueijan, p.137.
39: Q 13:22.
40: Caroline Franklin, *Byron's Heroines* (Oxford 1992), p.49.
41: Oueijan, p.107.
42: Bagabas, p.269.

Giaffir's love for his daughter is also tainted with signs of incest,[43] and it comes a very distant second in comparison to his own Oriental political ambitions and lust for power. Zuleika is practically sold as the "bride for Osman's bed".[44] Byron, writes Franklin, successfully "demonstrates the simultaneous extreme idealization and utter subjugation of woman in Islamic culture".[45] Critics do not recognise, however, that in Islam the dowry is given to the bride, and it belongs to her solely. According to Islam, no person, including the father, can force a woman to marry, let alone control her wealth or her dowry. In any case, Giaffir is not just presented as an evil person, his actions must be somehow attributed to Islam as well as to the inferiority of the monolithic Oriental culture and race.

Most critics who have commented on Zuleika's personality, agree that she represents a typically Oriental female, who lives in absolute subservience. She accepts the traditional social role of women, which makes her like an object in the hands of men. This, states Bagabas, is the role that Islam has given her and it is through an "Islamic marriage" that love, affection, and freedom of choice are denied to women.[46] Bagabas not only attacks Islam, but also claims that Turks are ignorant "of the significance of true feeling".[47] Also, it should be noted through, what Watkins calls "the ideological processes of this culture",[48] women are manipulated and taught that powerlessness is a virtue.

Giaffir represents both the ignorant and unfeeling Turk and the despotic Muslim (as Byron constantly interchanges the two terms). Not only does he choose Zuleika's husband for her, but he also chooses a much older man. The decision is presented as an act that furthers Giaffir's political and military ambitions in, what Oueijan declares to be, an Oriental world of brutality.[49] The fact that Zuleika's future husband is a "wretch"[50] from a "viler race", with "ill gotten wealth", and a very mean soul[51] is of little importance to her father. She will be one of Osman Bey's countless wives or slaves. Osman, like Giaffir, will teach her all her "sex

---

43: *BoA* 1, 147, 152-4.
44: *BoA* 2, 656.
45: Franklin, loc.cit.
46: Bagabas, p.269.
47: Ibid 270.
48: Watkins, pp.62-3.
49: See for example Oueijan, p.74.
50: *BoA* 1, 371.
51: *BoA* 1, 373.

hath need to know".[52] Watkins infers from this that the Oriental woman is "denied her basic humanity".[53] Marchand actually believes that Byron portrays the East in an unrealistically positive light with an overbalance of romantic sensibility in the speeches and actions of the "stolid Turks". The truth, Marchand continues, is that Zuleika is put:

> [...] on a pedestal in a manner that Byron would have ridiculed in his later satires, for he knew that in the East "wedlock and padlock mean the same".[54]

When Marchand states that the poet "knew" what the East was like, it implies that the critic shares this knowledge as well.

While conditions in the Ottoman Empire were definitely not based upon Islamic ideals or principles, it would be proper to keep in mind that at this time, as Mary Wollstonecraft pointed out, a married woman in England could legally hold no property in her own right, nor enter into any legal contract, nor for that matter claim any right over her own children.

In contrast to his Oriental affection towards Zuleika, Giaffir shows contempt for Selim, who in the first canto is portrayed as Zuleika's half-brother. This hatred is well manifested through racial insults directed at Selim's Greek mother.

> 'Son of a slave!' – The Pacha said –
> 'From unbelieving mother bred,
> Vain were a father's hope to see
> Aught that beseems a man in thee.[55]

Kidwai argues that Giaffir shows his contempt for women "in a true Oriental vein", when he mocks Selim's "less than woman's hand" which should, "Assume the distaff – not the brand".[56] Giaffir belittles Selim for being "Greek in soul",[57] thus showing that, similar to the fisherman in *The Giaour*, he is extremely racist. He speaks of "the dogs of Moscow"[58] and "the curs of Nazareth".[59] Giaffir also shows an equal amount of hostility towards Arab Muslims. While Giaffir reveals his religious and racial

52: *BoA* 1, 216.
53: Watkins, p.63.
54: Marchand, op.cit., p.64.
55: *BoA* 1, 81-4.
56: *BoA* 1, 99-100.
57: *BoA* 1, 87.
58: *BoA* 1, 96.
59: *BoA* 1, 98.

prejudices, Rishmawi points out that, he is "the most Eastern of *The Bride's* characters".[60] According to Bagabas, Giaffir represents not just himself but the reality of "Turkish social life".[61]

Selim's character is almost completely different from that of his uncle. What makes him distinct from his uncle and other Orientals is his Greek blood. In some ways, according to Joseph, he is similar to Romeo, because he is "Greek in soul, if not in creed".[62] According to Bagabas:

> His rebellion against his authoritarian and ruthless uncle have their origins in Selim's inheritance of love of freedom from his Greek mother. Thus he wants to redeem himself from his Turkish upbringing. Selim therefore unveils his Christian and western soul at the first opportunity he gets. He stands up for the Greek ideals of freedom he has inherited and studied as part of "The wisdom of the cautious Frank".[63]

Unlike Giaffir, whose sole entertainment is, "mimic war"[64] or even better put, "mimic slaughter",[65] Selim has a very sophisticated and civilized personality. He is thoughtful and has a gentle nature and he enjoys literature as well as nature. His uncle, who represents a full-blooded Muslim Oriental, despises these qualities. In the words of Giaffir, "We Moslems reck not much of blood".[66]

The Bride informs the reader that Islam endorses the spread of violence and despotic rule, and it is this, which, Watkins states, draws Selim towards moral destruction and decadence as the "existing social values" "actually control Selim's thinking and help to diffuse his planned insurrection".[67] When Selim ultimately decides to rebel against Giaffir, he already shows dangerous signs of Eastern passions. This is partially due to his love and reliance upon the Eastern Zuleika.[68] He does not realize that an unbridgeable difference exists between their two personalities and that is what brings about his undoing. He loves her not for what she is, but "for what he thinks she is". What influenced his decision to rebel, most of all, was his hatred for Giaffir who had murdered his father and usurped his

---

60: Rishmawi, George Khalil. *Oriental Elements in English Romantic Poetry: Shelley and Byron* (PhD Diss.), State University of New York (1983), p.111.
61: Bagabas, p.248.
62: *BoA* 1, 87.
63: Bagabas, p.271; the quotation is from *BoA* 2, 860.
64: *BoA* 1, 450.
65: *BoA* 1, 247.
66: *BoA* 1, 200.
67: Watkins, p.61.
68: *BoA* 2, 397.

position. His primary motive is revenge, which, Oueijan claims, is a virtue "highly regarded by the Orientals".[69] It is this Eastern part of his character that eventually prevents him from achieving the Hellenic values inherent to his mother's race.

According to Watkins, he is motivated by mere selfish and personal grievances,[70] and in this sense he is like the Giaour and Conrad, who were also infected by the East, and led astray from Greek ideals. Selim's position is especially difficult, though, because of his Oriental blood and his religion. He seeks guidance from the Qu'ran, "So may the Koran verse displayed / Upon its steel direct my blade".[71] However, his source of guidance is presented as an instrument of destruction, one whose verses give the civilized West a "severer wound". Like Giaffir, he thinks poorly of other races, an Oriental feature which, Kidwai believes, the poet has well portrayed. Complete redemption as a Greek or even a Christian figure is not possible, because of these racial flaws. Although the Greek part of him rebels[72] when he defends his dignity[73] and makes Giaffir quail,[74] his Oriental blood and environment are responsible for his inability to liberate his soul. The poem suggests that in the East men follow their wild passions and their blood boils in every vein.[75] It is here that brother kills brother, as masculinity means lust for power and killing innocent people to demonstrate power is commonplace.

While Selim rebels against what Joseph sees as the corruption and injustice of Ottoman society,[76] these social values eventually dominate his mind. In his endeavour to escape them, he speaks out against Giaffir's tyranny and vows to have "one only love",[77] or as Franklin puts it, he "offers a union based on Western monogamous romantic love".[78] Monogamous love is, apparently, non-existent in the East.

However, like his uncle, Selim too rules his followers like an Oriental despot and when he tells Zuleika, "Now thou art mine, forever mine",[79] he shows that he would own his bride like any Oriental would. Although he clearly prefers his Greek followers to the Muslims, his tyrannical Oriental

---

69: Ouijean, p.131.
70: See Watkins, p.64.
71: *BoA* 2, 671-2.
72: *BoA* 1, 118.
73: *BoA* 1, 110.
74: *BoA* 1, 130.
75: *BoA* 2, 207-8.
76: M.K.Joseph, *Byron the Poet* (Gollancz 1964), p.36-60.
77: *BoA* 2, 417.
78: Franklin, op.cit., p.61.
79: *BoA* 1, 346.

behaviour shows that he is not completely like them. The Greek pirates are "the last of Lambro's patriots"[80] fighting for freedom and equal rights. They are symbols of Western masculinity, as they are brave, faithful, and true (although they steal and plunder). Selim, however, sees them as slaves or tools[81] and he rules them as an Ottoman authoritarian.

His support for individual freedom and his decision to rebel are related to his desire to substitute Giaffir with himself. According to Watkins, this is another sign that he cannot escape the dominant social values.[82] Hence, he becomes the cause of the defeat of the Greek pirates in what Leask terms the "struggle between oriental and Hellenic norms"[83] that exists throughout the poem.

Perhaps, the most significant sign of *The Bride*'s Orientalism lies in Zuleika's relationship with Selim. This is where East meets West. Here Byron roughly adheres to the centuries-old theme, though focusing on Greek rather than Christian values. Zuleika is inferior to the Saracen women, though, because while they were fortunate enough to be redeemed, her attempt to switch to Hellenic values[84] ultimately fails.

Critics mostly agree that Zuleika represents the homogeneous Eastern woman; however, they have differing views regarding her personality. According to Watkins, she is passive and one-dimensional, while Sharafuddin claims that she is a symbol of innocence and sensuality. Watkins makes an important point when he states that her charm and sweetness towards her father, "seem to approve both him and his political position". Also, Sultana points out that, "from the very beginning her language is covertly sexual."[85]

Although Zuleika's general behaviour is childish throughout, when she learns that Selim is not her brother her response is even more abnormal. Instead of being relieved and thinking that now they could possibly be married, she says:

> Oh! Not my brother! – yet unsay –
> God I am left alone on earth? –
> To mourn – I dare not curse – the day
> That saw my solitary birth!

80: *BoA* 2, 380.
81: *BoA* 2, 302.
82: See Watkins, p.67.
83: Leask, p.41.
84: *BoA* 2, 496.
85: Fehmida Sultana, *Romantic Orientalism and Islam: Southey, Shelley, Moore, and Byron* (PhD Diss.), Tufts University, 1989, p.177.

Oh! Thou wilt love me now no more![86]

The Oriental female (like Giaffir) is infected with incestuous love, she shows no opposition to tyranny, and she is also ignorant as well as unintelligent.

Byron comments much about the East, however, one remark linked to *The Bride* is rather exceptional. Here he explains why Selim and Zuleika's relationship as brother and sister, was eliminated in the revision of the poem. He says:

> I had nearly made them rather too much akin to each other – & though the wild passions of the East [...] might have pleaded in favour of a copyist – yet the times & the *North* [...] induced me to alter their consanguinity & confine them to cousinship.[87]

Apparently, in the wild East, incestuous love is a natural and common thing. However, it is probably not coincidental that these tendencies, which supposedly existed in the Orient, coincide with Byron's own. However, the existence of these elements in the personality of Byron are rarely seen by critics as problematic when assessing the authenticity of his Eastern representations. According to Rishmawi, although the poem was written as a result of Byron's incestuous relationship, this does not necessarily mean that he is using or "exploiting the East for personal reasons".[88]

As Byron "was well aware" says Bagabas, that the East was "where indulgence in what is regarded as taboo at home is considered to be the norm".[89] Bagabas goes further and claims that in the East, Byron found the freedom to have an unlimited amount of sexual experiences with both men and women. However, elsewhere, Bagabas, whose major source for these claims is Crompton, contradicts himself. He writes that Byron "admits in his letters (BLJ I 241) that his acquaintance with females in a Turkish society was made inaccessible because of their seclusion ...".[90] This is consistent with Giaffir's warning in *The Bride*. "Woe to the head whose eye beheld / My child Zuleika's face unveiled!".[91] Byron and many Orientalist scholars seem to allow themselves to make contradictory, yet supposedly authentic claims.

86: *BoA* 2, 165-9.
87: BLJ III, 199.
88: Rishmawi, p.109.
89: Bagabas, p.131.
90: Ibid.
91: *BoA* 1, 38-39.

Through a close study of the text alone, numerous questions can be raised regarding its accuracy. As Selim and Zuleika are not actually brother and sister, how could it have been possible for the strict and stern Giaffir to allow Selim to "hold the Haram key"?[92] Even if he thought Selim and Zuleika did not know the truth that they were cousins, Giaffir did. Hence, if as Gleckner claims, it is a Muslim custom to veil "the faces of virgins from the eyes of all"[93] (which is, of course, not true), how would it have been possible for Giaffir to allow Selim access to the harem? Oueijan tries to resolve this problem of authenticity by claiming that Selim secures the key to the harem by bribing the guards. He supports his argument by informing the reader that, "love of money-renders bribery extremely effective in the East". The love of money is something which is inherent to the Muslim character and this knowledge, is presented as another reason for the work's authenticity.

Nevertheless, Oueijan's introduction of this stereotype does not resolve the problem in the text. Near the beginning of the first canto, Selim says to Giaffir, "I on Zuleika's slumber broke, / And, as thou knowest that for me / Soon turns the Haram's grating key".[94] While near the end of the same canto, Selim tells Zuleika that, "Thou know'st I hold a Haram key / ... and Haroun's guard / Have *some* and hope, of *more* reward".[95] It is quite clear that Giaffir knows about the key in Selim's possession. The bribes are probably paid to let Zuleika out of the harem tower. Therefore, the question about the harem key and Selim's access to Zuleika's chamber remains unresolved.

Zuleika represents the submissive Eastern woman, who is "a shimmering fetish object"[96] locked up in a tower. Through combining the imagery of different Oriental countries, Byron furthers the impression that the Oriental woman is homogeneous.

> And o'er her *silken Ottoman*
> Are thrown the fragrant beads of amber,
> O'er which her fairy fingers ran;
> Near these, with emerald rays beset,
> (How could she thus that gem forget?)

92: *BoA* 1, 475. "It was the office of Shaban, as Chief Eunuch, to keep the key of the Ladies' apartment" – Henley's note to *Vathek*, p.128 (1786 edition, pp.308-9).
93: Gleckner, op. cit., p.126.
94: *BoA* 1, 65-7.
95: *BoA* 1, 475, 478-9.
96: Mohja Kahf, *The Muslim Woman in Western Literature, from Romance to Romanticism* (PhD Diss.), Rutgers, The State University of New Jersey, New Brunswick, 1994, p.281.

> Her mother's *sainted amulet*,
> Whereon engraved *the Koorsee text*,
> Could smooth this life and win the next;
> And by *her Comboloio* lies
> *A koran* of illumin'd dyes;
> And many a bright emblazon'd rhyme
> By *Persian scribes* redeem'd from time;
> And o'er these scrolls, not oft so mute
> Reclines her now neglected lute;
> And round her lamp of fretted gold
> Bloom flowers in *urns of China's* mould;
> The richest work of *Iran's loom*,
> And *Sheeraz' tribute* of perfume.[97]

This highly romantic and sentimental view shows the oriental woman living in a world of Eastern wealth and charms that separate her from the world of reality. This is partially why she cannot understand that, according to Franklin, "she is not accorded spiritual equality with her father and brother by Islam".[98] Ironically, according to Islam the human soul is not divided into male or female.

According to Byron, women are viewed by the Prophet as so insignificant, that he thought it beneath his notice and unworthy of consideration to speak of the destination of the female soul:

> And oft her Koran conned apart,
> And oft in youthful reverie
> She dream'd what Paradise might be –
> Where woman's parted soul shall go
> Her prophet had disdain'd to show.[99]

An apologetic Sharafuddin tries to defend both the authenticity of these lines and provide an excuse for the Prophet at the same time. In support of Byron's Romantic realism, he claims that these lines rely:

> ... on many popular Islamic sources and Western commentaries which interpreted Muhammad's reluctance to promise women what he had promised to their men as a device to avoid arousing the latters' jealousy. The existence of the female soul is not denied, though its *exact* destination is unknown.[100]

97: *BoA* 2, 64-81.
98: Franklin, op.cit., p.51.
99: *BoA* 2, 103-7.
100: Sharafuddin, p.221.

There are a number of problems with Sharafuddin's argument, however. First of all, he does not name the Islamic sources that Byron apparently relies upon. Another problem is that he interprets, what Byron calls the Prophet's disdain, as mere reluctance, which cannot be true. In the time of Byron, as today, "to disdain" carried a clear negative connotation. What is most surprising, though, is that Sharafuddin agrees that the exact destination of the female soul is unknown. However, the Qu'ran makes absolutely no distinction between the souls of women and men or their destination:

> Whoever leads a righteous life whether be male or female, while he or she is a true believer, to them we will surely bestow a pure and good life in this world and We shall pay them surely a reward in proportion to the best of what they used to do.[101]

While critics often assume that Byron relies upon many Islamic texts, this example again reveals that his knowledge on the central Islamic text is severely flawed. The failure of literary scholars to recognize this, further questions their ability to pass judgement on Islam or the East.

Hence, when Byron claims that women are not allowed to approach the Ka'aba, nor can they be sure that they are worthy enough to be able to even make a vow, few of these scholars bother to see if this is true. Even when they do so, they regularly obtain their information from sources influenced by the same dominant discourse.

When Marchand claims that the work contains an "authentic background of Muslim customs", clearly he is authenticating among other things the completely erroneous lines that say:

> … I swear by Mecca's shrine
> If shrines, that ne'er approach allow
> To woman's step, admit her vow.[102]

This means that he is implicated in the misrepresentation of the Oriental.

It is the Oriental woman that ultimately brings about Selim's destruction. Although he throws aside his "Ottoman robe of pride"[103] as well as his turban, Selim makes a grave mistake about Zuleika, in thinking that she could be independent of any encounter with Giaffir. He does not

---

101: Q 16: 97.
102: *BoA* 1, 312-14.
103: *BoA* 2, 131.

understand, as Bagabas states, that he simply cannot keep her away from "the authoritative Oriental world to which Zuleika is deeply committed and connected".[104] This is impossible in an "Islamic environment". Hence, as Blackstone points out, it is this mistaken faith and fondness for the Oriental Zuleika, which causes his death.

> There as his last step left the land,
> And the last death-blow dealt his hand –
> Ah! Wherefore did he turn to look
> For her his eye but sought in vain?
> That pause-that fatal gaze he took –
> Hath doomed his death – or fixed his chain.[105]

This faith was ill-founded partially as the Oriental Zuleika was not as innocent as Selim thought. She was:

> Fair – as the first that fell of womanhood –
> When on that dread yet lovely serpent smiling,
> Whose image there was stamped upon her mind –
> But once beguiled – and ever more beguiling.[106]

Interestingly, the above lines are based on Genesis, which contradicts the Qu'ran's view that Eve was not responsible for The Fall. However, Byron and most of the critics quoted in this chapter do not know these simple facts. Nevertheless, these critics claim that Byron's characters could even "think, act, and talk as Easterners do".[107]

They are victims and perpetrators of a non-too-skilful confidence trick. Byron writes that *The Bride of Abydos* "is my story and my East".[108] He implies in doing so that he is privileged. He would have his readers believe that his extensive knowledge, and real intimacy, as opposed to bookish understanding, make him an authority on matters pertaining to 'the Other'. When he speaks of his East, in a sense he is correct. The monolithic Orient that he describes, with his friendly critics' approval, is truly an 'Other' of his own creation. It has little do with the Islamic people supposedly being represented. This East seems to reveal a great deal more about the poet and the Orientalism of these scholars than it does about any part of the lands, religions, and cultures east of Europe.

104: Bagabas.
105: *BoA* 2, 561-66.
106: *BoA* 1, 158-61.
107: Oueijan, p.97.
108: *BoA* 1, 158-61.

"Best Success Were Sacrilege": Investigating Antitheses in *The Siege of Corinth*

Robert McColl

Byron's letter to an anxious Tom Moore, August 28th, 1813, is much quoted: "Stick to the East" he writes; "– the oracle, Staël, told me it was the only poetical policy. The North, South, and West, have all been exhausted; but from the East, we have nothing but S**'s unsaleables".[1] Two years later, in 1815, he has, as he says, "apparently exhausted"[2] the East as well. He gives over to publication *Parisina* and *The Siege of Corinth*, and for six months or so enacts the silence *The Corsair*'s Preface "meditated". Meanwhile, the public agrees with him. Following *The Corsair*'s success, *Lara*, *Parisina* and *The Siege* are themselves increasingly "unsaleable".

But wherever Byron mentions Southey a character assassination is not far behind. "Unsaleable" for Byron may refer both to how many copies of Southey are bought up, and to how many should be. Then, concerning a writer whose "little book ... cast ... on the waters" *Don Juan* so savages (*DJ* I.222), Byron may intend a small pun on unsailable, or unseaworthy.[3] We may expect him to elide differences between commercial and aesthetic success. We may expect him to satirise both the hallowed authenticity of the unpopular poet, and the chameleonic commercialism of the popular

---

1: BLJ III, 101.
2: BLJ V, 45.
3: Byron likes conflating book and vessel, sale and sail. He hopes Hodgson and Bland "roll down the stream of Sale, with rapidity" (BLJ I, 241). To Henry Drury he extends the metaphor: "Hobhouse went to England to fish up his Miscellany, which foundered (so he tells me) in the Gulph of Lethe, I dare say it capsized with the vile goods of his contributory friends, for his own share was very portable. – However I hope he will either weigh up or set sail with a fresh Cargo, and a luckier vessel" (BLJ II, 59).

one. Byron's letter to Moore appears to merge a "poetical policy" with saleability. There may be something singularly *successful* about the lightness and fluency of saleability.

Venetian-occupied Corinth was besieged and taken by the Ottomans in 1710 under the Viziership of Comourgi, a history Byron read in *A Compleat History of the Turks* (1719). *The Siege of Corinth* is a chapter from that history, liberally modified. *A Compleat History of the Turks*, cited in the poem's Advertisement, speaks of the accidental explosion of a Turkish magazine which killed six or seven hundred. In the poem, it is the Venetians' magazine, stored in the vaults of a church, and deliberately fired by the despairing governor, Minotti.[4] The poem also renders the experiences of the fictional Alp, a Venetian convert to Islam attacking Christian Venetians, among whom is Alp's paramour, Minotti's daughter. Alp is the one of whom we read, his "best success were sacrilege":

> He felt how faint and feebly dim
> The fame that could accrue to him,
> Who cheer'd the band, and waved the sword,
> A traitor in a turban'd horde;
> And led them to the lawless siege,
> Whose best success were sacrilege. (396-401)

This describes a pointlessness, a choice without real difference. His only achievement can be to annul the standard by which they judge achievement. "Sacrilege" will mean not only a countering of religious tenets, but a more literal, material despoliation of them.

There is an analogy here, but how does it tally? Firstly, Alp's problem is the same as Tom Moore's, or any Orientalist poet's, locked into a subgenre whose poetic and commercial machinery he cannot escape. Moreover, the more the poet achieves popularly, the more he places himself outside the critical consensus. Indeed he appears to be effecting this separation of the popular and critical. Whether the siege will prove

---

4: Jerome McGann writes that it is the Venetians' magazine that was fired (CWP III, 482). He appears to be citing George Finlay's *A History of Greece* (1856), though he does not exactly specify his source. Finlay's *A History of Greece* however corroborates *A Compleat History of the Turks*, stating that it was indeed the Turks' magazine that was fired: "About noon a great smoke was seen from the Othman camp to rise over the Acrocorinth, and a loud explosion announced that from some unknown cause a powder magazine had blown up..." (from the 1970 reprint of the 1877 edition). *A Compleat History of the Turks* has it as Byron's Advertisement quotes.

successful – or the poem sailable, in any sense – is a nicety undermined by its inherent rejection of a critical standard. Both siege and poem will always be marked by this problematic disavowal of their reception. More particularly, of course, Alp is a surrogate Byron, attacking his compatriot critics, but destroying himself with them – a dubious self-sacrificer, brought down by desire for revenge. The problem for the critics is Byron's saleability. And saleability is Byron's great vengeance upon the critics.

Somewhere this serpent is still eating its tail. Byron is still taking revenge and many critics still have a problem with it. Jerome McGann writes that the poem "is, despite some careless passages, one of his [Byron's] strongest tales".[5] But for Marchand[6] and Gleckner[7] between them, the Oriental tales are "Hollywoody", and the *Siege* is "careless", "slipshod", "haphazard". Philip Martin doesn't like it any better. It is "impoverished", "pastiche", "sensationalist".[8] Frederick Shilstone[9] senses a precariousness and irrelevance to these aesthetic criteria. For him, the *Siege*, along with *Parisina*, is a postscript to the other tales, continuing *Lara*'s theme of lateness, or pastness. It does not have enough centrality to demand such an excommunication. Shilstone suggests Byron's proposed sequence of tales properly ends with *Lara*, and places *The Siege* outside it.

Jerome Christensen goes some way towards this viewpoint. He does not place *The Siege* outside the sequence of tales, because he sees all of the tales as necessarily sequential, but for *that* reason, he, too, implies an irrelevance to such decided aesthetic evaluations. He aligns the success of the Oriental tales to their "successiveness".[10] For him, their popularity is synonymous with their apparent ease and self-perpetuation. Success indeed is defined in these terms – perpetuation and popularity. "Byron's fragments," he says, "propose succession without consecution ... effects without causes, possession without conquest."[11] He finds repeated motifs across the tales, sliding from fragment to fragment, taking each poem beyond itself. The poems are a "system of signifiers", whose imperialism characteristically *survives*, to the service of a conservative and self-

---

5: CPW III, 481.
6: Marchand, *Byron's Poetry: A Critical Introduction*, pp.62-3 and 68.
7: Gleckner, *Byron and the Ruins of Paradise*, pp.164 and 167.
8: Martin, *Byron: A Poet Before his Public*, pp.45 and 60.
9: Shilstone, *Byron and the Myth of Tradition*, pp.92-6.
10: Christensen, *Lord Byron's Strength*, pp.96-7.
11: Ibid., p.104.

confirming commercial culture.[12] "The serpentine subjectivity of the Oriental tales unfolds without joints,"[13] he notes, as if seeing that same tail-eating serpent of popular success and critical sacrilege. Rather than taking part in that circle, Christensen observes it, and sees it as a part of the poems' procedure.

Christensen's critique raises a number of problems. Taking a lead from Said's *Orientalism*, he argues that *The Giaour* reinforces the premises of British imperialism, whereby the Orient corresponds to nothing "empirical", "nothing heterogeneous". Moreover, for Christensen, the "land of the cypress and myrtle" which *The Bride of Abydos* asks us if we know, is a nursery and drawing-room staple – a "garden of metaphors".[14] He imagines – or idealises – an "unresisting" reader, bound by *The Corsair* (just as Medora is bound), and "raped" by *The Giaour*, via the cycle of "consumption".[15]

Christensen extends his *Corsair* analogy, therefore, so that Conrad's locked cycle of turning and returning, his relentless serialism, becomes a figure for Byron's market-driven returns to the Oriental tale. Far from escape, the tales can deal only in repetitions and enclosure, having no external points to move to. In *Don Juan* he suggests, Byron's antitheses are tamed by their centrality.[16] They become equivocal rather than antithetical. Similarly, in *The Corsair*, Medora is captive to Conrad's and Byron's captivation with "structural opposition".[17]

It is particularly that "structural opposition" I want to address. Does *The Siege of Corinth* unsustainably pit poetic success against commercial success, or can it find a way around this jejune opposition? Does the poem understand and perpetuate only tamed antitheses? Answering these questions may give us an angle on Alp's apparently useless success / sacrilege paradox.

Certainly the poem is awash with genuine oppositions, strongly contrasted. Muslims fight Christians, East fights West and lover fights father. There is land and sea, within-city and without-city, past and present (a contrast both seen and felt), man and Nature, male and female meeting.

12: Ibid., pp.129-130.
13: Ibid., p.115.
14: Ibid., p.117.
15: Ibid., see pp.106 and 119.
16: Ibid., pp.96-7. Christensen cites the harem scene in particular as one where the antithetical risks becoming equivocal by virtue of being at "stage-centre".
17: Ibid., p.120.

Few things in the *Siege* are without their opposite. However, the hints and happenings documented in the narrative leave us in very little doubt what occurs when such ignorant opposites are allowed to clash. Catastrophe occurs. These opposites move with staggering violence and force toward a centre and interior (the church, notably the poem's only interior) and, too extreme to inhabit any interior, explode. And yet catastrophe means in this case less destruction than assimilation. In Christensen's words, "[n]othing heterogeneous can last in the face of the imperial coercion of reality called Orientalism".[18] The catastrophe eats up all the distinctions by which opposition feigned to operate. Witness –

> Christian or Moslem, which be they?
> Let their mothers see and say! (1041-2)

or:

> That one moment left no trace
> More of human form or face (1050-1)

But while the explosion is the acme of catastrophe and assimilation, this homogenising process has already begun before Minotti fires the magazine. The names on the vaults are, we read, "illegible with gore" (968), and there are "dead above, and the dead below…" (973), as if the two worlds were no different. Indeed, so *un*opposed are the Turks, they are gashing and decapitating the already dead (990-1). Even before the effects of slaughter, we begin to feel that what appear antitheses may amount to sameness. Like an image from *Inferno*, we find "the hero" – any hero – "mustering his last feeble blow / 'Gainst the nearest levell'd foe", and "grappling" with him upon the ground (841-6). This is an unspecified kind of hero, included now only in the list of things, and one who becomes ineluctably worthy of so undistinguished an opponent. Meanwhile the corpses around Minotti play a supporting role:

> The dead before him, on that day,
> In a semicircle lay; (784-5)

There is an absoluteness here, also a fluency, that brooks no question. "In a semicircle lay" is a line with one thought only – this semicircle – and advertises such with its dropped syllable, inviting silence before its accustomed time. Even Alp's death-shot, has its distinction strangely subsumed. So smooth it is that he falls "Ere an eye could view the wound"

18: Ibid., p.132.

(876). And if he dies before his time, neither is his tale really developed in *The Siege*, cut short before it gets going precisely because a tale already past. Seventeen lines later, another "Ere" affirms this sense of consummation without recognition:

> Ere his very thought could pray,
> Unanel'd he pass'd away (893-4)

Here, as often, when Byron wants to suggest effect without developed cause, the lines become shorter, punctuation is minimised, and their tenor more single. Opposition has no scope to contradict – his passing away is total.

The examples proliferate. The above all take place in what Byron calls "the after carnage" (770), but we could find more before that: in the dying's "downward borne" (746), in battle's "annihilating voice" (760) and, winning all particulars, in the unitary "muteness" of death (752). Indeed, "after carnage" and mere carnage resemble each other very closely. And since the poem begins not only *in medias res*, but in the *midst* of carnage, "before carnage", too, takes on these colours, "like the hands of dyers". As with Alp's death, we are not sure that anything here has its time, has any self-possession that is not either before or after. All things are seized by carnage, and the present struggles to make its presence felt. According to Francesca, Alp's life, even while alive, is "past" (634). Alp himself says, "'tis too late" (678).

This sense of the superfluous, of the "after-event" has been seen as particularly counterproductive to the poem's success, and the scene where wild dogs crunch on human skulls represents its quintessence. Instead of shortening to suggest singleness, here the lines lengthen to pentameters, suggesting looseness, lack of necessity. But the result of these long and shorts is the same: instead of tension, homogeneity:

> From a Tartar's skull they had stripp'd the flesh,
> As ye peel the fig when its fruit is fresh;
> And their white tusks crunch'd o'er the whiter skull,
> As it slipp'd through their jaws, when their edge grew dull,
> As they lazily mumbled the bones of the dead,
> When they scarce could rise from the spot where they fed;
> So well had they broken a lingering fast
> With those who had fallen for that night's repast. (458-65)

It is the excess the critics have reviled. They are, to use Gleckner's word, "overwritten".[19] Gifford, Byron's editor, crossed out the lines, but Byron insisted on their inclusion. "Lazily" is the key word in the passage, and is couched appropriately in an anapaestic twelve-syllables. Indeed, the passage as a whole is a rare instance in Byron of form's subjugation to content. In "when their edge grew dull", both "when" and "their" are repetitions lacking in tension. The "when" is handed down from "when its fruit is fresh", but looks gratuitous; we are going back to the tusks again. "Their" comes across from "their jaws", and though it refers to a different subject – the tusks – this hardly seems to matter. "Going back" is the mindset of the couplet here. The lines become a series of qualifiers. Even the "who" in line 465 looks like a "when" in disguise.

Finally, in the couplet 464-5, the dogs feed, or mumble, then cannot rise. But the place they cannot rise from is "where they fed", and cause and effect become likewise semi-consumed. The dogs are sunk in couplets which feign opposition only to undermine it. No wonder they cannot rise. The same is true of the following couplet, where the three-way figure of images introduces the repast (the breaking of a fast), then the fallen, then the repast again. Truly it is a repleting one.

Bernard Beatty has shown how Byron continues to use Augustan antitheses, but, via an "exploratory syntax", "dislodges" their accord with metre and grammar, showing what it is like to *have* antitheses, rather than focusing on the antithetical objects *per se*.[20] In *The Island* the couplet pointedly opens up antitheses and becomes a vehicle for the Romantic mode of consciousness – in Christensen's terms, "the lyric's complaint" at narrative's endless returning.[21] In *The Siege*, on the other hand, there is a gesture toward antithesis – the structural opposition the couplets are captivated by – but then another movement which faults the antithetical tension. Returning upon themselves, they reach no goal. They appear to confirm Christensen's view that, in Romanticism, it is the lyric which has the self-possession that narrative, in its returns, strives for but inexorably parodies.

By that token, it might appear that Byron is haunted by an Augustan order, and attempting by ways superficial, to return to it. Beatty however refutes the idea that Byron can only produce the appearance of an Augustan moral order in his verse. He does so with the paradox that

---

19: Gleckner, op.cit., p.171.
20: Beatty, *Continuities and Discontinuities of Language and Voice in Dryden, Pope and Byron* in *Byron: Augustan and Romantic.*
21: Christensen, op. cit., p.119.

continuity comes with discontinuity and, beyond intertextuality, is present in voice. I want to say that, insofar as *The Siege* returns upon itself in the manner shown in the "dogs" passage, it is parodic, but that it shows other modes by which to get away from parody. Its interest in "structural opposition" is not only an appearance and haunting. If it is consciously investigating those oppositions, they are nevertheless, like the Augustan idiom, present – this time outside the flow of the intertextual.

What are those modes which escape parody? The poem's chief antidote to homogeneity is its combination of historical sensibility and sense of structure. Alp is impressed not just with the signs of history but with its materiality, and is at his most unwritten – passing his hand athwart his brow – while reflecting upon history (literally reflecting *upon* it, because sitting on a "pillar's base"):

> He sate him down at a pillar's base,
> And pass'd his hand athwart his face; (507-8)

In that moment he is a part of that history, as that history is equal component in the playing-out of the present event. Indeed, history's material co-ordinates level out the event, and keep it from a consummation in teleology. How does the historical aspect of the poem keep the poem centred in event and not in result, and what part does fiction play in this? Focusing on these questions may suggest a different kind of reading from one emphasising tamed antitheses.

Firstly, more than the other tales, *The Siege* abounds with the names of historical places and people. The opening couplet gestures toward historical fact, despite its mistake. Then come the specifics of place we might expect from the other tales: Epirus, Acro-Corinth, Cithæron, the Isthmus, the Adriatic, Venice, St. Mark's palace, the plain of Carlowitz, Danube, Patra, Eubœa, and so on. Among the mythical or historical people, intermixed, we find Timoleon's brother (Timophanes), Persia's despot (Xerxes), Comourgi, Eugene, Sobieski, Menelaus, and Minotti. *The Siege of Corinth* is populated with facts – with names and places – and is so worldly as to count the co-ordinates of myth and religion among those facts, insofar as they are used and talked about, known and acted upon, in the present.

Secondly, these facts and names are necessary for the composition of what Byron envisaged as historical event, specific and localised, an idea which we can see taking shape in *The Siege*, and which roughly equates to his "truth of *history*".[22] It is not just its recourse to facts, its use of verifiable names or dates, that characterise the *Siege*'s historical nature, but also this identification of the event as a kind of temporal node. Though *The Giaour* may be based on amalgamated anecdotal histories, and the other tales allude to historical data – names, places, occurrences – *The Siege* is the only one to frame itself by one single, publicly acknowledged historical event, and to foreground its status *as* an event.

Daniel Watkins is good on this aspect of the poem. He reiterates that it was during the period of writing *The Siege*, Byron began and abandoned the historical narratives *Il Diavolo Inamorato* and *The Monk of Athos*, and started work on a version of the historical drama, *Werner*. For Watkins, Byron is not now looking only to describe historical episodes, but to "*imagine* historical processes at work ... pressures that constitute as well as shape both events and the individual experience of those events".[23] With *The Siege*, he says, Byron casts abstractions "within a framework that can explain them". Alp's story, or gestures, are contextualised and penetrated by historical event. This is not *his* tale; it is the tale of the siege of Corinth, and Alp is unable to absorb it. This is an important point. Compared with the other Oriental tales, *The Siege of Corinth* is barely a tale at all. It is the representation of a place and an event. Alp's tale, or idea of a tale, is carried within it. Moreover, according to Watkins, because Alp's past and motivations are abstracts, "we cannot construct a mechanical set of causes and effects to explain his exile .... This method of presentation not only emphasises "the present as history," but also decenters the narrative, denying the priority of a linear explanation of events and of individualist perspectives on events without denying the priority of historical context".[24]

Watkins' differentiation in Byron's procedure between "structural" and "causal" analysis is helpful. Byron chooses the 1710 siege of Corinth as subject matter for his poem for a reason. In choosing the siege of Corinth, *The Deformed Transformed*'s siege of Rome or *Don Juan*'s siege of Ismail, Byron is taking a historical event which has, as it were, an *a priori* completeness to it. He is attracted to the sieges of walled cities. Watkins suggests it is the moment of extreme upheaval and dramatic social change, but it is also the geographical circumscription which interests him. The sacking of a walled city is particularly localised. The circumscription which the walled city provides is as vital to the concept of

---

22: BLJ VIII 22.
23: Watkins, *Social Relations in Byron's Eastern Tales*, pp.108-9.
24: Ibid., p.111.

event as the more organic form the warring opposites generate. Organic and imposed forms combining, there is a self-address to the event we could call historical lyricism. For Byron's siege of Corinth, consequences are more like subsequences, and do not undermine the event's initial integrity. Narrative is "decentered", eluding the parody Christensen sees in the tales.

The notion of historical event, then, maintains antitheses which a more linear reading would domesticate. There is no need to impose them, or to look for their result, because their result is right there in the event itself. As we have seen, however, they are not now literary modes of procedure, but historical and geographical composites, situative more than situated. "The silent pillar, lone and grey" (410) is characterised above all by discontinuity. If the idea of Alp's tale gestures toward continuity in the tales, the pillar does not. Thus, the two armies, the city walls, the Isthmus, the spectacular pedestal of Acro-Corinth against the flat land, the two points in time between which the siege is played out − all of these are counterpointing, and measuring. But that they are found and proven by recourse to a register outside the literary, and that the historical event has such a formal character, argues that they continually escape the theoretical antitheses which lead to assimilation. This is precisely the premise Byron is testing in *The Siege of Corinth*.

But, beyond these geographical and dramatic counterpoints, the poem also has more conventional structural pointers, likewise resistant to assimilation. We see that in comparison with the other tales, and in pointed contrast to the long *Corsair* and repetitious *Lara* in particular, *The Siege* and *Parisina* have a natural sense of economy. Together they are the shortest of the tales to date, and *Parisina* in particular looks to be a length *The Giaour* was supposed to be, before it "somehow lengthened when begun". The parts, again in contrast to *The Giaour*, are not "fragments" but completed and distinct narrative episodes, easily characterised. They do not break within a train of thought, neither are the happenings they describe fragmentary or inexplicable ones, as in *The Giaour*. Like a book of *The Divine Comedy*, which, together with *The Iliad*, hangs so heavily over the poem, there are thirty-three of these parts, roughly eleven for each of the three sections of the poem − the setting, the night-scene and the war-scene.

Similarly, the poem makes much of mid-points, and uses them to temper as well as to demarcate its extremes. The setting on the isthmus of Corinth, between two waters, is as dramatic as it is appropriate. The poem finds a central locus in space, as indeed it does in time. Midnight, which opens the night-scene, also has a dramatic resonance, as it has in *Manfred* – the ability to draw things near its compass and hold them in suspense. It is reminiscent of a stage direction:

> 'Tis midnight: on the mountains brown
> The cold, round moon shines deeply down; (242-3)

The land too is the mid-point of the mutually-resembling sky and sea ("azure as the air"). Then we have the church as mid-point of the city, the city as mid point between two armies, and Greece as mid-point between Venice and the Ottoman empire. Stephen Cheeke attests that the part that Greece plays subverts the easy dualities of interpretation, even if it is partly suggested by them:

> The philhellenic idea of Greece is not easily accommodated within a system of Orientalism predicated upon the binarism of East-West relations, nor does it ever quite escape that system, but remains a ghostly and anxious presence.[25]

All of the tales, says Cheeke, have these metaphors of "hovering between"[26] to them. To some extent, via its visible scattered ruins, Greece also introduces a vein of Pagan plurality to the meeting of the great monotheisms. Bernard Blackstone speaks similarly of *The Siege*:

> Byron excels at these moments of suspense, of the poised wave, the tottering column: what in *The Monody of Sheridan* he calls the "breathing moment on the bridge where Time / of light and darkness forms an arch sublime". This breathing moment comes as the midpoint of an action which is easily seen as triple: Day- preparation (1-10); Night-pause (11-21); Day assault (22-33).[27]

In effect, what we find in these mid-points is not the barrier between two colliding opposites, but a temperance and measure that holds them buoyant. Midnight is repeated in line 267: "In midnight call to wonted prayer". Blackstone is wrong to find the Muezzin's call "arrogant", and Byron's use of "wonted" sarcastic.[28] "Wonted" denotes the ease and self-

---

25: Cheeke, *Byron and Place*, p.58.
26: Ibid., p.67.
27: Blackstone, *Byron: A Survey*, p.123.
28: Ibid., p.125.

appointment to voice – its usage, its anomalous desire, its being outside the pressures brought to bear by oppositions.

Within this measure, we find that the poem bears a different motivation from the siege itself. I mentioned earlier that at the siege's centre – and involved somewhere at the town's centre – is the church, also epicentre of the explosion. This, as we have seen, is the place to which the furious exchange of opposites are driven, and where they are forced to their ultimate sameness. It is also located at the poem's end. But the poem's centre is quite different from the siege's centre. It is the visitation of Francesca, and, more specifically, in a 1079 line poem, it is lines 538-41:

> His trembling hands refused to sign
> The cross he deem'd no more divine:
> He had resumed it in that hour,
> But conscience wrung away the power.

It is doubtful Byron plotted to situate these lines at the exact centre of his poem; nevertheless, in that he was thinking structurally and according to a sense of measure in writing *The Siege of Corinth*, the centrality of Francesca's visitation – and Alp's dilemma at its heart – is telling.

It's worth saying here that the scene represents the poem's most obviously literary moment – pointing as it does to similar scenes in the other Tales, and relating to a love-history quite literally "annaled" in a way that Alp's death is not. We know when we read it that we are coming to the formula, and foreground, in the poem. This Byron signals by a number of gestures which draw attention to the fact that the poem is being narrated, according to traditional narrative techniques, and by a conventional narrator. "'Tis midnight" could be said to begin this literary and readerly space within the poem. Then, the luck or providence which preserves Alp at the wall is an unanswered question:

> ...but they saw him not,
> Or how could he 'scape from the hostile shot? (442-3)

"How could he 'scape" indeed? It is the first of three unanswered questions, a formula with narratorial overtones which conjure briefly our narrator's first person ("I know not, in sooth"). Likewise, Alp finds the dogs "too busy to bark at him!" (457), and the exclamation is in part the frame of narrative. The dogs themselves, as we have seen, advertise a narrator toying with verse, and then the absurd-seeming comparison of

Alp's beating fingers to piano-playing ("Hurriedly, as you may see / Your own run over the ivory key") invokes again a genteel audience. Finally, the formula of three questions again, followed by an exclaimed answer, with archaism ("There sate a lady, youthful and bright!") advertises again the narrator's hand in the story – the introduction of this literary moment.

Then, linked to this conscious literariness, it is a fictional scene, as opposed to a factual or historical one. It is a different fiction from, for example, the explosion. Whether an accident or Minotti triggers the explosion does not matter particularly. Of course, Byron is concerned to show the effects of pride and obduracy, but this point is taken up into the overstatement which is the explosion. Death and waste neutralise all motivations and supposed causes. The fiction that it is Minotti who fires the magazine is part of the idea that history does not matter. Alp too is in the service of this historical iconoclasm, or sacrilege, when in the last part of the poem he continues to prosecute the siege. Alp and Francesca's fiction, however, represents an anomaly which upsets somewhat the totality of structural opposition. Because of it – because of its stylisation, its typology – and despite that later sacrilege, Alp's story as a whole does not take part in the linearization of history. On the contrary, it begins after, and ends before, the panorama of the siege. Alp can be an anomaly precisely because of this defined framework, whereas, for example, although piracy in *The Corsair* is imagined to be an anomaly, it ceases to be one, because piracy defines the poem. As the poem is all about the anomalous pirate crew, it creates no space for that anomaly to work in. What Byron communicates via Alp and Francesca is the allure of the exception among stark divisions. He finds something redemptive and anti-imperial in this inter-permeation of fiction and history, where neither represent exclusive totalities. Stephen Cheeke says something similar. For him, beyond the confines of the fiction / fact antithesis, Byron's Orientalism is about bringing out the *reality* of the East's "semi-fantastical nature".[29]

Chief among these anomalies, as we have seen, is Alp's hesitation to sign the cross. We can compare it with the signs of the cross which Francesca and Minotti insist upon and repeat. Those which they invoke exist not uniquely but in these repetitions. As if to confirm this, they echo across lines. Francesca asks:

> But dash that turban to earth, and sign
> The sign of the cross, and for ever be mine; (577-8)

29: Cheeke, op. cit., p.60.

as if one sign were not enough, while Minotti "made the sign of the cross with a sigh" (961), allowing for its joining with other, secular motivations, and the forthcoming explosion. It is as if the sign cannot exist without referring beyond itself. The overlaps in sign and sound in these lines do not allow for centring. To sign a sign, or to sigh a sign, is to interpret a symbol, to exchange spirit for letter. In Alp's irresolution, there is, contrarily, more of spirit. His non-sign is a withholding, existing between two antitheses, sacrilege and redemption and refusing both; one of the few things that pushes against the flow toward explosion. What it allows for is a more lateral reading – for history to maintain potentiality. The scene is not merely a mathematical centre but resonates after the teleology of catastrophe.

If such a moment is so central, if the poem is full of mid-points, is it not, to use Christensen's model, so central it becomes equivocal? Is it not too overdetermining, involving the poem again in self-enclosure? No, because, though literary or fictional moments, still they are not unitary. Alp's irresolution disrupts the unity of the Francesca scene. Similarly, Francesca is a spirit, and her semi-existence undoes the bond of two lovers meeting. There is much about the scene that is neither central, nor antithetical, and therefore, out of the nature of the circumscribed. The meeting takes place not at the centre of the city, but outside the city, at the wall's edge. The outside of walls is clearly a dramatic place for Byron. It is more or less where Cain meets Lucifer, where *The Vision of Judgement* is played out, and where Aurora Raby is seated. But there are no metaphysics here; this is the edge of a literal rather than heavenly city. This off-centre is the true middle of the poem, the middle which escapes away, is neither quite here, nor quite there. It is not an absolute and fictional nowhere, set, like *Lara*, on "The Moon".[30] Byron is consciously doing something very different from *Lara* here. This contrast between the city's centre – where the explosion happens – and the poem's centre is very illuminating. Byron pointedly contrasts dangerous centres with these persuasive "outsides".

The poem's stylistic gestures, its signs, are its other axis. There is Parnassus' light, frail, yet invulnerable "white veil" of snow (372). There is the hand that Alp passes "athwart his face", a subtle, theatrical gesture, reminding us how light he too is, how he too can be hidden (508). There is the hand that Francesca lays on Alp's, whose "thrilling" effect is out of keel with the effects most of the poem propounds. These neither come from, or go to, a particular point, but have a self-possession, allowing us

---

30: BLJ IV 146.

to read backwards and across, tempering an over-causal analysis of history, of which the assimilation of antitheses is the crude result. Success, also, is too crudely measured by such an analysis, which is why Alp appears stuck in the success / sacrilege paradox. "How could he 'scape?" The poem's sense of measure, also fiction's and history's off centres, elude capture by sacrilege, like the animals at its close. Likewise, the antitheses which threaten both Corinth and the poem, and which offer only a divided idea of success, are treated down to success, to a sailability, of a more singular kind. Rather than explode, and "exhaust", once and for all the Orient and its tales, in its treatment of historical event *The Siege of Corinth* looks toward the history plays and *Don Juan*.

Byron and the Other "Other" – Themes and Variations from Handel through Beethoven to Schoenberg

Gerald Silverman

Like many a young man just arrived in Cambridge for his first term, Byron was soon spending more than his allowance could bear. But in true "romantic" spirit he initially disclaimed the value of money as against "liberty". Though liberty then meant merely being away from his "tyrannical" mother. He wrote to Augusta on the 6 November 1805:

> I am allowed 500 a year, a Servant and Horse, so Feel as independent as a German Prince who coins his own cash, or a Cherokee Chief who coins no Cash at all, but enjoys what is more precious, Liberty. I talk in raptures of that *Goddess* because my amiable Mama was so despotic.[1]

By the end of the month, however, Byron was feeling the pinch. Writing to his solicitor, John Hanson, he complained that his financial provision was inadequate and that he felt let down and cheated.

The first term over, Byron moved to London, to lodgings in Piccadilly at the home of a widow who was a distant relative. From there, on Boxing Day of 1805, he wrote to Augusta again, now darkly hinting at some profound and secret emotional hurt that he would not yet fully confide in her. And on the heels of that letter, he wrote to her the next day confessing this much:

> The Affair is briefly thus; like all other young men just let loose, and especially one as I am freed from the worse than bondage of my maternal home, I have been extravagant, and consequently am in want of Money...[2]

1: BLJ I, 79.
2: BLJ I, 86.

Byron ended the letter by asking if Augusta would stand surety for him for a loan, for like many other Christian prodigals he would indebt himself to Jewish moneylenders.

A few days later, in another letter to Augusta, Byron hinted at a still darker problem, one that he refused to detail in writing, but which was causing him a deep 'melancholy'.

> My dearest Augusta – Your efforts to reanimate my sinking spirits will, I am afraid, fail in their effect, for my melancholy proceeds from a very different cause to that which you assign, as, my nerves were always of the strongest texture ... Suffice it to know that it cannot spring from Indisposition, as my Health was never more firmly established than now, nor from the subject on which I lately wrote [namely, his financial difficulties], as that is in a promising Train, and even were it otherwise, the Failure would not lead to Despair. – You know me too well to think it is Love; & I have no quarrel or dissention with Friend or enemy ... I fear the Business will not be concluded before your arrival in Town, when we will settle it together, as by the 20th these sordid Bloodsuckers, who have agreed to furnish the Sum, will have drawn up the Bond ...[3]

I would suggest that in this letter Byron, consciously or unconsciously, identified himself with Antonio in The Merchant of Venice. Here are the salient passages:

Antonio.	In sooth I know not why I am so sad ...
Salerio.	Your mind is tossing on the ocean,
	There where your argosies with portly sail
	Like signiors and rich burghers on the flood ...
Solanio.	Believe me sir, had I such venture forth,
	The better part of my affections would
	Be with my hopes abroad ...
Salerio. [...]	
	But tell not me, I know Antonio
	Is sad to think upon his merchandise.
Antonio.	Believe me, no ...
	... my merchandise makes me not sad.
Solanio.	Why then you are in love.
Antonio.	Fie, fie!
Solanio.	Not in love neither: then let us say you are sad
	Because you are not merry ...

3: BLJ I, 87-8.

Leslie Marchand has conjectured that Byron's melancholy at this time
sprang from a head-over-heels homosexual crush on a choirboy, a student
also at Trinity College, one John Edleston, and that much of Byron's then
self-confessed extravagance could have resulted from expenditure on just
this lad. Moreover, as Byron doubtless was aware, Shakespeare has
something similar going on also between Antonio and *his* friend Bassanio.
Here is Bassanio opening up his heart to Antonio very near the start of the
play:

<blockquote>

Bassanio. 'Tis not unknown to you Antonio
How much I have disabled mine estate,
By something showing a more swelling port
Than my faint means would grant continuance ...
...   to you Antonio
I owe the most in money and in love,
And from your love I have a warranty
To unburthen all my plots and purposes
How to get clear of all the debts I owe.
</blockquote>

And here is Antonio's reply:

<blockquote>

Antonio. ... be assur'd
My purse, my person, my extremest means
Lie all unlock'd to your occasions.
</blockquote>

Notwithstanding Byron's then *professed* "romantic" rejection of
material wealth, his undergraduate letters are peppered with reports of
pecuniary embarrassment and his resulting involvement with Jewish
moneylenders. On the latter he conferred various ethnic epithets –
"Israelites" – the "Tribe of Levi" – and, more straightforwardly, "Jews".

Coincidentally, at precisely this time, in 1806, Byron's idol since his
schooldays, Napoleon Bonaparte, who was now emperor of the French,
was consulting with Jewish representatives in France – the so-called
Jewish "notables" – about certain issues touching on the Jews as French
citizens. Not least he wished to clarify whether, according to their religion,
Jews were permitted to practice usury or not. He was assured they were
not (but that of course was only half the story). Soon this politically
convenient reply was, however, to be ratified even by the great Paris
Sanhedrin, which Napoleon convened the year following, in 1807. Maybe
Byron knew of this, for a Jew whom he had so far not yet met, but whom
he would eventually know well, was at this time writing an account of the
Paris Sanhedrin in the *Monthly Magazine* (see below).

To his credit, Byron never generalised his anger roused by Jewish *moneylenders*, some of whom did charge exorbitant rates of interest, uncritically against Jews as a whole. Otherwise two important future friendships with Jews might never have occurred. One of these was with Isaac D'Israeli, who was author of that article on the Paris Sanhedrin. D'Israeli's father had become rich in the world of finance, but Isaac chose a literary life, rejecting the cash-profitable careers that were on offer to him. He was lucky, however. His parents were indulgent, and from a grandmother he inherited a fortune that secured him materially for life. Among D'Israeli's literary works, Byron admired greatly his writings on the "curiosities" of literature (as their author called them), as well as those on the *psychology* of the literary character. In a volume of the latter, Byron wrote marginal notes that eventually found their way, via Murray, into the next edition of that work by D'Israeli. And on the 10 June 1822 Byron wrote to D'Israeli from Montenero confessing that, had he known his marginalia would eventually be printed, he would have made them far more copious, but that he was nevertheless not displeased with their publication. Then, in that same letter, he treated D'Israeli as someone whose opinion he regarded highly, and as one he could trust. He wrote:

> Mr Murray is in possession of an M.S.S. Memoir of mine (not to be published till I am in my grave) … In it I have told what, as far as I know, is the *truth* – *not* the *whole* truth – for if I had done so I must have involved much private and some dissipated history … I do not know whether you have seen those M.S.S.; but as you are curious in such things as relate to the human mind, I should feel gratified if you had.[4]

And he added:

> If there are any questions which you would like to ask me as connected with your Philosophy of the literary Mind (*if* mine be a literary mind), I will answer them fairly or give a reason for *not* – good, bad, or indifferent.[5]

Byron would be ever ambivalent not only towards Jews but also towards money, and in later life he identified himself somewhat more with Shylock than with Antonio, even while penning his notorious tirade against Jewish bankers in *The Age of Bronze*.

4: BLJ IX, 172.
5: BLJ IX, 172-3.

Byron and D'Israeli became excellent friends, and the proud Jewish father eventually introduced to the poet his prodigious young son, Benjamin. A touching footnote to this friendship is what happened to Byron's loyal Venetian servant, Tita, after Byron had died. Giovanni Battista Falcieri (to give Tita his real name) was then taken into the service of Isaac D'Israeli, who brought him back to England, there to be cared for even by Benjamin Disraeli also, who found for him government employment for a while. Thus Tita lived out his autumn days in comfort, not least basking in the celebrity of his former Byron connexion, to die aged seventy-six.

Byron's other Jewish friend, Isaac Nathan, rose from humbler stock than D'Israeli's. Nathan's father had sacrificed much to send his son to a Jewish boarding school in Cambridge (the first of its kind in England), there to study in order to become a rabbi, learning along the way Hebrew, Latin and mathematics. To study formally at the two great English universities was still barred to Jews (as also to Catholics and nonconformists), but Nathan could attend lectures informally at Cambridge University, and did so for a while. (Isaac D'Israeli was barred similarly from a university education, but was made an honorary Doctor of Civil Law by Oxford University in 1832 in recognition of his historical writings.)

The gift of a violin at an early age, however, made clear to Isaac Nathan that his real passion was for music, and he left his school prematurely to study music full time. Music was to be his destiny. He had a sweet voice, an instinctive gift for musical understanding, and more than average charm.

In their backgrounds the two Isaacs – D'Israeli and Nathan – differed sharply. Both were quintessentially "other" to Christians, but, to each other, each was *another* kind of "other". D'Israeli was a Sephardic Jew, while Nathan, the son of a Polish Jew, was Ashkenazi. The Sephardim, who derived from Spain, Portugal and the Middle East, were the first Jews to settle in England after Cromwell had raised the ban, and were initially more affluent and possibly more cultured (that is what *they* thought at least) than the later arriving Ashkenazim from Germany and central Europe. They looked down on the latter. Even when the Ashkenazim prospered also in England, the Sephardim looked down their noses at them as *arrivistes* and *nouveaux riches*.

Byron, though, was un-influenced by such intra-Jewish snobbishness, even if he was aware of it. And it was probably Nathan of the two Isaacs who was ultimately the more intimate with Byron. He seems genuinely to have captivated Byron, something that caused resentment eventually in not a few of Byron's *Christian* friends.

Unlike D'Israeli, Nathan had neither family wealth nor powerful family connexions to help support him. His material needs had to come from the sweat of his brow. Fortunately, in the first couple of decades of the nineteenth century there was a rising vogue for traditional national songs, and Nathan determined to cash in on this by composing music based on ancient *Jewish* melodies. Some were very old, it is true, though whether any dated from temple times, as he advertised, is arguable.

Nathan needed words to go with his music, and to this end he tried to interest an English poet to provide these. Walter Scott declined, but Byron's imagination was captured. Douglas Kinnaird, then Byron's gentile banker, catalyzed this collaboration, though afterwards he turned sour on Nathan and tried to undermine his relationship with Byron. Yet Byron stayed warmly disposed towards his new Jewish friend. This is illustrated in a touching exchange of letters between the musician and the poet that was prompted by Nathan's gift to Byron of some Jewish Matzohs before the latter's final departure from England:

> My Lord,
> I cannot deny myself the pleasure of sending your Lordship some holy biscuits, commonly called unleavened bread, and denominated by the Nazarenes Motsas, better known in this enlightened age by the epithet Passover cakes; and as a certain angel by his presence, ensured the safety of a whole nation, may the same guardian spirit pass with your Lordship to that land where the fates may have decreed you to sojourn for a while.[6]

> My dear Nathan,
> I have to acknowledge the receipt of your very seasonable bequest, which I duly appreciate; the unleavened bread shall certainly accompany me in my pilgrimage; and, with a full reliance on their efficacy, the *Motsas* shall be to me a charm against the destroying Angel wherever I may sojourn; his serene highness, however will, I hope, be polite enough to keep at a desirable distance from my person, without the necessity of besmearing my door posts or upper lintels with the blood of any animal. With many thanks for your kind attention, believe me ...[7]

6: Isaac Nathan, *Fugitive Pieces and Reminiscences of Lord Byron* (1829), pp.89-90.
7: BLJ V, 68-9.

One of Nathan's melodies which is of undoubted antiquity accompanies *On Jordan's Banks*. It is that of a Hebrew hymn sung by Jews the world over at the festival of *Chanukah*. Moreover Nathan brought his early if abortive rabbinical training to bear when consulting with Byron on some of the latter's texts. In his *Fugitive Pieces*, written after Byron's death, Nathan gives a lengthy discussion on the various Jewish scholarly arguments over the Book of Judges, though not dwelling overmuch as to whether Jephthah did in fact sacrifice his daughter or merely had her remain a virgin. This latter detail was then, in fact, in live debate amongst Anglican Christian theologians as well. In the former century Handel's librettist, Thomas Morrel, had departed from earlier tradition and kept the daughter alive in Handel's great last oratorio *Jephtha*, in conformity with English "Enlightenment" concerns to have the Almighty appear to behave as rationally and humanely as possible. But with the arrival of romanticism the aesthetic had been reversed once again. Thus, for example, Edward Smedley wrote in his advertisement for *his* poem *Jephthah* (which incidentally he sent to Byron around this time):

> The controversy in regard to Jephthah's sacrifice has been extended to considerable length; and like all other controversies is still undetermined – there can, however, be but little doubt that, for all poetical purposes, it is far more sublime to consider that Jephthah offered his daughter as a living victim on the altar, than that he devoted her to perpetual virginity ...[8]

That he was an aristocrat was important to Byron, even if he was also a great "Liberal", and a defender, for example, of the rebelling frame-workers. Perhaps this double-sidedness in his nature was a consequence of his childhood situation, which was relatively humble and seemed, at first, to offer little realistic hope of later ennoblement. But, even that ennoblement, when it did come, did little to impede Byron's enthusiasm for the French Revolution or for Napoleon Bonaparte (that Corsican-come-Frenchman who filled the role of a multipurpose "other" for so many romantics at that time); while it is noteworthy that Byron, the aristocrat, did not immediately or automatically take exception to Napoleon crowning himself emperor.

Ludwig van Beethoven, whose background was nowhere near so exalted, also professed "liberal" views, though still unable to resist pretending, on the bogus basis of the Dutch "van" in his name, that he had

---

8: Edward Smedley, *Jephtha: a poem* (London: John Murray, 1814), Advertisement.

noble blood (thus without success he tried to have his nephew Karl's custodianship case heard in the court of Nobles rather than in the Commoners' court on this basis).

Whereas it took Napoleon's military failure and subsequent exile to Elba to draw from Byron his tirade in the *Ode to Napoleon Buonaparte*, for Beethoven the final straw came years earlier. Hearing that the general had made himself emperor, Beethoven famously tore up the original dedication to him at the head of his *Eroica* symphony.

For some years Napoleon remained a central symbol of romanticism. He was Prometheus, having stolen fire from God's appointees, the old aristocracy, to give it instead to their erstwhile subjects. And art and literature pictured him repeatedly as Prometheus, with Promethean allusions pervading all kinds of romanticism anyway. Thus Byron wrote a *Prometheus* poem, Shelley a *Prometheus Unbound*, and Mary Shelley subtitled her *Frankenstein* "A Modern Prometheus' Furthermore, for the last movement of the *Eroica* symphony Beethoven had adopted a theme that he had composed first for his ballet score, *The Creatures of Prometheus*. And in his *Ode to Napoleon Buonaparte* also Byron managed a reference to Prometheus.

Now let us move to the twentieth century. On the 30 January, 1933 Hitler came to political power, and on the 31 October of that year, after much heart wrenching and vacillation, the renowned Austrian Jewish composer, Arnold Schoenberg, left Europe for sanctuary in America; where he was feted and made to feel thoroughly at home. He had been forced to flee Austria and Germany because he was Jew. It mattered not at all that, though he was born a Jew and circumcised, he had in his twenties converted to Lutheranism, and for a while even tried out Catholicism. Once a Jew, always a Jew. Thus, even before Hitler, other anti-semitic forces were driving Schoenberg back to his Jewishness. In time he fully re-adopted his parental faith, turned actively pro-Israel, and more than ever focussed much of his art on Jewish themes.

Schoenberg, like both Byron and Beethoven, was touched also by the shadow of Napoleon; and had, like them, eventually found this hero wanting. In 1942 he set to music, for Speaker, Piano and String Quartet, Byron's *Ode to Napoleon Buonaparte*. The vocal line is here in *Sprechstimme* (as in his earlier *Pierrot Lunaire*), in which speech and song are blended, pitches left only approximate. The musical language is twelve-tone serial atonality; which is, of course, Schoenberg's most identifying contribution to musical evolution. But, as in some other atonal works, Schoenberg ended the "Ode" with a tonal cadence – to close on an

E flat major triad – a symbolic nod almost certainly to Beethoven's *Eroica* symphony that is in that key also.

Just when or why Schoenberg first engaged with Byron's poetry we do not know; but in 1918 Schoenberg added to the catalogue of his private library a list of new purchases that included writings by Zola, Rousseau, Goethe, Balzac and *Byron*. According to his biographer, Stuckenschmidt, Schoenberg "recognized similarities in the figures of Napoleon and Hitler." But Schoenberg wrote to Stuckenschmidt in 1948:

> Lord Byron, who previously admired Napoleon very much, was so disappointed by his resignation that he overwhelmed him with the sharpest scorn; and I believe not to have missed this element in my composition.[9]

Here then is that old ambivalence about Napoleon still. At which point we have come full circle.

9: H.H.Stuckenschmidt, *Schoenberg: his life, world and work* (London: John Calder, 1977), p.453.

THE RECEPTION OF BYRON'S POETRY IN RUSSIAN LITERATURE AT THE BEGINNING OF THE NINETEENTH CENTURY

SVETLANA KLIMOVA

The fame of Byron's personality in Russian literature and culture, and Russian admiration for his poetry, are well-known. A passionate interest in him, both as a poet and as a man, began to appear in Russia in the second decade of the nineteenth century, and continues to this day. As is written by the renowned Russian Byronist Nina Diakonova, in her article "Russia and Byron", "his life and his works are as much studied, published and translated at the end of the twentieth century and the beginning of the new millennium as they were at the beginning of the nineteenth century."[1] The first Russian translations of Byron's poetry appeared in 1819, and the latest one (*The Prisoner of Chillon* by G. Usova) was published in 1989; and while the first Russian literary works about him date from the 1820s, the last ones date from the 1990s (they are G. Usova's *Veri Baironu / Believe Byron*, 1991, E. Manilova's *Ty tochno znal / You knew exactly what*, 1999, Yu. A. Dombrovskii's *Smert' lorda Bairona / The Death of Lord Byron*, 1999, plus others); and while his name was first mentioned by a Russian critic in 1815, studies of his art and mind continue in the twenty-first century. He appeal to Russian readers has endured for two centuries.

In 1815 in the journal *Rossiiskii Museum / The Russian Museum* V. V. Izmailov, a follower of Karamzin, mentioned Byron's name for the first time in the Russian press, reviewing *The Corsair* and noting his and Walter Scott's growing fame. By that time the Russian public had become acquainted among British writers mostly with Milton and Shakespeare, with Young, Gray and Ossian, with Sterne and Richardson. Until the seventies of the previous century Russian culture was mostly oriented on

Sections of this essay appeared in the *Byron Journal* 33:2 (2005) and are reproduced here with the permission of the Academic Editor.
1: N. Diakonova. *Russia and Byron // The Reception of Byron in Europe*, in 2 V. – L., N.-Y., 2004; II, 352.

the French model, and Russians knew almost nothing about British
authors, except for some essays and allegorical tales by Addison, Steele
and Dr Johnson. A. A. Bestuzhev, a Decembrist and a prominent man of
letters, noted in 1833, that England "was lying then for us at the sea-
bottom"[2].

The next review that mentioned Byron appeared a year later, in 1816,
and was written by another Karamzin follower, V. I. Kozlov, in the journal
Russkii Invalid / The Russian Invalid. The two journals represented the
late Russian sentimentalists' circle and gave the first interpretation of
Byron's poetry as that of "sensitiveness ever tender and vivid"
("chuvstvitel'nost' nezhnuyu zhivuyu"). Most probably, they bore in mind
British sentimental authors. The anti-Karamzinist journal *Vestnik Evropy /
The Messenger of Europe*, that began to publish papers on Byron's works
in 1818, stressed another feature of Byron's art – that of the "bleak
colouring" and "rebellious passions" ("mrachnyi kolorit", "miatezhnye
strasti") of the heroes. This point of view revealed the pre-romantic,
"Ossianic" understanding of it[3].

He became famous in Russia in the twenties and thirties of the
nineteenth century, among a new generation of critics, writers and readers.
Byron became the most important figure of contemporary European poetry
for the people whose minds were shaped by the French Revolution that
inspired optimism in the liberal-thinking Russian aristocracy and gave rise
to the political reaction of the tsarist government. The First Patriotic War
of 1812 influenced Russian society no less. The event was followed by
rebellions among peasants and soldiers in the next decade and by a strong
liberation movement among the nobility, which led some of them to the
Senate Square in Saint-Petersburg on December 14, 1825 and to the
scaffold or Siberia after the Decembrists' failure.

The following extract from a letter written in 1819 by count Petr
Viazemskii, a poet, a critic and a close friend of Pushkin, gives one of the
earliest examples of this new, and very enthusiastic, attitude towards
Byron's poetry:

> I am bathing in the depths of poetry, reading and rereading Lord Byron,
> certainly, in pale French translations. What a rock, from which the
> ocean of poetry is spurting! … Who reads English and writes Russian in

---

2: A. A. Bestuzhev. *O romane N. Polevogo "Kliatva pri grobe Gospodnem"*,
Moskovskii telegraph, 1833, N 15 / / *Dekabristy. Estitika i kritika.* – Moscow,
1991; 163.
3: N. Diakonova. *Russia and Byron / / The Reception of Byron in Europe*, in 2 V. –
L., N.-Y., 2004; II, 334.

Russia? Bring him to me! I'll pay him with my life for each Byron verse.[4]

Byron, both as a personality and a poet, became a symbol of the new epoch for Russian readers. As Viazemskii declared in 1827 in the article *Sonety Mitskevitcha / Mickiewicz's Sonnets*, "it is impossible in our time not to sound Byronic ... He set to music the song of the whole generation".[5]

The reception of Byron's poetry proved to be inseparable from interest in his life. He was one of the first two contemporary British authors known to Russians, the other being Walter Scott. As a contemporary writer and a conspicuous figure in European politics, Byron attracted people's attention to the smallest details of his life. In 1823, to satisfy the demands of the reader, the journal *Syn Otechestva / The Patriot Son* closely followed Byron's life in Greece. Its No 45 informed the public, that "Lord Byron is living on the island of Cephalonia. He has offered to Greeks a considerable supporting sum ..."[6] In 1830 Lermontov read Thomas Moore's memoirs about Byron and compared his own life with that of the British poet; and in 1835 Pushkin attempted a biography of Byron, never to be finished. From 1822 onwards Byron was spied on by the Russian secret services, his political activity being considered dangerous enough to cause a threat to the established political order in Europe; the new editions of his poetry were banned by the censorship, and all translations of his poems were heavily censored.

His liberal convictions, his revolutionary activity in Italy and Greece found an enthusiastic response in Russian "free-thinkers", especially in the future Decembrists, and provoked hot polemics in the press. Thus in 1823, reviewing *The Vision of Judgement*, *The Patriot Son* provided the official point of view on the poem in the following statement: "There is a character of high-handedness and disbelief, his permanent rules of anarchy and rebelliousness".[7]

Byron's death in Messolonghi, which became known in Russia in May 1824, aroused a most vehement reaction. The common feeling was that of loss, as can be seen in a letter written by A. A. Bestuzhev to his friend P.

4: *Ostafievskii arkhiv kniazey Viazemskih.* v 3 t., - St.-Petersburg, 1899; I, 326.
5: P. A. Viazemskii. *Sonety Mitskevitcha / / Dekabristy. Estitika i kritika.* – Moscow, 1991; 163.
6: M. P. Alekseev. *Byron i russkaya diplomatiya / / M. P. Alekseev. Russko-angliiskie literaturnye sviazi.* – Moscow, 1982; 419.
7: *Syn Otechestva*, 1823, N 32 / / *Dekabristy. Estitika i kritika.* – Moscow, 1991; 426.

A. Viazemskii: "We lost a brother ... in Byron, humanity its fighter, literature – its Homer of thoughts." In the same letter Bestuzhev revealed the connections between Byron and Greece, Byron and contemporary European history and politics: "He died, but what an enviable death ... he died for Greece, if not for Greeks. ... He acted ... for the sake of all humanity."[8] A huge number of poems devoted to Byron's death appeared in Russia in the mid-twenties, and these words reflect the ideas expressed in the majority of them. Among the authors of the poems is K. F. Ryleev, a Decembrist-poet, who wrote *Na smert' Bairona / To the Death of Byron* (1825) and V. K. Kiukhelbeker, a poet, critic, and friend of Pushkin, who created *Smert' Bairona / Byron's Death* (1824). There were published *Smert' Bairona / Byron's Death* (1829) by D. Venevitinov, *Bairon / Byron* (1824) by I. I. Kozlov, a prominent translator of Byron's poems, and another *Bairon / Byron* (1827) by P. A. Viazemskii. Pushkin is known to have ordered a funeral service for "Georgii" (George) in May 1824 in Mikhailovskoe, and to have written the poem *K moryu / To the Sea* the same year. In the poem Byron is described through the image of the sea and is given its characteristics of "mightiness" and "depth", "gloom" and "invincibility":

> Исчез, оплаканный свободой,
> Остав миру свой венец.
> Шуми, волнуйся непогодой:
> Он был, о море, твой певец.
>
> Твой образ был на нем означен.
> Он духом создан был твоим:
> Как ты, могущ, глубок и мрачен,
> Как ты, ничем неукротим.[9]

(He) disappeared, wept over by freedom, / Having left his wreath to the world. / Roar, swell with tempest: / He was, oh sea, thy bard. / Thine image was printed on him. / He was created by your spirit: / Like thee, he was mighty, gloomy and deep, / Like thee, he was invincible.

Ryleev, Kiukhelbeker and some other authors, according to their generally active political position, concentrated in their poems on the political and civic significance of Byron's art and life. Pushkin, Kozlov

---

8: A. A. Bestuzhev. Letter to P. A. Viazemskii. June 17, 1824 / / Ibid. – Moscow, 1991; 189.
9: A. S. Pushkin. *Polnoe sobranie sochinenie*, v 6 t. - Moscow, 1949 - 1950; I, 401.

and Viazemskii emphasized his "deep thoughts" (Pushkin, Kozlov), his "wild soul" (Viazemskii), his "invincible" fire (Pushkin) and his "secret sorrow" (Viazemskii) as the essential characteristics of Byron's works. But to oppose the two groups of the authors would be a simplification of the live literary process. For Ryleev, who was the most "political-minded" poet among Russian authors of that period, Byron's art was an expression of "men's passions, their deepest motives, the eternal struggle of passions with a secret longing for something high, for something infinite"[10]. On the other hand, the image of Byron in Pushkin's poem *To the Sea* is lucidly connected with the notion of freedom.

Byron's poetry as a model of the new literary epoch was ardently criticised, translated and followed. As far as criticism is concerned, the opinions were not always unequivocal. "Many of his pages" were acknowledged "eternal".[11] This "eternal quality" was, in the mind of the Russian reader, connected with the art with which he described human passions and feelings, with the "astonishing" ideas, colours and pictures (as pointed out by Kiukhelbeker and by Pushkin). Thus, analysing the peculiarities of his poetry, Viazemskii argued that the "ugliness" of its style, in which the "wild cries of his heart" were expressed, the "disorder" of its composition (meaning that of *Childe Harold's Pilgrimage* and the *Oriental tales*), the dominating gloomy power of the Byronic hero were the true ways of expressing the spirit of the time.[12] On the other hand, the "monotony" of his gloomy intonation (Kiukhelbeker), the subjectivity of his works, especially of his dramas (Pushkin), his adherence to "moral horrors", "ravaged souls" and "crushed hearts" (Kiukhelbeker) and something "terrifying and embarrassing for the soul" (Zhukovskii), even the irony of *Don Juan* (Kiukhelbeker) were not to be accepted by most of the critics with enthusiasm. Upon the whole, the general favourable attitude to Byron's rebellious spirit, to his deep insight into human psychology and men's society and to the new literary forms in his poetry was accompanied by disapproval of the despair of his world-vision. The gloom was interpreted as disbelief in political and social change, in the possibility of progress in human society and nature, and thus contradicted

10: K. F. Ryleev. *Neskolko mysley o poezii. Syn Otechstva*, 1825, N 22 / / *Dekabristy. Estitika i kritika.* – Moscow, 1991; 424.
11: V. A. Zhukovskii. Letter to I. I. Kozlov, Jan. 27. 1833 / / V. A. Zhukovskii. *Sobranie sochinenii*, v 4 t.– Moscow – Leningrad, 1960; IV; 600.
12: P. A. Viazemskii. Letter to A. Turgenev, 1819 / / *Ostafievskii arkhiv kniazey Viazemskih*, v 3 t. - St.-Petersburg, 1899; I, 327; P. A. Viazemskii. *"Tsygany", poema Pushkina. Moskovskii telegraf*, 1827, N 15 / / *Dekabristy. Estitika i kritika.* – Moscow, 1991; 112.

the social optimism characteristic of the "pre-Decembrists'" epoch in Russia. It was often understood as total disbelief in God, and that was, certainly, another point to provoke an ambiguous attitude from Russian critics. Before the Decembrists' rebellion in 1825 the profound stoic endurance of life in disillusionment and loss, characteristic of Byron's art, did not resonate among the majority of Russian readers. Understanding came in the thirties, to find its highest expression in Lermontov's poetry.[13]

As far as translations are concerned, the first two translations of Byron's poems into Russian appeared as early as 1819: they were N. P. Gnedich's translation of the poem *Impromptu, in reply to a friend* (under the title of *K drugu / To a Friend*, and without mentioning the fact that it was a translation) and K. Batiushkov's translation of an extract from *Childe Harold's Pilgrimage, Canto IV* (published only in 1828). The next year another Byron poem, *From the Portuguese*, was published under the title of *Portugal'skaya pesn'a / A Portuguese Song* in Viazemskii's translation. In 1821 the there were six translations of Byron's works, including three of the *Turkish tales* – *The Bride of Abydos*, *The Giaour* and *The Siege of Corinth* - and *Mazeppa*, all rendered in prose from French prose versions by M. Kachenovskii.

The *Oriental*, or *Turkish, tales* became the most popular among Byron's poems to be translated and imitated in the second and third decade of the nineteenth century. Their popularity among Russian interpreters can be judged by the following figures: from 1821 till the middle of the 1830s there were published three translations of *The Giaour*, plus two translations of some extracts from the poem; two translations of *The Bride of Abydos*; three translations of *The Corsair*, two of *Lara*, three of *Parisina*. There also appeared two translations of *Manfred* and one translation of an extract from it, and two of *Mazeppa*. *Childe Harold's Pilgrimage* was widely read (mostly in French versions), but was not translated as a whole during that time, most probably, because of censorship; beginning with 1825, nevertheless, about ten authors translated extracts from it. Zhukovskii's interpretation of *The Prisoner of Chillon* (1822) played a considerable role in forming Russian romanticism and made the poem a highlight of Russian literature. From 1825 onwards there appeared four interpretations of *Darkness*. *Hebrew Melodies* as well became a perpetual source of inspiration for Russian translators, especially after 1825: there were more than ten references to different poems in the cycle during the above-mentioned period. *Don Juan* is known to be read

---

13: *Istoriya russkogo romantizma*, v 2 t. – Moscow, 1979; I, 5-11.

with admiration, for instance, by Pushkin and Ryleev, but there were only four extracts from Byron's great poem translated at that time.

The *Turkish tales* proved to be not only the most frequently translated Byron's poems, but also the most influential model for Russian literature of the second and third decade of the nineteenth century. At the beginning of the twenties, when Russian romanticism was searching for new forms of expression, Byron's *Turkish Tales* provided a model for the new genre of the lyric poem that was to replace the genre of the classical epic poem for Russian poets. One of the peculiarities of Russian poetry at that time was that the tradition of the epic poem had ceased to exist some decades before, and the only "long" genre remaining was that of the descriptive poem. In 1821-4 Pushkin's "Southern poems" – *Kavkazskii plennik* / *The Captive in the Caucasus* (1820-1), *Brat'ya-razboiniki* / *The Robber Brothers* (1821-2), *Bakhchisaraiskii fontan* / *The Fountain of Bakhchisarai* (1821-3) and *Tsygany* / *The Gypsies* (1824) – appeared. They were once as strongly associated in the minds of the public with the name of Byron, as they were rightly understood in connection with the genre of the "long" poem, primarily the descriptive poem. Thus Viazemskii, speaking about the first of them, *The Captive in the Caucasus*, emphasized its significance in the Russian literary tradition and traced a clear connection between this poem and Zhukovskii's translation of *The Prisoner of Chillon*. In his words, *"The Captive in the Caucasus* and *The Prisoner of Chillon* ... interrupted the long silence that dominated our Parnassus."* Going on, he declares, that "the author of the tale *The Captive in the Caucasus* (following the model of Byron in *Childe Harold*) wanted to communicate to the reader the impressions that influenced him during his journey."[14] Analysing the last of Pushkin's "Southern poems", *The Gypsies*, Viazemskii concentrated on the similarities between its composition and the composition of Byron's *The Giaour*. According to his statement, "in the very form, or, better to say, in the very absence of ... a conventional form ... the author's reading of *The Giaour* is reflected. Byron also ... did not unite different parts of the whole, but he rather followed an order, or disorder which was imposed on him by the clear thought and the true notion of the character of his epoch."[15]

Pushkin's "Southern poems" together with Zhukovskii's translation of *The Prisoner of Chillon* began the tradition of the lyric, or romantic, poem in Russian literature. It was clearly stated and proved by the Russian

---

14: P. A. Viazemskii. *O "Kavkazskom Plennike", povesti soch. A. Pushkina. Syn Otechestva*, 1822, N 49 / / *Dekabristy. Estitika i kritika.* – Moscow, 1991; 45.

15: P. A. Viazemskii. *"Tsygany", poema Pushkina. Moskovskii telegraf,* 1827, N 15 / / *Dekabristy. Estitika i kritika.* – Moscow, 1991; 112.

scholar, academic V. M. Zhirmunskii in his monograph *Pushkin and Byron* that Pushkin's "Southern poems" followed Byron's model and preserved some particular features of Byron's *Turkish Tales*. Zhirmunskii also argued that most of the Russian romantic poems written and published after the "Southern poems" imitated Pushkin, and did not borrow straight from Byron. Thus, among the lyric poems written after Pushkin's Southern poems, Zhirmunskii distinguishes the group modelled on *The Captive in the Caucasus*, in which the authors imitated the motifs of the hero's captivity, love of a beautiful native girl for the captive, the arrangement of his escape by her and the escape itself (for example, D. Komissarov. *Turetskii plennik / The Captive in Turkey*. 1830; N Minaev. *Kirgizskii plennik / The Kirgiz Captive*. 1828; P. Rodivanovskii. *Plennik / The Captive*. 1832, and so on) Another group is modelled on *The Fountain of Bakhchisarai*, primarily not in its plot, but in the "harem" setting and in the central personages (a "pasha" and a "harem captive", his wife or daughter). (Oznobishin, *Selam, ili yazyk tsvetov / Selam, or the Language of Flowers*. 1830; Gerbanovskii, *Khadzhi-bey*. 1833; *Ziuleika*. 1839, etc.). *The Robber Brothers* and *The Gypsies* didn't prove to be so influential: the majority of the "family dramas" followed I. I. Kozlov's *Chernets / The Monk* (A. Podolinskii, *Borskii*, 1829; *Nishii / The Beggar*, 1830; P. Inozemtsev, *Ssyl'nyi / The Exile*, 1833, and so on). The motif of robbery was so popular at that time, that it cannot be traced explicitly in different poems back to Pushkin.

The importance of the place the new genre occupied in Russian romantic literature can, firstly, be testified to by the number of lyric poems modelled on Byron's *Turkish tales* that appeared in that period. According to the data given in Zhirmunskii's book, there were above two hundred poems of this kind, 120 of which were presented as complete, the rest published as parts of poems. Lyric poems became a mass genre in the late twenties and early thirties in Russian literature. Secondly, the fact that they were written and published all around Russia, in both the capitals and in provinces, proves both the genre's popularity and its importance. Thus in 1832 I. Kosiarovskii's poem *Peremetchik / The Defector* appeared in Odessa; in Kharkhov P. Inozemtsev's poems were published in the thirties, in Kazan – those by A. Fux, in Minsk, by D. Sergievskii. And, thirdly, as we've already seen in the comment made by Viazemskii on Pushkin's "Southern poems", they aroused a lively interest among literary critics and were acknowledged to be a new phenomenon in Russian literature.

In *The Captive in the Caucasus* the hero, a Russian officer, is captured by Circassians and imprisoned, but only so that he can observe the simple, savage life of the natives and become loved by a beautiful native girl. She soon discovers that he cannot reciprocate her feelings, because of the unhappy love he experienced in Russia, which, together with disappointment in society and human relations, still keeps him gloomy and desperate. She helps him escape, but refuses to follow him, and when he swims across the river and reaches the other side of it, the sound of a splash is heard, and the girl is nowhere to be found. Together with the "exotic scene" – the Caucasus here – and the love conflict at the centre of the poem's plot, the Russian author borrows from Byron's *Turkish tales* the composition, characteristic of which is the narration starting in the middle of the action and the plot not coinciding with the storyline. Pushkin also imitates the complicated relations between past, present and future in the poem, and between the author's and the characters' points of view, as well as the hero's and heroine's monologues, their dialogues, and the author's digressions, which are interrelated with each other. He also borrows the structure of Byron's tales: the poem consists of a dedication, a tale itself, an epilogue and a commentary explaining exotic words mentioned in the poem, the historical facts, and so on. He certainly borrows the image of the Byronic hero, and his dominant position in the poem. But at the same time, all these Byronic features undergo a considerable change in the new context of another author's art, of a different culture and literary tradition.

The "exotic scene" still plays an important role in the poem, bearing the meaning of particular unusual beauty of nature (the mountainous landscape of the Caucasus, as opposed to the flat one of central and Northern Russia), and of the unusual customs and beliefs of the native people (Circassians with their war-like games, their hospitality, and their cruelty to the enemy). It is worth noticing here that an interest in other cultures, particularly, in eastern cultures, was as characteristic of Russians at that time as of British or French people. As a result of this social interest, the Eastern Department was opened in the Main Pedagogical Institute in St Petersburg in 1818; a number of translations from Saadi and Hafiz appeared in the twenties, and in the period between 1825 and 1827 the journal *The Asian Messenger* was published. The "exotic scene" also, like Byron's tales, has particular political implications, the setting referring to the place of perpetual contemporary conflicts, caused by the politics of expansion, led by Russia at the end of the eighteenth and the beginning of the nineteenth century. The politics resulted in the fact that parts of Armenia, Georgia and other Caucasian states were brought under the power of the Russian monarchy. The Caucasus also meant at that time the place of exile for politically undesirable people – thus Pushkin was

exiled there in 1820 and Lermontov in 1837 and in 1840. At the same
time, the fact that the setting is so close to Russia (in fact, inside Russia),
that it is so "domestic", and the hero is Russian, captured by natives of the
Caucasus, emphasizes the meaning of "the opposite", or "the other" in a
way different from that of Byron in his tales. In fact, Pushkin's poem
appeals to the patriotic feelings of the reader, making him sympathise
strongly with the protagonist as his compatriot. If we look at the
background to this feature of Pushkin's poem, it becomes clear to what a
large extent it reflected the general atmosphere of the epoch. Patriotism,
aroused in Russia after the Napoleonic war of 1812 in all layers of society,
was realized in Russian literature in many ways, including attempts to
imitate folk songs, to adapt folk metres in literary verse, and to depict
events from the recent and remote past of Russian history. It was one of
the leading motives, if not the only leading motif, in the works of the
Decembrist-poet Ryleev.

The meaning inherent in the wilderness of nature and wild life of non-
civilized natives (as opposed to the civilized Russian), drawn by Pushkin,
does not seem to refer to Byron's tales either (compare his highly civilized
Turks), though a parallel can be drawn with his *Manfred* (the episode with
the Chamois Hunter). On the other hand, the opposition "harmonious
nature – disharmonious humanity" so characteristic of Byron's *Turkish
tales* is never carried over into the Russian poem.

In any case, in his next "Southern poems" Pushkin finds other "exotic
places", also inside Russia. In *The Robber Brothers* the action takes place
in the Volga steppe; in *The Fountain of Bakhchisarai* the Crimea serves as
the setting, and in *The Gypsies* it is the southern steppe where the events
are depicted. The places are not associated with any political message, and
are mostly significant as the places either of particularly beautiful nature
and Eastern Muslim culture with the accent on the peculiar roles of men
and women in the culture (*The Fountain of Bakhchisarai*) or of non-
civilized wild life where what is deemed "freedom" by the hero as "the
other" (Aleko in *The Gypsies*) is revealed a set of rules and traditions,
different from those he is accustomed to. In *The Robber Brothers* the most
obvious meaning of the setting is that of a place for outcasts. In the first
and the last cases there are apparent parallels with Byron's *The Bride of
Abydos* and *The Corsair*; in the second case again Byron's *Manfred* (the
episode with the Chamois Hunter) can serve as the parallel, though it is
much less obvious. Following Pushkin, other authors made the Caucasus
the scene of their poems: among them one can list *The Captive of
Dagestan* by A. Shishkov-the-Second (1824), *Nina* by Kosianovskii
(1826) and *The Cossack of Greben* by V. Yakovlev (1835), and others. A

number of poems depicting the Southern steppe and the Crimea was published as well. Siberia appeared among the favourite places for Russian romantic poems – most probably, under the influence of Ryleev's one completed poem, *Voinarovskii* (1825).

The hero is also modelled on the Byronic hero of the *Turkish Tales*, but again with some particular changes. Byron's emphasized descriptions of the hero's "pale face", "bent brow" and "glazed eye" (*The Giaour*) with generalizing comparisons and epithets adding to the emotional intense and general character of his psychological state ("pale as marble over the tomb", "the flash of that dilating eye", "ghastly whiteness") correspond in Pushkin's poem to more laconic and particular forms of expression. For example, describing the Captive, the narrator says:

> Таил в молчаньи он глубоком
> Движенья сердца своего,
> И на челе его высоком
> Не изменялось ничего.[16]

He kept all the movements of his heart in deep silence, and nothing changed on his high forehead.

We can state, in the words of the renowned Russian scholar Yurii Mann, that "the Russian romantic poem preserves the stamp of highness and significance in the portrait of the central personage. But it makes the image softer …"[17] We may add that it makes the image more particular.

The poem is concentrated upon the hero who is revealed, like the hero of Byron's *Turkish Tales*, to be a man superior in his nature to all the other men around him and disappointed in people, life and society. At the same time, he seems not to have lost all his hopes, for he goes to the Caucasus deliberately, longing for some illusionary freedom, and he does not die at the end of the poem, but returns to Russians. Accordingly the main motive of his despair seems to be less a total disappointment, or disillusionment with the whole Universe, causing a constant doubt poison each moment of his life, but more specifically the result of worn-out passions, betrayed friendship and unhappy love. Anyway, they are not to be forgotten, and he is not to achieve happiness or start a new life.

On the other hand, his superior and dominant position in the poem doesn't appear as absolute as that of the hero in Byron's tales. Thus, being

---

16: A. S. Pushkin. *Polnoe sobranie sochinenie*, v 6 t. - Moscow, 1949 - 1950; II, 342.

17: Yurii Mann. *Dinamika russkogo romantizma*. – Moscow, 1995; 90.

a captive, he cannot lead other people, so that his personality forms no
contrast to that of anybody around him and can be seen only from the
point of view of his keepers. Another factor that transforms the position of
the hero is the change of the position of the heroine: in the second part of
the poem she is described in no less detail than he, her feelings and
thoughts being revealed in her monologues and their dialogues, in the
author's address to her and in characteristics given to her emotional state.

The changes introduced by Pushkin into the image of the Byronic hero
found their way into his other "Southern poems"; they were later
developed by such authors as   K. Ryleev (in his *Voinarovskii*, 1825), I.
Kozlov (in his *Chernets / The Monk*, 1825; *Nataliya Dolgorukaya*, 1828
and *Bezumnaya / The Insane Lady*, 1839) and by E. Baratynskii (in his
Eda, 1825; *Bal / The Ball*, 1828 and *Nalozhnitsa / The Concubine*, 1831),
as well as borrowed and imitated by various authors of "mass" literature.
Thus, Voinarovskii's estrangement is caused particularly by his role in the
Russian-Ukrainian politics in the times of Mazeppa and Peter the Great
and by his exile to Siberia as Mazeppa's supporter and relative. He at least
can feel quite happy when he discovers that his wife has followed him. He
becomes nearly desperate again when she dies, but finds a true friend in
Doctor Miller who can share his feelings and ideas. His despair is anyway
never absolute, because there is something he firmly believes in, and feels
for, and lives for – and that is the prosperity of his native country, Ukraine.
And though he's never to see it again, the fire of patriotism warms his
heart.

In I. Kozlov's *The Monk* the motive of the estrangement of the hero is
also very particular – his orphan state and poverty. It comprises several
stages, as well. He first manages to overcome his gloomy emotional state
when he meets his future wife and marries her, but becomes miserable
again when she and their baby die. Once again he is restored to life when
after some time he realizes that he will meet them in heaven, but again he
falls into despair when, struck by a sudden fit of hatred and indignation, he
kills the man he thinks caused his wife's death. He then becomes a monk
and is no less ardent in his prayers than any of the other monks. Written in
the form of a confession-monologue pronounced by the dying hero to the
friar (compare *The Giaour*), the poem ends with his death, accompanied
by bell ringing.

In Baratynskii's *Eda* a Finnish peasant girl stands at the centre of the
poem. The author, describing her seduction by a hussar as the cause of her
estrangement, gives a detailed picture of the changes in her psychology
moving the whole poem towards psychological realism. The girl's despair,

the feeling of loss and guilt lead her to despair and death, according to the rules of the romantic poem.

The sentimental tradition had a strong influence on the majority of Russian Byronic poems, including those by Kozlov, Baratynskii and Pushkin, both in the choice of the hero and in how he is described. Thus, Kozlov has a poor orphan as his hero, Baratynskii has a peasant girl, and Pushkin also has an orphan (in *The Robber Brothers*). Kozlov's monk is said not only to pray before his death, but to cry, as well. Pushkin's hero Guirei (*The Fountain of Bakhchisarai*) is also portrayed crying when remembering the death of his beloved wife Maria. The traces of sentimentality that influenced Russian reception of Byron's art so profoundly, can be found in the half-ironic characteristic given to it in Pushkin's *Evgenii Onegin* (Part III, stanza XII):

> Лорд Байрон прихотью удачной
> Облек в унылый романтизм
> И безнадежный эгоизм.[18]

Lord Byron by a successful caprice / Cloaked in dejected romanticism / Even hopeless egotism.

Kozlov's poem *Byron* gives one of the brightest examples of the "sentimental Byronism" that tinged the image of Byron itself with the colours of Christian-like sentimentality, preserving, at the same time, the ambiguity of the romantic conflict:

> И даже в последний таинственный час
> Страдальцу былое мечталось,
> Что будто он видит родную страну,
> И сердце искало и дочь и жену,
> И в небе с земным не рассталось![19]

And even in his last mysterious hour / The sufferer was dreaming about the past, / He had the vision of his native land, / And his heart was searching for his daughter and wife, / And did not part with its earthly aspirations in heaven!

Following Byron in composition and in structure, Pushkin also begins his poem with description, though not of the natural beauty, but of the

---

18: A. S. Pushkin. *Polnoe sobranie sochinenie*, v 6 t. - Moscow, 1949 - 1950; III, 53.
19: I. Kozlov. *Bairon* / / I. Kozlov. *Stikhotvoreniya*. – Moscow, 1948; 59.

native people, after which a sudden introduction of the captured hero
follows. While the tale develops, the author's descriptions of the hero's
emotional state, of his thoughts are interrelated with the descriptions of
nature and the life of the natives, with the dialogues between the hero and
heroine, with their monologues and with the author's digressions. The
main change introduced by Pushkin here is that the author's digressions
tend to be ousted from the main body of the tale. Thus, there is only one
digressive generalization by the author in the first part of the poem, and
one address by the author to the heroine in the second, with the author's
"I" mostly concentrated in the epilogue. Significant is another tendency in
Pushkin's poem: the author's words in the epilogue appear to be more an
expression of a personal concern, than a generalization of the message
given in the poem, than an attempt to project the message to the whole of
humanity (in contrast to many of Byron's digressions). Thus the epilogue
of *The Fountain of Bakhchisarai* begins:

> Покинув север, наконец,
> Пиры надолго забывая,
> Я посетил Бахчисарая
> В забвеньи дремлющий дворец.[20]

Having left the North at last, / High merriments forgetting for long, / I
visited Bakhchisarai, / Its palace, slumbering in oblivion.

In the epilogue of *The Captive in the Caucasus* Pushkin refers to his muse
who chose the Caucasus as the right place to fly to because of its
"wilderness" and "crudity", its war-like inhabitants and their legends, and
the importance of recent historical events. He presents an equivocal
picture of these events in the following words:

> И смолкнул ярый крик войны:
> Все русскому мечу подвластно.
> Кавказа гордые сыны,
> Сражались, гибли вы ужасно:
> Но не спасла вас ваша кровь.[21]

The fell cry of war is stilled: / Everything is tamed down by the Russian
sword. / Sons of the Caucasus, you fought and perished terribly: / But
your blood did not save you.

20: A. S. Pushkin. *Polnoe sobranie sochinenie*, v 6 t. - Moscow, 1949 - 1950; II,
396.
21: Ibid., II, 352.

Similar changes can be observed in all the other "Southern poems": *The Fountain of Bakhchisarai* and *The Gypsies* have nearly the same composition, with the author's "I" relegated to the epilogue; and in his *The Robber Brothers* the author doesn't appear at all. I. Kozlov's *The Monk* follows Pushkin's model: the author's "I" appears only in the address to his wife before the actual beginning of the tale; there is no author's digression in the tale itself; the "voices" taking part in the narration being reduced to that of the hero and the narrator. Nearly the same can be said about Ryleev's *Voinarovskii*: inside the poem there are only two "voices" speaking – those of the narrator and the hero, "outside" it there is an introductory address to A. A. Bestuzhev to reveal the author. In Baratynskii's *Eda* the author's voice is heard only in his addresses to the heroine. Commentary and prose introductions, so important for Byron's *Turkish Tales*, were not strictly borrowed, either. There is no prose introduction to any of the "Southern poems", and only two of them – *The Captive of the Caucasus* and *The Fountain of Bakhchisarai* – have a commentary. Ryleev in his *Voinarovskii* gives two prose introductions, describing the lives of Mazeppa and Voinarovskii. There are neither commentaries nor introductions to either of Baratynskii's or Kozlov's poems.

Last, but not least, Pushkin closely follows Byron in arranging the narration around the love conflict and in introducing a novelistic plot into the poem. Love in Pushkin's poems, as well as in all other Russian romantic poems, becomes the embodiment of ideals, the highest realization of man's aspirations, feelings and values, of man's notion of happiness. It is always passionate, and to some extent rebellious, and it is never to be achieved as a permanent state in one's life: it must be confronted either with the death of the beloved woman (man) (in *The Fountain of Bakhchisarai*, in *Voinarovskii*, in *The Monk*), or with a rejection (in *The Captive in the Caucasus*), or with betrayal (in *The Gypsies*, in *Eda* and in *Nina* by Baratynskii). But, following Byron here, Russian romantic poems do not stress the contrast between the hero's and the heroine's love to one "chosen" person and hatred for, or estrangement from all the others. Thus, in *The Gypsies* the protagonist Aleko, having fallen in love with a gypsy girl Zemphira, joins her band, and even earns money, creating shows with a bear.

As far as the plot is concerned, the Russian romantic poem tends to reduce Byron's "horrors" – deaths, rebellions, robberies, incest and executions – to a more "usual" narration. Thus, in *Robber Brothers* the hero tells a story of his own and his brother's orphan state, their becoming robbers, his brother's death after their escape from prison, and his joining a band of robbers after that. In *Eda* the plot is even more trivial: the heroine falls in love with a Russian hussar, is seduced and abandoned by him; at the end of the poem she dies in despair.

So, Byron's *Turkish Tales* were received in the Russian literature of the second and the third decade of the nineteenth century as a genre of the new romantic poem, with a certain hero, with particular relations between the protagonist and the other characters of the poem, with a certain set of motives and themes, and compositional and structural elements. The model of Byron's poems was transformed by Russian authors according to the needs and demands of developing literary taste in a particular cultural and historical context. Upon the whole, Russian romantic poems kept particular Byron motives and figures of speech, such as the "exotic scene", the "high" portrait of the hero and heroine, the sudden introduction of the hero, rhetorical questions and exclamations to move the action, etc. They also kept the central dominating position of the hero, the complicated composition with the author's voice interrelated with those of the narrator and the hero and heroine; the general interpretation of the main conflict as that of love to reveal human inability to achieve the ideal. At the same time, the model of Byron's *Turkish Tales* undergoes a considerable change in the interpretation of Russian poets. The transformations introduced by them after Pushkin's "Southern poems" concentrate in the interpretation of the "exotic scene", in the depiction of the hero's or the heroine's estrangement; of their love; as well as in the plot, composition and structure of the poem.

Among Russian Byronic poems those written by Mikhail Lermontov stand out as an original and a rather late phenomenon. The number of the poet's works belonging to this genre is over twenty (exactly twenty if we count his completed poems). To specify the period of Lermontov's interest in the Byronic poem it is necessary to speak about his creative activity on the whole. He started writing his Romantic "tales" (as some of them are called) when he was fourteen – it was the poetic form he chose for himself one of the earliest. His two masterpieces – *Demon* / *The Demon* and *Mtsyri* – were completed in 1838 and in 1840 respectively, which means ten and more years later and the end of his life. The poet's constancy in developing one genre seems to have been supported, on the one hand, by his personal interest in the Oriental culture of Caucasian peoples and his actual participation in the military operations led by Russian troops in the Caucasus; and, on the other, by Lermontov's rapt attention to Byron's poetry and prose. The peculiarity of his "tales" might be connected, to some extent, with a fundamental change in the social and political atmosphere in the country after the Decembrists' defeat, with its reflection in the poet's tragic *Weltanschauung*, and, at the same time, with Lermontov's close reading of Byron's original texts, especially the *Turkish tales* and the mysteries.

It should be noted, though, that Byronism is to no extent limited in Lermontov's works by the genre of the Byronic poem, but plays a significant role in his lyric pieces and in his prose novel *A Hero of Our Time* (1838-9).

Lermontov's earliest Byronic poems – *Tcherkesy / Circassians* (1828), *Kavkazskii plennik / The Captive in the Caucasus* (1828), *Korsar / The Corsair* (1828) and *Prestupnik / The Criminal* (1829) – in their basic features reproduce the model of the Byronic poem as it was created by Pushkin and Zhukovskii and developed by Kozlov, Baratynskii and Ryleev. These basic features include the Caucasus as the setting of the first two works, deliberately modelled on Pushkin's *The Captive in the Caucasus*, and the plot built around the idea of capture (*Circassians*, *The Captive in the Caucasus)* and of orphanage and robbery (*The Corsair*, *The Criminal*). The author's "I" is significantly reduced in the poems as compared to Byron's tales: thus the number of digressions in *Circassians* is limited to one, *The Corsair* and *The Criminal* bear the form of a monologue and a dialogue respectively, so that the author's voice does not sound in them directly at all. The hero's estrangement appears to have such traditional motives for the Russian Byronic poem as the hero's capture, his orphan state in his childhood and the heroine's unrequited love. The hero's estrangement seems to be non-absolute: thus the captive in *The Captive in the Caucasus* shares his depression with other captured Russians. The heroine in *The Captive in the Caucasus* behaves actively, and much attention in the poem is concentrated on her image. A significant role in the hero's description is played by sentimental elements (e. g. his "dejection", his "tears" in *The Captive in the Caucasus*).

At the same time, even in these early poems Lermontov is somewhat different from other Russian authors of romantic poems. The main elements distinguishing him from others concentrate in the setting and the plot: in *The Corsair* the hero mentions the Danube as the river of his motherland and says about his being a corsair in Greece. In *Circassians* one of the main episodes depicts in detail a cruel battle between Russians and Circassians. In both the poems Lermontov's introduction of the elements that can be considered "unusual" for the Russian romantic poem seems to be connected with the direct influence of Byron's works (mainly *The Corsair* and *Lara*). The supposition can be confirmed by the fact that in 1830 Lermontov worked at prose translations of Byron's *Darkness*, *Napoleon's Farewell*, *The Giaour* and *Beppo*, and created verse

translations of the first two mentioned Byron's works and some other ones
in 1830 and 1831.

Gradually some of the structural elements of the Russian romantic
poem, used in Lermontov's early "tales", disappeared in the poet's later
works, giving way to the features some of which might be described as
more clearly Byronic and the others as more personally Lermontov's.
Thus beginning from *Poslednii syn volnosti / The Last Son of Freedom*
(1831) no sentimental elements can be traced in the hero's
characterization: the conventional "dejection" corresponds to the hero's
"grief", "despair", "vengeance" and the "emptiness" of his soul; as well as
the hero's "tears" to his "silence", a monumental pose and acts of
retaliation. In *Ispoved / Confession* (1830), *Azrail* (1831), *Angel smerti /
The Angel of Death* (1831), *Ismail-Bei* (1832) and some other later
Lermontov's "tales" the hero's estrangement is depicted as pronouncedly
total, directed against the whole world and – in its absolute form – against
God the Creator. In connection with that the heroes of *Azrail* and *The
Angel of Death* are non-human beings of the Promethean type. As if
referring to Byron's *Lara* and *the Siege of Corinth,* Lermontov creates
images of war in *Ismail-Bei* and *The Angel of Death* and uses in the first of
them the plotline of the heroine masked as a man following the hero in his
battles. Also partially changed are the role and the character of the
author's digressions: his words, though quite laconic, can sound directly
and serve not to refer to a certain situation or emotion but to make a
general conclusion, or to correlate the episode described with general
qualities of human nature. Thus, in *The Angel of Death* "the East" is
characterised by the "beauty" of the times, 'when by the stamp of the evil /
the soul of people, following its fatality, / was not yet disgraced ..." A
motion to the Byronic might be seen in the way Lermontov treats
patriotism in his "tales": though the motif of patriotic feelings aroused in
the hero is present in some of them, they never play the leading role in his
psychological state or his decision-making. The position is clearly stated
by Leila in *Khadzhi Abrek* (1833): "The divine world is beautiful
everywhere / There is no motherland for the heart!" More specifically
Lermontov's seem to be the motives of prison, of the superfluous man and
of disbelief: the first, shaping in *Circassians* and *The Captive in the
Caucasus*, appears in its more or less complete form in *Confession*, and
then serves as the central image for *Moriak / The Sailor* (1832) and *Mtsyri*
(1839-40). Lermontov's is the semantic development of the motif: the
action of the poems focused on real prisons, by the end of the poems the
whole world appears a prison for a human soul aspiring to personal
freedom. The motif of the superfluous man, the image of whom seems to

be a particular development of the Byronic hero, for the first time is introduced in *Ismail-Bei*: the hero is said to be born "as if superfluous among mankind" and to be "lonely" even in his early childhood. Lermontov's superfluous hero is revealed in the poem as a man of "great passions", fatally ousted from any human society even at his birth. "Superfluous" is said to be Selim in *Aul Bastundzhi / The Village Bastundzhi* (1833) and is described to be Arsenii in *Boyarin Orsha / The Boyar Orsha* and Mtsyri in *Mtsyri*. The motif of disbelief in Lermontov's poems is expressed in the author's digressions. First in *Ismail-Bei*, then in *Litvinka / A Lithuanian Woman* (1832), *The Boyar Orsha* and *The Demon* the author is looking for the roots of the hero's unhappiness in his disbelief in the good, in his doubt in the existence of something "above", or beyond this world. Thus the author comments on Arsenii's fate in *A Lithuanian Woman*:

> ...он век счастливый свой
> Определил неверящей душой;
> Он кончил жизнь с досадой на челе,
> Жалея, мысля об одной земле ...[22]

...his happy days / He determined by his disbelieving soul; / He finished his life with disappointment on his brow, / Feeling sorry, thinking only about the earth ...

Lermontov's late works – *Beglets / The Fugitive* (1838), *Mtsyri* and *The Demon* – in their own organic way unite the features of the Russian Byronic poem, Byronic elements as they were received by the Russian poet, and specifically Lermontov's motives. The setting of all the three poems is the Caucasus; the author's "I" is reduced to the figure of the epic narrator; the epic distance between the narrator and the events is emphasized by the reference to the past. In all the three poems the estrangement of the hero appears absolute, though its causes are different. In *The Fugitive* and *Mtsyri* the causes are certain: in the first "legend" (as it is called by the author) the hero is estranged, on the one hand, from the enemy of his people – Russians, and, on the other, from his family and compatriots because he bridged their laws of courage and vengeance. He is a *re*creant in the eyes of "his" people and in his own eyes, because he is a coward, but he is not a *mis*creant. In this sense he is Byronic and anti-Byronic at the same time: humanity in his image is maximized and

22: M. Yu. Lermontov. *Litvinka* / / M. Yu. Lermontov. *Sobranie sochineniy*, v 4 t. – Moscow, 1976; II, 308.

heroism is minimized. Some sentimental features are preserved in his characterization, such as "a tear" and "groans": in this respect his image is also opposed to the images of "his" people, including his stoical mother. On the other hand, the poem makes the reader perceive the values of human society, according to which the law is placed above human life and feelings, as something extremely ambiguous.

In *Mtsyri* the hero's estrangement is caused by his orphan existence in a monastery where he was placed in his early childhood. Mtsyri seems to be Byronic in his exceptional passions, in his passionate wish to be free, and in his indifference to death and the mystery of life-after-death. But he is non-Byronic, or Russian-Byronic in his being a child and in his ability to cry and to be afraid of the unknown, in his non-disdainful attitude to other people and in his "private", little life and thoughts. His aspiration to freedom, at the same time, though described as "private", appears to be connected with human society, more precisely with Russian imperial politics (for he is brought to the monastery as a captive by a Russian general) and to be directed against the whole world – and against the Creator. Associated first with the monastery, the image of prison by the end of the poem covers the forest, the mountains, the two houses the hero comes across on his way to the place of his birth, and even his own body. Accordingly, the image of freedom becomes more and more ephemeral as a material phenomenon while the place of the hero's birth is being revealed as the concept of his paradise, a notion of his heart, associated with "the golden times" of his early childhood.

The totality of the Demon's estrangement in *The Demon* is obvious: the disbelieving and non-loving "spirit of expulsion", he is opposed to the Creator and to the created world. Going away from Pushkin's tradition, Lermontov draws a global picture of the existence of the one, whose "proud" and "doubting" spirit refutes the whole world-order. In this sense the Demon seems to be much closer to Byron's titanic heroes than a lot of other central personages of Russian Byronic poems. On the other hand, the central motif of the plot seems to be personally Lermontov's: wishing to be reconciled with the Creator, the Demon chooses to struggle with himself to open his soul to the good. Tested through his "love" for Tamara, a beautiful Georgian woman, the Demon's intention is revealed as false in its essence: by the end of the poem he is as "doubting", "disdainful" and non-loving as he was at its beginning. In contrast to the Demon's, Tamara's struggle with herself is shown as less unequivocal: her pride and passions, aroused by the spirit, make it possible for him to kill her body, but her soul, having "suffered and loved", is taken to heaven by an angel, and the Demon appears to have no power over it. Paradoxically,

Tamara as man and thus a being ready and able to change stands out as the
central personage of Lermontov's poem.

The Byronic, having been elaborated in Lermontov's "tales", served as
a prototext for *A Hero of Our Time*. Thus, Lermontov carefully uses
Byronic features in the image of Pechorin, the hero of the novel. On the
one hand, Pechorin looks and behaves very much like the conventional
Byronic protagonist. He has small, delicate hands, curly hair, and a pale,
noble brow; at twenty-five he is bored with society, learning, warfare, and
women. Death in an Orient, West or East, is his natural destination:

> ... любовь дикарки немногим лучше любви знатной барыни;
> невежество и простосердечие одной так же надоедают, как и
> кокетство другой. ... Как только будет можно, отправлюсь – только
> не в Европу, избави боже! – поеду в Америку, в Аравию, в Индию,
> – авось где-нибудь умру на дороге![23]

> ... A native girl's love is little better than that of a lady of rank; the
> ignorance and simplicity of the one are as tiresome as the coquetry of
> the other ... As soon as I can I'll leave - not for Europe, though, God
> forbid! I'll go to America, Arabia, India, – with luck I'll die somewhere
> on the way.

He enjoys dressing as a stylish Asiatic tribesman, adores the novels of
Scott (particularly *Old Mortality*), and prefers to doubt everything. He also
has a destructive influence on the lives of nearly everyone he meets. It
comes as no surprise when he describes himself as one of those who start
life expecting to end up as Alexander the Great, or Lord Byron.

On the other hand, Pechorin is depicted in such a prosaic and detailed
way that his image seems to be much more human and much less titanic
than is expected from the Byronic prototype. Accordingly, Lermontov's
Caucasians are described as unscrupulous rogues whose way in this life is
to cheat and rob unwitting Europeans:

> Ужасные бестии эти азиаты! Вы думаете, они помогают, что
> кричат? А черт их разберет, что они кричат? Быки-то их понимают;
> запрягите хоть двадцать, так коли они крикнут по-своему, быки все
> ни с места... Ужасные плуты! А что с них возьмешь?.. Любят

23: Text from http: / /lib.ru /LITRA /LERMONTOW /geroi.txt; see also HAУK
Lermontov (Moscow /Leningrad 1962), vol. 4, p.316.

деньги драть с проезжающих... Избаловали мошенников! Увидите,
они еще с вас возьмут на водку. Уж я их знаю, меня не проведут![24]

Dreadful villains, these Asiatics. Do you really think they're doing any
good with all that yelling? God alone knows what it's all about! But the
oxen understand them. You hitch up twenty bullocks if you like, but
they won't budge an inch when they shout at them in that lingo of theirs.
Terrible rogues they are! But what can you do with them? They enjoy
fleecing travellers … They've had it too easy, the swine. And just you
wait and see – they'll get a tip out of you too. But I see through them!
they won't get me.

Not only have the "Asiatics" seen the westerners coming, but they've
trained their beasts of burden to join in the conspiracy. The style of his
realist Orientalism is closer to that of Hobhouse's diary than to that of
Byron's Turkish Tales.

There are other more or less significant aspects which differentiate
Pechorin from his English original. The major aspect is stressed by the
author himself in his introduction: his hero is *not* an exception, not a titan
opposed to the crowd by his passionate and highly conscious nature, but a
'type':

Герой Нашего Времени … точно, портрет, но не одного человека:
это портрет, составленный из пороков всего нашего поколения, в
полном их развитии.[25]

A Hero of Our Time … is really a portrait, but not of one person: it is a
portrait, composed of the vices of our generation, in their full
development.

Other aspects include his non-creative nature; the shallowness of his
life, of his aspirations and his actions; and the absence of any believes,
including political ones. Thus, in his Diary (the part called "Princess
Mary", June 16th) Pechorin reflects on his life:

Моя любовь никому не принесла счастья, потому что я ничем не
жертвовал для тех, кого любил: я любил для себя, для собственного
удовольствия …[26]

24: Text from http: / /lib.ru /LITRA /LERMONTOW /geroi.txt; НАУК
Lermontov, vol. 4, p.279.
25: Text from http: / /lib.ru /LITRA /LERMONTOW /geroi.txt.
26: Text from http: / /lib.ru /LITRA /LERMONTOW /geroi.txt.

My love did not bring happiness to anyone, because I did not sacrifice anything to those whom I loved: I loved only for myself, for my pleasure ...

***

Russian Byronism is an extensive phenomenon: it covers such ways of reception as critical essays and articles devoted to Byron and his works, observations in official and private conversations, letters and diaries, translations of his works into Russian, and generic models used by Russian authors in their original works. The first and the main genre received by Russian poetry from Byron's works is the genre of the Byronic poem. Having been thoroughly developed in Russian poetry in the 1820s and 1830s, the Byronic poem came to its conclusion in Lermontov's *The Fugitive, The Demon* and *Mtsyri*. It was jettisoned from the live literary process in the forties – a phenomenon connected with the growing dominance of prose and with new realistic tendencies. Its experience nevertheless was preserved, e.g. in the subjective, lyrical manner of narration in romantic and early realistic prose and "melodramatic" plots and Byronic heroes in it, never to be annihilated.

APPENDIX

BYRON'S TURKISH FRIENDS

Byron was nothing if not inconsistent – or rather, like Pierre Bayle in his Dictionary, anxious to do justice to all sides of any question, even at the expense of seeming self-contradictory. It should therefore come as no surprise that, so famous as a friend of, champion of, and finally martyr for Greece, he should have been on such good terms with the Turks – particularly during his first trip to the Levant, in 1809-11. In a note to *Childe Harold* II he writes:

> I have in my possession about twenty-five letters, amongst which some from the Bey of Corinth, written to me by Notaras, the Cogia Bachi, and others by the dragoman of the Caimacan of the Morea (which last governs in Vely Pacha's absence) are said to be very favourable specimens of their epistolary style. I also received some at Constantinople from private persons, written in a most hyperbolical style, but in the true antique character.[1]

In the last two years of his life he met fewer Turks, but he was charitably disposed towards those he did meet, adopting a Turkish girl, and interceding for some Turkish prisoners. It looks as if what we have in the letters below – all that seems to remain of the "twenty-five" – is the tip of an iceberg. On November 27th 1810, in a letter to Francis Hodgson, he describes his Athenian social milieu thus (this is after Hobhouse has gone home):

> I am living alone in the Franciscan monastery with one Fri*ar* (a Capuchin of course) and one Fri*er* (a bandy legged Turkish cook) two Albanian savages, a Tartar, and a Dragoman, my only Englishman departs with this and other letters. – The day before yesterday, the Waywode (or Governor of Athens) with the Mufti of Thebes (a sort of Mussulman Bishop) supped here and made themselves beastly drunk

---

1: CPW II pp.207-8.

with raw Rum, and the Padrè of the convent being as drunk as *we*, my *Attic* feast went off with great éclat …[2]

Notice there are no Greeks in the picture at all. Byron writes an additional note to *Childe Harold* II, in part of which he refers to the same gathering as in the letter to Hodgson:

> It is hazardous to say much on the subjects of Turks and Turkey; since it is possible to live amongst them twenty years without acquiring information, at least from themselves. As far as my own slight experience carried me I have no complaint to make; but am indebted for many civilities (I might almost say for friendship), and much hospitality, to Ali Pacha, his son Veli Pacha of the Morea, and several others of high rank in the provinces. Suleyman Aga, late Governor of Athens, and now of Thebes, was a *bon vivant*, and as social a being as ever sat cross-legged at a tray or a table. During the carnival, when our English party were masquerading, both himself and his successor were more happy to "receive masks" than any dowager in Grosvenor-Square.
>
> On one occasion of his supping at the convent, his friend and visitor, the Cadi of Thebes, was carried from table perfectly qualified for any club in Christendom; while the worthy Waywode himself triumphed in his fall.[3]

The Waywode of Athens, Suleiman Aga, is author of letters 8 and 9 below.[4] There being no Greek aristocracy, the elitist side of Byron was naturally more attracted to the ruling class, and these, in Greece in 1809-11, were mostly Turks (an exception was Andreas Londros, the *cogia bashi* at Patras, who was so moved at a rendition of Rhigas' version of the *Marseillaise* that he fell off his chair).

Byron's involvement with the Turkish ruling class began very well with his meeting with Ali Pacha, the Graeco-Albanian-Turkish rogue who ruled Albania and much of north-western Greece, and is author of Letter 1 below. Byron was very impressed by Ali's social polish, which contrasted strikingly with what people told of his casual brutality elsewhere.

When he and Hobhouse went to see Ali, in October 1809, neither the twenty-one-year-old Byron nor his friend seem to have known much about the politics of the area. It was not till December 10th 1809 that Hobhouse recorded, "… we have observed the profess'd hatred of their masters to be

---

2: BLJ II, 27.
3: CPW II 209.
4: Though see BLJ II, 262: "If you mention my name to Suleyman of Thebes I think it will not hurt you" (letter to William Bankes, December 26th 1812).

universal amongst the Greeks." But seeing the light politically made no difference socially. Trelawny, who can be trusted on the subject of Greek good manners, records Fletcher as saying, in 1823, "The Turks were the only respectable people in the country. If they go, Greece will be like bedlam broke loose. It's a land of lies, and lice, and fleas, and thieves".[5]

The politeness of many of the letters below is laid on so thick ("written in a most hyperbolical style"), that the translators have felt it unnecessary to convey it all: nevertheless, such elaborate and well-ingrained good manners could not but make a pleasant effect, though even Byron was a bit overwhelmed by it on occasion:

> Velly Pacha [*writes Byron to Hobhouse*] received me even better than his Father [*Ali*] did, though he is to join the Sultan, and the city is full of troops and confusion, which as he said, prevents him from paying proper attention. – He has given me a very pretty horse and a most particular invitation to meet him at Larissa, which is singular enough as he recommended a different route to Ld. Sligo who asked leave to accompany him to the Danube. – I asked no such thing, but on his enquiring where I meant to go, and receiving for answer that I was about to return to Albania for the purpose of penetrating higher up the country, he replied, "no you must not take that route, but go round by Larissa where I shall remain some time on my way. I will send to Athens, and you shall join me, we will eat and drink well, and go a hunting." – He said he wished all the old men (specifying under that epithet *North*, *Foresti*, and *Stranè*) to go to his father, but the young ones to come to him, to use his own expression, "vecchio con vecchio, Giovane con Giovane." [*the old with the old, the young with the young*] – He honoured me with the appellations of his *friend* and *brother*, and hoped that we should be on good terms not for a few days but for Life. – All this is very well, but he has an awkward manner of throwing his arm round one's waist, and squeezing one's hand in *public*, which is a high compliment, but very much embarrasses "*ingenuous youth*". – The first time I saw him he received me *standing*, accompanied me at my departure to the door of the audience chamber, and told me I was a παλικαρι [*palikari: brave young man*] and an εὔμορφω παιδι [*eumorfu paidi: beautiful boy*]. – He asked me if I did not think it very proper that as young men (he has a *beard* down to his middle) we should live together, with a variety of other sayings, which made Stranè stare, and puzzled me in my replies. – He was very facetious with Andreas and

---

5: Trelawny, *Records of Shelley, Byron, and Author*, ed. Wright, Harmondsworth, 1975, pp. 228-9.

Viscillie, and recommended that my Albanians' heads should be cut off if they behaved ill.[6]

Well-disposed as he may have been in theory to the downtrodden Greeks, it was with the Turks that Byron felt instinctively at one; and it's clear that they returned the feeling, as these letters show. Most of them date from the last months of Byron's first trip east, and reveal what a considerable network of contacts he had by then built up amongst the Turkish community in Greece during his year there without Hobhouse. Via the Marquis of Sligo and Stratford Canning, he has a hotline straight to the Sultan in Constantinople; via Suleiman Aga he has a hotline straight to Ibrahim Effendi, the governor of Cairo; he can get the Bey of Corinth to apologise to him, and the Caimacan of the Morea to apologise on behalf of the Bey of Corinth. One Turkish family has lent him money; another Turkish friend asks for a gold watch and a gun to be sent back to him from London.

Byron further writes, in his note to *Childe Harold* II:

With regard to presents, an established custom in the East, you will rarely find yourself a loser; as one worthy of acceptance is generally returned by another of similar value – a horse, or a shawl.[7]

Byron's Turkish friends seem an amiable, considerate, helpful, well-mannered lot. We realise that none of the heroes of the Turkish Tales are Greek, except Selim in *The Bride of Abydos,* who is half-Greek. By way of summing-up, here is another section from the note to *Childe Harold* II (the note is worth reading in its entirety):

The Ottomans, with all their defects, are not a people to be despised. Equal, at least, to the Spaniards, they are superior to the Portuguese. If it be difficult to pronounce what they are, we can at least say what they are *not*: they are *not* treacherous, they are *not* cowardly, they do *not* burn heretics, they are *not* assassins, nor has an enemy advanced to *their* capital. They are faithful to their sultan till he becomes unfit to govern, and devout to their God without an inquisition. Were they driven from St. Sophia to-morrow, and the French or Russians enthroned in their stead, it would become a question, whether Europe would gain by the exchange. England would certainly be the loser.[8]

6: BLJ II, 9-10.
7: CPW II 209.
8: CPW II 210.

On the other hand, Byron's low opinion of Greeks is all too thoroughly documented. In 1811 he wrote,

> It may be true that the Greeks are not physically degenerated, and that Constantinople contained on the day when it changed masters as many men of six feet and upwards as in the hour of prosperity; but ancient history and modern politics instruct us that something more than physical perfection is necessary to preserve a state in vigour and independence; and the Greeks, in particular, are a melancholy example of the near connection between moral degradation and national decay.[9]

In 1823 he was still franker:

> ... all the foreigners that I have hitherto met with from amongst the Greeks – are going or gone back disgusted. – Whoever goes into Greece at present should do it as M[rs] Fry went into Newgate – not in the expectation of meeting with any especial indication of existing probity – but in the hope that time and better treatment will reclaim the present burglarious and larcenous tendencies which have followed this General Gaol delivery. – When the limbs of the Greeks are a little less stiff from the shackles of four centuries – they will not march so much "as if they had gyves on their legs". – – At present the Chains are broken indeed; but the links are still clanking – and the Saturnalia is still too recent to have converted the Slave into a sober Citizen. – The worst of them is that (to use a coarse but the only expression that will not fall short of the truth) they are such d——d liars; – there never was such an incapacity for veracity shown since Eve lied in Paradise. – One of them found fault the other day with the English language – because it had so few shades of a Negative – whereas a Greek can so modify a No – to a yes – and vice versa – <that> by the slippery qualities of his language – that prevarication may be carried to any extent and still leave a loop=hole through which perjury may slip without being perceived. – – –[10]

For reassurance, I've included three short Greek items on the last page, including a Greek poem in praise of Byron. There seem no other Greek letters from this period. In the headers, "DLB" is "Deposit Lovelace Bodleian", and "Journey" is Hobhouse's *A Journey through some Provinces of Turkey*.

I'm extremely grateful to David Holton and Hassan Toussoun for their assistance with this project. In the notes, "B." is "Byron," and "H."

9: CPW II 206.
10: BLJ XI, 32-3.

"Hobhouse." Material from the Lovelace Papers in the Bodleian is quoted by permission of Pollinger Ltd., and the Earl of Lytton.

1 / *Journey*) Ali Pasha to Elias Bey Jacob, October 10th[11] 1809

[The army of bodyguards with which Ali surrounded Byron and Hobhouse on their return to the Gulf of Corinth from Tepellene was a mixed bunch, some Christian, some Moslem, some neither, some both, and showed the English how Ali's men stood in relation to the locals by beating up old ladies and knocking down the doors of houses which wouldn't open to them at once. But their songs, stories and dances gave Byron much material for his poetry, especially *Childe Harold* II.]

To my beloved Elias Bey Jacob
Bey and director of the treasury
Joseph Aga   Health
                        Vrachore

My beloved Jacob Ali Bey and whichever of my Bolu-bashees is to be found at Vrachore, after my salutation, I make known to you that these two English Gentlemen[12] my friends, come hither in order to go to Messalonge. Do you receive them with every respect and attention, and give them men sufficient to guard them on their way as far as Messalonge, and do not let them meet with any difficulty at all.

1809

October 10

TEPELTES[13]

[postscript:]

Jacob Bey you must send together with them your brother; the director of the treasury Joseph Aga even without him, must go with them as far as Messalonge without fail.

(J.C.Hobhouse, *A Journey through Albania*, 1814, II p. 1152, translation only. Rearranged.)

11: This is the date H. seems to give; but the two men stayed with Ali from October 19th-23rd.
12: B. and H., who have just stayed with Ali.
13: H. writes that this is the name of the secretary who wrote the letter.

2 / DLB f.160) Unknown correspondent to unknown correspondent, perhaps Byron, no date.

[This intriguing letter seems to give us a peep into an argument in which someone has flouted either the law or social conventions, and in which a Turkish party or the Turkish party feels it necessary to point out that things are no better in allegedly civilised England.]

[No date, no signature. No names mentioned. The letter is well written, probably by a government official or "learned man".]

I was happy to remind you how equitable and friendly this report[14] is. Indeed, all that is written is in an imposing tone. But this salutary declaration, by accusing someone unjustly of lies, calumny and false accusations, is distressing[15] to those who have sent this command. The above-mentioned [*person*] does not obey orders, nor does he refrain from doing what is prohibited. In this case, it is clear that these sorts of people are liable to be punished by law, and by the rules in force between nations.

Some time ago, in England, somebody, because of his opposition to some ministers of the government, was offered other affairs, and was attacked and pelted with stones, earth and mud during fights. Finally war was declared, and he was encircled, caught, and thrown into prison. Was all that great pain necessary?

(Deposit Lovelace Bodleian 155-6,[16] f.160:[17] translation by Hassan Toussoun.)

3 / DLB ff.165-6) The Caimacam of the Morea to Byron, 8th February 1811.

[For the origin of this and of Letter 5, see Byron to Stratford Canning, English ambassador in Constantinople:

> Athens. October. 13th. 1810 / Sir, – I cannot address you without an apology the more especially as I write in the character of a complainant. – In travelling from the Morea to Athens, the Bey of Corinth for some

---

14: Or "official note" or "statement".
15: Or "damaging".
16: The Lovelace documents are in a folder (f.171 ult.), with the words "Turkish & Romaic MS."
17: A single sheet (11.5 x 22.3 cm) with seven-and-a-half lines of Ottoman script sloping at the top of one side; thick laid paper. Second side blank.

time refused me a lodging, and this at a time when the inclemency of the weather made it an act not only of impoliteness, but of inhumanity. It was indeed one of those days when "an enemy's dog" would have been sheltered. – The Greek Cogia Bachi was equally unwilling to order a house, and I at last with difficulty procured a miserable cottage. – As the last circumstance has happened twice to myself in the same place, and once to others, I have nothing left but to request your interference. – I know no circumstance of extenuation, as a word from the Bey or the Cogia Bachi, would have admitted me into any house in the village, where I had before (in the time of Vely Pacha) found much better accommodation. – I therefore do hope and venture to request that this "circumcised dog" may not pass (I cannot say unpunished) but unreprimanded. – I believe it to be the inclination, as I know it to be in the power of the British minister to protect the subjects of his Sovereign from Insult. – I conceive that brutality will not be countenanced even by the Turks, as we are taught that hospitality is a Barbarian's virtue. – Your interference may be esteemed a favour not only to me but to all future travellers. – By land or sea we must pass the Isthmus in our excursions from Athens to the Morea, and you will be informed of the accuracy of my statement of the Bey's conduct, by the Marquis of Sligo, who does me the honour to deliver this letter. – I again solicit your interposition, and have the honour to be, Sir, / your most obedient humble Servant / BYRON'[18]

The Caimacam, or Caimacan, of the Morea was the superior of the Bey of Corinth. Here, perhaps under pressure from Constantinople, he apologises for the Bey's lack of consideration when, one wet night, Byron could find no shelter in the vicinity of Corinth. He writes his letter three days before the Bey writes his – see next item but one.]

Most excellent, most eminent, and desired friend of mine milord Byron, I greet you in friendship and affection and request your favour, which is dear to me.

After my friendly greetings, I announce to you that I received your friendly [letter] of the 30th of the past month, together with that of my brother pasha bey efendi,[19] and I rejoiced at your good health which is dear to me. I am well aware of the things you write to me concerning Nuri Bey, and I was much grieved at the displeasure which you received from him, to his misfortune, and I was amazed on account of this. Know that from the very beginning he is a noble person and descended from a

---

18: BLJ II 21-22.
19: That is, the Bey of Corinth (letter 4).

great family, and all the travellers, English milord ambassadors and various others who passed through, and guests who came by, he received them and treated them with great entertainments and ministrations, and they always departed with much satisfaction and obligation. But now, seeing your friendly [*letter*] I was much puzzled, and examining the matter I learned from many that on those days when your eminence was going to Corinth, Nuri Bey was not there but was absent in Tripolitsa, and at that time it happened that the baggage and retinue of our supreme master, Veligioun[?] by name, was setting out, and the armies of his highness, with great haste and no little impatience, but amidst great confusion, seized the horses and went off, and perhaps it was thus and for this cause that your complaint followed. None the less, on account of your favour and affection, and that you might receive satisfaction, I did not fail to summon him and give him a scolding and reprimand, as he himself of his own accord will write to you, begging you to forgive him, as he himself on account of this has punished those whom he had as agents and commissaries in Corinth. So, in view of the fact that it was unintentional, and Nuri Bey did not commit such a great fault, and on account of the great affection and friendship which you have with our supreme master, Veligioun[?] by name, I also beg you and implore you to overlook and forgive the unintended past mischance, inasmuch as he himself was absent from there at that time, as I have been assured by many, and he was not informed. Being acquainted with your noble self, and the courteous disposition which you have, on account of which we hope that from henceforth you will grant forgiveness. And I beg you to write to me in friendship about your health, which is of concern to me; fare you well with good fortune.
1811: February 8:
Tripolitsa Serif Mustafa Bey
Kaymakam of the Morea

(Deposit Lovelace Bodleian 155-6, ff.165-6:[20] translation by David Holton.)

20: A bifolium (41.5 x 31 cm) written on one only of its four sides (f.165), with a seal-mark identical to the Bey's seal-mark on f.169 (Letter 4); white laid paper, watermark knight with lance on horseback (f.165) and bull (f.166) with "GIUSTI".

4 / National Library of Scotland 12604 / 4197) "Konstantinos" to Byron, 8th February 1811.

[The tone of this letter from the otherwise unidentified Konstantinos is so hyperbolical – along with most of the others in this appendix – that one can't tell whether he is offering his services as servant, as lover, or as both. But the respect and affection he expresses seems sincere. The date is identical to that in Letter 3.]

Most excellent, most distinguished and most noble signor Byron, I humbly pay my respects [literally: I servilely do obeisance] to your excellency.

In humble servitude(?), I do not fail to make manifest to you that, on seeing your man Dervish Aga here, and having been informed by him as to the condition of your distinguished health (which is dear to me), with great pleasure and satisfaction I took the trouble to enquire, by means of the present letter, after paying my humble respects, about your distinguished health (which is dear to me), boldly beseeching you to hold me in the memory of your affection. For, when asked as to your natural nobility and kindly disposition, I am hopeful that you love me [or feel affection for me?]; which I would have as my great boast and an excellent treasure. Knowing therefore the humble inclination and respect which I maintain towards your distinguished personage, from the moment that, to my good fortune, I had the honour to make your acquaintance, I pray you to number me your servant in the list of your faithful servants, commanding me as far as is in my power, through your distinguished declaration of your health which I desire more than anything else.
Your excellency's

     your humble servant

     and at your command
servant Konstantinos ??imou
humbly pays his respects to you

1811: 8 February In Tripolitsa

     [*indecipherable signature*]

(John Murray Archive / National Library of Scotland 12604 / 4197: translation by David Holton.)

5 / DLB f.169) The Bey of Corinth to Byron, February 11th 1811.

[The letter Byron received in February 1811 from the Bey of Corinth was first published as a facsimile with *Childe Harold's Pilgrimage*, Cantos I and II.

Byron made two journeys from the Morea to Athens in the second half of 1810. The first, on which he was accompanied as far as Corinth by the Marquis of Sligo, was in July and August – shortly after he had returned to Greece from Constantinople.[21] In December 1812, Sligo was tried for abducting between twelve and fourteen members of the crew of HMS *Pylades,* the ship which took Byron and Hobhouse from Athens to Smyrna: he was fined £5,000 and sentenced to four months in Newgate.[22] On this journey Byron visited Vostitza, Patras, and Tripolitsa, where he met Vely Pasha (the son of Ali Pasha, and ruler of the Morea) who remonstrated with him about his "relationship" with Ali, saying "vecchio con vecchio, Giovane con Giovane",[23] and presented him with a "pretty stallion".[24] His second journey was in September, when he fell seriously ill at Patras.[25] He was back in Athens by mid-October.[26] It *seems* to have been while passing through Corinth while returning from the second of these trips that he encountered the foul weather, and the uncharacteristic failure of Turkish hospitality, about which he writes in the letter, printed above, to Stratford Canning in Constantinople.

It is strange that Byron refers to the "Insult" in no other document, even though he stresses that it has occurred "*twice*". It is also strange that he refers to "the time of Vely Pacha" as one in which he was better treated, for two of his visits to Corinth took place when Vely Pacha was in the Morea. Perhaps the "twice" refers to passing the Isthmus en route for Patras on his second journey, and then re-passing it on the way back. Very bad luck to have inclement weather on both occasions.

Corroboration of the story is to be found in part of a letter to Byron from the Marquis of Sligo himself. It is dated November 5th, 1810:

21: BLJ II, 5.
22: *Annual Register* for 1812, pp.279-89.
23: BLJ II, 19.
24: BLJ II 14-15, 18.
25: See William A. Borst, *Lord Byron's First Pilgrimage*, Yale 1948, rpt. Archon 1969, pp.156-7.
26: BLJ II, 23-4.

I have delivered your letter concerning Nouri Bey to M^r. Canning, and have <c/>Conjoined my testimony to that contained in your letter, the effect of which will be a certain reprimand to the aforesaid Bey.[27]

On receipt of Byron's letter, Canning sent a reply, and a letter from himself as Plenipotentiary, to the Caimacan of the Morea – the Bey's immediate superior, whose headquarters were at Tripolitsa, whence, in Byron's words, he "governed in Vely Pasha's absence". Vely had, since Byron had met him in August, left the Morea, with troops with whom he was supposed to help the Sultan on the Danube, although he had in fact taken them to assist his father, Ali Pacha, with his military problems at Iannina. As Byron explains to Hobhouse on October 4, during his second stay in the Morea:

> Ali Pacha is in a scrape, Ibrahim Pacha, and the Pacha of Scutari have come down on him with 20000 Gegdes and Albanians, retaken Berat, and threaten Tepaleni, Adam Bey is dead, Vely Pacha was on his way to the Danube, but has gone off suddenly to Yanina, and all Albania is in an uproar … Sultan Mamoud is in a phrenzy because Vely has not joined the army …[28]

Then, on "February 20th 1812" (sic: for "1811") the Bey sent a letter to Byron, apologising. It seems that Byron's complaint had had the desired effect.

The name of the Bey was Nuri, and that of his secretary, who actually wrote the letter, was Sotirakis Notaras: Notaras was the second son of an illustrious, highly educated Corinthian family ("a descendant of the great duke of that family who was put to death soon after the capture of Constantinople" is Byron's description). Byron lost no time in telling Canning what he had received:

Athens. Feby. 26th. 1811
Sir, – I have forwarded to the Caimacan of the Morea the letter which accompanied that of your Excellency, & it has produced a long apology from the Bey of Corinth, which is all that can be wished of Turk or Christian. – I took the liberty of correcting a small mistake in the said remonstrance, & of exchanging the word *Coronna* & substituting that of *Corinth* in its stead, it being the Governor of the latter city of whom I had occasion to complain – I have now only to return my thanks to your

---

27: John Murray Archive / National Library of Scotland.
28: BLJ II, 40.

Excellency for your interference which has had all the effect which
could be desired, & have the honour to be your obliged
& very obed^t. humble Servant
BYRON[9]

When in the following year Byron was putting together the package in
which *Childe Harold* I and II were to be presented to the public, he
decided to make use of the Bey's letter. For, as Roger Poole has written,[29]
the book which John Murray published on March 10, 1812 contains far
more than just *Childe Harold,* the two-Canto poem – which takes up only
115 pages. Not only are there (by the time of its seventh edition of 1814,
from which I am working) twenty-nine extra poems, taking up 71 pages,
but 67 pages of Notes to *Childe Harold* itself, and, at the end, a 33-page
Appendix, much of it in Greek. It was not, in aggregate, a book intended
for the many. As Jerome McGann writes,

> Its publisher conceived its audience to be a wealthy one, people
> interested in travel books and topographical poems, people with a
> classical education and with a taste for antiquarian lore and the
> philosophical musings of a young English lord. As it turned out, all of
> England and Europe were to be snared by this book's imaginations.[30]

Byron's idealistic aim seems to have been to use his knowledge of
both Greeks and Turks to enlarge the minds of his countrymen, or at least
the minds of those qualified in the way McGann describes: to make them
see the Greeks as more cultured than they were normally taken to be, to
see the Turks as more civilised than they were normally taken to be, and to
see the Frankish nations as by no means superior to either. One section of
the notes quoted above continues:

> The reader will find a fac simile of the handwriting of a good scribe,
> with specimens of the Romaic, in an appendix at the end of the
> volume.[31]

In the Appendix, he adds

29: Roger Poole, *What Constitutes the "Real" Childe Harold?* in *Lord Byron the
European*, ed Cardwell, 1997, pp.149-207.
30: Jerome J. McGann, *The Beauty of Inflections*, Oxford 1985, p.259.
31: *Childe Harold's Pilgrimage, A Romaunt* John Murray, seventh edition 1814
(hereafter CHP) pp.181-2.

The letter given in the *fac simile* was signed and sent by the Bey of Corinth, and was written I believe by Notaras the Cogia Bachi, a descendant of the great duke of that family who was put to death soon after the capture of Constantinople. It contains merely an apology on account of some complaints lodged against Nouri Bey (the only complaint I ever had occasion to make against a Moslem) by my friend the Marquis of Sligo and myself with the minister at Pera. I will not affront the learned by deciphering it in a printed copy; a slight acquaintance with the written character in a couple of perusals will render it very easy. The contents merely regarding private business are not worth a translation; but as a specimen of the manner of writing in a character generally deemed elegant amongst the modern Greeks, the *fac simile* is annexed to this Appendix.[32]

It was therefore as an example both of the refinement of contemporary Turkish manners, and of the beauty of contemporary aristocratic Greek calligraphy, that Byron appended his letter from the Bey of Corinth to *Childe Harold* II. But we may wonder how successful his pro-Turkish ambition for it was, because although the calligraphic beauty of its Greek is clear at once (see illustration below), it is very difficult to transcribe and translate. Byron's penultimate sentence, in the note just quoted, is some distance from the truth. Some of the words in the letter are loanwords from Turkish, some of the Greek words (though not many) are mis-spelled, and the grammar is not always perfect. Like Byron's letters to Canning, with their canine quotations from *King Lear* and *Othello*, it is in a mixture of registers. Some words still cannot be understood fully. What has most baffled scholarship, however, is the handwriting, which seems to have proved – until now – an insurmountable barrier to reading the letter. But here it is, in its first-ever English garb, which has been created for it by Professor David Holton, who has been helped with the Turkish words by Dr Mehtin Kunt, and by a literal translation into modern Greek by Professor Vasileios Katsaros.]

Most excellent, most eminent, most highly noble, and desired friend of mine milord Byron, I salute you affectionately and in friendship, and request your kind favour.

After my friendly greetings and inquiry about your health which is dear to me, I announce to you that, finding myself in Corinth at this time, there came suddenly to me an order from the most glorious and distinguished *kaymekam bey efendi*, and they conducted me to Tripolitsa, subjecting me

---

32: CHP pp.295-6.

to a great scolding and reprimand, on account of the displeasure which
your eminence received from me while passing through Corinth, and at
this I was amazed and much sorrowed, without having the least idea about
it. I assure you, Excellency, that as far as I myself have known and as
long as I have been in our *khan*, I am not aware of ever having failed to
receive or attend to any one of those travellers, English milords, who have
passed through here. On the contrary: and especially to such persons as
your eminence, whom it would have been my greatest pleasure to see, and
to become acquainted with your worthy self; however, my ill fortune
determined that I should not be in Corinth, but in Tripolitsa, where at that
time the baggage and retinue of my supreme master were leaving. There
the armies of his highness, with great haste and impatience, were setting
forth. Amidst great confusion they began seizing the horses and going on
their way. And on account of this, and my own absence from Corinth,
your complaint followed, without any fault on my part, but in
consequence of my sins. For all this, I have not ceased to punish severely
the agents and my commissaries, which I had in Corinth. Therefore, my
most eminent friend, in as much as my fault was unintentional, without
my being aware, I pray you to forgive me, and to assign me to your noble
friendship and affection, by writing to me of your good health, in which I
shall rejoice, and by recognising me as your sincere friend. This much in
friendship, and I remain: 1812 : February : 20:
[signature in Turkish]
[Ottoman date corresponding to 11 February 1811 in the Julian calendar]

To the most eminent and most noble milord Byron. Most courteously –
at Athens –[33]

[Professor Holton writes, about the clearly inaccurate date: "The problem
of the date remains unsolved. There is a Turkish date which translates as
11 Feb. 1811 in the Julian calendar. If we hypothesise that the Greek
secretary was using the Gregorian calendar (twelve days difference) for
Byron's benefit, and that Gregorian 20 February (= 8 Feb. Old Style) was
when he did his calligraphy, but Nuri Bey signed and dated it a few days
later, the only mystery is 1812. It has to be a slip, but a very strange one."
    It may be doubted whether publishing the *fac simile* ever had quite the
educative effects Byron intended. But at least we now have a clearer idea
of what its contents signify. However, reading the letter in the light of
what we know was going on at Tripolitsa is again strange, for it seems that

33: DLB 155-6, f.169, which does not have the last line and a half; facsimile at
CHP I-II, seventh edition, 1814, pp. 262-3.

Nuri Bey received the complaint while he was witnessing a huge troop departure ("the baggage and retinue of my supreme master were leaving", and so on). This sounds like the departure of Veli Pasha ("my supreme master" … "the most high one") and his army, off to help Ali at Iannina, which must have been *before* Byron's *second* trip, which in turn means that Nuri Bey's neglect, occasioning the affront, occurred during Byron's *first* trip, while Veli Pacha was at Tripolitsa – which Byron, in his first letter to Stratford Canning, says was a time when he had found "much better accommodation" at Corinth.

Perhaps Nuri Bey is either confused about when exactly his alleged inhospitality is supposed to have occurred, or is thrashing about in desperation for an excuse.

I am very grateful to Professor Holton for the time he has taken in transliterating and translating the Bey's letter. I am also grateful to Professor Nora Liassis for her advice.]

The facsimile letter from *Childe Harold's Pilgrimage* I and II

6 / *Journey*) An unknown Turkish official to Byron, mid-March 1811.

[Hobhouse did not translate this letter, which he too seems to have included – on the very last page of *Journey* – as an example of Turkish script. In fact it's in a Greek secretary's hand. We do not know which of Byron's servants needed a horse to get to Patrass at this time.]

Most excellent and most honourable Lord Byron, greeting your Excellency in friendship I ask your noble favour.

After my dear and friendly greetings, and the enquiry of your good health, for which I pray, I declare to your Excellency that I previously received your friendly letter to me, and in accordance with your request I did not fail to be bestirred by my duty to your Excellency, to give horses immediately to your emissary for Patras, and to arrange to bring him the "order of free passage" for his passage through the *defile*,[34] and henceforth, having an inclination to manifest by deeds to your excellent personage the characteristic signs of a sincere friendship, I beseech you to honour me with your noble letters, and command me in whatever is needed,[35] and you will find me ready to carry out your service, in accordance with my friendly duty, as I subscribe myself in sincerity.
March 17th[36] 1811, In Corinth.
[Signature in Ottoman Turkish script: could be "Ali Mehmed"]

(J.C.Hobhouse, *A Journey through some Provinces of Turkey* (1814) vol II, p.1153, final page: translation by David Holton and Hassan Toussoun.)

7 / DLB f.163) The sons of Suleiman Abd-ül-Medjid to Byron, Thursday April 11th 1811:[37]

[We have no information about the sons of Suleiman Abd-ül-Medjid. It looks as if the family have been prevailed upon to lend Byron money.]

34: This might be a place-name, Derveni, a present-day village on the Gulf of Corinth.
35: Unclear.
36: This date could be "12" or "13".
37: B. leaves Greece on April 22nd 1811.

[After the usual compliments, the authors[38] of this letter ask, in conformity with his sincere friendship, news of the health of his "Beyzâdé,"[39] then starts his letter:]

A couple of days ago, your note reached us, as did the letter you sent asking news about our health, which gave us great joy.

In your letter you also ask us to send you a thousand piastres. As at this moment our agent Edhem Agha has to go to your place[40] to settle some business, he will remit you all the money.

Would you be kind enough to write a promissory note and to send it to us, in conformity with the close friendship that exists between us.

In your letter, you also let us know that you intend to go home[41] on board a government vessel. May God grant that you reach your destination in safety.

We hope that in the future you will not forget the friendship that exists between us. When you receive and have read our affectionate letter, it is our most sincere hope that the Almighty may let neither distance nor forgetfulness erase our friendship from your mind.

Signed

The sons of Abd-ül-Medjid   Dated: 17 Rabi-ül-evvel 1226
Süleyman.   [*Thursday April 11th 1811.*]

(Deposit Lovelace Bodleian 155-6, f.163:[42] translation by Hassan Toussoun.)

8 / DLB f.158) Suleiman Aga to Byron, Friday April 19th 1811.

[This item is paraphrased at CMP pp.525-6. Suleiman Aga seems to have lent Byron some more money: either that, or this is the money from the sons of Suleiman Abd-ül-Medjid in Letter 7. Byron purchased some guns and a gold watch (the watch cost £31.10s) in London in 1813, in

---

38: Or "author".
39: Byron's name is not mentioned.
40: No details are given as to where this place is.
41: "Vilayet" means province, principality: sometimes used as "your country of origin".
42: A single sheet of thick white laid paper (22 x 33 cm), with writing on one side in very neat script in Ottoman and signature and seal-mark identical to those on ff.158 and 161 (Letters 7 and 8), but not identical with those of the Bey of Corinth on f.169 (Letter 4), or of the Caimacan of the Morea on ff.165-6 (Letter 3).

preparation for a Levantine journey that never transpired; so Suleiman Aga may have waited in vain.]

[*In Byron's hand:*] Received from Suleyman Aga Waywode[43] of Thebes this Letter <March> April 17th 1811 / B. / Athens

[*Envelope:*] To the English Beyzâdé[44] now residing in Athens, the reverend, honourable, intelligent, and my affectionate friend, your Honour, Lord Byron.
May it [*the letter*] reach him with the help of God.

(Deposit Lovelace Bodleian 155-6, f.159:[45] translation and commentary by Hassan Toussoun.)

[The main letter and the bottom postscript are written by Suleiman's secretary; the upper postscript, hastily, by Suleiman himself. Byron is called a Beyzâde – a nobleman. There are a lot of repetitions, especially in relation to the gun and the clock / watch. Repetition is common in Ottoman letters, and the dragoman or interpreter would miss them out and go straight to the next subject.]

Reverend, honourable, intelligent, shrewd, Excellency, lord of high rank, my dear friend.[46]

As our affection to your Excellency is at its highest point of perfection, you must expect us always to ask news of your health.[47]

The hearty letter you have sent me through the means of your agent has reached me. As the friendly words and expressions contained in it consist of what obligation and friendship is all about, they have strengthened still more the affectionate relations that exist between us. May it always be so.

Lately, a thousand piastres[48] were sent and remitted to our friend the *Beyzâde*, and your agent remitted the receipt. I was very happy, because the henna[49] which was sent has also arrived.

43: A Waywode ("Voyevode") was a Turkish governor.
44: "nobleman, gentleman".
45: The envelope for f.158 (Letter 8), with three sealing-wax blobs and what appears an address, in Ottoman script; thick laid paper (23.7 x 37 cm), watermark "AC". Second side blank.
46: This was the usual salutation among the Turkish upper classes.
47: Ibid.
48: CMP 525 has "*kuruş* (Turkish piastres)".
49: CMP 525 has "*kinakina* (Cinchona bark, or quinine)".

May God grant you safety and facilitate your journey so as to enable you to reach home[50] with health and security.

On the other hand, my faithful friend, you write in your letter that if we desire something we should let you know, and you will be happy to send it from your country. As it is useless to point out that between us there is no place for ceremony, when, thanks to God, you arrive, we should like a pair of pistols of the best quality, sumptuous and ornamented with gold, and long enough to receive bullets of ten *dirhem*.[51] We desire also a watch[52] made of gold. We should like the size of the gun to be equal to the piece of cord we put in our letter. *[The last paragraph is then repeated.]*

I am ready to pay up to five hundred piastres for the two pistols. If God wills, when you arrive I shall send you the money wherever you want.

My dear friend, I write you this letter to let you know that I shall never forget in the slightest way the obligation and friendship which has existed until now between us, and to tell you that every time you depart, whether it is to a faraway destination or not, my friendship to you will always increase.

If God wills, when my letter reaches you, and when you are acquainted with its contents, I hope that in the future you will never forget to express your friendly thoughts to me.

Suleiman   25 Rebi'-ül-evvel 1226 [Friday April 19th 1811]

[Bottom postscript:] My dear friend, as I have been for a long time on sociable and friendly terms with Ibrahim Effendi, the Seal-keeper of our Lord the Governor of Cairo, Egypt, I have written and sent you a letter. If God wills, when you have an interview with the Effendi, you will remit it to him. You will be very satisfied with the meeting you will have with him.

I beg you: the watch and the pistols mentioned in the letter must be of the finest quality. I shall pay the price, wherever you desire: at Athens, at Izmir,[53] at the capital,[54] or at any place you wish.

50: "your province / principality".
51: A measure of weight. Metric equivalent not clear.
52: "saat" is either a clock or a watch; wristwatches did not exist at that time, only fob-watches.
53: Smyrna.
54: Constantinople.

I expect that you, at all times, to pay particular attention to the fact that they should be of the best quality.

[*Upper postscript:*] My faithful and sincere friend, as I write to you in my letter, if I did not need the pistols and the watch badly I should not have disturbed you. Knowing the character of your Excellency, I have not the least doubt that you would satisfy our demand. As you are going to England, I dared to ask you to perform this commission. As I mentioned in the addendum to my letter, please be sure that, with God's will, I shall without fail send the money, to wherever you wish. There is no problem at all, my dear.

(Deposit Lovelace Bodleian 155-6, f.158:[55] translation, commentary and notes by Hassan Toussoun.)

9 / DLB f.161) Suleiman Aga to Ibrahim Effendi, April 19th 1811:

[The generosity of Suleiman Aga seems considerable. Doubtless the Byronic charisma helped. Byron mentions that he plans travel further east; but money runs out and he has to come home.]

[The address is on an envelope with three red sealing-wax blobs.]

To the ruler of the province of Cairo, Egypt, our benefactor, member of the imperial diwan [*council*] and seal-keeper of our Master the Sultan, our Lord, the generous Ibrahim Effendi.

(Deposit Lovelace Bodleian 155-6, f.164:[56] translation by Hassan Toussoun.)

[There is much repetition and formal padding in this letter.]

Illustrious, generous, kind, benignant, noble and generous, my Lord, high in dignity ...

55: A single sheet (20 x 36 cm) of strong white laid paper folded in four with the body of a letter in Ottoman in the centre of folds 1-4, and addenda to the letter written horizontally on folds 1 and 4. Signature and seal-mark identical to those on ff.161 and 163 (Letters 8 and 6). Second side blank.

56: An envelope (33x x 22.5 cm) with three sealing-wax blobs and an address, in Ottoman script so neat as to resemble print; the size suggests it held ff.161 and 163 (Letters 8 and 6); watermark three crescents. Second side blank.

I have the honour to write this letter because I should like to let you know that according to the impulse of my sincere heart I continuously express my best wishes towards you. I should like also to inform you that I have, at the city of Athens, been for more than a year on friendly and familiar terms with an English *Beyzâde*, the revered and intelligent Lord Byron, my friend, who is now longing to travel to Egypt, in order to visit Cairo, and, having recently left for that destination, I told him that between us there exist relations of friendship to the degree of brotherhood.

As a matter of fact, my friend the Lord is influential, and considered so by his peers. As such, he merits a friendly welcome on your part. When you meet him, you shall receive him accordingly.

I took the liberty to write this letter to you because I am confident that you will take all the steps necessary for this purpose, and you will be content and satisfied at having had a meeting with him.

With God's will, when our friend the lord shall arrive, there is no doubt that you will welcome him, and treat him warmly and in the best manner possible.

Suleiman   25 Rebi-ül-evvel 1226 [*Friday April 19th 1811*]

(Lovelace Bodleian 155-6, f.161:[57] translation, commentary and notes by Hassan Toussoun.)

10 / DLB f.157) A firman from Sultan Mahmoud II, giving Byron permission to travel.

[Byron mentions receiving this firman, or visa, as we would say, on February 1st 1811.[58] To travel further east than Constantinople was standard for English aristocrats. One went to Jerusalem, Cairo, up the Nile, and still further – to Damascus, Baghdad, and even Tehran. But it was risky, expensive, and everyone was terrified of the plague. Byron made no use of this firman, and in 1813 it was news of an outbreak of plague which prevented him going back to the Levant with the Marquis of Sligo. Obtaining the document seems not to have been hard. Sligo writes, "I have just got your Ferman which I have paid the enormous sum of 12 Piastres

---

57: A large (36 x 52 cm) folded sheet on very strong white laid paper, with Ottoman script on one side (18 x 52 cm) only, and a signature and seal-mark at the bottom identical to those on ff.158 and 163 (Letters 7 and 6).
58: BLJ II 38, 39.

which will pretty nearly balance the 18 Shillings &c which I owe you for our supper at the Masquerade Shop".[59]]

To all the illustrious Kadis,[60] Valis, Governors, Kethüda,[61] Commanders of Janissaries, and all other officials of all the districts on the road from Cyprus and all the below-mentioned places to the capital:

When my firman containing my Tura arrives, be it known to you that the Ambassador of England, resident at my capital, with the title of Minister Plenipotentiary, a model of the great men of the Christian nations, Stratford Canning (may his latter days end with good),[62] has presented a sealed official note to the *Rekab hümayun*[63] saying that the *Beyzâde*, named Lord Byron, who is accompanied by a guard and four Christian servants, has expressed the wish to make a journey in order to visit Cyprus, Akka,[64] Jerusalem, Damascus, and from thence to Egypt and finally from Egypt back to the capital.

In my Imperial firman, I therefore order you to act as it is desired in my Imperial firman, that is, to bestow great care [*on Lord Byron*], and to pay particular attention to the following matters:

When the *Beyzâde*, accompanied by a guard and his four Christian servants, arrives at the above-mentioned places, in his journey on the roads and at the post- and halting-places and stations, they will not be molested by the tax-collectors of the *Jüziye*,[65] and other taxes, and will be treated with civility, and received assistance and protection, and that, when they cross dangerous areas, they will be accompanied by useful paid guides, so that they can pass through safely and with security.

(Lovelace Bodleian 155-6, f.157:[66] translation, commentary and notes by Hassan Toussoun.)

59: John Murray Archive / National Library of Scotland 12604 / 104.

60: Islamic judges.

61: Deputies.

62: This actually means, "according to the faith of Islam": that is, it is a wish to see the person in question become a Moslem. It is usually addressed to ambassadors and sovereigns. Dragomans did not normally translate it, or changed it to "may his mission end in success".

63: A sort of court composed of high dignitaries close to the Sultan.

64: St John of Acre.

65: The capitation-tax.

66: A sheet of very strong white laid paper so large as almost to defy measurement (app. 76 x 53cm) with on one side five Ottoman characters and on the other eight-and-a-half lines of Ottoman script, a very large (20 x 16 cm) signature at the top

11-13 / DLB ff.167, 168, 170) A poem by Demetrios Zograffos, and two addressed envelopes 1811(??).

10) [Demetrios Zograffos ("painter") was one of two servants whom Byron brought back to England in 1811; the other was Spiro Saraci. Zograffos returned to Greece in 1812, having assisted Hobhouse with the vocabulary to *Journey*. In 1821 he headed the Athenian part of the Greek Revolutionary War; see BLJ VIII, 211 and IX 23.]

> Everyone embrace the distinguished Lord Byron!
> Wish him a fortunate life!
> A worthy young man like him
> Of most acute intellect
> Truly honours his race and family.
> If we had five or six young men like him
> We should have great honour from the Europeans![67]
> Your most humble servant
> Demetrios Zograffos

(Deposit Lovelace Bodleian 155-6, f.168:[68] translation by David Holton.)

Two envelopes addressed to Byron, in Greek:

[The letters which these envelopes contained do not seem to have survived.]

11) To the most excellent most distinguished dear-to-me friend My Lord Byron
(Deposit Lovelace Bodleian 155-6, f.167:[69] translation by David Holton.)

---

and a smaller signature at the bottom; watermarks three crescents and a heraldic device.

67: A doggerel poem in fifteen-syllable rhyming couplets.

68: A single sheet of thin, laid blue-grey paper, 19.2 x 26 cm, watermark "CARLO", with six lines of Romaic script and a line-and-a-half of signing-off. No other item in the collection is on paper of this kind.

69: An envelope 14.5 x 10.5 cm internal area, with address in Romaic, similar to but not identical with the address on 170; watermark knight on horseback with lance (matador??) and "GIACOMO".

12) Humbly in Athens / To the most distinguished most noble My Lord
Byron / In all affability
(Deposit Lovelace Bodleian 155-6, f.170:[70] translation by David Holton.)

BIBLIOGRAPHY

The books listed below by Kidwai and Ouijean have substantial bibliographies, of which Kidwai's is supplemented by Demata, Massimiliano. *A Bibliography of Byron's Oriental Reading: Addenda and Correction. Notes & Queries* 46.1 (March 1999) pp 39-41.

Byron

The Works of Lord Byron: A New, Revised and Enlarged Edition with illustrations. Poetry, ed. E.H.Coleridge, seven vols, John Murray, 1898-1904.

Ashton, Thomas L. *Byron's* Hebrew Melodies (London: Routledge and Kegan Paul, 1972).

Burwick, Frederick, and Paul Douglass (eds.), Byron, and Isaac Nathan, *A Selection of Hebrew Melodies, Ancient and Modern*, (Tuscaloosa: University of Alabama Press, 1988).

Byron's Letters and Journals, ed. Leslie A. Marchand, 13 vols, John Murray, 1973-94.

Lord Byron: The Complete Miscellaneous Prose, ed. Andrew Nicholson, Oxford, Clarendon Press, 1991.

Lord Byron: The Complete Poetical Works, ed. Jerome J. McGann and Barry Weller, 7 vols Oxford, Clarendon Press, 1980-93.

Marchand, Leslie A., *Byron: A Biography*, 3 vols Alfred A. Knopf, New York, 1957.

MacCarthy, Fiona. *Byron. Life and Legend*, London, John Murray, 2002.

Southey and Moore

Southey, Robert. *The Life and Correspondence of the Late Robert Southey*, ed. C.C.Southey, Longman, Brown, Green and Longmans, 6 vols 1849-50.

—. *Selections from the Letters of Robert Southey*, ed. J.W.Warter, Longman, Brown, Green and Longmans, 4 vols 1856.

—. *The Correspondence of Robert Southey with Caroline Bowles*, ed. Dowden, Longman 1881.

—. *New Letters of Robert Southey*, ed. Kenneth Curry, Columbia University Press, 2 vols 1965.
—. *Poetical Works, 1793-1810*, ed. Lynda Pratt, 5 vols Pickering and Chatto, 2004.
Moore, Thomas. *The Poetical Works*, ed. A D Godley (London: Henry Frowde, Oxford University Press, 1910).
—. *Lalla Rookh, An Oriental Romance*, first edition, Longman, 1817.
—. *The Letters of Thomas Moore*, ed. Wilfred Dowden, 2 vols Oxford, 1964.
—. *The Poetical Works of Thomas Moore Complete in one Volume*, Longman, 1855.

Contemporary books about the Orient known to Byron

At the end of each entry, where applicable, is a note saying where evidence of Byron's reading the item is to be found. I have included doubtful items. I am grateful to Andrew Nicholson for his assistance with this section. I have included works on Greece because of their Ottoman content. Likewise works about Africa.

BLJ: Byron, Letters and Journals, ed. Marchand.
CHP: *Childe Harold's Pilgrimage*.
CMP: Byron, Miscellaneous Prose, ed. Nicholson.
CPW: Byron, Complete Poetical Works, ed. McGann and Weller.
HD: Hobhouse diary entry. Not all these entries have been published in book form. All are days when Byron was in Hobhouse's company, far from libraries. The relevant volumes of the diary are in B.L.Add.Mss. 56527, 56529, and 56536-7.
SoC: *The Siege of Corinth*.

Anon. *A Compleat History of the Turks, from their origin in the year 755 to the year 1718*, 4 vols 1719. *SoC*, Advertisement.
Belzoni, Giovanni Battista. *Quarterly* review of *Travels in Egypt and Nubia*, 1820. CMP 253.
du Bocage, M. Barbié. *Maps, Plans, Views and Coins Illustrative of the Travels of Anacharsis,* 1793. English translation of *Le Voyage du jeune Anacharsis en Grèce au IVe Siècle del'ère vulgaire,* by Jean-Jacques Barthélemy (1716-95). See B.'s Appendix to *Childe Harold* I and II, where it is called *Marmartouri's Prospectus of a Translation of Anacharsis ... who wished to publish it in England* (a section not printed in CPW II). HD 11 Feb 1810.

Bruce, James. *Travels to Discover the Source of the Nile* (1790). CMP 5.
Bryant, Jacob. *Observations upon A Treatise, entitled a Description of the Plain of Troy, by Monsieur le Chevalier (1795), and Dissertation concerning the War of Troy, and the Expedition of the Grecians, as described by Homer, shewing that no such Expedition was ever undertaken and that no such City of Phrygia existed* (1797; 2nd edn. corrected, 1799. BLJ VIII, 22.
Burckhardt, Jacob. *Travels in Nubia* (1819). CMP 253.
——. *Travels in Syria and the Holy Land* (1822). CMP 253.
Cantemir, Demetrius, Hospodar of Moldova. *The History of the Growth and Decline of the Othman Empire*, 1734. *Don Juan* V, 147, 7 and VI, 31, 5. CMP 3, 4 and 220.
Castellan, Antoine Louis. *Mœurs, Usages, Costumes des Othmans, et abrégé de leur histoire* 6 vols Paris 1812; Eng. tr. in *The World in Miniature*,1821. BLJ III, 102 and 104.
Chandler, Richard. *Travels in Asia Minor and Greece, 1775-76*, 1817. HD 30 Dec 1809.
Chardin, J. *Voyages en Perse et autres lieux de l'Orient par Langles*, 10 vols Paris 1811. CMP 233.
Clarke, Edward Daniel. *Travels in Various Countries of Europe, Asia and Africa*, 1816-20. CMP 236 and 253.
de la Mottraye, Aubry. *Voyages en Europe, Asie et Afrique*, tr. as *Travels through Europe, Asia and into parts of Africa*, 1732. No evidence of Byron's reading.
D'Herbelot, Barthélemy. *Bibliothèque Orientale*, 1697. CMP 239. Byron owned a 1776 edition: CMP 238.
D'Ohsson, Mouradja. *Tableau Général de l'Empire Ottoman*, Paris 1787. No evidence of Byron's reading.
Eton, William. *A Survey of the Turkish Empire*, 1798. HD 18 Feb 1810.
Fitzclarence, George. *Journey from India to England*, 1819. CMP 254.
Galt, John. *Letters from the Levant*, 1815. BLJ XI, 233.
Gell, William. *The Topography of Troy* (1804??).
——. *The Geography and Antiquities of Ithaca* (1807).
——. *The Itinerary of Greece* (1810).
——. *Narrative of a Journey in the Morea* (1823). BLJ X, 171
Goldsmith, Oliver. *The Grecian History*, 1774. HD 5 Jan 1810.
Hanway, Jonas. *An Historical Account of the British Trade over the Caspian Sea*, 2 vols 1754. No evidence of Byron's reading.
Holland, Henry. *Travels in the Ionian Isles, Albania, Thessaly, Macedonia &c. during the Years 1812 and 1813* (1815). Sent by Murray to Byron: letter of March 8 1815.

Jones, Sir William. *Works*, ed. Lord Teignmouth, 13 vols 1807. CMP 5.

Kinneir, John. *A Geographical Memoir of the Persian Empire*, 1813. CMP 237.

Knolles, Richard. *The Generall Historie of the Turkes*, 1621. *Don Juan* V 147, 7. CMP 3, 4 and 220.

Lavallée, Joseph. *Letters of a Mameluke*, 2 vols 1804. CMP 231.

Leake, William Martin. *Researches in Greece* (1814). CMP 48-50 and 317-22

——. (possibly) *The Topography of Athens* (1821).

Macmichael, William. *Journey from Moscow to Constantinople*, 1819. CMP 254.

Malcolm, Sir John. *History of Persia,* 2 vols 1815. BLJ IV, 147-8 and CMP 243.

Meletios, Bishop. *Geografia Palaia kai Nea* (1728). BLJ II, 60 and CMP 238.

Mignot, Vincent. *The History of the Turkish or Ottoman Empire*, 1787. No evidence of Byron's reading.

Mitford, William. *History of Greece* (1784, 1790, 1810). Several BLJ references, inc. VIII, 13-15.

Montagu, Lady Mary Wortley. *Letters,* 2 vols Paris 1800. *Don Juan* V, 3, 8. Numerous references in BLJ; CMP 125-6 and 172.

Montesquieu, Charles-Louis de Secondat, Baron de. *Lettres Persanes*, 1721. No evidence of Byron's reading. The name Astarte is found here, but it is also in Voltaire's *Zadig*.

Morier, J.P. *Two Journeys through Persia, Armenia and Asia Minor in 1808 16*, 2 vols 1812-18. No evidence of Byron's reading.

Olivier, Guillaume Antoine. *Voyage dans l'Empire Othoman, l'Egypte et la Perse* (1802-7) tr. as *Travels in the Ottoman Empire, Egypt and Persia*, 2 vols 1801. Includes atlas. HD 26 June 1810.

Orme, Robert. *A General Idea of the Government and People of Indostan* (1752, first pub'd. 1805). CMP 3.

——. *A History of the Military Transactions of the British Nation in Indostan from the Year 1745* (1763-78). CMP 3.

——. *Historical Fragments of the Mogul Empire, of the Morattoes, and of the English Concerns in Indostan from the Year 1659* (1782). CMP 3.

Park, Mungo. *Travels in the Interior of Africa* (1799). CMP 5.

Potter, John. *Archælogia Græca, or The Antiquities of Greece*, 1697-8. HD 20 Feb 1810.

Pouqueville, F.C.H.L. *Travels in the Morea*, 1806. *CHP* II, 47, Byron's note.

Rays-Effendi, Mamoud. *Tableau des Nouveaux Réglemens de l'Empire Ottoman, composé par Mahmoud Rayf-Effendi, ci-devant Secrétaire de l'Ambassade Impériale près de la Cour d'Angleterre. Imprimé dans la Nouvelle Imprimerie du Génie sous la direction d'Abdur-rhamin Effendi, professeur du Géometrie et d'Algébre, à Constantinople,* 1798. HD 27 May 1810.

Richardson, John. *A Dictionary, Persian, Arabic, & English, to which is prefixed a dissertation on the languages, literature and manners of the eastern nations,* 2 vols 1777. CMP 241.

Rollin, Charles. *Histoire ancienne des Egyptiens, des Carthagenois, des Assyriens, des Babyloniens, des Mèdes, et des Perses, des Macédoniens, des Grecs* (1730-8). CMP 3.

Rubruquis, Guillaume de. *Voyages remarquables de Guillaume de Rubruquis en différentes parties de l'Orient,* 1735. HD 25 May 1810.

Rycaut, Paul. *The Present State of the Ottoman Empire,* 1668. CMP 3, 4, and 219-20.

Sale, George (tr.) *The Koran, Commonly called the Alcoran of Mohammed, Preliminary Discourse,* 1734. No evidence of Byron's reading.

Scott, Jonathan (tr.) *Arabian Nights,* 6 vols 1811. CMP 232.

Sonnini, Charles Sigisbert. *Travels in Upper and Lower Egypt,* 1800. CMP 243.

Southey, Robert. *Letters From England,* ed. Jack Simmons (London: The Cresset Press, 1951).

Taylor, John. *Travels from England to India,* 1799. CMP 242, HD 17 Feb 1810.

Thornton, Thomas. *The Present State of Turkey,* 1809. BLJ II, 106 and 115.

Tott, François Baron de. *Memoirs ... containing the state of the Turkish Empire, during the late war with Russia,* 2 vols 1785. *Don Juan* VI, 31, 5. CMP 220.

Tournefort, Joseph Pitton de. *A Voyage to the Levant,* 1741. *Giaour,* 755, Byron's note.

Tully, Richard. *A Narrative of a Ten Years' Residence at the Court of Tripoli,* 1816. BLJ VIII, 186, and HD 13 Sep 1816. The book is by either Tully's sister or sister in-law.

Turner, William. *Journal of a Tour in the Levant,* 3 vols 1820. BLJ VIII 80-3.

Valentia, George, Viscount. *Travels to India, Ceylon, the Red Sea, Abyssinia and Egypt in the Years 1802-6.* HD Sep 11 1809.

Vertot, René Aubert de. *Histoire des chevalier hospitaliers de Saint-Jean de Jerusalem* (1726, tr. 1728). CMP 3.

Walpole, Robert. *Travels in Various Countries of the East* (1820). CMP 254.

Wheler, Sir George. *A Journey into Greece* (1682). HD Jan 8 1810.

Whiston, William and George. *Mosis Chorenensis Historiae Armeniacae Libri III* (1736). CMP 336.

Anon. Review of Thomas Moore's *Sacred Songs*, in *Blackwood's Edinburgh Monthly Magazine* 1:6 (September 1817) 630-631.

Anon. Review of Thomas Moore's *Sacred Songs*, in *Monthly Review (2nd ser.)* 90 (December 1819) 413-420.

1930-1990

Abrams, M H. *The Mirror and the Lamp: Romantic Theory and the Critical Tradition* (Oxford: Oxford University Press. 1953).

Borst, William A. *Byron's First Pilgrimage 1809-11*, New Haven 1948.

Brown, W.C. *Byron and English Interest in the Near East, Studies in Philology* 34, 1937.

Butler, Marilyn. *Romantics, Rebels and Reactionaries*, Oxford 1981.

—. *The Orientalism of Byron's Giaour,* in Beatty, Bernard and Vincent Newey, eds., *Byron and the Limits of Fiction*, Liverpool University Press 1988.

Chew, Samuel Claggart. *The Crescent and the Rose*, Oxford 1938.

Conant, Martha Pike. *The Oriental Tale in England in the Eighteenth Century*, New York 1908.

Culler, Jonathan. *Framing the Sign. Criticism and its Institutions* (Oxford: Basil Blackwell, 1988).

Curran, Stuart. *Poetic Form and British Romanticism* (Oxford: Oxford University Press, 1986).

DeFord, Miriam Allen. *Thomas Moore* (New York: Twayne Publishers, 1967).

Gleckner, Robert F. *Byron and the Ruins of Paradise* (Baltimore: Johns Hopkins Press, 1967).

Hepworth, Brian. *Robert Lowth* (Boston: Twayne Publishers, 1978).

Marchand, Leslie A. *Byron's Poetry: A Critical Introduction* (London: John Murray, 1965).

Shilstone, Frederick. *Byron and the Myth of Tradition* (Lincoln: University of Nebraska Press, 1988).

Slater, Joseph. "Byron's Hebrew Melodies," in *Studies in Philology* 49:1 (1952) 75-94.

Wiener, Harold S. L. *Byron and the East: Literary Sources of the* Turkish Tales, in Herbert Davis, DeVane, William S., and R. C. Bald (eds.), *Nineteenth-Century Studies,* Cornell University Press, Ithaca, NY, 1940, pp.89-129.

Post-1990

Allen, Elizabeth Cheresh. *Lermontov's Not-Byronism: A Reconsideration,* in *Romantic Russia* 1998, pp.2-34.

Bagabas, Omar Abdullah, *Byron's Representation of the Orient in Childe Harold's Pilgrimage, Don Juan, and the Oriental Tales* (PhD Diss.), Essex University 1993.

Ballaster, Ros. *Fabulous Orients: Fictions of the East in England 1662-1785*, Oxford 2005.

Beatty, Bernard. *Byron's Oriental Wardrobe*, 1998 *Newstead Abbey Byron Society Newsletter*, pp.67-75.

Blackstone, Bernard. "Byron's Greek Canto: The Anatomy of Freedom", *Yearbook of English Studies*, 4 (1974): pp.172-89.

—. *Byron and Islam: the Triple Eros*, in *Journal of European Studies* (1974) 4, pp.325-63.

Butler, Marilyn. "Orientalism", in David B. Pirie (ed.), *The Penguin History of Literature: The Romantic Period*, Penguin, London, 1994, pp.339-447.

Cardwell, Richard A. (ed.), *The Reception of Byron in Europe*, Thoemmes-Continuum Press, London, 2005, pp.434-47.

Cochran, Peter. *Byron and "Tully's Tripoli", Byron Journal*, 1992, pp.77-88.

—. *Byron and the Birth of Ahrimanes, Keats-Shelley Review*, Autumn 1991, pp.49-59.

—. *Byron and Castelnau's* History of New Russia, *Keats-ShelleyReview* October 1994, pp.48-70.

—. *Nature's Gentler Errors: Byron, Ali Pasha and the Ionian Islands, Byron Journal*, 1995, pp.22-35.

—. ("Petros Peteinaris"). *The Bey Apologises, Newstead Byron Society Review* July 2001, p.13. Translation by David Holton of the facsimile letter in CHP I and II.

—. *Byronic Heroes (III): Sultan Selim III; Newstead Byron Society Review 2003* p.91.

—. ("Zosya Propisetskaya"). *Lermontov's* Izmail Bey: *A Byronic Poem for our Time; Newstead Byron Society Review* 2005, p.32.

—. *Byron, Greece, and Guilt, ΚΑΜΠΟΣ* (*Cambridge Papers in Modern Greek*), No 13, 2005, pp.63-88.

—. *Byron and Islamic Culture*, Keats-Shelley Review, XXI, 2007, pp.65-78.

Donovan, J.P. *Don Juan in Constantinople: Watching and Waiting;* 1993 *Byron Journal*, p.23.

Felsenstein, Frank. *Anti-Semitic Stereotypes 1660-1830* (Baltimore: Johns Hopkins University Press, 1995).

Franklin, Caroline. *'Some Samples of the Finest Orientalism': Byronic Philhellenism and Proto-Zionism at the Time of the Congress of Vienna*, in *Romanticism and Colonialism: Writing and Empire, 1780-1830*, by Tim Fulford and Peter Kitson (Cambridge: Cambridge UP, 1998) pp.221-42.

Graham, Peter W. *Don Juan and Regency England* (Charlottesville: University Press of Virginia, 1990).

Heinzelman, Kurt. "Politics, Memory and the Lyric: Collaboration as Style in Byron's *Hebrew Melodies*," in *Studies in Romanticism* 27:4 (1988) 515-27.

Kahf, Mohja. *The Muslim Woman in Western Literature, from Romance to Romanticism* (PhD Diss.), Rutgers, The State University of New Jersey, New Brunswick, 1994.

Kelsall, Malcolm. *Once did she hold the gorgeous east in fee ... Byron's Venice and Oriental Empire*, in Raizis, M. Byron (ed). *Byron and the Mediterranean World, Proceedings of the Twentieth International Byron Conference in the University of Athens 20-21 September 1995*, Athens 1995.

—. *Reading Orientalism: Woman: or Ida of Athens*, in *Review of National Literatures and World Report*, 1998, pp.11-20.

—. *Once did she hold the gorgeous East in fee ...: Byron's Venice and Oriental Empire*, in *Romanticism and Colonialism: Writing and Empire, 1780-1830*, ed. Tim Fulford and Peter J. Kitson (CUP, 1988) pp.243-61.

Kidwai, Abdur Raheem. *Samples of the Finest Orientalism: Image of the Orient in Lord Byron's Turkish Tales,* in *Aligarh Critical Miscellany* 1996, pp.65-84.

—. *Orientalism in Lord Byron's "Turkish Tales"*, The Edwin Mellen Press, Lewiston/Queenston/Lampeter, 1995.

Leask, Nigel. *British Romantic Writers and the East,* Cambridge University Press, Cambridge, 1992.

—. *Childe Harold II and 'The Polemic of Ottoman Greece'*, in Drummond Bone (ed.), *The Cambridge Companion to Byron*, Cambridge 2004.

Liassis, Nora. *Oriental Females in Byron's Verse Narratives* in Raizis, M. Byron (ed). *Byron and the Mediterranean World, Proceedings of the Twentieth International Byron Conference in the University of Athens 20-21 September 1995*, Athens 1995.

Lowth, Robert. *Lectures on the Sacred Poetry of the Hebrews*, trans. G Gregory, 2 vols (London: J Johnson, 1787; facsim. rpt. London: Routledge / Thoemmes Press, 1995).

Makdisi, Saree. *Romantic Imperialism*, Cambridge University Press, Cambridge, 1998.

Marandi, Seyed Mohammad. *Byron's Infidel and the Muslim Fisherman*, 2006 *Keats-Shelley Review*, pp.133-55.

—. *The Concubine of Abydos*, 2006 *Byron Journal*, pp.97-108.

Melikian, Anahid. *Byron and the East*, American University of Beirut, Beirut, 1977.

Mole, Tom. "The Handling of *Hebrew Melodies*," in *Romanticism* 8.1 (2002) 18-33.

Ouijean, Naji B. *Byron's Eastern Literary Portraits*, in Raizis, M. Byron (ed). *Byron and the Mediterranean World, Proceedings of the Twentieth International Byron Conference in the University of Athens 20-21 September 1995,* Athens 1995.

—. *Orientalism: The Romantics' Added Dimension* in *Review of National Literatures and World Report*, 1998, pp.37-50.

—. *Western Exoticism and Byron's Orientalism, in Prism(s): Essays in Romanticism* 6 (1998)pp.27-39.

—. *A Compendium of Eastern Elements in Byron's Oriental Tales,* Peter Lang, New York, 1999.

—. *Futile Encounters between East and West: Islam and Christianity in Byron's* The Giaour, in Reiko Aiura, Itsuyo Higashinaka, Yukihito Hijiya, Takehiko Tabuki, and Koichi Yakushigawa, (eds.) *Byron the Traveller*, Japanese Byron Society 2003.

Poole, Roger. "What Constitutes, and What is External to, the Real Text of Byron's *Childe Harold's Pilgrimage, A Romaunt and Other Poems* (1812)?" in Richard Cardwell (ed.), *Lord Byron the European. Essays from the International Byron Society,* The Edwin Mellen Press, Lewiston/ Queenston/Lampeter, 1997, pp.149-207.

Procházka, Martin (ed.) *Byron: East and West / Proceedings of the 24th International Byron Conference /* Charles University Prague, Prague 2000. Includes Franklin, Michael. *The Building of Empire and the Building of Babel: Sir William Jones, Byron, and their Productions of the Orient*; Beatty, Bernard. *Calvin in Islam and Calvinism: A Reading of* Lara *and* The Giaour; Oueijan, Naji B. *Western Exoticism and*

Byron's Orientalism; and Liassis, Nora. *The Crescent O'er the Cross: Byron and Apostas*

Reibel, David A. 'Introduction' to Robert Lowth, *De Sacra Poesi Hebræorum* (London: Routledge / Thoemmes Press, 1995).

Reiman, Donald H, ed. *The Romantics Reviewed: Contemporary Reviews of British Romantic Writers* (New York: Garland, 1972).

Rishmawi, George Khalil. *Oriental Elements in English Romantic Poetry: Shelley and Byron* (PhD Diss.), State University of New York (1983).

—. *The Muslim East in Byron's* Don Juan. PLL 35.3 (Summer 1999) pp.227-43.

—. *Islam and Muslims in Byron's* The Corsair, *International Journal of Arabic English Studies*, Dec 2000, pp 299-312.

Said, Edward. *Orientalism*, Penguin, 1991. First published in 1978.

—. *Culture and Imperialism*, London, Vintage, 1994.

—. *Covering Islam: how the Media and the Experts determine how we see the rest of the World*, London, Vintage, 1997.

Saglia, Diego. *I Discorsi dell'Esotico: L'oriente nel romanticismo britannico 1780-1803*, Naples 2002.

Sampson, Kathryn Ann. *The Romantic Literary Pilgrimage to the Orient: Byron, Scott and Burton* (unpublished dissertation), Austin 2000.

Sharafuddin, Mohammed. *Islam and Romantic Orientalism*, Tauris, London, 1994.

Sultana, Fehmida. *Romantic Orientalism and Islam: Southey, Shelley, Moore, and Byron* (PhD Diss.), Tufts University, 1989.

Thomas, Gordon. "The Forging of an Enthusiasm: Byron and the *Hebrew Melodies*," in *Neophilologus* 75.4 (1991) 626-36.

Vail, Jeffery. *The Literary Relationship of Lord Byron and Thomas Moore*, Johns Hopkins, Baltimore and London, 2001.

Unterman, Alan. *Dictionary of Jewish Lore and Legend* (London: Thames and Hudson, 1991).

Weinbrot, Howard D. *Britannia's Issue: The Rise of British Literature from Dryden to Ossian* (Cambridge: Cambridge University Press, 1993).

INDEX

Flaubert, Gustave, 139.
Fletcher, William, 33, 88, 288.
Foresti, Spridion, 288.
Forster, E.M., 196.
France, 17, 18, 82.
Franklin, Caroline, *Byron's Heroines*, 224&n, 228&n, 229&n, 232&n, 236&n.
Franklin, Michael, 6-7 & 7n, 79-80&n, 156, 196, 197n.
Franks, Tommy, 63.
Frere, John Hookham, 66.
Fry, Mrs Elizabeth, 290.
Fulford, Tim, 6, 8&n, 9.
Fux, A., 270.
Gadamer, 191.
Gamba, Pietro, *Lord Byron's Last Journey*, 225&n.
Garber, Frederick A. *Self, Text and Romantic Irony*, 2n, 156-7&n, 223&n.
Garrick, David, 60.
Gell, William, 117.
George III, King, 21, 31, 120, 182.
George IV, King, 31, 142, 199.
Georgia, 271.
Georgio, pirate, 68.
Gerbanovskii, *Khadzhi-bey*; *Ziuleika*, 270.
Germany, 84, 258, 262.
Gibb, Sir Hamilton, 192, 193.
Gibbon, Edward, 157, 179.
Gibraltar, 155.
Gifford, William, 45, 58, 245.
Gillray, James, 76.
Girey, Khan, 33.
Gleckner, Robert F., 206n, 226&n, 228&n, 240&n, 245&n.
Gnedich, N.P., 268.
Godfrey, Mary, 177.
Goethe, Johann Wolfgang von, 83, 99&n, 190, 191, 262.
Goldsmith, Oliver, *Citizen of the World, A*, 86.
Good Hope, Cape of, 73.
Gordon, Lord George, 203, 212.

Goza, 38, 39.
Graham, Peter (ed.) *Byron's Bulldog*, 117n; *Don Juan and Regency England*, 215n.
Gray, Thomas, 60, 263.
Greece, 18, 20, 85, 155, 155, 220, 257, 258.
Gregory, Allan, 1, 96.
Gronow, Captain, *Reminiscences*, 132&n.
Guiccioli, Teresa, 23; *My Recollections of Lord Byron*, 1n.
Gulbeyaz, concubine to Mahomet IV, 94.
Guneche, wife to Mahomet IV, 94.
Hafiz, 6, 17, 45-6&n, 70&n, 263.
Hammersley's Bank, 87, 88.
Handel, George Frederick, *Jephtha*, 260.
Hanson, Charles, 86.
Hanson, John, 157, 255.
Hearn, Lafcadio, 196.
Heinzelman, Kurt, *Politics, Memory and the Lyric*, 211&n.
Henley, Samuel, notes to Beckford's *Vathek*, 64, 65, 68, 124, 235n.
Hepworth, Brian, *Robert Lowth*, 213n, 207n.
Herakles (Hercules), 37.
Herbelot, Barthélemy d', *Bibliothèque orientale*, 6, 69-70, 179, 193.
Herder, 191.
Higashinaka, Itsuyo, 139&n.
Hitler, Adolf, 261, 262.
Hoare's Bank, 89n.
Hobhouse, Sir Benjamin, 117.
Hobhouse, John Cam (subs. Lord Broughton), 19, 21, 22, 24, 31, 35, 42, 43, 45, 46, 50, 69, 86, 92, 100, 108, 113, 116, 120, 126, 135, 142, 274, 275, 276, 277, 287, 288, 296, 289, 297. Diary quoted, 24, 24-5, 26, 27-9, 29-31, 42, 71n, 85.